Praise for

GOD —
the World's Future

"The systematic comprehension, clarity, and brevity (given its ambitious scope) arguably make *God—the World's Future* the best introduction to this kind of theology available. . . . Peter's remarkable ability to draw analogies which illumine the meaning of an ancient claim or symbol, and to simplify complex issues in short, pithy statements, make this an excellent choice as an introductory textbook."

—Douglas J. Schuurman
The Cresset

". . . clearly written and tightly argued, yet gently beckoning—especially to those who are used to pondering the postmodern world of 'holism' and postcritical reconstruction. In this respect, Peters's book is a significant attempt to do classic theological work in a way that takes our contemporary context with radical seriousness."

—Donald K. McKim
Reformed Review

". . . rich and comprehensive. . . . a welcome addition to the relatively small list of one-volume interpretations of the Christian tradition—hence made-to-order for seminary studies and for college students and others who have an advanced interest in theology. . . . The task that this work has set for itself, to plant its feet firmly in what appears to be the trajectory of history's future, places it in such a pathbreaking role."

—Philip Hefner
Dialog

"*God—the World's Future* will be especially helpful for conservative Christians who need help in entering the postmodern world of wholism and postcritical reconstruction under the guidance of an author devoted to the authority and relevance of classic Christian symbols and doctrine."

—John P. Newport
Southwestern Baptist
Theological Seminary

GOD —
the World's Future

*Systematic Theology for
a Postmodern Era*

Ted Peters

FORTRESS PRESS   Minneapolis

Interior design: ediType
Cover illustration: *Cosmogenesis,* by Blanche M. Gallagher
Cover design: Terry W. Bentley

Library of Congress Cataloging-in-Publication Data

Peters, Ted, 1941–
    God—the world's future : systematic theology for a postmodern era
  / Ted Peters.
        p. cm.
    Includes index.
    ISBN 0-8006-2542-0
    1. Theology, Doctrinal.   I. Title.
  BT75.2.P48 1992
  230—dc20   91-43158
                                                     CIP

Manufactured in the U.S.A.   AF 1-2542

01   00   99   98   97   3   4   5   6   7   8   9   10   11   12

CONTENTS

PREFACE

Faith is believing and trusting in God. Theology is the discipline of thinking about God in light of our faith. But many people in the modern era have experienced a crisis of faith. This crisis has caused doubts regarding the ability of theology to speak intelligibly or meaningfully about the reality in which we live. If our trust be in God and God alone, however, then both our faith and our intellectual honesty will require that we face the crisis squarely and seek to reassess the potential of theology to present the ultimate truths that govern our lives. I write as one who has personally experienced the crisis and who wishes to suggest a postcrisis method for pursuing the theological task.

My story is not at all unusual; nor does it hinge upon dramatic external events. It is a story of the inner life and may be all the more instructive because of this. I was raised in a devout Protestant family in the Midwest. We attended church frequently and my parents took their turns at Sunday school teaching and serving on the church council. The Christian symbol system imbued my daily life. God, heaven, hell, and the drama of salvation were as real to me as George Washington, the Declaration of Independence, and General Motors. The only threat to the validity of my family's faith was a rumor about godless university professors who were teaching the theory of evolution, which contradicted the Genesis creation account. I dreaded the thought that I should ever come under the influence of such idea mongers who might puncture the sealed world of religious truth in which I lived.

But then I turned eighteen and went off to the big state university— straight into the den of intellectual iniquity. The rumor became reality. Some professors laughed overtly at the beliefs of the more fundamentalistic students. It seemed that my freshman English teacher asked at least once a week: "If God is omnipotent, can God make a stone so heavy even he can't lift it?" This question was always followed by a smirk and a chuckle. My biology professor was much more sympathetic and spent considerable time assuring us that there need be no conflict between science and religion as long as they—like church and state—did not mix. But I could only recall Shakespeare's "me thinks thou dost protest too much," and the professor's protestations created more suspicion that I had come to the either/or fork in the road.

My response was to plunge headlong into studying the philosophies of atheism, concentrating on the works of Friedrich Nietzsche and Jean-Paul Sartre. Although genuinely concerned about my soul, my father kept asking me to study something that would get me a job and to stop studying philosophy. But I was concerned with truth. So I pushed on.

I now describe those college years as my critical stage, a stage from which I have not yet thoroughly emerged. By "critical" I mean I was learning to stand back and examine my religious beliefs and symbols from an alien point of view. I was learning how to offer alternative explanations for religious phenomena, thinking about them without loyalty to Protestant Christianity and even without reference to the reality of God. In short, I was entering the world of doubt.

This meant that whatever I would eventually affirm positively in the way of religious commitment would henceforth have to be done freely, done alone, and done on the basis of my own resources rather than simply inherited from my past. Instead of remaining solely a doubter, in time I came around to reaffirming the basic tenets of Christian belief. Making such affirmations of faith constituted a move beyond criticism to a postcritical belief system. In retrospect, I believe this is one form of experiencing what Saint Paul meant when he wrote of leaving the milk toast to eat solid meat—that is, of maturing in Christ.

The postcritical reaffirmed faith does not produce exactly the same theology as the original naive faith did, however. It is still faith in the same God and the same religious symbols, to be sure. Yet there is a change in how one thinks about such matters. A theologian's task is to trace such steps in the change of thinking. The task of this volume is to examine the precritical symbols of Christian faith, to explicate them in light of critical and postcritical modes of thinking, and to suggest a coherent scheme for organizing Christian doctrine and theology.

Ecumenical and Ecumenic Courage

As I attempt to organize and explicate Christian theology, I wish to maintain an *ecumenical* and an *ecumenic* mood. With the term *ecumenical* I wish to affirm at the outset what I believe to be the God-intended unity of all Christian believers, the unity of the one body of Jesus Christ. I take it that when Saint Paul describes Christ as having "broken down the dividing wall" (Eph. 2:14) he leaves no room for the kind of parochial prejudice that most Christians somewhat innocently but no less viciously grow up with. I have had the fortunate experience in my adult years of working quite closely with Christians of various stripes. My dissertation adviser at the University of Chicago was a Roman Catholic, David Tracy. Later I had the opportunity to teach in a Jesuit institution, Loyola University in New Orleans. Such experiences taught me how theologically emaciated would be my own denominational life if it were to sever all ties to the richness of the Roman tradition. Presently I teach at the Graduate Theological Union in Berkeley, where I work daily with Presbyterians, Baptists, Methodists, Anglicans, Disciples of Christ, the Eastern Orthodox, and others, as well as with my own group, the Lutherans. I can no longer conceive of affirming "one Lord, one Faith, and one Baptism" without doing so in concert with my sisters and brothers across denominational lines. There is in the last analysis only one Christian faith, and it is an ecumenical faith.

When engaged in theological thinking, however, one must not let the ecumenical spirit devolve into a mushy sentimentality that discourages rigor or weakens intellectual commitment. The task is to explicate the gospel in ways that maintain integrity in our time; and this often means following the trail of hard-nosed honesty no matter where it leads. It may lead to criticism of someone else's understanding of things. It may lead to criticism of one's own understanding of things. In those sorts of situations the ecumenical principle means that theological criticism need not be church-dividing. Christians can disagree theologically without running their opponents out of the church. Christians can honestly debate the meaning of the gospel within the framework of an acknowledged unity shared in Christ.

The second term, *ecumenic*, is closely related to but still distinguishable from *ecumenical*. Both words come from the Greek root, οἶκος, meaning house. When I use the term *ecumenical* to refer to interdenominational yet still intra-Christian relations, I am talking about the one, all-inclusive household of faith in Jesus Christ. The term *ecumenic* is a bit different. It points to the window of faith that opens out toward the world beyond. It opens out to the universe that lies beyond the church. It is interreligious, concerned with non-Christian points of view. It connotes the sense of oneness of the human race and perhaps even the sense of ecological oneness—our human bond with nature as a whole—that are indicative of the emerging elements of postmodern culture. Whereas the term *ecumenical* reminds us of the implicit unity of the church, the term *ecumenic* reminds us of the unifying power of the kingdom of God.

The term *ecumenic* means two things for the present work in systematic theology. First, it means no field of knowledge is off limits. Everything one can learn about the inner life of the human spirit or about the outer world is relevant to our knowledge of God. Second, it means that persons of faith need to identify with the unity of all things, with the whole of God's reality. If God be the creator and redeemer of all that is, then nothing within God's creation is too dirty or too inimical to identify with. If it is because "God so loved the world that he gave his only Son" (John 3:16), then we can love it too, in its entirety.

Significant things are happening on the ecumenical and ecumenic fronts. Theologians are talking seriously with one another across denominational lines and are using one another's insights to enrich their own respective traditions. In addition, the present generation seems to be experiencing a deepening of concern for the whole of which we are a part, for the whole human race to which Christians belong, and for the whole of nature understood as our home. New doors seem to be opening. It will take some courage to walk through them, however.

In 1983 the now late Edmund Schlink published a systematic theology, *Ökumenische Dogmatik*, which was aimed at pursuing theology with an inclusively ecumenical scope. In the fall of 1967 I had the privilege of hearing Schlink's lectures on twentieth-century theology at the University of Heidelberg. The lectures included one presentation on the signing of the Barmen Declaration, the 1934 document of the confessing Christians that declared a resounding yes to Jesus Christ with an accompanying no to Nazism, to Hitlerism, to totalitarianism, to anti-Semitism, and to the capitulation of the Christian faith to the whims of a powerful culture and a powerful body politic. Schlink told how Karl Barth and others put their names on the line, knowing they might be putting their careers or even their lives on the line at the same time. As Schlink finished his lecture in the somewhat dispassionate style characteristic of German scholars, he removed his glasses and announced: "That was the way it was at Barmen." The 120 or so students were so moved by the presentation that they rose to their feet and with tears in their eyes applauded spontaneously as the professor walked out of the room. We knew that we were sitting in the historical shadow of great courage, that we were vicariously living again one of those moments when the power of faith casts out fear and faces the challenges Jesus had once forecasted would come our way.

The present time calls for a similar courage. The courage of 1934 reported by Schlink was exercised for the purposes of separating and dividing, for the purposes of distinguishing as sharply as possible between what the Christian faith stood for over against a society that was hostile to it. In his own career, however, after Nazism became mostly a memory, Schlink himself showed a kind of courage by investing his energies in a movement away from division and toward reunion—that is, toward reunion of separated Christian communities. This is where the present generation finds itself: called upon to consider with courage the possibility that something new might be in the offing, that the pain of division that separates Christians might be healable, and that a new sense of the oneness of the body of Christ and of the kingdom of God might be realizable in our own generation.

There should not be any anxiety over competition between an ecumenical Christian faith and a shared ecumenic spirit. They complement one another. God works in both spheres, although differently perhaps. If we press the household analogy, ecumenical or intra-Christian relations could be likened to a conjugal family, to an intimate bond. Ecumenic relations such as we find in interreligious dialogue or in shared strivings for social justice and ecological health could be likened to close friendships. We need to feel unity both in family life and in warm friendships if our life is to be rich.

Proleptic Explication of the Gospel

The sense of oneness of which I speak is something borrowed from God, the world's future. Ecumenical and ecumenic consciousness anticipates the unity of all things that God has promised will come as a gift of divine grace. With this in mind, the central theme of this book is the concept of prolepsis, whereby the gospel is understood as announcing the pre-actualization of the future consummation of all things in Jesus Christ. The world has been given God's promise that in the future all things will be made whole. The promise comes to us through Jesus who died on Good Friday and rose from the dead on Easter Sunday. He embodies the promise because he anticipates in his person the new life that we humans and all creation are destined to share.

The argument all the way through this volume will affirm faith in the God of the future. The God of Israel is mysterious on many counts, but one salient feature of the revelation in Jesus Christ is that this is a God of faithfulness. This God is trustworthy. In addition, this trustworthy God has given us a promise. The divine voice has spoken to us through the prophets and through the Son with the message that a new and transformed world is coming where swords will be beaten into plowshares, lions will lie down with lambs, and there will be no more tears in our eyes. Now, this claim is either true or it is not. The Christian faith is constituted by trust that it is true. Its truth is nothing that can be discerned philosophically or deduced from the structure of natural phenomena. Its truth is dependent solely on the faithfulness of the God who promised that these things would come to pass.

As a confirmation of the promise and as an appearance of its fulfillment ahead of time, history has experienced the incarnation of the Son of God. The paradoxical presence of the incarnate Logos in Jesus of Nazareth meant that in that time and place the universal will of God was at work under the finite conditions of human personality. On the one hand, Jesus was subject to transiency, to the evil designs of others, to the power of present fixation and denial of futurity, or, in short, to death. Jesus was a part, not the whole, of creation. The cross on which he died signified that God's will is not "done on earth as it is in heaven." On the other hand,

Jesus' own unyielding faith in God meant the incarnate Logos never broke relationship with God's future. Even when facing death and praying in Gethsemane, Jesus said, "Thy will be done." The Easter resurrection was God's act wherein the faith of Jesus was vindicated and his oneness with the coming consummate fulfillment was affirmed.

The imagery attached to the traditional picture of the incarnation is that of a heavenly being coming down to take up residence on earth. It is spatial imagery. What would happen should we temporalize incarnation imagery and locate God's creative power at the consummation? We would get prolepsis. By prolepsis here I mean anticipation of future reality in a concrete preactualization of it. Jesus Christ is the future made present. He is the first fruits (1 Cor. 15:20), a foretaste of the great banquet yet to be enjoyed in the consummate kingdom of God. The good news of the gospel is that the kingdom of God has arrived ahead of time in Jesus of Nazareth and is the promised destiny of the whole of creation.

The exhilarating impact of the gospel is that it evokes in us the life of beatitude. In the Sermon on the Mount Jesus describes the life of beatitude as living a blessed life today in light of the coming of God's kingdom *tomorrow*. "Blessed are the peacemakers," says Jesus, because "they *will be* called children of God" (Matt. 5:9). God's future wholeness exerts its healing power now. In the life of beatitude the Holy Spirit collapses time, so to speak, so that believers can share ahead of time in the oneness of all things that is yet to come. Eyes of faith can catch a glimpse of the unity beyond the division and conflict that seem to be so destructive to our race and to the realm of nature to which we belong. Amid the viciousness of devouring competition, one can envision the lion lying down with the lamb. Amid the desert of portending mass destruction, one can glimpse the river of life flowing from the throne of God. Amid the wanton lack of care for the beings and things of this world, one can feel the heart beat with the rhythms of the divine love that pervades and promises wholeness throughout creation.

The Emerging Postmodern Context

The emerging postmodern consciousness and its vision of integrating wholeness constitute the primary context within which I seek here to understand and explicate the gospel and in which I wish to evoke the life of beatitude. The modern world—the world we have lived in since the Enlightenment of the eighteenth century—is the critical world that has torn apart the relation between the human mind and objective reality. Through the specialization of knowledge into separate disciplines, modernity has broken our naive sense of oneness with the whole of the world. Emerging schools of postmodern thought, however, are searching for ways to reunite what has been separated, to fix what has been broken apart. As I try to explicate the significance of the gospel in this context,

I will ask just how God's promise of future wholeness for all creation affects our life now amid a world of brokenness. My suggested answer is that it does so proleptically and beatitudinally.

Male and Female in Theology

The present period is a time of acute gender consciousness. We can no longer define the human simply in terms of what both sexes share in common. What is distinctive must be taken into account.

The bulk of the inherited tradition of Christian literature has come from male theologians. Today's scholars are asking: might the distinctively male apperception of things have slanted the direction taken by theology in the past? Are there nuances and insights drawn from the way women experience the world that could enrich the theological enterprise? With these questions in mind, I am here adopting a principle of gender complementarity. According to the complementarity principle operative in this book, whenever concepts are explored that are based upon analogies to what is human, these concepts should take both genders into account.

Gratitude

Some words of gratitude are in order. I did not write this book in isolation. Numerous parties have given me encouragement. I wish to thank the Board of Trustees of Pacific Lutheran Theological Seminary and its past president, Dr. Walter Stuhr, for granting me sabbatical time away from my teaching responsibilities in order to concentrate on research and writing. I wish to thank as well the Lutheran Brotherhood for including me in its Seminary Sabbatical Fellowship Program, and I am especially grateful to the Aid Association for Lutherans for awarding me the Fredrik A. Schiotz Fellowship for 1983–84. Such fellowship programs are a tribute to the farsightedness of these organizations that see the need for sponsoring ongoing scholarship intended to enrich the life of the Lutheran church.

I am indebted as well to Professor Wolfhart Pannenberg for his gracious hospitality and sound advice while I pursued research in Munich during 1984. I wish to express appreciation also to my teaching colleagues and student friends at the Graduate Theological Union who have examined various parts of the manuscript and offered critical but helpful advice. In particular I wish to mention David Stagaman, S.J., Durwood Foster, Bob Russell, Martha Stortz, Victor Gold, Nancey Murphy McClendon, Michael Morrissey, Tom Ross, Susan Nachtigal, John LaMunyon, Tom Struck, Beth Purdum, Jon Christianson, Kurt Christianson, Randall Lau, Tim Huff, and David Parks. I want to thank Carol Tabler for indexing.

I dedicate this work to Jenny, my beloved wife and devoted companion for more than a quarter century. She along with the rest of my immediate family—Paul, Kathy Kim, and Elizabeth—deserves a thank you. They have been most tolerant and patient during those long periods when my body was present but my mind was buried in one or another chapter of the yet-to-be-written book. They flatter me by saying that now with the book finished they are glad to have me back again. It is still nice to be welcomed home, even if you have never really left it.

I also wish to memorialize the whole family in which I grew up. I refer particularly to my father, Theodore Frank Peters, Sr., and to my mother, Lillian May (Tesch) Peters, who first demonstrated the love of God in my life and who never ceased to encourage me to live graciously and responsibly. Unfortunately, both my mother and father died during the decade in which I was working on this book. I pray that the oneness we previously shared in Christ will soon be realized once again as a oneness we can share together.

I also wish to express gratitude and appreciation to Robert N. Peters and to Helga (Busch) Peters for the continuing bond and friendship that we share; and to my aunt Edna (Tesch) Carpenter, whose gestures of kindness proved her to be a stalwart friend to a little boy growing up.

Finally, I offer this book to those students of the Christian mysteries who seek a better understanding of the symbols of our faith and who wish to pursue the loving life as a response to God's gracious love for us.

ABBREVIATIONS

BC   *The Book of Concord*, edited by Theodore G. Tappert. Philadelphia: Fortress Press, 1959.

CD   *Church Dogmatics*, by Karl Barth. 4 vols. Edinburgh: T. & T. Clark, 1936–62.

Chr.D.   *Christian Dogmatics*, edited by Carl E. Braaten and Robert W. Jenson. 2 vols. Philadelphia: Fortress Press, 1984.

CT   *The Christian Tradition: A History of the Development of Doctrine*, by Jaroslav Pelikan. 5 vols. Chicago: University of Chicago Press, 1971–89.

ILL   *An Inclusive Language Lectionary*. Atlanta: John Knox Press; New York: Pilgrim Press; Philadelphia: Westminster Press, 1983.

Inst.   *Institutes of the Christian Religion*, by John Calvin. Vols. 20 and 21 of The Library of Christian Classics, edited by John T. McNeill. Philadelphia: Westminster Press, 1960.

LW   *Luther's Works, American Edition*. Vols. 1–30, edited by Jaroslav Pelikan. St. Louis: Concordia Publishing Company, 1955—67. Vols. 31–55, edited by Helmut T. Lehmann. Philadelphia: Fortress Press, 1955–86.

TI   *Theological Investigations*, by Karl Rahner. 22 vols. London: Darton, Longman & Todd, 1961–76; New York: Seabury Press, 1974–76; New York: Crossroad, 1976–88.

WW   *The Works of John Wesley*, edited by Thomas Jackson. 14 vols. 3d ed. 1829. Reprint. Grand Rapids, Mich.: Baker, 1978.

GOD —
the World's Future

P A R T   O N E

THEOLOGY'S
CONTEXT AND
METHOD

INTRODUCTION

Systematic theology explicates the content of Christian belief, often by expanding the trinitarian structure found in the Apostles' and Nicene Creeds. This content is normally termed *doctrine*. The doctrinal content sits in the center, usually preceded by a section on *methodology* and followed by a discussion of *ethics*. The section on methodology consists of a prolegomenon that is occasionally called "foundations" or "fundamental theology." The discussion of ethics, which sometimes appears in a work separate from the systematic theology itself, attempts to discern what conduct should flow from doctrinal belief.

The explication of doctrinal content will occupy Parts Two, Three, and Four of the present work. The current situation—what I call *context*—is the first topic within Part One, the section on methodology. Here the basic principles that will guide this systematic theology are laid out within the framework of the current context of emerging postmodern consciousness, a context that seems to require a new explication of Christian belief.

The fundamental assumptions and method of inquiry are additional preliminaries that need to be clarified in Part One. At the center of this method is a focus on the heart of Christian conviction—the gospel of Jesus Christ that establishes Christian theology's purpose and provides the norm against which everything else is measured. The components of Part One are the methodological foundation upon which the systematic theology later builds.

1

ADDRESSING
THE POSTMODERN PERSON

Aristotle says that philosophy begins with wonder; not as in our day with doubt.

—Søren Kierkegaard, *Journals*, 1841

We require nothing less than a paradigm shift to a holistic view of the entire human family, now inextricably linked by our globe-girdling technologies.

—Hazel Henderson

Painted at the intersection of the longitudinal and transverse axes of the central nave ceiling in the little chapel at Wies in southern Germany is Jesus sitting on a rainbow. Below him is the judgment seat. It is empty. Above and to the left two angels are pointing to the empty cross, the cross upon which the judge himself made the sacrifice that frees the accused captives. The rainbow recalls the covenant sign given by God to Noah, revealing divine sadness at the sight of human destruction and promising a life forever secure from the ravages of deluge. Jesus is pointing to his broken heart. In front of the church and above the altar one finds the mother pelican, tearing open its breast in order to feed its young with its own living flesh. The viewer knows, then, that Jesus points to the divine heart, a heart broken so that the covenant could be sealed in blood. The entire scene displays the gospel in all its glorious color.

The artist, Johann Baptist Zimmermann (1680–1758), painted the Wieskirche ceiling in Bavarian rococo style, a style deeply imbued with the spirit of the Counter-Reformation and instituted in part as a bastion of defense against the challenges of the Age of Reason. The symbols used

4

to convey the gospel here are the ancient symbols, the biblical symbols. One of their duties is maintaining unbroken continuity with the ancient worldview, the only worldview that the Bavarian kings thought could give life its meaning. This part of southern Germany in the eighteenth and nineteenth centuries became an island of naive if not reactionary faith that sought to protect itself from the strong currents of the modern world swirling about it.

In the twentieth century the island of safety has been sorely eroded. The tides of modern life are everywhere sweeping away traditional verities. So, like the Bavarian kings before them, many people of Christian faith throughout the world today wonder if there can be—or even if there ought to be—a safe island of belief that will not be washed away by the eroding eddies of the modern mind.

One can identify the modern theologian as a person who is willing to jump off the island and attempt to swim amid the currents of modern consciousness. He or she is aware of the risks of leaving the dry land of biblical naiveté behind, but hopes that farther out at sea another island of meaning will appear. If none does appear, then perhaps with strong faith one can simply learn to enjoy the unending swim.

THE HERMENEUTICAL QUESTION

What makes a modern theologian modern is knowing and accepting that the temporal currents have borne Christianity quite a distance from where it started its journey. This temporal distance, a distance of at least twenty centuries, is reflected in what I call the hermeneutical question. This question and its proposed answers are at the center of every theological enterprise that can be called modern. That question is this: how can the Christian faith, first experienced and symbolically articulated in an ancient culture now long out-of-date, speak meaningfully to human existence today as we experience it amid a worldview dominated by natural science, secular self-understanding, and the worldwide cry for freedom?

This question provides the backbone and establishes the posture of a wide variety of schools of thought, whether it be Rudolf Bultmann's demythologizing, Paul Tillich's method of correlation, Dietrich Bonhoeffer's religionless Christianity, Vatican II's *aggiornamento*, David Tracy's revisionist theology, James Cone's black theology of liberation, or Sallie McFague's feminist hermeneutic. Regardless of what answer is offered, this question makes modern theology modern and distinguishes it from what went before. Modern theologians seek to pour the nectar of an ancient faith into the cup of modern consciousness, a stiff cup of machined steel upon which is engraved the pattern of nonreligious thinking and living. Theologians have been careful and cautious because the fear is high that the new cup will change the taste or perhaps even poison the faith. But the pouring is taking place, and many have become quite used to the blended taste of modernity and Christianity.

Now, what happens when modernity gives way to something else? What happens when the cup is returned to the engraver and upon it is inscribed a new religious sensibility? Something like this seems to be happening right now to the modern world. Complaints are being raised in many quarters about the narrowness of secularism, the limits of materialism, and the dangers of scientism. Those complaining often ask for something more than modernity has been able to offer, for a renewed sense of transcendent meaning and personal wholeness. Struggling to be born in our time is a nascent postmodern consciousness, a postmaterialist vision that has the marks of a romantic if not outright religious worldview. Should one try to pour the faith into this cup as well? This question will be addressed in the present work.

We find ourselves at what may be the first phase of a change in the overall theological agenda. Rather than modernity, we must inquire about the meaning of the Christian faith in the context of an emerging postmodernity. Without in any way abrogating the hermeneutical question as I have already stated it, I need to offer an amendment: how can the Christian faith be made intelligible amid an emerging postmodern consciousness that, although driven by a thirst for both individual and cosmic wholeness, still affirms and extends such modern themes as evolutionary progress, future consciousness, and individual freedom?

I am working with the assumption here that Christian theology is contextual in character—that is, it attempts to make the symbols of the faith understandable in the context within which it is working. To do so one must understand the present context, both modern and postmodern. It is to that context that I now turn.

THE CHALLENGE OF THE MODERN MIND

The modern mind poses a challenge to Christian theology because it makes assumptions that are essentially hostile to the symbols of the Christian faith. The most devastating assumption is that Christian symbols are old-fashioned and out-of-date. In fact, it is only because of modern thinking that one could even suggest the possibility that the Bible's meaning is strange, anachronistic, or no longer valid. Augustine in the fifth century did not think the Bible was out-of-date. Nor did Thomas Aquinas in the thirteenth century or Martin Luther and John Calvin in the sixteenth century think of the Bible as old-fashioned. Only those who come after the rise of natural science and the Enlightenment pit what scripture says against what we learn from other sources. This distancing of ourselves from what was said in the ancient world of the Bible is due to a fundamental shift in our way of thinking, a shift that marks the difference between the premodern and the modern eras.

The hermeneutical question characterizes the modern era in terms of the prominent place it gives to natural science, secular self-understanding, and the worldwide cry for freedom. Philosopher and mathematician Bertrand Russell once told a BBC audience that "what science cannot tell us, mankind cannot know." Russell believed that we do not know of a God existing beyond the empirically observable world, and therefore any claim to have knowledge about God is actually a psychological fabrication produced by our unconscious fear of power. For him modern science necessarily entails humanism and atheism.

That there has been an ongoing struggle between science and religion over the last three centuries, with science coming out the victor, is an interpretation of history preferred by the modern mind. The early pioneers of the new knowledge of nature—Copernicus, Kepler, Galileo, Newton, Descartes—were all devoutly religious. But when they began to describe the movements of natural things in terms of calculable natural laws, the need for religious insight to understand our world appeared to become superfluous. The world came to bed pictured as a great machine, as a cosmic Volkswagen, so to speak, within which each part acts on the others in a way that engineers can understand and put into mathematical formulas. The world machine is now running properly on its own, so there is no need for a divine mechanic, a God outside the machine, or even for a God inside the machine. Thus, when it came to the relevance of God for explaining how the world works, Laplace could say he had no need of a divine hypothesis. Modern science may not require outright atheism, but it does go about its business without reference to things divine.

This attitude among natural scientists spread so that modern people began to think that they could organize society without reference to religious beliefs or churchly authority. What emerged was secular self-understanding and the process of de-Christianizing Western culture and political life. No longer do we need to follow a transcendent model of the perfect society existing in heaven. The spread of democracy is assumed to be a human achievement. We moderns no longer count on angels to help us. Secularity is a way of understanding life that simply accepts the natural world to be the only world. It does not look behind things or under things to find some spiritual realities. What is natural seems to be enough. We do not need or even want anything supranatural. The secular point of view is this-worldly, not other-worldly. It rejects the transcendent dimension of reality.

Many modern people have rejoiced at the arrival of secular thinking because it seems to liberate them from outdated tradition and from demands to obey divinely decreed laws about human behavior. This has led to the modern world's reverence for freedom above all other concepts. What is freedom? Because the objective world is thought to operate like a Volkswagen—that is, according to a closed system of fixed mechanical laws—the search for freedom turns to the inner world of the human subject. Even if the outside world is determined, the inside world is not. The locus of freedom has become the human self. We believe we are free to make decisions: we are free to vote, free to choose which brand of breakfast cereal to buy, free to decide what career we will pursue. We moderns have come to believe that this freedom to decide puts us (not God) into the driver's seat of the cosmic Volkswagen. As these trends have proceeded, the more we have removed the sacred element from nature and from society, the more liberated has become our interior life, and the more direction we have exercised over the course of events.

Therefore, we have come to think of freedom as an achievement. For many Westerners it is something our ancestors won for us in the eighteenth century when they liberated us from the power of the king to tell us what to do and from the power of the church to tell us what to think. We have come to identify freedom with the autonomy of the individual, with the release of external constraints so that we can think or act solely on the basis of subjective desires. Enlightenment philosopher Thomas Hobbes spoke of liberty as the "absence of external impediments" that keep us from doing what we wish. And Immanuel Kant spoke for the age when he defined freedom in terms of autonomy, as "the property of the will to be a law unto itself." Liberation is the process of breaking the chains that constrain us, and freedom is the state of existing without encumbrances to self-expression.

The advance of psychotherapy has accelerated and extended the process of liberating the human subject. Modern culture has begun seeking to release the self from internal impediments right along with the external ones so that liberation becomes a continuing process of unbridling human passions. This has led to increasingly deeper understandings of just what the human self is, defining it more and more sharply over against everything that is the nonself or even the unauthentic self. If there is a mission in the modern world, it is a dedication to the advance of freedom by throwing off the external impediments of poverty and political oppression along with the internal inhibitions of a distorted self-image. All of this is done so as to realize the autonomy of the free and unencumbered human ego.

Postmodern critics are dissatisfied with these modern developments. They say they are divisive. What is wrong is that they break up, separate, and fragment. A natural science and a secularism that are unable to comprehend spiritual realities are too narrow and restricted. Freedom understood as the autonomy of the individual ego divides the human reality into separated persons who distance themselves from the best interests of the race as a whole. Freedom understood as radical individualism destroys community.

Postmoderns go on to charge that academic specialization prevents people from catching a glimpse of the whole of things, that the efficiency of large political and economic institutions destroys the personhood of the people involved, that unbridling individual human passions without regard to valuing human community let alone the ecosphere as a whole has led to wanton pollution of our environment and the competition that has put us on the brink of thermonuclear disaster. All of this—rightly or wrongly—is blamed on the modern mind, which postmoderns believe is essentially divisive in its mode of thinking.

When one looks back on all this, one can see that the divisiveness of the modern mind is due to a three-legged structure of consciousness that lies at the foundation of modernity, the three legs being science, secularity, and autonomous freedom. This structure stands at the heart of the challenge to premodern religious faith and at the heart of the postmodern critique. I call it "critical consciousness."

Critical Consciousness

The essence of critical consciousness is distance. Distance takes the forms of objectification, nonparticipation, and alienation. When theologians bump into it they call it the "hermeneutical gap," referring to the interpretation gap between the ancient worldview of scripture and that of its modern readers today. This historical distance between the Bible and the modern reader is, however, only a symptom of a much larger problem, a problem that has left our whole culture in a state of alienation. The very structure of modern consciousness is founded on the principle of distanciation. Some have called it the "onlooker" or "spectator" consciousness, according to which we assume the real world consists in a drama on stage while we sit in the audience and watch it. We moderns have separated our subjective consciousness from the objective drama that constitutes what is real.

This distanciating structure is best illustrated by the work of René Descartes, who is considered to be the father of modern philosophy. The Cartesian approach has become so much a part of our education process that we no longer recognize it as just one form of thinking among others but rather as the only form of thinking a rational person would judge sane. Descartes has bequeathed two legacies that have greatly shaped our minds, the subject-object split and the principle of doubt. I will briefly review them in turn.

Descartes formulated the question of truth as if the truth had nothing to do with himself. He asked: how can I as a human subject be sure the ideas in my mind correspond accurately with the way the objective world out there really is? Just in posing the question this way he presumes there is a distance, a separation, an alienation between his own subjectivity and the real or objective world outside it. He implicitly cedes the content of truth to the objective world and not to himself as a subject.

This led eventually to the present widespread standard for truth— that is, the assumption that truth must be objective. Truth must be free of any subjective opinions or prejudices. Genuine knowledge is impersonal. One's scientific research is considered valid only if the data can be verified independently by other anonymous scientists. Police investigators attempt to focus solely on the facts because they assume that only on the basis of objective knowledge can we judge someone guilty or innocent in a court of law.

Descartes and the modern mind that followed taught us to objectify everything in the world. We have come to assume that nature is an agglomeration of disparate things that are related to one another by impersonal laws, and the object of science is to learn what these laws are so that we can manipulate the things through technology. Social scientists over the last century have taught us even to objectify ourselves, to treat ourselves as things subject to statistical laws. The social sciences concern themselves not with persons but with concepts of persons. So now we can step out of ourselves and look at ourselves as objects. We can understand ourselves in terms of ethnic background, social contexts, demographic trends, or psychological principles. We can hear ourselves spoken about, even if not spoken to.

The flip side of this objectivity is unchained subjectivity. Such things as value and worth, beauty and ugliness, good and evil, and importance and triviality are removed from the objective sphere and turned completely over to the subjective. Each of us individually can now decide on the basis of our own self-determined criteria what is valuable, beautiful, good, or important. Taste has become a private affair. It is not proper to say that the Mona Lisa is a beautiful work of art in any objective sense. One can only say, "I like it."

Pluralism

This split between object and subject in the critical consciousness of the seventeenth century has led to a curious conceptual tension in our own century, namely, the battle between objectivism and relativism. The objectivist believes that there exists an overarching framework of laws of nature and laws of reason and that rational thought consists in discovering what these laws are. The relativist disagrees, denying the existence of such an overarching framework. The relativist believes that what we think to be rational thought is relative to the specific cultural or social context within which we do our thinking. Because a plurality of such contexts exists, we can never escape speaking of "our" and "their" standards of what is reasonable. To be truly modern, the relativist claims, is to accept the fact that we live amid a pluralism of perspectives. The relativist thus translates the perspectivalism of the individual subject into the perspectivalism of the social or cultural group and then denies us access to the universal realm of objectivity.

As the battle rages, the relativists accuse the objectivists of mistaking their own culturally determined perspective for what is universal or permanent, which means the objectivists are blindly purveying ethnocentrism. The objectivists counter by accusing the relativists of self-contradiction: if the relativists claim that their position is universally true, then the relativist position itself is said to transcend the limits of its own cultural conditionedness, and, hence, the position undermines itself. Although it may appear that these two positions are radically distinct, they are both children of the modern mind. The battle is a form of sibling rivalry. Most of us are likely to hold both positions, perhaps arguing one way on some occasions and the opposite way on other occasions. Some of us take the easy way out and make objectivist assumptions when dealing with matters of natural science and then support relativism when dealing with the social sciences, humanities, and the arts. This conceptual split reflects the pressure toward dichotomous thinking that seems to be built into the critical consciousness of the modern mind.

We need to challenge such dichotomous thinking in the attempt to apprehend a more inclusive notion of truth. Critical distance through objectification has made us forget that there is only one reality that includes both external objects and human subjects in relation to one another. Our personal feelings, inclinations, perspectives, evaluations, and biases are just as real as the objects we study; and if truth is to be comprehensive, it must include the human subject and the cultural context as well as the natural world. Truth cannot be limited to objectivity; nor ought it be denied in the name of cultural relativity. I believe we need to think of truth comprehensively. Subjective feelings and cultural perspectives are not strictly epiphenomenal to an otherwise value-neutral cosmos. Their very inclusion in the whole of what is makes the one reality of which we are a part a reality that itself makes value judgments and has value.

This means as well that to think of freedom strictly in terms of individual autonomy is a delusion, because each individual is in fact granted what measure of freedom he or she has by the release of constraints by other free individuals. In other words, free or not, we are all in this together. It takes the whole human community for us to be who we are. The recognition of this fact has led postmoderns to advance the theory of holism. But more about that later.

Doubt

Another Cartesian legacy that imbues the sciences and secular self-understanding is the principle of doubt. Doubt sounds like a negative principle. It is. Yet over time it has led to a positive principle, namely, commitment to pluralism. If one can always doubt one's own position, then one must grant the possible truth of an opponent's position. Nevertheless, as soon as this is done, the opponent ceases to be an opponent and becomes a fellow traveler along the path that takes us toward greater and greater uncertainty about everything except pluralism itself.

We tacitly believe doubt should be systematic and exhaustive. One should doubt everything except that which is shown to be indubitably true. Nothing could be exempt from doubt, said Descartes, nothing except the presence of the doubter. Hence, *Cogito, ergo sum:* I think, therefore I am. In order to doubt, one cannot doubt the doubting process. So, for there to be a doubting process there must be a doubter, a thinker, a human subject. Descartes's own subjectivity was indubitable. Having passed the test of doubt, the indubitable knowledge of his own subjectivity provided Descartes with the foundation for his philosophy.

The principle of doubt has become the cutting edge of modern critical thinking. By honing the insights of relativism, the nineteenth and twentieth centuries have sharpened the blade of doubt so that it cuts ever more deeply. Karl Marx, Friedrich Nietzsche, and Sigmund Freud added subjectivity itself to Descartes's list of things to be doubted. Knowledge of oneself is no longer indubitable. We ourselves cannot be fully aware of what constitutes our own consciousness. When we articulate beliefs about God's will, for example, Marxists suspect that we are unconsciously giving voice to middle-class or bourgeois economic interests cloaked in religious language. Freudians suspect that we are repeating parental or cultural values that we introjected into our superego prior to the age of five. Depth psychologists may say we have unconsciously created the image of a loving Father in heaven in order to overcome the shock of growing up and realizing that our earthly fathers are unable to protect us from the vicissitudes of life or from the fear of death. Feminists may say similarly that we have created the image of a heavenly Father who rules over earth in order to garner religious sanction for a social structure of oppression in which earthly fathers rule over women, children, and households. Operating in all of these analyses is the principle of critical doubt, which some philosophers now dub the "hermeneutic of suspicion." The hermeneuts of suspicion, in short, accuse religious people of having a false consciousness, of projecting their own quite mundane self-interests onto God and heaven, where they do not belong.

This critical consciousness accounts for the so-called death of God. The hermeneuts of suspicion invert the authorship of the divine-human creation. Instead of God creating us, they say we have created God. Thus, atheism has arrived full force in the modern mind. But it is not the assertion of an atheistic position per se that accounts for the alleged death of God. Rather, it is the critical consciousness that raises the specter that our language about God can be looked at in another way. It is the suspicion—whether proven or unproven—that our talk about heaven is a disguised form of talking about earth. The net impact is that religious authority appears to have lost its transcendental grounding and, hence, is no longer for us an authority.

There is no longer any way to prove with certainty that what theologians say about God is true or false. Hence, one must doubt the validity of theological assertions by considering the possibility that what is said about God may have more than one meaning, more than one interpretation. So we find ourselves in a situation where there is always a plurality of interpretations of any statement about God, and there is no objective means for adjudicating decisively between them. Pluralism has made its nest in the modern mind and plans to stay for the foreseeable future.

Thus, modern critical consciousness has proven to be a formidable challenge to religious people whose theological doctrines were first formulated in a premodern age. We can with the tools of suspicion take our belief systems and objectify them, analyze them, depersonalize them, and criticize them. We can compare them to what other people think. We can also doubt them, doubting not only their objective truth but suspecting false motives on the part of the faithful who hold them. In sum, modern consciousness distances us from the source of religious life found in the ancient Christian symbols.

Hermeneutics as Theological Response

Now, how have Christian theologians responded to this challenge of the modern critical consciousness? The first thing has been to formulate the theological task in terms of the hermeneutical question. The hermeneutical question presupposes that the context has changed and that theology consists primarily in a form of translation from one context to the next. Sometimes cast in terms of the "hermeneutic problem," the task most modern theologians set for themselves is that of reinterpreting the original meaning of what the Bible says in light of the new situation. Much as a translator interprets meaning from one language into another, modern theologians have been seeking new formulations for apparently out-of-date symbols and beliefs. They seem to assume that the meaning of the Christian faith could be cut loose from its original situation. As a letter mailed to an overseas address passes from one country to another, so also the gospel has been thought to travel from one worldview to another and, when delivered, be read and understood. Because the gospel can travel, the theologian could serve as the travel agent to arrange its jet-propelled flight across the abyss that separates the time of the Bible from the time of the modern world.

It is my position that the hermeneutical question has been the proper question to ask over the last century or two and, furthermore, that most of the assumptions made by modern theologians are worth maintaining for the foreseeable future. As we move from modern to postmodern consciousness, however, the value and role of these assumptions become a good deal more subtle than first suspected. This subtlety will require that we modify—if not abrogate—the translation model for moving from the period of the biblical experience to our own. I say this for two reasons. First, the language of the Bible is not as foreign to our modern way of thinking as is widely assumed. Yes, of course there is a difference between biblical and modern worldviews, but when we seek the roots of modernity we see that they reach back to the ancient world in such a way that we moderns are deeply dependent upon what went before. The revolution of the modern mind is not as radical as is sometimes thought. What is needed is a theological method that assumes that both ancient and modern understandings belong to a single and more inclusive tradition-history—to the single story that is Western civilization—and that this tradition-history will eventually participate in the one comprehensive story of humankind on earth.

Second, although there is some validity to thinking that the Christian faith is constituted by a linguistically independent meaning that can be translated from one language to another, there are certain basic symbols of the faith that are not translatable and simply must be present wherever one finds the faith. The basic symbols that are tied to the original experience of the revelation from God are irreplaceable and even untranslatable. All one can do is continue to interpret their meaning in light of new contexts. One cannot translate them exhaustively into a new mode of discourse. The symbol of the cross, for example, is requisite for Christian faith regardless of what language one speaks or what historical context one finds oneself in. If the cross is not present, the faith is not present. What permits the gospel to ride out the centuries, traveling from one age to another and one language to another, is not its translatability. It is rather the protean power of its symbols to emit new meaning in new contexts.

I will attempt to show how this is the case in the chapters that are to come. In the meantime, we need now to turn our attention to postmodern consciousness proper in order to note where it diverges from the modern mind even while maintaining continuity.

THE CHALLENGE OF THE POSTMODERN MIND

Postmodernity as an independent mode of consciousness is not here yet, if it is ever to come to full term at all. It is at present a babe struggling to emerge from the womb of modernity, and as it does so its first cries are of protest. There is growing disenchantment with the brokenness and fragmentation left in the wake of modern objectivism, mechanicalism, technologism, and individualism. We moderns, say the postmodern critics, have separated human consciousness from the world of extended objects, separated value from truth. We have separated humans from nature, from God, and from one another; and should we finally detonate our nuclear weapons—weapons that represent the height of the modern achievements in technological thinking—then we may even separate ourselves from our own future. Our world continues to break into more and more pieces. Voices from many quarters can be heard crying out, "Enough of this! Let's put the world back together again!"

The Quest for Wholeness

Of all categories, that of wholeness most thoroughly embraces the variety of proposals to put the world back together again. The cardinal doctrine of postmodernity is that the whole is greater than the sum of the parts, and the problem with us moderns is that we look only at the parts while ignoring the whole. An important corollary to the cardinal principle is this: everything is related to everything else. The problem with us moderns is that we foolishly think we can operate as isolated individual egos and ignore everything else. This ignoring of the relation between our internal world and the whole of reality is being attacked as the root cause of the dichotomous thinking and fragmentation that are narrowing our vision and threatening to destroy our world. A philosophy of holism can overcome this tendency toward fragmentation.

This message comes from many quarters. This is the message of revisionist physicists who wish to understand the apparent chance movement of electrons as directed by a unifying and comprehensive reality that can be best understood in terms of Asian mysticism. In a different but parallel fashion this is the concern of postcritical modes of philosophical thinking in such schools as process metaphysics and continental hermeneutics. We hear it as well from the growing global consciousness of futurists who advocate a "new holism" and "ecological humanism." We hear it from feminists who claim that women can see the whole of things intuitively and that we need to redress the modern imbalance that tips in favor of the left-brain or objectivist thinking of men. Finally, we hear it from various aspects of new age consciousness with its emphasis on such things as human transformation, holistic health, biofeedback, the paranormal, mystical religion, and Aquarian visions of a utopian future. The postmodern mood is succinctly expressed by the New England Network of Light, an informal association of new age organizations that considers its members to be "seeds of a new culture and civilization, based on cooperation rather than competition, on love and respect for all of life, and on living in harmony with the earth, with each other, and with God." What all of these expressions of an emerging postmodern consciousness have in common is a desire to transcend the boundaries of modernity and to find healing for the wounds it has left.

Postmoderns of various types seem to agree that the fundamental cause of this fragmentation is the modern habit of divisive thinking, or, more precisely, it is the destructive assumption that the fragmentary nature of human thought corresponds with an actual fragmentariness characteristic of reality itself. Because we are finite and our thoughts tend to seek out differences and draw distinctions, we get into the unreflective habit of assuming that these are real differences and distinctions. We then experience the world as broken up in fragments. Hence, many people today believe the cure for the ills wrought by modernity must begin with healthier thinking.

The first division that needs healing is epistemological. It is the gash that presumably separates objective reason from subjective feeling. A holistic understanding of human reasoning will recognize that love, compassion, trust, and faith are feelings that help compose knowledge. The category of imagination is inclusive of both thinking and feeling, and imagination places the human being in a context of intelligibility that spans the cleavage between subject and object, a context of meaning that includes both.

But the wholeness and healing postmoderns seek are more than epistemological. They are also ontological. They apply to reality, to our cosmos. To illustrate, we note that the basic principles of holism in its current form were developed early in the twentieth century by the South African philosopher J. C. Smuts. Smuts sought to conceive of the whole of things according to the model of biological evolution. This means things move through time. They change and develop. What makes temporal movement significant, according to Smuts, is that it is accompanied by genuine creativity, by epigenesis.

There are two basic and incompatible ways of conceiving creative activity within the cosmos. They are the *unfolding view* and the *epigenetic view*. According to the first view, everything is in one way or another given at the beginning. The universe consists in an unfolding or realization of potentialities already present at the starting point. This view assumes the created order was in principle complete and final at the point of origination, so that all subsequent events and changes consist only in rearrangements and reshufflings of the original material and forms. The present and future have been predetermined or at least delimited by the past. All fresh initiative, novelty, or creativeness are effectively banned from the universe. In the course of this book I will refer to this as the *archonic view*, using the Greek root ἀρχή , which means both "beginning" and "rule." Popular versions of postmodernity such as the human potential movement—which interprets human liberation as the unfolding of potential already existing within us—unknowingly espouse this more conservative of the two alternatives.

Smuts, in contrast, proffers the epigenetic view. Evolutionary theory emerging from the nineteenth century rejects the notion of a completed beginning in the past. Instead we have "a real progressive creation still going forward in the universe" so that "the sum of reality" is not constant but is "progressively increasing in the course of evolution.... Evolution is not merely a process of change, of regrouping of the old into new forms; it is creative; its new forms are not merely fashioned out of the old materials; it creates both new materials and new forms from the synthesis of the new with the old materials."[1] From this arises the view that evolutionary development is an epigenesis rather than an unfolding of a previously fixed genetic reality. Epigenetic movement is understood as creative of the new, as displaying novelty and initiative, as opening up new paths and rendering possible new choices, as creating freedom for the future, and in a very real sense as breaking the bondage of the past and its fixed predeterminations.

When one combines essential temporality with this emergent creativity as Smuts does, it leads rapidly away from the holism characteristic of classical ontology. One could say that the metaphysics of the ancient Greeks was holistic in the sense that the monistic question was constantly raised: how are all things finally related to one another? Simplicity was the virtue. Plato argued that oneness was prior to plurality. Anything that is a composite of two or more elements is subordinate because it is dependent upon each of those elements for its reality. Therefore, what is simple, indivisible, and indestructible is ultimate.

What we see developing in postmodernity is a concept of emergent holism, wherein composite actualities produce new wholes that are not simple but that represent higher levels of complex and integrated being. Whereas for classical ontology the move from the simple to the composite is almost a degeneration, for epigenetic holism ever-new composites—if they become genuine wholes and not mere aggregates—constitute an achievement. The ancient metaphysic left virtually no room for change or development. It was a form of the unfolding view of creation. The evolutionary and epigenetic ontology, in contrast, incorporates temporal movement and foresees new and equally ultimate realities appearing in the future. "The pull of the future" is as essential to the life of an organism as "the push of the past," and the new wholes that arise are the center and creative source of reality.[2]

In short, postmodern thinking seeks to overcome the fragmentation of the modern mind by employing the concept of holism. By giving priority to the whole, postmodernists believe we can reintegrate thought with feeling, objectivity with participation. This means that we need to get beyond the machine model of the world. The model of the living

---

1. J. C. Smuts, *Holism and Evolution* (New York: Macmillan, 1926), 89.
2. Ibid., 115–16; see also 102.

organism appears better because it integrates things around the dynamic movement of life.

It should be obvious that this is not simply a return to the premodern understanding of things. The emerging postmodern worldview can be distinguished from the premodern because it seeks wholeness through synthesis, not through a return to the simple origin. It is dynamic. It recognizes that significant change takes place. It embraces creativity. Because the whole is both creative and synthetic, it has the potential for uniting what has been fragmented, for healing what has been broken.

Toward a Postmodern Theology

Now I must state that it is not my intention here to render a wholesale endorsement of things that bear the postmodern label. My primary motive for addressing postmodernity issues from the contextualization principle, according to which the church's theology and ministry need to be made intelligible and effective in each context to which we are called to bear witness to the gospel of Jesus Christ. Postmodernity belongs to our current context. This alone justifies addressing it theologically.[3]

Beyond its contextual significance, however, it may have constitutive value as well. The medium of postmodern thinking itself draws theological explication in directions of greater comprehensiveness and coherence than were possible during the modern period. The whole-part dialectic in particular provides systematic theology with a potent auxiliary concept for

---

3. At present there is no single agreed-upon usage of the word *postmodern*. Many competing schools of thought are filing for a patent in the intellectual community. My approach here differs sharply from theologians who employ the deconstructionist literary criticism of Jacques Derrida and who substitute the literary text for the transcendent self. This approach, it seems to me, is a mere extrapolation of modern commitments to the point of producing nihilism. See Mark C. Taylor, *Erring: A Postmodern A/Theology* (Chicago: University of Chicago Press, 1984). Postmodernity in essence is the recovery of meaning, not its dissolution. Therefore, my sympathies lie closer to those of process theologian David Ray Griffin, founder of the Center for a Postmodern World (located in Santa Barbara), and history of religions scholar Huston Smith, because these two wish to engage in constructionist or revisionary thinking and to do serious business with holism. I wish to start where these scholars start. However, my emphasis on eschatological ontology means I can borrow only meagerly from the Whiteheadian metaphysics Griffin espouses; and my emphasis on history as reality makes me reluctant to embrace the mysticism of Smith's perennial philosophy. See David Ray Griffin, ed., *Spirituality and Society: Postmodern Visions* (Albany: State University of New York Press, 1988); Huston Smith, *Beyond the Post-modern Mind* (New York: Crossroad, 1982); David Ray Griffin and Huston Smith, *Primordial Truth and Postmodern Theology* (Albany: State University of New York Press, 1989); and my own assessment in "Toward Postmodern Theology," *Dialog* 24, no. 3 (Summer 1985): 221–26, and 24, no. 4 (Fall 1985): 293–97. I am less than fully sympathetic with Thomas C. Oden, who believes he can avoid the wilderness of modernity by returning to the Eden of orthodox Christianity in the first millennium. He in effect equates the postmodern with a desired return to the premodern (*After Modernity... What? Agenda for Theology* [Grand Rapids, Mich.: Zondervan, 1990]). I have more affinity for the position of Hans Küng, who wants a postmodernity that preserves the critical consciousness of modernity while avoiding its reductionism (*Theology for the Third Millennium* [New York: Doubleday, 1988], 8–9).

drawing out the implications of the Christian understanding of God, creation, eschatology, and ethics. In the pages to come, I hope to show how this might be done through the cultivation of a proleptic consciousness of the yet-to-be consummated whole of reality. By *proleptic consciousness* I am referring to our awareness and anticipation ahead of time of the future whole. Such awareness and anticipation are based upon God's promise and upon faith in God's faithfulness.

The blueprint for structuring such a proleptic theology will follow a destiny–wholeness–integration formula. We will see that the gospel of Jesus Christ is essentially a promise for the future. In fact, it is more than just a promise. It actually embodies ahead of time the future God has promised for the whole of creation, namely, new creation. If the gospel be the key to understanding reality, which I believe is the central Christian commitment, then it seems to follow that what is real is future-oriented. Destiny determines and defines what things are. Further, only at the fulfillment of the divine promise will reality itself become a whole, and only with this whole of wholes will the true nature of all the participating parts—including ourselves—be revealed. Only in light of the God-determined whole can we apprehend the purpose according to which all the world processes and human enterprises will be integrated, according to which separated and fragmented parts will be transformed into an integrated unity. Of course, that God-determined whole is not yet actual. It does not yet exist. But it has been revealed—it has been incarnated—ahead of time in the life, death, and resurrection of the Nazarene. Hence, it is to Jesus Christ that one must look to find human destiny, to gain a vision of the whole, and according to which people can integrate the disparate elements of their lives. A life so integrated around Christ is a proleptic life. It is the future life actualized ahead of time. It is new life in the midst of the old life. It is beatitudinal life because it is true life. It is beatitude.

THREE STAGES ALONG FAITH'S WAY

The very fact that I have posed the hermeneutical question and then followed with an attempt to identify the emerging postmodern consciousness raises the prospect of thinking about the Christian faith in terms of at least three phases: premodern, modern, and postmodern. One of the curious things about history is that it seldom really leaves anything behind. It accumulates. The premodern way of thinking has not been totally abandoned. It is still with us and continues to exist side by side with the more recent innovations.

There is another way to look at this matter. It may be helpful not only to think of these three phases as different chapters in the story of Western civilization, but also as chapters in one's life story. Using the tools of philosophical hermeneutics we can draw a fascinating parallel between the morphology of human consciousness in general and that of our history up to this point. It may be more than just a coincidental parallel because we are becoming increasingly aware that how we think is determined in large part by the language and tradition within which we do that thinking. The history of our culture lives and moves within us. Therefore, the pattern we follow in developing modes for interpreting the symbols of our faith can rightly be pictured as a microcosm of the development of our culture as a whole, the macrocosm.

I suggest that we think of faith in terms of three levels or stages of consciousness: (1) naive world-construction, (2) critical deconstruction, and (3) postcritical reconstruction. These characterize my own spiritual biography as described in the preface, just as I believe they characterize the discipline of theology as it tries to respond to currents in our culture.

Each stage, I maintain, has its own integrity; and when we fail to distinguish the stage in which we are thinking it may lead to confusion. Therefore, let me invoke three cautions at this point. First, the term *naive* connotes nothing pejorative. When it comes to one's belief in God, a naive faith is by no means inferior to a critical faith. Second, the three stages are not intended to establish a hierarchy, so that one would necessarily be motivated to leave one level completely to go and live at the next. I suspect that it is possible for a person of faith to live simultaneously at all three levels.

The third caution comes from Eric Voegelin, who warns constantly about the danger of tripartite thinking wherein we conceive of history as proceeding from innocence to fall and then rising again to a higher stage of innocence. The problem with such a tripartite scheme is that we are tempted to put ourselves at the stage of higher innocence. The temptation is always great to absolutize the present, especially our version of the truth that exists in the present. This is a form of narrow-mindedness that does violence to great moments of truth in the past and fails to acknowledge the finite character of our own present knowledge.

Despite Voegelin's caution, we need to employ the idea of three stages because it reflects the actual experience of faith in our own era. Here I will insist that Christian faith can be authentic and fulfilling at each stage, and, further, I will contend that it is not the mission of the church to seek routinely to advance a person from one level to the next. The mission of the church is primarily to proclaim the gospel and encourage faith, and it can do so best if it takes into account the integrity of each stage of consciousness.

Naive World-construction

The first stage is the one I experienced at home prior to attending the university. Let us characterize it in terms of compact consciousness and refer to it as the *first naiveté* or *natural literalism*. The first naiveté is that stage in which we exist in simple harmony with the symbols of our world of meaning, our lifeworld. It is characterized by immediacy of belief, by an unbroken ecology of meaning in which everything fits together and makes sense. There is no clear differentiation between one's own basic concepts and those that are the common fund of the surrounding culture or subculture. It is the everyday swim in the stream of language and thought prior to critical consciousness, prior to stepping out of the flow and viewing it from the dry island of objectivity. Paul Ricoeur describes the first naiveté as a sort of blindness in the very heart of seeing.

Our understanding of the world at this stage of compact or predifferentiated consciousness operates at the level of what we might call *naive realism*. We assume that the ideas in our mind and words in our mouths correspond with the world the way it really is. We assume that when scientists engage in research, they uncover the hidden mechanisms of the world of nature and show us what is actually there. We assume that when the Bible speaks of the kingdom of God, we can imagine God as wearing a crown, sitting on a throne, and being waited on by servants. It is life lived amid the objective world before it requires a doctrine of objectivism to justify itself. It is the feeling of being at home with our ideas and language.

For Christians at the level of the first naiveté, the word *God* is part of the everyday furniture of their symbolic home. This certainly was the case with people living in antiquity in general and with the writers of the Bible in particular. Visions of heaven and hell, interventions by angels and demons, miraculous cures, divine guidance in the course of events, and such matters were all accepted at face value as part and parcel of the world. The Bible did not need to argue for the existence of God. It assumed it, and so did the bulk of its first readers. Quite the same situation exists for children today who are raised in Christian families. The watchful presence of guardian angels, providential interpretations of tragedy, and thinking that deceased relatives are now happy in heaven and getting ready for the last judgment—all these make good common sense. This is the naive oneness with our symbolic world that Zimmermann relied on when painting the nave ceiling of the Wieskirche.

Essential to this lifeworld is an experience of tension. But it is not an intellectual tension. It is moral. Religion at the level of the first naiveté reflects the tensions of human existence through a set of dualisms that organize moral thinking and social awareness into categories that distinguish right from wrong. The paramount dualism is the antagonism between God and Satan. The other more modest dualisms are variants of this: good versus evil, obedience versus disobedience, spirit versus flesh, commitment versus self-indulgence, virtue versus sin, confession versus denial, heaven versus hell. Individual thinking and acting have meaning because they participate in the cosmic contest between God and God's enemies. The object of religious devotion is to make a willful choice—that is, to decide to commit oneself to the divine mission and to fight against the forces of evil at work within one's own soul and in the exterior world.

Thus the fundamental existential issue at the level of the first naiveté becomes the degree of personal commitment. How much faith do I have? Does my conscience guide me to live righteously? Will I be brave enough to die for what is right and true? Am I really sincere in my belief? These are deep and conscience-gripping questions that lead the sensitive soul down under the surface of the culturally shared Christianity and into the depths of spiritual turmoil. The inner pain of authentic faith coming to birth is a labor that can be faced only by the individual. No surrogate can walk that dark valley for you or me. Only when one has personally traversed that valley can there be a faith that is truly sincere and fully committed. The tension of human existence becomes articulated in terms of the struggle of faith versus unfaith; and the tension is thought to be relieved when one can say that "Jesus Christ is my personal savior."

What is the role of theology at the level of the first naiveté? It is basically world-constructing. By "world" here I mean *lifeworld* or world of meaning, the realm of signification within which we understand ourselves. This world can be distinguished from what we ordinarily mean by environment, the universe as viewed through the objective lenses of the scientific gaze. Our world is something to which we are personally related. It is usually prior to and inclusive of our objectified thinking and our subjective reflection. We are able to achieve self-understanding only through the language and symbols given us by our lifeworld.

This world is not the result of pure projection or individual imagination. It is shared. It is bequeathed to us by our intimate family, our surrounding culture, and our linguistic tradition. It provides the fundamental system through which we understand ourselves, external reality, and what is of ultimate importance to both.

For theology to serve the task of world-construction, then, means that it will seek to present, re-present, and think through the primary symbols of the Christian faith in terms of naive realism. By retelling the Bible's stories and by reciting the creeds it will provide a vocabulary through which we can bring to articulation our innermost thoughts and personal feelings in conjunction with a mental picture of how God's world works. The very language and concepts we use to describe the world and to understand ourselves will connote and refer us constantly to the reality of God.

As I said before, thinking at the level of the first naiveté has its own integrity. It is not necessarily anti-intellectual, dishonest, or spiritually shallow. It is natural, an inevitable stage of consciousness from which some people never emerge but which all of us must go through. The gospel of salvation is as true and meaningful for children and naive adults and was as true and meaningful for the people of antiquity as it is for anyone else.

Nevertheless, once a person undergoes the purging fires of modern critical consciousness there is no going back. Theology, as we shall see, is both challenged and immensely enriched by modern criticism.

Critical Deconstruction

As we saw earlier, the seventeenth and eighteenth centuries have brought us into the modern era with its increasingly differentiated consciousness. To the heart of modern thinking belong critical awareness and the distance it sets up between our interior subjectivity and the outside world of objective things. It also sets up a distance between the ancient or premodern world and today's world. In the case of the Bible we have come to call it the hermeneutical gap, the interpretation gap between the ancient worldview of scripture and its meaning for modern readers today. Think of the familiar contrasts between the Bible's then and our now. The Bible describes the intervention of supranatural powers into the course of human events; we today describe events in terms of the laws of nature. The Bible assumes that heaven is above, somewhere near the clouds; we today fly above the clouds in jet airplanes. We can no longer live naively in the world of the Bible. We live twenty centuries distant from it. We can objectify it, can see it in its strangeness, and can treat it as if it has no direct meaning for our lives. In short, our naive relationship to the symbolic world of the Bible is broken.

I could at this point rehearse the development of lower criticism and higher criticism that led to the modern techniques for interpreting the Bible. But this might sidetrack us from apprehending the central impact of the modern mind on Christian consciousness, namely, the loss of divine meaning for the objective world. Because the natural world is thought to be running according to a closed system of natural laws discernible by science, and because nothing like spiritual presence or divine intervention can be perceived through scientific analysis, religious faith has become relegated to private subjectivity (or sometimes cultural relativity) right along with value, meaning, and autonomous freedom. The modern mind can no longer find God in nature. The world around us has ceased to become a mode of divine presence. It has became secularized and reified. If the divine is to be found at all, God would have to be found in the human subject along with valuing and decision making. The world itself has become religiously meaningless. The question of the meaning of life has become the overriding concern of modern artists, philosophers, and theologians alike. The trauma has shaken us deeply.

What has happened to theology? The liberal Protestants and their heirs, the neoorthodox and existentialist theologians, decided to leave the realm of objective meaning entirely to natural scientists and to secular experts who would treat it as a value-neutral reality. They then retreated to the interior realm of the human subject. They took the original Christian symbols—such as the doctrines of creation and consummation—that seemed to indicate that God has a relationship with the world as a whole and translated them so that they would refer only to personal faith. By relegating faith statements to the domain of human subjectivity, modern theologians thought they could avoid encroaching on the province bequeathed to the natural scientist. God's creative and transformative activity became focused entirely upon the individual human consciousness and its decision-making power. In short, theologians joined the conflict between the objectivists and the relativists, consigned the objective realm to the scientists, and took up residence in the humanities departments of universities.

The net result was that the basic symbols and doctrines of Christian faith could no longer illuminate the wider world. The doctrine of creation lost its ability to enhance understanding of galactic formation or biological evolution. The doctrine of providence seemed to have nothing to say about the law of gravity or the fission of the atom. Bible-based beliefs became ghettoized within the human soul, within university courses on the history of Western civilization, and within the community of shared symbolic meaning, the church.

But the loss of the world was not all bad. In the process of making the shift to the human subject, the neoorthodox and existentialist theologians reinterpreted in a powerfully new way the first commandment and its call to faith in God alone. "You shall have no other gods," the commandment reads. What does it mean to have a god? Existentially speaking, a god is that in which we believe, that upon which we place our trust. A god is that to which we yield ourselves. While trying to recover some of the spiritual treasures of the Reformation of the sixteenth century, many modern theologians read with great care what Martin Luther says in his Large Catechism when commenting on the first commandment:

A god is that to which we look for all good and in which we find refuge in every time of need. To have a god is nothing else than to trust and believe with our whole heart. As I have often said, the trust and faith of the heart alone make both God and an idol. If your faith and trust are right, then your God is the true God. On the other hand, if your trust is false and wrong, then you have not the true God. For these two belong together, faith and God. That to which your heart clings and entrusts itself is, I say, really your God.[4]

Luther is saying that the dynamics of faith appear to be quite the same whether one believes in the true God or in an idol. Faith entails seeking goodness, entrusting oneself, and yielding oneself. Idolatry is not the absence of faith. It is faith in the wrong thing. The primary issue is not

---

4. Luther, BC, 365.

whether or not one has faith, but whether or not one's faith is in the true God. Luther is so employable by modern theologians because he places the burden of faith on the human subject, not on objective reality. The result is idol analysis.

To engage in idol analysis we must ask, who is the true God? The modern neoorthodox theologians answer: the true God is not of this world. This is the important thing. God is not a part of the world like other parts are, is not one being existing side by side with other beings, is not one object among others. For those of us thinking at the level of critical consciousness, this means that we cannot objectify God. As the Hebrews were enjoined not to construct graven images, we must avoid constructing conceptual images. Images, graven or conceptual, objectify. To objectify God is to risk creating a conceptual idol, to risk alienating ourselves from God.

How can this alienation from God be overcome? Through faith. Faith at the level of critical consciousness requires two things. First, persons of faith accept the fact that God transcends the cosmos; God is not one reality among others within the world. Second, persons of faith recognize—personally and subjectively—that they are already in relationship with God and that they cannot set out to establish a relationship when it already exists. They do not need to pursue a relationship with God in the objective world outside if they already have a relationship with God inside. The result of these two observations is the call to faith in the true God and not in a conceptual idol. Faith is not faith in an object, but rather faith in that which transcends all objectivity. Relationship to God is discerned not through the world but solely through a decision of faith, a decision to trust God and God alone.

This daily faith at the level of critical consciousness now includes a paradoxical component, namely, doubt. If faith is the result of a subjective decision, how can one know for certain he or she made the right decision? Answer: there is no certainty. One cannot simply go to God and ask if one made the right decision. There is no place one can go to find God because God is not locatable. God transcends all locations. There is no way to verify statements of belief. Hence, doubt must always accompany faith.

But how can that be faith? It is not faith in the sense of simple or naive belief. It is a trust in things unseen, a devotion to a presence that transcends beliefs, a commitment to a divine reality that cannot be conceived. It rests upon a fundamental biblical tenet, namely, that Jesus Christ is the truth (John 14:6). To believe that Jesus Christ is the truth means, among other things, that no genuine pursuit of truth will lead us away from Christ. The purpose of doubt in modern thinking is to serve the truth, and a person who genuinely doubts is paradoxically expressing faith in truth. Doubt is pressed into the service of faith as a tool for discovering and dispensing with idols, for unmasking and disempowering those images of God that make God only one more component of the mundane world. Modern or critical faith is courageous faith because it seeks radical obedience to the first commandment by incorporating doubt and leaping into the realm of the unknown and unknowable.

Of course, very few people live with the brute courage of critical faith that this theology calls for. For many modern people the fires of criticism have purged Christianity not only of its conceptual idols, but of belief in the true God as well. Many people have gone ahead and thrown out the golden truth along with the idolatrous dross. Critical consciousness most often produces skepticism and alienation from religious symbols entirely. Secularism rather than radical faith becomes the option most people choose. Hence, the modern period has been one of widespread nonfaith.

The task of theology at the level of critical consciousness, as might be obvious here, is to be world-destroying. The overt purpose of theology is to deconstruct or even to demolish our world of meaning. This is based on the insight that God is not of this world, is transcendent to it, and stands over against it. Nothing in the world can adequately represent the divine reality. Therefore, as long as we find our life's meaning totally or exhaustively in terms of this world—in terms of the language, concepts, and values of our culture or even our religion—then the only result will be idolatry. We are trusting something other than the true God. Critical theology uses all the tools of objectification and suspicious doubt (even when supplied by atheists) necessary to demolish the false security of our present world. The first commandment is a call from the beyond. It is the voice of God saying that we must put our faith in God and God alone.

Within many churches there is resistance to such critical theology. We should probably expect that because critical consciousness poses such a severe threat to naiveté, a defensive posture is almost inevitable. The form it usually takes is atavistic fundamentalism, a defiant defense of biblical literalism. Fundamentalists are literalists who have been confronted with critical consciousness and who do not want their world of meaning torn away from them. They do not want to surrender the objectified world of nature to the secular worldview; nor do they want faith directed toward a nonobjectifiable God. At its worst, reactionary literalism risks putting faith in the wrong thing—that is, it risks putting faith in the world of biblical meaning rather than in the transcendent God who shatters our meaning and calls us to radical obedience. This is why the Bible and its authority have moved to the center of the debate. Within the Bible the unchallenged world of archaic meaning seems to remain intact. From the point of view of liberal and neoorthodox Christians, however, the fundamentalists border on idolatry—sometimes called bibliolatry— by choosing meaning within this world over pure faith in the transcendent

God who is beyond this world. The story of the bitter debate contains countless dramatic chapters.

One aspect of the debate that makes it unnecessarily bitter is the frequent failure on the part of liberal and neoorthodox proponents to distinguish between the first naiveté and fundamentalism. These two are not exactly the same. Naive literalism is precritical. Fundamentalism is anticritical. There can still be considerable intellectual integrity at the level of compact naiveté. The problem of bibliolatry arises only as a defiant response to the attack launched by critical consciousness. Bibliolatry does not belong to the first naiveté proper.

The temptation to idolize the Bible arises when critical consciousness assails the foundations of one's identity as a person of faith living in relation to God. Once a person of naive faith is attacked by the weapons of modern criticism, he or she seems to have only two options: to retreat and defend the old worldview or to press on aggressively toward a critical faith in the God who transcends the world, Bible included. Fundamentalists flirt with idolatry because they tend to allow the Bible, which belongs to this world, to become the object of worship and devotion rather than the divine reality to which it points—the divine reality that transcends this world. This is not the mistake of the first naiveté per se. Hence, the first naiveté should not be the target of denunciation.

Postcritical Reconstruction

Modern critical consciousness in general leaves us is in a desert of suprasubjective meaninglessness. This may be true of modern critical theology as well. At this moment in the history of Western culture theologians are being called upon to go beyond the modern mind, to reconstruct modes of meaningfulness issuing from the symbols conveying revelatory truth.

Postmodern voices complain that moderns have blithely accepted the erroneous notion that the meaning of life is something strictly subjective. The terrifying problem with accepting this notion is subjective loneliness. If we insist that meaning is created by the self and not found in the external world, then we end up finding our self utterly alone. The self becomes an isolated oasis of meaning in a vast wasteland of meaningless objectivity. Modern critical consciousness has left us bereft and alone amid a desert of meaninglessness.

"Beyond the desert of criticism we wish to be called again," writes Paul Ricoeur.[5] What we need, he contends, is an interpretation of the ancient symbols—symbols that come to us initially from outside our own subjectivity—that lets us be taught by them, that lets us share their world of meaning. But just how can we do this without returning to the immediacy of belief of the first naiveté? Ricoeur's answer is the wager.

---

5. Paul Ricoeur, *The Symbolism of Evil* (Boston: Beacon, 1967), 349.

A wager is a risk, a bet. In this case—and in this book—we are betting that a hermeneutic of belief in the Christian gospel will be more fruitful for living in the world than the skeptical conclusions produced by a hermeneutic of suspicion. We will not forget our doubts. But we will press on, trying to understand ourselves and the world around us in light of the symbols of divine revelation. The wager is a form of hypothetical belief, a self-entrustment to the world of meaning created by Christian language.

The wager takes us into theology's hermeneutical circle. Ricoeur describes the circle this way: "We must understand in order to believe, but we must believe in order to understand." When approaching the claims of the Christian faith, we do so with at least a hypothetical believing in order to begin to understand them. What we are asking for here is a post-Cartesian version of Saint Anselm's definition of theology as faith seeking understanding. Once we have entered the belief-understanding circle, the process of interpreting Christian symbols begins to illumine our own life and makes it understandable in relation to the divine reality.

Christian symbols are reality-detectors. They enable us to confront truth and to discern life's meaning, something we could not do apart from symbols. Hence, we need the wager so that we can attend to the gospel, share the gospel's realm of meaning, and let it speak to us. If we treat Christian symbols only from a distance, only across the gap of twenty centuries, only as meaningful to another culture of another time with another worldview, then we will be unable to hear what they might be saying to us. By betting that the gospel can be meaningful, we will open ourselves to the possibility of constructing a new self-understanding and a new world-understanding. Postcritical thinking is both personally participatory and world-constructive, or better, world-reconstructive. It is integrative and holistic consciousness at work.

The participatory quality to postcritical theology makes it integrative and holistic. We recognize here that when thinking about God we are not thinking simply about a thing, about an object. When we ask a question about the reality of God, we must acknowledge that it is not just in the answer that the reality of God appears. God is already present in the act of our questioning. When we focus our attention on theological questions, we do so within the horizon of the Christian symbols. These symbols reflect a prior experience with the divine presence, an experience that continues to give rise to the awareness of an encompassing reality that answers to the name "God." Pursuing theological reflection is a process of refining and, in a sense, enhancing our already existing understanding of God at the compact level of symbolic meaning.

This process makes theology participatory also because the questions we pose regarding God become simultaneously questions God poses to us. We ourselves become part of the questioned reality. Who am I as a finite creature looking into the abyss of infinity? Who are we as mortal human beings standing in the face of an awesome and eternal holiness? When we reflect upon biblical symbols such as God's love, God's justice, and God's grace, we can but ask ourselves: am I loving? Am I just? Am I gracious? Or, what is my relationship to a God who is like this? Hence, to enhance our understanding of things divine is simultaneously to enhance our self-understanding.

This also enhances our understanding of the world. We can get at this by asking the following questions: even if critical theology has rid us of the idolatry of this world and we now place our faith in the transcendent God of the first commandment, is it possible to live day to day without any meaningful concept or image of the relationship between God and the world? Does obedience to the first commandment require that we lead our daily life bereft of this-worldly meaning? Not necessarily. It requires rather a reorientation or a deepening of the fragments of meaning already present in our world. Trusting God rather than this-worldly idols does not actually leave us alone in the desert of Cartesian objectivity and doubt. Rather, belief in the transcendent God reorients our life in this world around the point where the divine touches the mundane, where God has revealed Godself, namely, in Jesus the Christ. Because we have no direct or immediate access to the transcendent divine, the point of orientation must be the symbols that refer us to this revelatory event. The Christian symbols exist at what we will call the *metaxy*, at the inbetween where the ineffable God beyond touches the mundane realm in which we live. Or, as in the case of the proleptic arrival of the divine kingdom in the incarnate Son of God, the symbol marks the overlap of the future and the present.

Systematic theology becomes reconstructive when it asks the question: how should we understand our world now that we know it has been touched by God? If the ancient symbols indicate that God is a gracious creator, we wager that we can better understand our world if we conceive of it as a divine gift. If the saving event of Jesus Christ indicates that God acts out of redeeming love, we wager that social interaction is most authentic when pursuing reconciliation. If the scripture promises the comforting presence of the Holy Spirit, we wager that in our moments of despair we have good reason to believe we are not alone. Such integrative thinking requires imagination and willingness to hypothesize and speculate. It mandates the theologian to reconstruct a picture of the world and of ourselves in which everything can be seen in relation to its destiny in God.

FUNDAMENTAL QUESTIONS AND PRINCIPLES

As we pursue the tasks of Christian systematic theology in our own context characterized by modern and emerging postmodern consciousness, we will constantly bear in mind the hermeneutical question: how can the ancient symbols of the Christian faith speak meaningfully to us today? Noting that this question has been the hallmark of modern theology, I acknowledge that the agenda of the present work is modern in this sense. This is the fundamental question around which the contents of this book are organized.

In addition, there are two principles of postmodern thinking that will be of value for pursuing the answer to this question. The first is the principle of holistic thinking. I will presume that there is something intrinsically healthy to working with a holistic framework. The desire for synthesis or integration points to the deeply experienced human need for healing, for the assurance of oneness, for salvation. In the explication of the originary symbols of the Christian faith I will ask again and again how and to what degree visions of the whole—visions of a divinely graced whole—help to make the content of Christian faith meaningful in our time.

The second postmodern principle employed here is a version of the wager, namely, hypothetical reconstruction. What we do theologically must be hypothetical because it is postcritical. There is no intellectually honest way for us to return to the first naiveté without risking a fall into the deformation of fundamentalism. We must press on, incorporating our doubt and our acknowledgment of a pluralism of perspectives along the way. We must also be reconstructive because the very idea of meaningfulness implies that we live in a world of meaning. We cannot live meaningful lives in isolation. Meaning is always communal. It is shared with other people, with the world, and with God. The task of systematic theology is to show how this is the case, to show how the world is meaningful because it is loved by the God who creates and redeems it. It is loved by the God who makes it whole.

In sum, I believe it is possible for a person of Christian faith to emerge from the critical consciousness of the modern mind, to enter again into the nave of the Wieskirche and find it a meaningful experience to look up at the dome-shaped ceiling. There in the archaic but still living symbols we can be led to understand that the law of God inspires while it condemns, that the gospel of God forgives and promises, and that the closed doors of death open out on the other side to a wholesome and everlasting life.

2

EXPLICATING
THE CHRISTIAN SYMBOLS

The Symbol opens up levels of reality which are otherwise closed to us.
—Paul Tillich

There is need of a method for finding the truth.
—René Descartes

Method? Hell, we gotta get something done around here!
—Thomas Edison

Christian theology is the explication of the basic symbols found in scripture, appropriating them to the current context within which the theologian is working. Theology is the church thinking about what it believes. In itself theology is not the content of what the church believes. Rather it is reflection on the content of that belief. One puts faith in God, and this faith comes to expression in the way life is lived and in what is believed. The content of belief is found in the symbols that accompany faith. Theology is a form of thinking about these symbols; it is a form of explicating these symbols to show what they mean. As such it is a subject area to ponder, a discipline of research, a pattern for argument. Theology is not synonymous with the Christian faith itself; it is rather a way in which that faith seeks to understand itself.

How shall one go about this task of faith pursuing understanding? What should be assumed? What procedures should be followed? What are the sources and norms? By what criteria shall one's work be evaluated? We turn to theological methodology to answer these questions. Methodology is the stage in any academic discipline where foundational

31

questions are asked, alternative paths are entertained, terms are defined, goals and objectives are presented, assumptions and presuppositions are spelled out, criteria are stipulated, and procedures are adumbrated.

Now it may seem at first that methodology is a particularly modern function, hearkening to the increasingly faint voice of Descartes when he uttered in *Rules for the Direction of the Mind:* "There is need of a method for finding the truth." Yet in Christian theology the specification of a method is premodern, harking back at least to Clement of Alexandria in the second century. Clement said theologians should study both "divine scripture" and "common notions," and that the procedure for this study includes defining important words clearly and then inquiring whether or not any reality corresponds to these words. He also believed that if we sincerely ask questions regarding the truth and if we pursue a logical investigation, then God will illumine our soul. Hence, the purpose of method in theology is to advance "by scientific demonstration, without love of self, but with love of truth, to comprehensive knowledge."[1] In sum, the theologian answers the call of truth by designating a particular theological method.

The term *method* refers to a way or means for disclosing the truth, implying a movement from the compactness of primary understanding through interpretive differentiation toward theological explanation. The Greek roots for the term, μεθ and ὁδός, mean literally "with a way." The word *method* denotes a way, a road, or a highway, often with connotations of conduct—for example, a way of eating. We should note in passing that the terms *method* and *methodology* are not synonymous, and, although they are often confused, they can be distinguished. Methodology, like other names for disciplines ending in "logy," refers to general reflection over problems of method in research. It can refer to the establishment of the philosophical foundations or outline of a given method, or it can refer to a study that compares various methods. Method refers to a particular procedure for pursuing the systematic and ordered inquiry itself, to one or another way of doing things. The adjective *methodological* refers to the concerns of methodology, while *methodical* or *methodic* ought to be understood in the ordinary sense of conformity to a designated procedure. Thus, the theological method I propose here is a specific way of pursuing the truth through explicating the meaning of what Christians believe to have been originally experienced in the gospel of Jesus Christ.

SYMBOL AND REALITY

A theological method is comprised of sources, norms, assumptions, and procedure. With regard to sources, theologians in the tradition of Richard

---

1. Clement of Alexandria *Strometa* 8.1.

Hooker and John Wesley since the sixteenth century have usually designated four: scripture, tradition, experience, and reason. Of these four sources, scripture is usually thought of as primary and the others as secondary—that is, as dependent upon scripture. Here I will designate as the primary source the *biblical symbols*. I employ this term because it does double duty: it gives primacy to scripture while reflecting the delicate interdependence of the four sources through history. This interdependence is reflected in two assumptions I make. First, there is a tradition of symbolic speech about God that precedes scripture as well as follows it. Second, these symbols are associated with an originary experience that is tied to God's self-revelation, and internal to symbolic experience there is an inherent thrust toward reasoning, toward the process of interpretation. Because of this I define theology's procedure as the explication of symbols.

Symbol as Prism

Symbols are reality-detectors. In this regard, the symbols of Christian faith can be compared to a prism. Brought home from a science fair and given to me by one of my children, this wedge-shaped piece of glass sits on my desk and serves as a paper weight. As a mere decoration it occasionally gets moved about the room as more functional objects usurp its place. It is just one more thing that clutters up my study.

But a prism has an unusual revelatory quality. If you pick it up, focus your eyes on it, and turn it carefully until you find just the right position, then suddenly a whole rainbow of color breaks out. The prism does not create the color, of course. The colors were there all the time. It may seem under ordinary conditions that the room is bathed in white, colorless light, but the prism reveals that the whole spectrum of color is co-present. The key to knowing this is looking through the prism to see the otherwise invisible truth.

Christian symbols work somewhat like the prism. When we look through them we see truths that we would otherwise miss. During the modern period Christian symbols have often been treated like I treat the paperweight on my desk. They may be thought of as attractive to some, but functionally they are nearly superfluous ornaments to our civilization. Delicate crosses of gold or silver dangle from pierced ears and neck chains, yet the beauty of this jewelry hides the ugliness of the original cross that once revealed something about the scope and depth of innocent suffering. We glibly talk of our cities, almost forgetting that many of their names still bear the dignity of the apostles and saints of the church: St. Petersburg, St. Paul, San Francisco. In promoting a new government policy we just might describe it as an "economic gospel." An invading army is said to go on a "mission." And not infrequently the words "Jesus Christ" or even "Jesus H. Christ" can be heard amid a streak of profanity.

These are instances in which the Christian symbols invisibly decorate or punctuate modern life. Even if temporarily overlooked, however, they have by no means lost their revelatory power. Once we begin to focus our attention so that we look at things through the symbols, a whole spectrum of realities is opened up to our vision and insight.

Symbols live. They live in the sense that they participate in the metaxy, in the tension of life. *Metaxy* (μέταξύ), Plato's term, literally refers to the inbetween, to the edge of human existence, to the limit beyond which we find either God or nothingness. It is the tension we experience between finite human knowledge and infinite reality, between burying ourselves in the mundane soil of daily life and opening ourselves to the power of the Spirit, between life this side of death and the call that comes from beyond.

Symbols vibrate at the point of tension between what is obvious and what is hidden, between the visible and the invisible, between what is seen and what is unseen, between the shallow and the deep, between what is now and what will be. A symbol is what it is, but at the same time it points beyond itself to a greater reality. In fact, this greater reality is somehow present to the symbol and efficacious through it. Symbols live because they bear us gently from this world to the next without ever leaving this world behind.

Four Levels of Symbolic Function

Christian symbols are complex. They function simultaneously at four different but mutually interpenetrating levels. The first two I designate the primary levels, because here the symbols are equiprimordial with experience itself. The fundamental Christian experience is with certain physical or linguistic symbols. Primary symbols belong to compact consciousness because the symbol, its meaning, and the experience are all monomorphic, all part and parcel of a single revelatory experience. The primary symbols theologians seek to explicate are associated with the message communicated to us by scripture. At the two secondary levels, namely, conceptual symbols and confessional doctrines, we witness a developing differentiation of consciousness and the articulation of symbolic meaning at higher levels of abstraction. Such secondary-level discourse over time, however, returns to influence the primary level so that later generations within the living Christian tradition may believe they are experiencing the secondary as seemingly primary. When living within the house of symbolic meaning it is not immediately obvious that these four levels exist. Let us look at these in turn.

Physical symbols. The first of the primary levels is the physical symbol. A number of symbols belonging to the Christian understanding of self and world exist on the border between linguistic expression and extralinguistic things. The cross is perhaps the preeminent physical symbol.

One cannot imagine a Christian worship service being held in a church building without the cross being physically present as either an icon or an object of genuflection or both. In itself the cross is only a shape, a form. But this shape points beyond itself to a transcendent reality. The cross in worship is a re-presentation of the original historical cross on which Jesus was crucified, the cross that belongs inextricably to God's act of salvation and self-revelation. It calls to mind the moment in history when heaven and earth clashed in a violent struggle to the death, when the divine that lies beyond this world became fully present within our mundane existence and absorbed all its destructive terrors.

But the cross in church does not simply remind worshipers of what happened many years ago at Golgotha. The sign of the cross made by the priest or minister in benediction makes that ancient event contemporary. God's act of salvation many years ago becomes present today, and we sense its presence because of the cross's presence.

Similarly, the bread and the wine of the eucharist along with the water of baptism provide us with additional physical symbols that constitute the identity of the church. They not only re-present the original bread and wine consumed at Jesus' last supper or the waters of the Jordan with which Jesus was anointed messiah; they also continue today to bear the saving power of God's presence. They are a means of grace. Hence, like the symbol of the cross, they provide a focus around which Christian worship revolves.

We are familiar with other physical symbols, such as postures, places, and people. Prayer postures, such as kneeling as if to show respect to a queen or with hands outstretched as if inviting someone into an embrace, are ways we exercise our bodies in worship. Geographical places are far less significant to Christian consciousness than to the consciousness of other religious traditions, such as Islam, but such significance is not absent from Christianity. Mount Sinai and the city of Jerusalem are symbolic because they are locations of theophanies, of revelatory events.

The symbolizing process is dynamic. It is still going on. Physical symbols establish our identity as Christians, even if they do not belong to the reservoir of primary symbols in scripture. In India most Christians are very careful not to use brass oil lamps in their liturgy. They use only candles, even though candles are more expensive. Why? Because brass oil lamps are what Hindus use in their polytheistic worship and meditation. Hindus do not use candles. Therefore, liturgical candles have provided a means for establishing Christian identity in this context. Indian Christians are well aware that candles are only wax and string. They are also well aware that candles do not replace the originary physical symbols such as the cross. Nevertheless, the place of candles in worship signifies that these people have heard the witness to the gospel and are responding with faith and commitment. Candles can have symbolic power.

Metaphorical symbols. The second of the two primary levels is the metaphorical symbol. With metaphor we have arrived at the level of linguistic discourse. In the form of metaphors we find the basic utterances that were voiced concomitantly with the originary experiences that led to the Christian faith. This matrix of symbols includes such phrases as the "word of God," the "kingdom of God," and the "lamb of God." God does not literally have a word, a kingdom, or a lamb, but each metaphor constitutes an utterance that posits a reality to which it refers. Some metaphorical symbols come in mutually reinforceable complexes, such as the relationship between our understanding of God as Father and of Jesus as the Son of God. Although these statements are not literally true, they affirm a reality genuinely experienced and revealed in the original compact experience of revelation.

Metaphorical symbols yield a double signification and exist at a point of tension that opens out toward a surplus of meaning. Three elements in the general structure of a metaphor are particularly important to understanding linguistic Christian symbols, namely, the contrast-kinship dialectic, new insight, and the necessity for interpretation.

By *kinship* I refer to the ability of a metaphor to bring two things together through the recognition of some similarity, some quality held in common. What metaphors share with similes is their ability to show one thing is like another. But the two things that the metaphor brings together are normally—or we might say literally—not associated with one another. The metaphor finds, or maybe even creates, kinship amid contrast. Jesus' metaphorical statement, "I am the good shepherd" (John 10:11), is an example. Literally this sentence is not true. As far as we know historically Jesus was never a professional shepherd. More than likely he worked as a carpenter for a time, and we know he spent a good deal of his time as a peripatetic teacher. Even if Jesus did have a part-time job watching sheep, it would be irrelevant. This metaphor seeks to carry us beyond its literal designation to a second meaning where Jesus and shepherds have something in common. Good shepherds care for their sheep. Jesus cares for those who follow him. Amid the contrast at the literal level where the statement seems to be false, we penetrate to a second level of meaning where kinship is discovered.

Metaphors do not stop with the discovery of kinship, however. They press on toward redefinition. This is the second characteristic of the metaphor, namely, the introduction of new insight. To assert that Jesus is a shepherd is to redefine this carpenter turned teacher as a shepherd. Jesus is the *tenor* of the metaphor, to borrow the terminology of I. A. Richards, and its *vehicle*, the shepherd, helps us to understand Jesus in a new way. Jesus is defined not simply as shepherd but as the good shepherd. What is a good shepherd like? A good shepherd, in contrast to a hireling, "lays down his life for the sheep" (John 10:11) just as Jesus gives his life on the cross. To be a good shepherd is to care and to be ready to sacrifice for all. Something new is revealed about Jesus, but at the same time we are drawn into a new perspective on shepherding.

What impact this has had on the wool industry is difficult to say. But its impact on the church has been noticeable. The Second Vatican Council, for example, asserted that the bishop should learn something from the symbol of the good shepherd—namely, the bishop should not expect to be "ministered unto but to minister." *Lumen gentium* (27) says the bishop should "be able to have compassion on the ignorant and the erring. Let him not refuse to listen to his subjects, whom he cherishes as his true sons and exhorts to cooperate readily with him." This seems like good advice for today's ecclesiastical shepherds.

This brings us to the third characteristic of metaphorical symbol: the need for interpretation. What makes a metaphor a metaphor is that the two levels of meaning—the literal and the new insight—are held together in tension. To eliminate one or another level is to lose the metaphor. Consequently the literal predication cannot be discarded once the secondary kinship has been located. This is an important emphasis of recent philosophical research into the dynamics of metaphor. Paul Ricoeur, in contrast to Aristotle, stresses that metaphor is a phenomenon of predication and not simply one of decorative or rhetorical naming. In our example, Jesus is predicating something of himself. He "is the good shepherd." Because of the difficulties this creates at the literal level, we must resort to a deeper interpretation in order to know what this means. Because it is literally false to say "Jesus is a shepherd," we must interpret it to find its surplus of meaning. We must think about what is said. Metaphors live through the process of interpreting them. They give rise to further thought. Christian theology—defined as the explication of symbols—will best be understood as the inevitable extension of the dynamic of meaning already at work within the metaphorical symbols.

Having said that symbols give rise to interpretation, let me rise from the primary levels of physical and metaphorical symbol to the secondary levels of Christian discourse. I describe them as secondary because they are initially dependent upon the primary physical objects or persons and metaphorical utterances. The life of faith in the Christian church, which includes the work of theology, enjoys an ongoing thought process wherein the extraliteral or surplus meaning of the primary symbols undergoes further articulation and elaboration. What is implicit becomes explicit. The result of this process is the theological concept.

Theological concepts.   The theological concept is the third level of symbol. It is secondary because it reflects on the two previous or primary levels.

At the level of theological concepts we locate the great religious ideas that have stirred Christian imaginations through the centuries and have provided an unending array of protean notions that help to explain reality to us and to organize many of our institutions. The interpretation and explication of the primary symbols as found in scripture have in time produced the overarching concepts of the Trinity, creation, providence, sin, grace, reconciliation, justification, sanctification, and so on.

Such concepts are not objects of worship but objects of thought. Assuming that the primary symbols are the doors to transcendent reality, conceptual theology seeks to take what has come to us through these doors as the basis for explaining mundane reality in relation to the transcendent. Theology abstracts from the concrete historical events belonging to the originary gospel experience in order to proffer generalizable principles regarding the reality in which we live. From the basic self-world-whole understanding into which the Christian symbols had assimilated our ancestors, theological conceptualization ever since has been moving through interpretation toward explanation.

There are some who might object to engaging in this process of moving through interpretation toward explanation. They would choose rather to live permanently at the primary level of symbolism where the full surplus of meaning is vitally present. This position holds that the conceptualization process is a limiting process, because no concept can fully exhaust the richness of symbolic meaning.

Now I readily concede that conceptual language cannot exhaust the meaning emitted at the primary levels of symbolization. But as we have seen, the dynamic of interpretation is intrinsic to symbolic meaning itself. The tension between the visual or literal dimension and the hidden or surplus dimension requires an interpretive process even at an unconscious level in order for one to become assimilated into the symbol's realm of meaning. In the case of the cross, to return to one of our examples, any old set of crossed lines such as one might see on a telephone pole or plus sign will not do. The crossed lines must evoke an identity with the event of Jesus' crucifixion if the symbolic power is to be released. In the case of the good shepherd, we must ponder what *good* can mean and to whom the designation *sheep* applies. All this requires active intellection and the movement through interpretation to the concept. Conceptualization is inevitable. "There is no need to deny the concept in order to admit that symbols give rise to an endless exegesis," comments Paul Ricoeur.[2]

One might then ask why we should label such concepts symbols. Why not simply refer to concepts and such thinking as reflection upon symbols,

---

2. Paul Ricoeur, *Interpretation Theory: Discourse and the Surplus of Meaning* (Fort Worth: Texas Christian University Press, 1976), 57.

while not going so far as to classify them as symbols? The answer has to do with the observation that the symbolic process is ongoing, and that we can perceive its dynamic within the movement of the Christian tradition through the centuries. Theological thinking is initiated by the primary symbols, to be sure, but once it has produced a rich and protean concept, this concept itself has the potential for garnering a certain degree of symbolic power on its own. It may even enter worship life as well as provide guidance for ecclesial organization. Theology itself gives rise to further thought, and it is not at all unusual for the theologian to think about the work of a previous theologian instead of turning directly to the originary symbols.

The concept of the Trinity is an example. This is not an originary symbol but rather a conceptual construction that was built up over a period of a few centuries. Building upon a foundation of basic biblical metaphors such as God the Father, God the Son, and God the Holy Spirit, the trinitarian doctrine is a superstructure that seeks to explain at the conceptual level just how the surplus meaning of each metaphor creates a relationship with the others.

But the concept of the Trinity has not remained in Christian consciousness as strictly secondary discourse. It is no longer merely an abstract reflection on a more fundamental experience with reality. It has gained liturgical status, so that we find visual figures of three interlocking rings, the shamrock, and the fleur-de-lis on our paraments. We invoke the Holy Trinity through prayer and hymn. In the Eastern Orthodox tradition the Trinity has become not an explanation but rather a mystery, the ultimate mystery conveying the holiness of the divine reality.

Not every theological concept gains such symbolic status, of course. Many retain their status as intellectual abstractions that help to inform and explain; but they do not themselves seem to participate in the bearing of transcendental presence. No matter how valuable they might be to the theologian at work, such concepts as the distinction between primary and secondary causation, the teleological suspension of the ethical, demythologizing, or anonymous Christianity are not themselves likely to become vehicles of liturgical expression.

If this consignment to abstraction is the fate of most theological concepts, it ought not to be counted as a weakness in the thinking process. Concepts are the result of the interpretive process. They help us to interpret and explain with greater clarity. They seek to broaden and find new application. If we can think of the originary symbol as a moment of enlightenment that illumines a field of life's meaning, the task of theology is to raise and direct that light source so as to illumine a wider area of understanding. But in pursuing conceptual thinking we are ever aware of our source and the inexhaustible supply of light generated by the symbols. Concepts that carry us beyond the field of illumination or that fail to extend the field can legitimately be turned off while we return to the source of our original enlightenment, the primary symbols.

Confessional doctrines. The fourth level of symbolic meaning is the identity level, namely, that of creeds, confessions, doctrines, and dogmas. At this level we are dealing with conceptual symbols that have taken on an official ecclesial status. Doctrinal commitments as articulated in the ecumenical creeds, Roman Catholic dogmas, or Protestant confessional statements consist in systems of theological ideas with a high degree of specificity. They are usually proffered initially in order to clarify ideas that are being rejected. The simple creedal statement of New Testament times, "Jesus is Lord," for example, is intended to reject its competitor, "Caesar is lord." The more complex conceptual development in the Niceno-Constantinopolitan Creed, wherein Christ is proclaimed to be eternally "of one being [ὁμοούσιος] with the Father," was intended as a rejection of the Arian slogan, "There was when he was not." Born out of intellectual conflict, creedal concepts become symbolic because they represent and embody a commitment to transcendental truth.

In a fashion similar to conceptual symbols but much more readily identifiable, creeds and doctrines rebound within the tradition so as—sometimes, not always—to circle back and become thought of as bearers of divine truth. The Apostles' and Nicene Creeds function this way for nearly all Christians. Something similar happens with the Book of Common Prayer for the Anglicans and the Augsburg Confession for the Lutherans. They reflect simultaneously the insights into divine reality gained through reflection upon the revelatory symbols as well as our own often courageous commitment to these insights.

Not all Christians have been happy with this. Seeing how creedal and dogmatic statements in the past had so divided the household of faith over theological issues, some ecumenically minded individuals during the Great Awakening of the eighteenth century sought to avoid conceptual divisiveness by restricting their allegiance to the primary symbols. John Wesley, for example, wanted to expunge theological opinions from determining church organization. "Think and let think," he said. In the next century Thomas Campbell, who was distraught over sectarian divisions that he believed were caused by creedal subscriptions, believed he could foster Christian unity with his slogan: "Where the scriptures speak, we speak; where the scriptures are silent, we are silent." Although such energetic leaders wished to unite all believers under the general name Christian, the actual historical result was new and separate denominations such as the Methodists and Disciples of Christ.

The irony is that such commitments against creeds turn out themselves to be creeds. The word *creed* comes from the Latin *credo*, meaning "I believe." Any time one states what one believes, it automatically distinguishes one from others who do not believe in the same way. To affirm "No creed but Christ! No book but the Bible!" is itself a creedal statement that separates one from those who subscribe to the Nicene and Apostles' Creeds. It is an identity principle and, although it by no means is the decisive factor, it becomes a partial factor in church division.

But this is insufficient reason to try to avoid confessions. Confessing one's beliefs goes to the heart of the Christian faith. It exists already within the New Testament when Mary Magdalene, after talking with the risen Jesus, ran to the disciples saying, "I have seen the Lord" (John 20:18). Paul says that confessing Jesus as Lord is itself part of the work of salvation: "If you confess with your lips that Jesus is Lord and believe in your heart that God raised him from the dead, you will be saved" (Rom. 10:9). Such confessions include both objective content (Jesus is Lord and giver of salvation) and existential significance (in Christ is *my* salvation).

The church continued this New Testament practice of confessing after the New Testament period. Already in the Roman period we find that the *regula fidei*, the "rule of faith" also known as *Romanum*, served as a precursor to the Apostles' Creed. The practice of formulating Christian beliefs continues down to the present day. Confessions of belief are endemic to the Christian symbol structure.

The upshot of all this is that confessions that result in creeds, doctrines, and dogmas function as more than simply abstract or second-order discourse within church life. They establish identity. Consequently, they along with the primary-level symbols become the subject matter for further theological research and analysis. In its mode as critical explication, theological reflection will analyze the relationship between existing creedal or doctrinal formulas and the primary symbols of which they are an interpretation. It will ask questions of validity, asking whether or not a given confessional position is faithful in its re-presentation of the original biblical witness to God's revelation.

SUSPICION AND CONSTRUCTION

Although the postmodern task of theology is the construction of a world of meaning through the explication of Christian symbols, we do not want to set aside critical consciousness in doing so. In the last third of the twentieth century, one acute form of critical consciousness has been the feminist hermeneutic of suspicion. There are problems with Christian symbols, feminists say. The preponderant number of male images—God as Father, king, Lord, and such—have the impact of reinforcing oppressive patriarchies in society.

Feminist critics are for the most part aware that Christian theologians have never conceived of God as ontologically male. Masculine appellations have been metaphorical from the beginning, and some patristic thinkers such as Gregory of Nazianzus even pointed it out. The problem lies elsewhere, namely, in the world of meaning constructed by these symbols. Sandra M. Schneiders, as a case in point, says that "the real problem is not in the area of systematic theology but in the area of religious experience or spirituality."[3] By this she means that the masculinity of God and of Jesus has been used, in the practical sphere, to give support from divine revelation for the patriarchal claim that maleness is normative for humanity and that men have a right to rule over women in family, society, and church. The originary symbols of the Christian faith have been prostituted so as to become weapons of oppression. This requires a hermeneutic of suspicion to ferret out the oppressive trajectories of interpretation.

How should we do this? Some, such as Sallie McFague, have suggested a method of piling up metaphors. That is, we should add to the biblical inventory of masculine symbols a list of feminine symbols. We should create new metaphors such as God as mother, lover, or friend.[4] We generate innovative images of God and then set them down next to those biblical images in order to reduce the hegemony of the Bible on contemporary consciousness. This is a divide-and-conquer method. It seeks to dilute the male metaphors by pouring them into a sea of feminine or neuter options. From where do these new symbols come? From the Bible? No, not necessarily. They may come from contemporary women's experience and from our human imagination; that is, they are independent of scripture.

I do not recommend the McFague method. To project motherhood onto God on the grounds that it is necessary to promote gender justice in human society is to give the case away to the other hermeneuts of suspicion, namely, the atheists. Ludwig Feuerbach and Sigmund Freud criticized the Christian religion because it projects human needs onto God without realizing that it creates a God that would not otherwise exist. If we grant that divine metaphors such as mother, lover, and friend are the creation of contemporary human imagination; and if we grant that these created metaphors have the same status as the metaphors associated with the biblical revelation; then, how can we say that God in Godself is not the creation of human imagination? The source of divinity is assumed to be human subjectivity. We create God in our own preferred image, rather than the other way around. God serves us, rather than the reverse. Any atheist can recognize the process of oblique self-divinization.

Christian theology, in contrast, begins with the assumption that it is trying to interpret an event in which God has become revealed. We are responding to God, not creating God. That event to which we are responding comes to us already packaged in the Bible. It comes wrapped in the language and symbols of those who experienced the revelation and

---

3. Sandra M. Schneiders, *Women and the Word* (New York: Paulist, 1986), 6–7.
4. Sallie McFague, *Metaphorical Theology* (Philadelphia: Fortress, 1982); idem, *Models of God* (Philadelphia: Fortress, 1987).

then wrote about it the best they knew how. We have no access to the God revealed here except through the symbols in which the testimony is enshrined. What we have to learn about God comes from the interpretation of this first testimony. If the task of theology is not conceived of in this way—if we conceive of theology as beginning with human experience and imagination independent from scripture—then we have no way of knowing whether or not we are speaking about the God of Israel who raised Jesus from the dead. We have no way of identifying our theology with revelation. Hence, I believe Christian theology must remain hermeneutical theology—that is, remain rooted in the task of interpreting the originary biblical symbols.

The key to a postmodern hermeneutic is surrender. We need to surrender ourselves to the symbols so that they can lead us into their world of meaning. We need to listen, to follow. To do this, we must trust. We must trust that the Christian symbols will not betray us by leading us into untruth or into false consciousness. Our wager is that if these symbols be of God, they will lead us to an understanding of ourselves, of our world, and of the divine that will bring wholeness.

The problem with McFague's proposal is that it is ruthlessly modern. It seeks to control meaning by controlling which symbols we use and just what they will come to mean. There is no surrender here. The resulting world of meaning can be nothing more than the projection of our own subjectivity.

Nevertheless, feminists such as Schneiders and McFague are right when they say systematic theology must serve Christian spirituality and the cause of justice in the wider society. Yet, we ask: how? The answer must come from the hermeneutical process itself. Once we surrender to the world of the symbols, and once these symbols have communicated that the God of Israel is a God of justice and love, then we need to explicate what this means for our life and our world. We need to ask especially in this context what this means for the liberation of women from the injustices of patriarchal abuse. To interpret biblical symbols such as God the Father or Jesus the Son as buttressing injustice is to misinterpret them, to misuse them. But in saying this I am making an assumption, namely, that there is a norm of some kind that gives shape to the hermeneutical process. Such a norm will have to come from the revelatory symbols themselves while, at the same time, it must function as a guide for interpretation. What is that norm, the norm for everything we do in theology? It is the gospel.

THE GOSPEL OF JESUS CHRIST AS MATERIAL NORM

If we were to think of Christian systematic theology as a wheel, the gospel of Jesus Christ would be located at the center. It is the hub around which everything else revolves. No other form of Christian theology—if it is to be rightly dubbed Christian—is conceivable. Non-Christian theologies are certainly conceivable, but the gospel is that which establishes one's identity as Christian. Hence, its position at the center is vital.

If systematic theology consists in organizing Christian affirmations in light of the contemporary context, it is the central theme of the gospel that provides the normative principle according to which things get organized. The theologian may draw from a range of sources: scripture, tradition, experience, reason. Theologians may investigate as well the history of religions, social and natural science, ancient and modern literature, art, philosophy, and even their own biographies. How does one corral this herd of theological sources, especially when each one claims a certain integrity and is bucking to go its own way? How does one know when to let some go and when to bring others in? Once in the corral, according to what normative principle do things get branded? My answer is that the gospel functions as the norm.

What is the gospel? We go to scripture for the answer and find these words: "The beginning of the good news [gospel] of Jesus Christ, the Son of God." These are the words with which Mark opens his telling of the story of Jesus. Because the word *gospel* (Greek: τὸ εὐαγγέλιον) means "good news," we take it that Mark is referring to the story or the report or the good news regarding the events surrounding the biography of this man, Jesus. The structure of Mark's Gospel is that of a narrative, a story, a history, an announcement of something that happened. My thesis is that the gospel, formally understood, is the act of telling the story of Jesus with its significance. This is what Mark and the rest of the Bible do. Materially understood, the gospel is the content of the story of Jesus and its significance; and this constitutes the material norm for systematic theology.

The story of Jesus and its significance come to us as a single piece. To say that the story of Jesus is good news already involves a certain level of confession, of commitment to the meaningfulness or significance of this story. In fact, the story in its most compact form of symbolization never appears in the Bible apart from this interpretive perspective. With the Bible as our source we have no access to Jesus apart from this interpretation. The news of Jesus and its goodness are found together, inseparable. Just how and why it is good news are reflected in the most primitive confessional or kerygmatic formulas.

The sermons of Peter and Paul in Acts provide excellent examples. Because of their function as the first evangelization in the ministry of the early church, we can expect that although brief they will include the essential and unmistakable heart of the primitive Christian message. Four quite consistent elements appear whenever the story of Jesus is told: (1) the fulfillment of Old Testament expectations; (2) the unwarranted death of the righteous one; (3) the resurrection from the dead; and (4) the forgiveness of sins. Whether addressing the people from Solomon's portico or responding to the threat of prison for preaching in the name of Jesus, the apostles typically recited briefly the history of Israel understood as pointing forward toward fulfillment. This was followed by reporting the execution of Jesus on the cross and his vindication by God through the Easter resurrection. It was further explained that all this happened to effect the forgiveness of sins and the redemption of Israel (Acts 3:12-26; 5:24-32; 10:34-43; 13:16-41). This preaching seems to have come as bad news—as judgment—to those who rejected it, because it appeared "to bring this man's blood upon us" (Acts 5:28). But to those among the "great numbers of both men and women" (Acts 5:14) who became believers it was good news because it brought healing into their lives.

It is likely that the speeches of Peter and Paul reported in the book of Acts are not word for word records of what the apostles actually said. They are probably the compositions of the author of Acts. Yet it is quite likely that they accurately reflect the original, and I say this for three reasons. First, because of the "we" passages scholars are generally agreed that the author of Acts must have been a traveling companion for at least some of the adventures reported. Having actually heard the original addresses, the writer could certainly remember the general content of what was said. Second, the writer declares himself or herself to be a historian who is attempting to present "an orderly account" of what happened so that the reader can "know the truth" (Luke 1:3, 4). There is an avowed attempt to be accurate and to present the truth. This leads directly to the third and most important reason: it appears that the objective of the original speeches and the objective of the book of Acts are nearly the same. Both are trying to present the gospel. Both constitute a form of evangelization. Even if we do not know word for word what Peter and Paul said on the reported occasions, the author of the Gospel of Luke and the book of Acts is trying to do the same thing as Peter and Paul, namely, to tell the story of Jesus with its significance.

The book of Acts is not the only New Testament source for such brief presentations of Jesus and his significance. For example, 1 Peter 3:18-22 offers a complementary form of gospel presentation. It appears to be an early creedal summary that most probably predates the letter itself. Some scholars contend that behind this text is an early Christian hymn similar to the ones quoted in 1 Timothy 3:16 or even Philippians 2:6-11 and Colossians 1:15-20. In a mode of expression anticipating the Roman Symbol and the Apostles' Creed, the 1 Peter text follows Christ's resurrection with his exaltation to the right hand of God and its efficacy for the believer in baptism. The heart of the statement is the report of the righteous one who died for the unrighteous, resulting in the forgiveness of sins—Χριστὸς ἅπαξ περὶ ἁμαρτιῶν ἔπαθεν (or ἀπέθανεν), δίκαιος ὑπὲρ ἀδίκων—in order that he might bring us to God. The substitution of the righteous Christ for the unrighteous sinner, perhaps connoting a sacrificial offering (Lev. 14:19 in LXX), establishes for us a new rapport with God. We might consider 1 Peter 3:18 the gospel in a single sentence, the story and its significance in a single statement.

The longer accounts of Jesus' life in the four Gospels are probably narrative expansions of briefer apostolic creeds, hymns, and sermons. Given the consensus regarding the time of composition of Luke-Acts after the fall of Jerusalem, more than likely the account in Luke's Gospel is not an expansion of these sermons per se. As we have them they are probably part of Luke's own reiteration. But we can surmise that in those very early years following the events of Jesus' life as the church began to move out from Jerusalem there was an identifiable kerygma that provided the core story of Jesus with its interpretive significance. It is generally agreed, for example, that Paul's kerygmatic formulation in 1 Corinthians 15:3-8 is exemplary and includes many of the elements we identified in Acts: "Christ died for our sins in accordance with the scriptures, ... was buried, ... was raised on the third day, ... appeared to Cephas, then to the twelve." Hence, by "story of Jesus with its interpretive significance" I do not necessarily mean the full-blown narratives of the Synoptic Gospels. These came later. What I mean is the reference to certain indispensable historical occurrences in the career of Jesus that establish that God has worked definitively to accomplish salvation.

The significance of the story of Jesus is that it announces our salvation. We may spell out this significance in terms of three New Testament themes: the gospel as new creation, justification, and proclamation.

The Gospel as New Creation

As we have seen, the resurrection of Jesus is an essential part of the gospel in the New Testament. This includes Paul as well. The power of resurrection is tantamount to the power to create, and this power belongs to God alone, "who gives life to the dead and calls into existence the things that do not exist" (Rom. 4:17). It is also significant for Paul because the resurrection of Jesus confirms the long-standing Hebrew hope for the final triumph of God's justice. The end of the age and the resurrection of the dead envisioned by apocalyptic seers have already occurred in Jesus Christ, and those who are united with Christ through faith are already participants in the new creation that is yet to come for the whole cosmos. The gospel communicates that on account of Christ, God's future is spiritually present now, imbuing us with newness of life and inspiring hope while granting us peace of mind.

In Christ, God's justice has triumphed. Justice (or righteousness, Hebrew: צדקה, *sdqh*) is the central concept in the Old Testament for discerning the quality of all relationships between God and humanity, within human community, and even with nature. *Sdqh*, translated δικαιοσύνη in the Septuagint and *justitia* in the Vulgate, is the highest value in life, that upon which all reality rests when properly ordered. The king as Yahweh's messiah, the one anointed to rule, is supposed to govern with righteousness and justice, and this means protecting the poor and caring for the widow and orphan (Ps. 72:1-4). With the Babylonian captivity Israel begins to hope for the future, to hope for a messianic king who will establish a kingdom of divine justice (Jer. 23:5; Isa. 51:5; 54:14-17; 59:16-17).

During the intertestamental period this hope is cosmicized and transmuted to the age to come. The apocalyptic pessimism regarding the present aeon and doctrine of the two ages accents the need for God to intervene in terrestrial affairs and "bring in everlasting righteousness" (Dan. 9:24). Where human justice is so lacking, only the justice of God will do. So Jews under the oppression of the Seleucids longed for the age to come. The sign of the arrival of the new age would be the resurrection of the dead. This apocalyptic vision of resurrection and transformation decisively conditions Paul's experience and evangelical explication of the gospel.

Jesus Christ is "the first fruits of those who have died," Paul tells the Corinthians (1 Cor. 15:20b; cf. Rom. 8:19; Col. 1:18). Recall how he opens chapter 15 with a creedal summary of the gospel as story reminiscent of the sermons in Acts: "Christ died for our sins in accordance with the scriptures.... He was buried.... He was raised on the third day" (1 Cor. 15:3-4). Now he is unpacking this compact formula in light of the Corinthian situation. Questions have come to Paul concerning such things as a case of incest, marriage, decorum at the Lord's table, spiritual gifts, and so forth. Paul is trying to answer such questions to Christians in Corinth, a city and culture enshrouded in a Hellenistic cosmology quite foreign to the apocalyptic dress of Paul's gospel exposition. Although the two worldviews are each dualistic in their respective ways, the spatial-vertical categories of the Greeks do not coincide with the temporal-historical mindset of the Hebrews. A historical perspective ascribes more reality and value to the physical world of the body than does a vertical dualism that considers the body irrelevant if not harmful to the health of the human spirit. In light of this, someone in Corinth has been teaching some sort of escapist or strictly spiritual salvation that denies the resurrection of the dead. Therefore, the transformation of history and the resurrection of the body require of Paul judicious apologetic description.

Of course the dead will be raised! exclaims Paul. If this were not so then there would be no gospel and no forgiveness and no hope: "For if the dead are not raised, then Christ has not been raised. If Christ has not been raised, your faith is futile and you are still in your sins. Then those also who have died in Christ have perished. If for this life only we have hoped in Christ, we are of all people most to be pitied" (1 Cor. 15:16-19). There is no doubt here that there is no gospel without resurrection.

Paul then proceeds as he does in Romans 5 to contrast the present age identified with Adam and death with the future age identified with Christ and resurrection to life. Christ is the avant garde, the embodiment in advance of the new order that is to come. Employing apocalyptic imagery Paul looks forward to the ultimate future when the messianic king will establish the age of God's justice: "Then comes the end, when he hands over the kingdom to God the Father, after he has destroyed every ruler and every authority and power. For he must reign until he has put all his enemies under his feet. The last enemy to be destroyed is death. . . . When all things are subjected to him, then the Son himself will also be subjected to the one who put all things in subjection under him, so that God may be all in all" (1 Cor. 15:24-26, 28). Salvation does not consist in some sort of individual escape from the physical realm of history into a transcendent realm of soul or spirit. Rather it is contingent upon the transformation of the created order, on the divinely promised redemption of the cosmos. The victory of Christ over the grave and the new life promised to us are part of something much bigger, namely, the triumph of God over the enemies of divine justice, including the triumph over death.[5] The resurrection victory of Christ is an advance incarnation of the yet-to-come new order of creation.

The gospel message, then, is that we have grounds for hoping in the transformation of a world gone astray and that through faith in Christ the power of the future new creation and the justice of God's future rule become part and parcel of our life today. "So if any one is in Christ, there is a new creation: everything old has passed away; see, everything has become new. . . . For our sake he made him to be sin who knew no sin, so that in him we might become the righteousness of God [δικαιοσύνη Θεοῦ]" (2 Cor. 5:17, 21; see Rom. 6:1-11).

The Gospel as Justification

Thus the story of Jesus is significant first of all because it signals the coming of the new creation. It is the power of new life. But this is not the only way of expressing its significance within the matrix of New Testament symbols. The notion of justification by faith is tied intimately to the gospel as well.

Justification is the means by which God saves us. The gospel "is the power of God for salvation," writes Paul (Rom. 1:16). He makes this point especially in the context of Jewish-Christian relations in the letters to the Galatians, Philippians, and Romans.[6] The situation in Galatia is

---

5. See J. Christiaan Beker, *Paul the Apostle* (Philadelphia: Fortress, 1980).

6. One of the key passages enunciating the notion of justification by grace apart from human works is Rom. 3:24-26. Ernst Käsemann, followed by Lutheran John Reumann and Catholic Joseph Fitzmyer of the Lutheran–Roman Catholic Dialogue, contend that this is pre-Pauline. See John Reumann, Joseph A. Fitzmyer, and Jerome D. Quinn, *Righteousness*

that Paul has to defend his gospel and apostleship against the attacks of interlopers who teach "another gospel" (Gal. 1:7, 9; 2:12; 3:1; 5:7, 9, 12), those whom he calls "dogs" in Philippians 3:2. The dogs are barking out a false gospel and confusing the churches. Presumably they are Jewish-Christian missionaries rivaling Paul by teaching that outside the Torah there is no salvation. They are requiring that in order to obtain justification—that is, righteousness in the eyes of God—believers in Christ must become circumcised and fulfill additional requirements of the Jewish law. Paul responds categorically: "A person is justified [δικαιοῦται] not by the works of the law but through faith in Jesus Christ" (Gal. 2:16). Paul excludes works of the law from the content of the gospel. If this were not true, he says, "then Christ died for nothing" (Gal. 2:21). If Christ is the proleptic embodiment of the fullness of God's justice in the new creation, and if we are united with Christ through faith and therefore with that righteousness, then conformity to the laws of the old creation simply has no influence on our salvation.

The net effect of this interpretation of the gospel in this context is to establish equality at the foot of the cross. It counters the claim for superior status by Jewish Christians within the church. With eloquence and passion Paul trumpets: "There is no longer Jew or Greek, there is no longer slave or free, there is no longer male and female; for all of you are one in Christ Jesus" (Gal. 3:28).

We should note that the explication of the gospel in terms of justification is at least in part dependent upon its explication in terms of new creation. The justice of God of which Christ is the proleptic embodiment is for us still an eschatological hope. We are still sinners, still participants in the injustice of the old order. Yet in Christ we participate as well in the justice of the expected new order.

Thus there is a double character to justification. On the one hand, it is a firm and present possession that yields peace in our lives (Rom. 5:1-5). On the other hand, it lies in the future. "For through the Spirit, by faith, we eagerly wait for the hope of righteousness [δικαιοσύνη]" (Gal. 5:5). Joachim Jeremias calls this an "antedonation" of God's final salvation, the beginning of a movement toward a goal, namely toward the hour of the definitive justification, of the acquittal on the day of judgment, when the full gift is realized.[7] Instead of *antedonation* I prefer the term *prolepsis*, indicating that the future reality is here ahead of time. Through faith in Christ we are citizens of two aeons, the future and the present. We

---

in the New Testament (Philadelphia: Fortress, 1983), 36, 74, 205. The importance of this is that the understanding of salvation as a gift from God is buried deep within the gospel story itself. It is already inherent in the compact symbol and comes to specific expression during Paul's explication in the context of Jewish-Christian relations.

7. Joachim Jeremias, *The Central Message of the New Testament* (New York: Charles Scribner's Sons, 1965), 65.

are justified because participation in the future consummation of God's justice is given to us now through faith.

The Gospel as Proclamation

I have been saying that the gospel is the report of divine grace that establishes justification and opens the door to new creation. But it is more than a report, much more. The very telling of the gospel participates in the reality of the gospel itself. The gospel by definition is news, and as such presses to be told and retold. The gospel when preached is not merely information or even revelation about justice; rather, the very preaching itself makes that divine justice a possibility for the hearer. The proclamation of the news itself bears the power of salvation.

Because the power of the gospel is borne by preaching, it has an ambivalent relationship to written scripture and tradition. On the one hand, Paul denies any dependency upon the apostolic tradition that preceded him. "I did not confer with any human being," he declares in Galatians 1:16. He received the gospel from direct revelation, from his vision of the resurrected one on the road to Damascus and perhaps an ecstatic experience in the desert of Arabia. Paul does not need to appeal to the authority of the original apostles because the gospel is not simply a bundle of teachings or traditions that can be memorized and transmitted. It is not a finished *depositum fidei* or timeless dogma. It is itself the manifesting of the Spirit in the world. Hence, it is something that lives.

On the other hand, he occasionally talks about the gospel as a tradition (παράδοσις) or teaching (διδαχή) that can be handed down and that needs to be preserved. In Paul's preaching he passes on what he has received (1 Cor. 15:1-4). What had he received? Most probably a version of the Jesus story told by Christians in Antioch. This he passes on to the Corinthians and others. Nevertheless, his radical appropriation and reinterpretation of such things as the Jewish law in the doctrine of justification show a creative appropriation of what he received. Paul does more than merely repeat what he has heard. Even the "ancestral traditions" (Gal. 1:14) come to life in a new way for Paul when they help bear the gospel, when they become part of the nascent new tradition. Thus, a gospel-oriented tradition is being born in the era of Paul. The gospel has a flexible content that can be passed on through teaching. Be that as it may, the content of the gospel comes to life only through its proclamation. Tradition clearly stands in the service of preaching, not vice versa. There is something elusive and alive about the gospel that makes it subject to tradition, yes, but always something more than tradition.

The idea of the spoken word—the word of God—is key to understanding the living tradition of the gospel. The whole life and destiny of Jesus are in their unique way God's word spoken to the world. Jesus Christ is the living word, the *viva vox*. This makes telling the story of

Jesus divine address. So for the church to present the gospel through preaching or teaching is to participate in the very activity whereby God addresses the world. Through our re-presenting the originary symbols of the gospel experience as reported to us in the New Testament, God actually calls people to live in the light of the revelatory action. Telling and listening to the story of Jesus with its significance are themselves part of the ongoing work of God.

In sum, I have said the material norm for systematic theology is the gospel. Where do we go to learn the gospel? To the Bible, of course. Because we have little if any access to Jesus and his significance that is independent of canonical scripture, we must think of the Bible as the indispensable criterial source for the living tradition of God's word.

THE BIBLE AS CRITERIAL SOURCE AND FORMAL NORM

I am defining theology as the explication of Christian symbols, and I am designating the gospel as the norm for this explication. What is the role of scripture? It functions as the source of primary symbols, and because of this it plays a unique if not criterial role.

Earlier I mentioned the quadrilateral sources: scripture, tradition, experience, and reason. Of these four, Protestants frequently speak of the Bible as the norm, making the remaining three dependent or secondary.[8] Roman Catholics are prone to claim in one fashion or another that church tradition in conjunction with the Bible establishes what is normative for Christian belief, although the Bible is certainly the high point in the tradition of the church.[9] Anglicans, who have tried to bring together both Roman and Protestant emphases, tend to begin with contemporary experience, experience rationally scrutinized according to the criteria of tradition and, of course, scripture.

Now the question: what is the relationship between the Bible and the gospel? Are they equivalent? No. Although they have a very close relationship, they can be distinguished. The Bible contains the gospel, yet

---

8. There is less than full agreement regarding the status of each source. A recent United Methodist commission examining the Discipline stated: "The Bible is the decisive source of our Christian witness and the authoritative measure of our theological statements." John B. Cobb, Jr., objects, saying this is tantamount to dismissing the quadrilateral. Each of the four sources deserves equal and independent status, he believes. Kenneth C. Kinghorn counters that the Bible has primacy and the other three serve biblical interpretation. This, he holds, is the proper use of the quadrilateral (*Circuit Rider* 11, no. 5 [May 1987]: 4–9).

9. Francis Schüssler Fiorenza includes in tradition what he calls "background theories"—that is, the history of theological theorizing. He also wants to pack the rendering of judgments tightly in with the sources. "Theological method does not consist simply in correlating contemporary questions with traditional answers or symbols. Instead theological method consists of making judgments about what constitutes the integrity of the tradition and what is paradigmatic about the tradition" (Francis Schüssler Fiorenza and John P. Galvin, eds., *Systematic Theology: Roman Catholic Perspectives*, 2 vols. [Minneapolis: Fortress, 1991], 1:84).

it contains more than the gospel. Because it appears that we have no access to the gospel prior to its transcription in scripture, the Bible functions for us as the author and hence the authority of the gospel content. The gospel is the norm, but we cannot know what the gospel is without the Bible. Scripture is the criterial source for the gospel. Therefore the thesis: whereas the gospel functions as the material norm, the Bible necessarily constitutes the formal norm for theology. As the formal norm, the Bible is the place to which theology goes again and again to discern the message of the gospel. As the material norm, the gospel is what theology looks for in the Bible. On account of scripture's role as the formal norm or criterial source, it is proper to ask of any theological commitment: is it biblical?

Scripture as Canon

To assume it is decisive to ask whether or not a theological commitment is biblical is to treat the Bible as canon. The term *canon* (Greek: κανών) means rule or measure, and it was used frequently in the first couple of centuries to refer to the rule of faith, the *regula fidei*. The Christians were the first to apply the word *canon* to scripture. The rabbis of earlier generations had spoken only of "sacred writings," although Josephus used the concept of canon to refer to divinely inspired writings. The idea of scripture as a measure to evaluate truth claims begins in the early centuries of Christian history as an extension of the confession regarding the significance of Jesus. Clement of Alexandria about A.D. 200 advocated the use of scripture to distinguish between truth and heresy. His disciple Origen appealed to scripture as the decisive criterion of dogma. A century later Athanasius contended that scripture is sufficient for the proclamation of truth.

The Protestant Reformers agreed with these early fathers. They protested excessive ecclesial authority by invoking the principle of *sola scriptura* (scripture alone!), and the Formula of Concord describes scripture as "the only judge, rule, and norm according to which as the only touchstone all doctrines should and must be understood and judged as good or evil, right or wrong."[10] John Calvin, in declaring the doctrinal authority of scripture alone over against that claimed by church councils, says he denies "they are gathered in his name who, casting aside God's commandment that forbids anything to be added or taken away from his Word, ordain anything according to their own decision; who, not content with the oracles of Scripture, that is, the sole rule of perfect wisdom, concoct some novelty out of their own heads."[11] In his "Character of a Methodist," John Wesley reiterates this commitment: "We believe the written word of God to be the only and sufficient rule both of Christian

---

10. *BC*, 465.
11. Calvin, *Inst.*, 4.9.2.

faith and practice."[12] Thus, the notion of scripture as norm is a familiar one to Christian tradition, especially to Protestants.

But treating scripture in this way as the sole norm does not settle all matters. The question of how to interpret the norm keeps the discussion going indefinitely. There can be different techniques for interpreting what the Bible says, just as there can be different groups who claim the privilege of offering the authoritative interpretation. This raises the issue of authority. Who has the right to offer the official interpretation?

To illustrate, let us note how during the developing centuries of Eastern Christendom a distinctively spiritual method of interpretation arose. A literal understanding of what scripture says is not enough, said the Eastern Orthodox theologians. A natural reading of the Bible yields only a natural interpretation, whereas what is required is a supranatural interpretation. Because the truth scripture conveys is mystical and ineffable, as Origen in the third century and Maximus the Confessor in the seventh century would say, it requires a mystical and inspired interpretation. Who, then, is so inspired and hence worthy to lead us into the proper interpretation? Answer: the church fathers and their descendants in the Orthodox tradition are worthy. Thus, what we end up with as a norm is in effect not scripture, but a self-appointed authoritative group for interpreting scripture. Hence, it does not necessarily simplify things to designate the Bible as norm. You cannot have a Bible without interpretation and a tradition of interpretation, and this easily becomes the justification for erecting a hierarchy of privileged interpreters.

Scripture and Tradition

Here perhaps I should distinguish between two overlapping uses of the term *tradition*. It can refer either to vital growth or to dogmatic authority. The vital growth image recognizes that once the seed of Christ's gospel is sown we can expect growth, development, expansion, and branching out into ever-new applications. Confessions such as the *regula fidei* or the Nicene Creed represent one of the branches of growth. Theology as a discipline represents another one, or perhaps a leaf on the confessional branch. Vital growth is expected and welcomed. I should add here, however, that this growth consists of an expansion of understanding, not an increase in the number of fundamental commitments. Cardinal Newman in the nineteenth century reminds us that "the river does not rise above its source."

There is, however, a second use of the term *tradition*. It can also refer to the dogmatomachy (rule by dogma) of institutional authority—that

---

12. Wesley, *WW*, 8:340. Elsewhere Wesley cries, "Let me be *homo unius libri* (a person of one book)" (*The Standard Sermons of John Wesley*, annotated by E. H. Sugden [London: Epworth, 1956], 50:31–32).

is, to the official authority to determine just how everyone ought to interpret the Bible. The Roman Catholic variant of establishing its own tradition as authority is illustrated by *Dei verbum* (12) of Vatican II: "For all of what has been said about the way of interpreting Scripture is subject finally to the judgment of the Church." This represents the power to dogmatize without specifying the content of the dogma. According to this second use, tradition functions as a formal norm concomitant with that of scripture.

This observation requires acknowledgment of an important assumption I am making here: it is difficult to draw the line marking where scripture ends and subsequent tradition picks up. Assessments of early church history show a reciprocity between scripture and ecclesial tradition that prevents any simple identification of scripture as norm independent of tradition. It was the church that decided which books belonged in the canon and which were to be excluded. In the second century Marcion was arguing that the Christian church should cut itself loose from its Hebrew background and its dependence upon the Jewish scriptures. Irenaeus and Tertullian invoked the rule of faith in part to counter Marcion. Because they believed that the significance of Jesus could not adequately be apprehended without the antecedent Hebrew writings, the Old Testament became canonical for Christians. The Old Testament canon did not establish the rule of faith. Rather, the rule of faith yielded the Old Testament canon.

Thus, historically speaking, the fixing of the Old Testament as canonical is itself a result of a church confession that developed over time. So also is the New Testament. The four Gospels and the thirteen Pauline epistles gained favor in the church spontaneously until they were put on equal footing with the Old Testament between A.D. 170 and 220. Other New Testament writings were received later, doubts persisting in the cases of Hebrews, Jude, 2 Peter, 2 and 3 John, and Revelation. But eventually they were added. Athanasius's Festal Epistle of A.D. 367 marks the fixing of the canon as we know it now. Thus, spontaneous authority was met with official authority. Even though we can say that it was scripture that normed the tradition, it was tradition that determined the canon and, in a sense, its own norm. Whatever scripture as canon means, it cannot mean that scripture stands in sharp contrast over against ecclesial tradition. It is not a purely independent norm. The canon is itself a product of doctrinal confession.

Scripture's Inspiration

In the post-Reformation era, however, some have sought to raise scripture to a status of supreme canonical authority in such a fashion that it is set over against tradition. On what grounds? On the grounds of inspiration. The Bible is said to be inspired by the Holy Spirit. The implication is that all other writings and all other aspects of church tradition are either noninspired or less inspired. Therefore, the Bible alone is thought to be our canon. The Westminster Confession of 1643 declares that the books of the Old Testament written in Hebrew and the New Testament written in Greek were "immediately inspired by God, and by his singular care and providence kept pure in all ages." The assumption here is that we can distinguish what is inspired from what is not, as evidenced by the statement that "the books commonly called the Apocrypha, not being of divine inspiration, are not part of the canon of the Scripture." In short, noninspired writings belong outside the canon. Thus, for all Christians, the Bible—because it is inspired—becomes the "supreme judge by which all controversies of religion are to be determined."

How do we know that the Bible is so inspired and carries this supreme authority? By the inner witness of the Holy Spirit. Origen along with John Calvin had earlier spoken of the inner testimony of the Spirit, so along with the Belgic Confession of 1561 the divines meeting at Westminster could "acknowledge the inward illumination of the Spirit of God" that leads to "our full persuasion and assurance of the infallible truth and divine authority" of the Bible. Thus, at Westminster a doctrine of double inspiration emerged: an immediate inspiration of the Bible's authors plus a witness within the hearts of the Bible's readers. These two inspirations yield scriptural canonicity, according to which the Bible is confessed to provide what is necessary and sufficient for our salvation, making it the final judge in all doctrinal controversy.

Over time this doctrine of immediate inspiration has led to the curious concept of the Bible's inerrancy. The composers of the New Hampshire Baptist Convention spoke with eloquent force: "We believe that the Holy Bible was written by men divinely inspired, and is a perfect treasure of heavenly instruction; that it has God for its author, salvation for its end, and truth without any mixture of error for its matter." In the twentieth century this became the first of the Five Fundamentals adopted by the General Assembly of the Presbyterian Church in 1910: the inspiration and infallibility of scripture.

This isolation of scripture due to its inspiration and infallibility is by no means a mere denominational issue. It has spread to numerous Protestant traditions. With the fundamentalist-modernist controversy raging during the 1920s among the Baptists and Presbyterians, the Lutherans began to think that no other denomination ought to be thought of as "more biblical" than the one that had introduced the concept of *sola scriptura* in the first place. So there began a tradition of confessional wording that persisted through the history of Lutheran groups in North America and that treats "all the canonical books of the Old and New Testaments as a whole and in all their parts as the divinely inspired, revealed, and inerrant Word of God, and submits to this as the only infallible authority in all matters of faith and life." The wording here is noteworthy. The phrase "as a whole and in all their parts" implies the doctrine of plenary inspiration, according to which inspiration is distributed evenly throughout the Bible making all parts equal in authority. This is the doctrine that dominates fundamentalism and much of contemporary evangelical Christianity. The point in reporting this confessional history is to document the recently developed belief that the canonical or normative status of the Bible is dependent upon its inspiration.

This was not always so. The ancient church that determined which sacred writings belonged within the canon and which should be excluded did not use inspiration as the criterion. The fathers of the church certainly agreed that the Old and New Testaments were inspired by God. But they did not thereby assert that nonscripture is necessarily noninspired. They believed that the inspiring activity of the Holy Spirit was at work in many aspects of the church's life, scripture being only one.

The early church fathers assumed there was a continuity between the work of the Holy Spirit in New Testament times and in their own times. They could affirm with 2 Timothy 3:16 that "all scripture is given by inspiration from God." But the term for "inspiration from God" (θεόπνευστος) could also be used by Gregory of Nyssa to describe Basil's commentary on Genesis as an "exposition given by inspiration of God." Everett R. Kalin, who has studied this matter, contends that a thorough search through the writings of the fathers up to the year A.D. 400 has failed to turn up a single instance in which any of these writers referred to an orthodox writing outside the New Testament as noninspired. If the scriptures were the only writings of the fathers considered to be inspired, one would expect them to say so, at least once in a while.[13]

This means that it is not the doctrine of inspiration that establishes the Bible as canon. We think of the Bible as canon or measure not because of some contrived doctrine of its inerrancy "as a whole and in all its parts." What does in fact make it canon for Christians is the church's firm belief that it is trustworthy. The people of the church, gathered together under the guidance of the Holy Spirit, are confident that it will convey to us the gospel of Jesus Christ. The Westminster Confession is right in asserting that the Holy Spirit did not stop working once the New Testament was written. The Spirit continues to work within the hearts and minds of believers who read what the Bible says and who receive the good news that the gospel proclaims. The Bible is authoritative because it is the indispensable source for the truth to which the Spirit continually witnesses. Hence, our posture toward the scriptures should be one of

---

13. Everett R. Kalin, "The Inspired Community: A Glance at Canon History," *Concordia Theological Monthly* 42 (September 1971): 541–49.

trust, one of confidence that here the truth of the gospel will be made known.

The Canon within the Canon

The gospel of Jesus Christ is the material norm with which I am working. The gospel is the proclamation of the redemptive act of God in Jesus Christ, an act of divine grace by which sinners are forgiven and incorporated into the eternal life of the risen savior. The gospel is a report of this action, and in reporting it actually participates in the word of God itself. It is the word of God to the hearers. This is an important emphasis of Martin Luther. For Luther, the gospel is closely tied to the living voice (*viva vox*) that brings life. The gospel is oral proclamation, personal conversation, and this takes priority over the written word. "Christ did not command the apostles to write, but only to preach," he said. Or, "The church is not a pen-house but a mouth-house." And, "The gospel should not be written but screamed."[14] This emphasis on the interpersonal dimension of communication reveals a subtlety and delicacy of the gospel that can easily be lost. A divine action is taking place and perhaps even can be experienced in the reporting and hearing of the gospel. The gentleness and power of the word of God are themselves present. Preaching and responding to the gospel are events in the word of God just as was the event that the gospel reports. Hence the living voice.

Thus, scripture should be understood as the word of God in a derived yet participatory sense. The word is first event. Then the word is proclamation. Then, in scripture, the word becomes written. The scriptures too participate in the word of God and may properly be called by that name. Nevertheless, some of the subtlety may be missing unless scripture is read by an open heart and mind seeking guidance from the Holy Spirit. The guidance of the Holy Spirit leads the reader to Jesus Christ. Jesus Christ is the heart of scripture. This apperception leads to what is widely known as the "canon within the canon."

What could "canon within the canon" possibly mean? It means that we look behind and under the verbal phrases of the Bible to find its deep structure, to find the hidden hinge upon which its basic message swings. The uniting subject matter of all scripture is the relationship between the divine and the human. Once we have the divine-human relationship in mind, we can ask: who initiates this relationship? There are two alternatives: the initiation can come either from God or from us. What became crystal clear to Luther was that, because of what occurred in Jesus Christ, we must say that the initiative comes from God. This is the essential message of scripture: God freely and graciously acts in behalf of humankind.

---

14. Cited by Jaroslav Pelikan in *Luther the Expositor* (companion vol. to *LW*), 57. See also Paul Althaus, *The Theology of Martin Luther* (Philadelphia: Fortress, 1966), 73.

Unless this truth be understood, the Bible is not understood. Regardless of what the words say, the deep content of scripture is the message that in Jesus Christ God has acted decisively in behalf of our salvation. This is the gospel.

From the above it should be clear that Luther did not believe every individual item in holy scripture to be gospel. The scripture contains and presents the gospel, to be sure, but every individual text does not present it equally or identically. Luther accepted the traditional twenty-seven books of the New Testament plus the Old Testament, but within this scripture he isolated the gospel as a normative theological principle. That principle, in brief, is Christ. The heart of the scriptural message is Christ, and whatever presents and carries Christ (*Christus treiben*) issues from that heart. Luther writes,

All the genuine sacred books agree in this, that all of them preach and inculcate [*treiben*] Christ. And that is the true test by which we judge all books, when we see whether or not they inculcate Christ. For all the Scriptures show us Christ (Romans 3:21); and St. Paul will know nothing but Christ [1 Corinthians 2:2]. Whatever does not teach Christ is not yet apostolic, even though St. Peter or St. Paul does the teaching. Again, whatever preaches Christ would be apostolic, even if Judas, Annas, Pilate, and Herod were doing it.[15]

With this criterion in mind, Luther could go to the extreme of ranking the books within the New Testament according to their proclamation of Christ. The result was three levels of apostolicity: (1) level one contains those books that preach the gospel of Christ directly and hence provide the norm for the others, namely, the Gospel of John, Paul's writings, 1 Peter, and 1 John; (2) on the second level are the Synoptic Gospels, Acts, 2 Peter, 2 and 3 John; and (3) on the lowest level are James, Jude, Hebrews, and Revelation. In his 1522 translation of the Bible Luther arranged the materials in such a way that these last four at level three were printed at the end of the corpus on unnumbered pages.

Jaroslav Pelikan describes Luther's attitude toward the canon as both "critical" and "pragmatic." Luther was critical in the sense that he did not accept a book as eternally binding simply on the grounds that it had been accepted as binding for a long time. Both his Roman Catholic and Protestant opponents chided him for this. But Luther was also pragmatic

---

15. *LW*, 35:396. J. Christiaan Beker's interpretation of Paul follows the same line. He says that for Paul scripture is not the gospel; it is promise. Paul's hermeneutic of scripture establishes "a canon within the canon" and interprets with "pneumatic" freedom. "Where the Spirit of the Lord is, there is freedom" (2 Cor. 3:17). Beker writes, "Luther understood Paul's sure grasp of Christ as the hermeneutical key to Scripture when he formulated as the key to all Scripture, *was Christum treiben*. Therefore, Scripture (*graphe*) remains a dead letter (*gramma*) unless the Spirit of Christ intervenes" (*Paul the Apostle*, 121). A contemporary argument for a canon within the canon is offered by Carl Braaten, "Prolegomenon to Christian Dogmatics," in *Chr.D.*, 1:61–78.

in that he did not pretend that either he or church bureaucrats could undertake the construction of the canon anew, or that we could open up the canon on both ends. Never, even at the height of his criticism of books such as James, did Luther consider dropping any books from the Bible. He did not even drop the Old Testament Apocrypha, which, as we saw earlier, was dropped by the Westminster Confession. From his own experience he could testify that often he found one or another book of the canon difficult or useless to him at a particular time, only to discover later that it was just what he needed in a time of trouble or temptation. If someone in the previous tradition had been permitted to re-edit the canon on the basis of some passing mood, then we today might be deprived of the comfort and the new insight that the scriptures afford us in the times we need them most. Within the historic canon Luther was critical enough to make distinctions based upon his Christ principle. But he was realistic enough to know that an honest theologian has to operate with the canon given by tradition.[16]

This idea of a canon within the canon is not universally approved by Christian theologians. Let us look briefly at three objections to the concept. First, many Roman Catholics fear that introducing a procedure of selection, *sola pars scriptura*, would downgrade certain books of the canon and elevate a few select ones to the status of speaking for the whole New Testament. This would tend to undercut the whole tradition of apostolic authority upon which the original notion of canonical scripture was established.

This criticism is instructive. The phrase "canon within the canon" should not be used as Luther did on occasion to rank the various books within the Bible. If we employ the concept today we do not want to establish a reductionist method wherein some individual texts will be designated gospel and others disregarded as nongospel and hence inconsequential. When I use the phrase here I do not intend to incite a search through the scripture with scissors in hand to find those passages that are more canonical, and then to cut out those that are less canonical and throw them away (as Thomas Jefferson did with his Jefferson Bible) so that Christians can live under the authority of an abbreviated Bible. What "canon within the canon" does positively is open ears and hearts to listen to scripture to discern the particular spirit of Christ's gospel. Writing in his preface to the third edition of his commentary on Romans, Karl Barth judges it impossible to "deal out praise to some passages, and to depreciate others. . . . The problem is whether the whole must not be understood in relation to the true subject matter which is—the spirit of Christ."[17] The canon within the canon is the proclamation of the gospel of Jesus Christ,

---

16. Pelikan, *Luther the Expositor*, 87–88.
17. Karl Barth, *The Epistle to the Romans*, 3d ed. (London: Oxford, 1977), 17.

which is found not simply in some of the parts but which is rather the spirit of the whole.

There is a second group that would object to the idea of a canon within the canon, namely, conservative and fundamentalist Protestants who hold to the doctrine of plenary inspiration. The doctrine of plenary inspiration requires that every aspect of the Bible—the whole and all its parts—be equally inspired by the Holy Spirit. This makes all parts inerrant and grants all equal authority. The idea of a canon within the canon would be objectionable, then, because singling out a theological norm from within scripture and according to which the rest of scripture could be evaluated might imply an unevenness in the work of the Holy Spirit. The doctrine of plenary inspiration seems to forbid our thinking that the Holy Spirit could inspire deeper or more basic truths on some occasions and shallower or more trivial truths on others. Thus the words of Balaam's ass become equally normative to those of Jesus or Paul, and the search for a norm centering on Jesus Christ within scripture becomes systematically unscriptural. Plenary inspirationists unnecessarily assume an evenhandedness on the part of the Holy Spirit that would forbid a canon within the canon.

There are two obvious weaknesses to the doctrine of plenary inspiration. First, there is no warrant for the assumption that such a thing as inspiration can be quantified and measured so that the category of equality of inspiration can make sense. What is the warrant for assuming that the Spirit must inspire every text equally? Why is it not possible for the Spirit to have some favorite Bible passages just as we do? Even if we were to grant the idea of plenary inspiration, it would still miss the point I am working with here. The purpose of a canon within the canon is not to discriminate between those parts of the Bible that are more inspired and those that are deficient in inspiration. Rather, it commits us to interpreting the Bible as a whole rather than reducing it to a ranking of individual passages.

This brings us to the second weakness of the plenary inspiration theory—that is, its fallacious reasoning. The doctrine of plenary authority commits the fallacy of division, a fallacy that is committed when one argues that the qualities of the whole belong to each part individually. An example of this fallacy would be to argue that because an office building is very large my office within it must also be very large. But it does not follow that the quality of the whole, in this case the building's largeness, applies individually to each part, in this case to my office. It is in fact possible for large buildings to have small rooms and for my office to be only the size of a closet.

In the case of the plenary authority theory of the Bible, the fallacy is committed when one argues from the premise that the Bible as a whole is the word of God to the conclusion that the individual parts are the words of God. It is quite possible to think of the scripture taken as a whole (that is, the book in its entirety plus its ongoing life directed by the Holy Spirit) as the word of God without attributing equal authority to each and every word or phrase that appears on its pages. The notion of canon within the canon reminds us that not every individual item in the Bible is gospel simply because it is found between its covers. There is much in scripture that overlaps with other literature and that provides contextual background to the peculiar message of the gospel. We can and must distinguish between what is occasioned by the Bible and what is to be derived from it. What is to be derived from the Bible is the gospel, and the gospel is the hermeneutical key for unlocking the meaning of the whole with all its parts.

We have looked at Roman Catholic and fundamentalist objections to the idea of a canon within the canon. There is a third position on this matter, but it does not actually come in the form of a criticism of the notion of a canon within the canon. It is better thought of as a parallel alternative. Liberal Protestantism of the nineteenth century sought a canon not within but beyond scripture, namely, in the history that scripture records. Historically conscious scholars began to acknowledge that the Bible itself is not only part of the church's tradition but that it has various traditions within its official canon. Consequently, the Jesus of history became the object of a historical-critical search, a quest that carried the scholar back behind ecclesial and biblical traditions to the original events that gave birth to those traditions. The originary history would allegedly provide the norm, should we be able to find it. These scholars tried to find the natural Jesus before the biblical writers purportedly interpreted him in light of their theological interests. Should they find this Jesus, then the Bible itself would be measured by this historically determined yardstick.

The problem, however, was that the Jesus of history could not be found apart from or independent of these biblical and theological traditions. All of our extant sources already contain a theological overlay, an interpretive framework with an identifiable point of view. The biblical books are already witnesses and confessions and testimonies. In order to counteract the existing interpretive frameworks of the biblical writers, the historical scholars had to substitute an interpretive framework of their own. Therefore, when modern historians claimed to have found the original Jesus, the picture they painted was of a strictly human Jesus divested of unique divinity and miracle-working powers and whose teachings constituted an ethical code for today's living. The Jesus they found looked curiously like themselves, a modern and secularized human being. He had to. What else could be produced from de-theologizing the Bible? In other words, the so-called historical Jesus was not found but invented. He had to be invented because the only sources we have—the biblical sources—confess Jesus as the Christ, the miracle-working, unique Son of

God who is our Lord. There is no ancient disinterested or theologically neutral rendering of Jesus' actual words and deeds. We have no historical access to Jesus except through the biblical claims that Jesus is the Christ. Consequently, *solus Jesu historicus*—the Jesus outside the Bible—cannot provide a theological norm because no one has direct access to him. We are thrown back again to the witnesses to Jesus inside the Bible. The Bible is all we have. It is our criterial source.

Gospel and Scripture

Hence, none of the three opposing positions mentioned is without problems. Could the idea of a canon within the canon have sustaining value in our context? To see if this is the case, let us try to clarify the relationship between gospel, scripture, and systematic theology. Let us reiterate the distinction between norm and criterial source, between material norm and formal norm. I suggest that we think of the material norm as the gospel that announces the historical event of God's decisive action in Jesus Christ. What we know about the event of Jesus Christ is the material content and hence the final norm, the *norma normans sed non normata*, the norm that norms other norms but is itself subject to no further norm.

Yet the phrase *norma normans*, the norming norm, has traditionally been ascribed to canonical scripture. Nevertheless, we have seen here that scripture is dependent upon something prior. It is the product of someone's confession, of a statement of belief subject to the event of the gospel. The confession that "Jesus is Lord," just like the reciting of the Apostles' Creed, reports or re-presents the Christ-event, and the New Testament consists in this kind of confession and re-presentation as well. The Bible is a large confession, and when we subscribe to its authority we share in making this confession too. This confession commits us to the belief that the Holy Spirit works in such a way that this very re-presentation participates in the speaking of God itself.

The Holy Spirit continues in our own time to employ the Bible for the purposes of eliciting knowledge and faith, and that affords to this book its special status. In this sense, scholars as disparate as Thomas Aquinas and John Calvin are right in saying that God is the author of scripture.[18] The Bible continues to be the word of God in a mediated and participatory sense. Although the Bible itself is normed by Jesus Christ, for us the Bible is the inescapable source of the criterion for norming theology.

The term *criterion* indicates a standard of judgment, a rule or principle for testing. The church has historically invoked the Bible to play the role of canon—the role of measure or rule, the *regula fidei*—for determining the Christianness of contemporary activity. In this functional sense it has played the role of *norma normans* so that the church's extrabiblical creeds

---

18. Thomas Aquinas, *Summa Theologica*, I, q. 1, a. 10; Calvin, *Inst.*, 1.7.4.

and confessions have the status of *norma normata*—that is, norms that are normed by something else. The creeds are normed by scripture. I am suggesting here that the Bible be designated normative for Christian systematic theology in this derived yet criterial sense.[19] The Bible is the formal norm, whereas the gospel is the material norm.

One does not need to be a fundamentalist, then, to affirm belief that in some sense the Bible must be considered inerrant or, better, infallible.[20] By this I mean that we put trust in the scripture to keep us on the track of truth, that the Bible will not ultimately mislead us. To affirm scriptural infallibility by no means commits us to affirming that every sentence or proposition or allusion is error-free. Rather, in the very act of employing the scripture in a criterial role we are implicitly affirming that we trust its reliability to impart the truth of the gospel.

In sum, the material norm for systematic theology is what we know of the gospel of Jesus Christ. The indispensable source of what we know is scripture, although we cannot simply equate gospel and scripture. Therefore, scripture functions as the source of our knowledge and hence as the criterial locus to which we must appeal when making theological judgments.

REVELATION, FAITH, AND ILLUMINATION

Which comes first, revelation or faith? Some say that faith is a human response to divine revelation. Others say that we have to have faith first, that faith is necessary to perceive God's self-revelation. Premodern orthodox theology, both Roman Catholic and Protestant, for the most part thinks of revelation as a body of divinely given doctrines (deposit of faith) that, if believed, produces faith. The biblical message is thought to be God's revelation whether anyone believes it or not. Modern neoorthodox theology, in contrast, reverses the priority. Assuming that the events recorded in the Bible can be understood objectively, the neoorthodox tell us we must look at these events through the "eyes of faith"; that is, we need to superimpose a subjective religious interpretation upon them. Revelation, then, results from the interpretation produced by the prior perspective of faith. The orthodox approach thinks of revelation primarily as already existing in objective form, whereas the neoorthodox approach thinks revelation is dependent upon subjective interpretation.

The postmodern approach of integrative consciousness that I suggest here says yes to both but, of course, offers some qualifications. We must

---

19. Schubert Ogden makes a parallel distinction (not separation) by designating Jesus Christ as the "primal authorizing source" and the Bible as the "primary authority" (*The Point of Christology* [San Francisco: Harper & Row, 1982], 103). On the distinction between norm and criterion, see also Charles M. Wood, *The Formation of Christian Understanding* (Philadelphia: Westminster, 1981), 101–2.

20. Avery Dulles, *Models of Revelation* (New York: Doubleday, 1983), 204.

distinguish between the logic of faith and the history or experience of faith. According to the logic of faith, revelation from God comes first and faith is understood as our response to what God has done. In fact, it would be nonsense to think it happens any other way. If faith means believing something, then one first has to have something to believe. If faith means trusting God, then one first must be told that God is trustworthy.

But the way we experience faith is not in its pure logical form. We usually find ourselves right in the middle of it. Even the New Testament found itself in the middle of an existing faith, the faith of Israel. The definitive revelation in Jesus Christ did not simply appear *de novo*. A knowledge of God already existed for the Hebrews in Old Testament times. Jesus Christ did not reveal God's existence for the first time. The gospel of Jesus Christ assumed knowledge of God and then went on to define a new understanding of God.

In a parallel fashion this is how we describe the psychological movement of faith for most people living today. For those who were born into Christian families and baptized as infants, knowledge of God and faith in God just seem to grow naturally due to the nurture of family life. They cannot pinpoint an actual time prior to faith in which they had knowledge of God; nor can they pinpoint a time in which they had faith but no knowledge. Attempts to do so usually reveal themselves to be quite artificial.

The same thing is true for those who convert to Christianity from Hinduism or Islam. They already have some knowledge of God prior to making a firm faith commitment to Jesus Christ. Some of that knowledge comes from the religious tradition being left behind. Some of that knowledge also comes from the converts' initial learnings about what Christians have to teach before those teachings are accepted. Then, when the step of faith is taken and full faith commitment to Jesus Christ is declared, the new believers' eyes are opened to still further understanding. Commitment to Christ so informs their vision of reality that they begin to see things in a different light. Faith illumines their lives.

Experientially no specific sequence is uniform. For some individuals illumination might be the factor that leads to faith, and faith in turn adds to illumination. Yet there is a discernible logic—namely, revelation is required for faith, and faith then illumines daily life.

What I propose is a hermeneutical scheme for understanding the relationship between these various phases: the logical sequence of revelation–faith–illumination. This scheme assumes that we could not have faith in the God of the gospel unless knowledge of God was first revealed in the event of the gospel. But faith by no means stops with an isolated event of hearing the news and making a commitment. It constantly goes back to review the revelation—that is, to retell the story of Jesus or to reinterpret the originary symbols. This in turn produces illumination—that is, a new and broader insight about the relationship God has to one's life and to the destiny of the cosmos.

The transition factor here is faith. Faith is born from the marriage of gospel proclamation and conscientious response that together produce the life of beatitude. Faith has three dimensions: belief, trust, and oneness with Christ.

First, faith is belief that certain things are true. It includes intellectual assent (*assensus*) to things known (*notitia*). Because Christian faith is a response to the hearing of the gospel, it presupposes a minimum of knowledge regarding the historical events surrounding the life and meaning of Jesus, knowledge of the events of revelation. Persons of faith have listened to the report about Jesus and then appropriated it, understood it as a promise that applies to them.

This results in confessions of faith, in statements of belief. As I mentioned earlier, the Apostles' and Nicene Creeds begin with the Latin word from which they receive their names, *credo*, meaning "I believe." The authors of such statements of belief were inextricably part of the originary experience of Christian faith. As we saw earlier, such creedal statements appear already in the New Testament. They constitute the symbolic structure that is equiprimordial with the initial hearing of and responding to the gospel revelation.

Such confessions are already theological in character. Theology is faith in the act of reasoning. Believing and reasoning, although related, however, are not identical. Reasoning itself is not the act of believing. As the act of thinking, reasoning does not believe per se. Rather, it reflects and extends by implication what is already believed. Of course, there can be a circular movement of reinforcement. One's reasoning may lead to things that can be believed. Theological reasoning, then, is the activity whereby faith brings to articulation what is already believed, but it is possible that the products of theological reasoning may lead to items to be considered for further belief. Because the activity of faith takes this spiraling form, we cannot expect ever to find pure faith separate from at least a modicum of theology. Where there is faith there is theology.

Yet faith can by no means be reduced to intellectual *assensus* or *notitia*. Faith has a second and much more dynamic dimension. It is trust in the God of the future. As such it is existential in character. It is much more than historical knowledge or even intellectual assent. It is something that envelopes the whole person, including his or her will. It is based upon knowledge, to be sure, but it is the personal knowledge that God is trustworthy. Faith is based upon knowledge of God's promise, of the prophetic commitment by God to be gracious to us, to forgive us, and to make us a part of the eschatological new creation. Article Twenty of the

Augsburg Confession makes this clear: "Faith is not merely a knowledge of historical events but is a confidence in God in the fulfillment of his promises."

At its deepest personal level faith takes the form of trust (*fiducia*), an underlying and continuing confidence in the faithfulness of God. Because it trusts in God, it is open to the future. It is ready to accept new things without fear, ready to embrace divine destiny. As trust it expresses itself in obedience (*obedienza*), in a daily life understood as a vocation given by God and characterized by deeds of love and service. The Augsburg Confession continues: "When through faith the Holy Spirit is given, the heart is moved to do good works." This is how trust and confidence in God come to expression. They issue in hope for the future and love for the neighbor.

No one, of course, wants to believe something that is false or to put trust in someone who will violate that trust. To understand faith as belief or trust, however, is to open up to the truth question. We must ask: is our faith valid? There is no absolute certainty in this regard. The knowledge upon which faith is based is knowledge of "things seen and unseen." We must wait to see what is now unseen to be certain that our faith has not been in vain. We must wait for God to confirm our faith. In the meantime, while we await divine confirmation, our faith cannot but help make us open to the future and what it will bring. We put our trust in that open future not because we know exactly what will happen, but because the as-yet-unseen God has made us a promise that there will be a new creation that will validate what we now believe. Faith consists in trusting God to keep the divine promise.

I have said that faith includes belief and trust. Now, thirdly, Christian faith also involves a supramundane and supratemporal union between the person of faith and Jesus Christ himself. "Christ is not outside us," writes John Calvin, "but dwells within us."[21] Article Twenty of the Augsburg Confession says that the Holy Spirit is given in faith. What does this mean? I interpret this to mean that there is an undeniably mystical quality to faith. It recognizes the presence of the Holy Spirit who ties us to the crucified Jesus on Golgotha and to the yet-to-come Christ of God's consummate future.

Christ is actually present to faith. He is present within the human soul as it ponders, plans, and prays. He is present in the faces of the poor and oppressed who call us to respond, whose weeping and murmurs call up and out of our own souls the same compassion that Jesus of Nazareth had embodied. He is present in, with, and under the water in the font and bread and wine on the altar. The living Christ is present in the world, and his life is the very life of Christian faith.

---

21. Calvin, *Inst.*, 3.2.24.

Christ is not present to our faith for any ontological reason. His being is not stuck in the world, so to speak. We do not have access to the being of Christ because of some metaphysical principle that identifies his being with ours so that to attain a mystical experience we simply need to raise our consciousness regarding who we are. The mysticism of Christian faith is not itself a source of knowledge emerging from an ecstatic experience of meditation. Rather, we know of Christ's presence because we know the promise. We know that Christ is present to our faith in the sacramental elements or in the faces of the poor and oppressed in our world because he has promised he would be there, and in faith we have believed the promise.

This third or mystical element of faith is what reconstitutes the identity of the believer. The self of a person of faith is not simply an autonomous subjectivity separate from the external objective world. Faith is not simply what the ego does, as if trusting and believing were simply activities that leave one's identity intact. Rather, Christian faith is a result of the Spirit's presence within the soul. When the divine Spirit enters the human soul, it is time for the ego to move over and make room. When the living Christ becomes present, the self moves beyond its ego interests. The self expands. Who we are begins to include who Christ is. Our identity is changed. We become something new and different.

There is more. We discover God not only present within us but without as well. God is present in the things of the objective world. As if to verify the childish taunt "It takes one to know one," our divinely inspired eyes can suddenly see the divine presence elsewhere. This produces a feeling of kinship, of connectedness, of oneness, of sharing, of participating in the divine love that unites all things.

Now we do not continually experience this transtemporal and transmundane union in its bare reality. It is always mediated—always incarnated—so that what we experience is the world that God so loved that God sent the Son into it (John 3:16). Therefore, we actually experience the world in conjunction with our trust and belief in God. A conjunction of our self- and world-understanding mediated by Christian symbols tells us we have responded to the hearing of the gospel and have embraced it as a promise for future salvation.

The three dimensions of faith—belief, trust, mystical union—are not to be confused with the three stages of faith: first naiveté, critical consciousness, and postcritical naiveté. All three dimensions can be present at each stage. Our concern here has been with the logical sequence of revelation, faith, and illumination. Let us turn now to the principles of systematic theology—the explication of Christian symbols—that seek to keep the process of illumination ongoing.

THEOLOGY AS EVANGELICAL EXPLICATION

Thus far I have defined theology as the explication of Christian symbols. The material norm for that explication is the gospel of Jesus Christ, and the formal norm or criterial source for primary symbols is scripture. I will now proceed to describe the principles of explication.

Two Functions of Evangelical Explication

The gospel is first and foremost a compact experience with God through faith that is presented in the form of a message. As the faith-experience of revelation works its way toward articulation in the message, the interpretive process moves toward an explanation of life in terms of God's reality. This interpretive process we call "evangelical explication."

The term *evangelical explication* simply means the explication of the evangel, of the gospel. Like unpacking a suitcase it seeks to draw more and more out of the compact gospel to dress if not address more and more of contemporary life. It is basically world-constructing and seeks to answer the question: what does it mean to believe and behave as a Christian? It poses this question when analyzing scriptural sources and when trying to understand life in the modern and postmodern worlds of today.

Given the hermeneutical question and the two temporal poles that it tries to connect—ancient scripture and contemporary intelligibility—let us consider a definition of the task of systematic theology as evangelical explication in terms of two functions and seven corollary principles. The first function is exposition. According to its *expository function*, systematic theology attempts to elucidate the content and meaning of the Christian faith in a manner that is faithful to the primary symbols found in scripture. Exposition of scripture is essential for identifying Christian theology as Christian.

The second function is construction. According to its *constructive function*, systematic theology attempts to provide the most adequate, intelligible, and meaningful explanation of the basic structures of reality shared by the theologian and those in her or his context. Some would call this application, but it is more than simply applying an old idea to a new situation. Constructive theology is synthetic and transformatory. It does not leave the contemporary situation to interpret itself but rather constructs new perspectives for understanding. Consequently, we can establish the second criterion for evaluating the success or failure of a given theological venture: is it intelligible to its context? Or, more severely, is it explanatorily adequate?

Seven Principles of Evangelical Explication

These two functions of evangelical explication—the expository and the constructive—are accompanied by seven identifying principles. The first is the *creedal ordering principle*. The form the exposition and construction takes follows roughly the order of the basic affirmations presented in the Nicene and Apostles' Creeds. The subject matter derives from the Bible, but the structure derives from these two confessional statements. The creeds are very short summaries of Christian belief, and they divide the subject matter into three basic parts or articles that correspond loosely with the three persons of the Trinity: Father, Son, and Holy Spirit. This structure is not particularly mandated by the Bible or any other authority. It seems to have grown up historically and provides the basic outline for most systematic theologies produced in Western Christendom. The trinitarian structure serves as the grammar for theological discourse. Should careful explication of the biblical symbols at some time in the future warrant a different structure, then the creedal ordering would certainly be subject to revision. In the meantime, the present work in systematic theology will follow this basic trinitarian outline.

I have begun this book with a methodological prolegomenon in which I describe the contemporary context and describe the task of theology. I will later move to Part Two, "The Fountain of Creation," which corresponds to the First Article of the Apostles' and Nicene Creeds. My concern in Part Two will be with ancient and contemporary understandings of God and the creative process of the human condition, sin, and the need for redemption. This will be followed with Part Three, "The Foretaste of New Creation," which corresponds roughly with the Second Article. Here I will take up redemption by examining the person and work of Jesus Christ. Part Four, "The Life of the New Creation," explicates the content of the Third Article, focusing on the Holy Spirit, the church, and the things to come. The final section, Part Five, "Proleptic Co-creation," adds agenda items not anticipated in the creeds such as the challenge of pluralism and social ethics. Again, this ordering principle is not mandated by the Bible or any other authority. It comes rather from the tradition that has found it adequate in many different centuries and many different contexts as a means for covering the essential ingredients of a Christian theology.

The second principle of evangelical explication is *the systematic principle*. It should also be obvious by now that systematic theology in its constructive mode has a highly speculative character. It is essentially a thinking discipline that engages in conjectural reflection. It employs the powers of imagination to make new connections and draw out implications for differing modes of understanding. It attempts to answer questions, solve burdensome problems, and create new visions of reality.

But speculative theology is not simply unbridled free-thought association. It is responsible speculation. This responsibility is entailed in the systematic principle that strives for coherence. Each of the central Christian teachings must be seen in coherent relation to the others. To be a system the various parts of a theology must cohere with one another—

that is, they must imply and not contradict one another. To be systematic in this sense is to be philosophically sound. Systematic theology tries to construct adequate explanations of reality.

The third principle of evangelical explication is *the ecumenical principle*. Faithfulness to the scriptural message makes theology ecumenical rather than parochial. All Christians of all times and all places must appeal to the Bible as the criterial source for what they believe. This is the fate bequeathed us as a tradition founded upon a historical event of revelation. Consequently, no matter what language we speak or cultural customs we adopt there will be certain persistent symbols that will always link us with the communion of saints around the world and across the centuries. Only some Christians lend obeisance to the magisterium in Rome. Only some Christians make the Augsburg Confession or the Book of Common Prayer or the Westminster Confession their founding document. All make the Bible their founding document. By returning constantly to the originary symbols of scripture, the agenda of today's theologian can transcend the parochial fixations of various denominations and various ethnic traditions within the wider Christian church. The expository function of theology naturally yields this ecumenical principle.

Here I take with utmost seriousness George Lindbeck's call for *ressourcement*—returning to the Bible as source—to achieve the *consensus fidelium* that might be able to reconcile the various confessional traditions.[22] An important variant is the first thesis of the proposal by Heinrich Fries and Karl Rahner regarding the possibility of attaining church unity in our time. The thesis is this: "The fundamental truths of Christianity, as they are expressed in Holy Scripture, in the Apostles' Creed, and in that of Nicea and Constantinople are binding on all partner churches of the one Church to be."[23] This means that the basic Christian symbols as found in the Bible and shared by virtually all of Christendom up until the fourth century provide fundamental identity for Christians. What comes later distinguishes one group of Christians from another. After the dispute over *filioque* and the role of the papacy in the eleventh century, we could distinguish between the Eastern Orthodox and the Roman or Latin churches. After the Reformation of the sixteenth century, we could distinguish between the Protestants and the Roman Catholics. Subsequent disputes created subsequent subidentities within the one identity that all Christians share—namely, all Christians understand themselves as trying

---

22. George Lindbeck, "Ecumenical Theology," in David F. Ford, ed., *The Modern Theologians*, 2 vols. (Oxford and New York: Basil Blackwell, 1989), 2:269.

23. Heinrich Fries and Karl Rahner, *Unity of the Churches* (Philadelphia: Fortress, 1985), 7. This proposal follows the spirit of Vatican II's Decree on Ecumenism, *Unitatis redintegratio*, where Catholics are encouraged to "acknowledge and esteem the truly Christian endowments from *our common heritage* which are to be found among our separated brethren" (no. 4; emphasis added).

to explicate the meaning of what God has revealed in Christ. The ecumenical principle applies to Christians today as they seek to reemphasize their common identity rooted in the events witnessed to in the Bible and confessed at Nicea. It is an identity of roots with a plurality of branches. The ecumenical principle is the principle of unity amid our support for plurality. When the theologian returns repeatedly to the originary sources of the faith, he or she is tacitly reaffirming the oneness of the faith shared among all those who take the name of Christian.

The ecumenical principle understood in this way is an expression of what John Wesley refers to as the true "catholic spirit." It is an affirmation of the one originary gospel amid differing opinions about that gospel. It means that we should "think and let think" and we should "love alike," but it does not mean that we must politely nod in agreement to whatever anyone says. "It is not indifference to all opinions: this is the spawn of hell, not the offspring of heaven," writes Wesley. What passes too frequently for ecumenical dialogue is limp irenicism, what Wesley calls "muddy thinking." So he enjoins us to "go first and learn the first elements of the gospel of Christ, and then you shall learn to be of a truly catholic spirit."[24] What Christians have in common and what potentially unites them are the first elements of the ancient truth of the gospel.

At this point one might object, saying that this proposal seems to send us backward just at the time when ecumenism should be moving forward. Does not the ecumenical movement depend upon a vision of future church harmony if not unity? Yes, it does. But the nature of that envisioned harmony is important. It must consist in a community of shared understanding, in particular a shared understanding regarding the fundamental Christian symbols that Christians hold in common. Ecumenism can move forward only if Christians pursue the task of interpreting the ancient symbols in light of an anticipated future harmony.

The fourth principle of evangelical explication is *the contextualization principle*, which applies primarily to the constructive function. Theologians explicate the meaning of Christian symbols with conscious attention to the understanding of reality regnant in the particular context within which they are working. The term *context* refers to the concept of reality dominant in a given cultural situation. The term *particular context* refers to whatever conceptual situation the theologian finds himself or herself working in. It is not limited to the modern West, by any means, although my primary concern in the present work is the contemporary context in

---

24. Wesley, *Standard Sermons*, 2:142–44. See also Michael J. Hurley, ed., *John Wesley's Letter to a Roman Catholic* (London and Nashville: Epworth and Abingdon, 1968), 56; and Colin W. Williams, *John Wesley's Theology Today* (Nashville: Abingdon, 1960), 19. Wesley, like Rahner, places high regard upon the ante-Nicene fathers because of the undivided nature of the church of their time (see John Telford, ed., *The Letters of John Wesley*, 8 vols. [London: Epworth, 1931], 7:106).

which modern culture is being challenged by an emerging postmodern consciousness.[25] Perhaps it goes without saying, in addition, that systematic theology in the constructive sense can and should be pursued in every culture and epoch, whether at the first naiveté or at postcritical reconstruction.

I believe we should think of the ecumenical principle and the contextualization principle as polar complements. They perform slightly different tasks, yet both are needed to pursue the task of systematic theology. We cannot afford to lose one in behalf of the other. Should we hold on to the ecumenical pole to the exclusion of the contextual, our religion would become irrelevant. Should we grasp the contextual pole and shun the ecumenical, in contrast, we would create a parochialism. In our own time, there seems to be a potent temptation afoot to do the latter—that is, to cut the contextual pole off from the ecumenical pole and risk a new parochialism. This is neither desirable nor necessary.

The issue can be clarified by distinguishing between contextual theology and nativistic theology. Nativists advocate a theology "made in Asia for Asians" or "made in Africa for Africans." A nativistic theology yields to the temptation to make the already existing values and beliefs indicative of a given culture the inviolate norms to which Christian teaching must be made to conform. If it fails to conform, then what is ecumenically Christian is blackballed as allegedly foreign, alien, or the imposition of Western imperialism. Nativistic theology permits no criticism of the status quo by gospel proclamation.

Contextualization, in contrast, does not seek to create an exclusivist version of Christianity that belongs to only one corner of the world. Contextualization seeks rather to educe a genuinely Asian expression of the one ecumenical faith, or African expression, or American expression, or even an expression for the context of a smaller subgroup within these larger continental categories. We must remain clear on this subtle but important distinction. The point is reiterated in the document *Ministry in Context: The Third Mandate Programme of the Theological Education Fund (1970-1977):* "False contextualization yields to uncritical accommodation, a form of culture faith. Authentic contextualization is always prophetic, arising always out of a genuine encounter between God's word and his world, and moves toward the purpose of challenging and chang-

---

25. Marjorie Hewitt Suchocki makes our contextualization point this way: "If the dominant understanding of the world is through categories of interrelationship, process, and relativity, then this sensitivity must be picked up by the language of faith" (*God, Christ, Church: A Practical Guide to Process Theology* [New York: Crossroad, 1982], 3). I share this methodological concern but, in explicating the language of faith in light of the present context, I tip less toward process metaphysics and more toward the eschatological ontology of Wolfhart Pannenberg in *Theology and the Kingdom of God* (Philadelphia: Westminster, 1969). Context necessarily influences but does not automatically determine the concept of reality produced by the theologian.

ing the situation through rootedness in and commitment to a given historical moment."[26] In short, the context does not replace the text. It interprets it.

The definition of systematic theology with which I am working here requires a fifth principle, namely, *the engagement principle*. I believe I have already made it clear that constructive thought ought to engage the fundamental understanding of reality indicative of the context within which it works. Chinese Christians ought not simply baptize Confucianism or Maoism, but rather engage in a critical reassessment of these bodies of thought in light of the Christian symbols. The same follows for Christians in India vis-à-vis the Upanishads, just as it did for the early Christian apologists vis-à-vis Platonic philosophy.

The particular application of the engagement principle in the present book deals with the understandings of reality indicative of the modern and emerging postmodern mind in the West. This may at first seem narrow, but it actually is quite broad. This is because within the postmodern mind itself there is a consciousness of pluralism as well as an ethic that calls us to work for global unity. But these are not unique to the postmodern West by any means. Many spokespersons in Third World countries are enunciating the same things. The dialectical relationship between maintaining the integrity of a particular ethnic tradition while at the same time affirming a single universal humanity is part and parcel of contemporary consciousness, both inside and outside the church, both in the West and around the world. Trying to work through this issue on the basis of New Testament resources will be intelligible to many people today whether they live in the West or not.

The sixth principle of evangelical explication is *self-criticism*. The self-critical principle begins with the all-important question: is it true? Or, if it is true, how is it true? It compels us to ask: what are the alternatives to the Christian commitment? Are they better? It invites the critical thinking of the philosophy of religion into the house of systematic theology.

The self-critical principle similarly opens the door to the hermeneutic of suspicion. It is willing to ask the hard questions such as whether or not certain theological positions serve class interests. Do our symbols and concepts serve the interests of patriarchy and repress women? Do our doctrines serve to undergird ecclesiastical authoritarianism? Does the church function as an opiate to numb the revolutionary spirit? The self-critical principle within systematic theology helps us to clean our own house. This critical component to theological method is more than a mere intellectual technique for clarifying what we think. It ultimately derives from the theology of the cross.

---

26. See discussions on contextualization in Douglas J. Elwood, ed., *What Asian Christians Are Thinking* (Quezon City, The Philippines: New Day Publishers, 1976), esp. xxvii and 47–58.

The theology of the cross begins with the disappointment of Jesus' followers, many of whom were hoping that in this carpenter from Nazareth they might find the hoped-for revolutionary leader who would lead Israel to independence from Rome and establish an independent kingdom. Some had even more grandiose hopes that he would be the messianic king who, according to the apocalyptic prophecies, would usher in the full glory of God's kingdom and the establishment of the everlasting new aeon. Jesus' followers were trusting God to fulfill the divine promise made in God's covenant with the chosen people, Israel. How disappointing to have such hopes smashed on the rocks of Golgotha! Peter could not accept the prospect of having this messiah suffer and die like a common criminal in Jerusalem (Matt. 16:22). The two disciples on the road to Emmaus "had hoped that he was the one to redeem Israel," but they could only mourn their disappointment while talking to the unrecognized resurrected one in their midst (Luke 24:21). By allowing the undignified death of God's chosen servant, God simply was not behaving as everyone had expected.

Such unexpected divine activity can disorient us and even make us angry. If one has placed high hopes on some form of accomplishment, reward, glory, success, honor, or such, then the sheer humility of God's activity comes as a disappointment that can be disorienting, leaving one to think that life is meaningless. "It is most difficult...to recognize as King one who has died such a desperate and shameful death," writes Martin Luther. "The senses are strongly repelled by such a notion, reason abhors it, experience denies it, and a precedent is lacking. Plainly this will be folly to the Gentiles and a stumbling block to the Jews (1 Cor. 1:23) unless you raise your thoughts above all this."[27] But, of course, in the face of tragedy it is difficult to raise one's thoughts; and the temptation is to pour out one's frustration and hostility against God. The temptation is to lay the blame for what goes wrong on the divine doorstep. Yet it is in the face of just this temptation that we need a theology of the cross, one that calls us to obey the first commandment—to trust God and only God—when all other apparently trustworthy hopes, dreams, ideas, and theoretical constructions seem to be falling apart. Thus, the event of the cross builds a critical principle right into the interpretive process of theological explication. The ongoing interpretation of the symbol of the cross requires that the systematic theologian be ever ready to challenge his or her most sacred beliefs.

The seventh principle of evangelical explication is the standard for measuring the success of constructive theology in the arena of competing worldviews, namely, *explanatory adequacy*. The explication of Christian

---

27. Luther, *LW*, 14:342.

symbols sets as its goal the construction of the most adequate explanation of reality possible. There is a way in which the Christian explanation is measured against competing visions of reality offered by secular philosophies and other religious traditions. We must ask: does the Christian vision offer a more comprehensive accounting or more fruitful illumination of the human experience with oneself, the world, and God?[28]

How can one know if a theological scheme is more or less adequate? If it makes more sense, how does it make more sense? It makes sense by meeting four criteria—that is, by being applicable, comprehensive, logical, and coherent.[29] By *applicable* I mean that there are some instances of actual contemporary experience to which theology applies. This is the bite, the point where theology digs into real life. Theology is not simply the telling of stories about other people in other times and places. There must be at least one or more present personal experiences for which theology gives the decisive—the most existentially meaningful—explanation.

By *comprehensive* I mean that there are no significant experienced realities that in principle are not interpretable and explainable according to the theological scheme. Because of the finite limitations of every thinker, it is impossible and unnecessary actually to explain every aspect of reality. Nevertheless, the texture of the proposed system should be porous so as to admit new experience with honest and meaningful incorporation.

Comprehensiveness is perhaps the most severe challenge confronting theology, or any system of thought for that matter. In the pluralistic setting of contemporary life we are well aware of competing symbol systems, all claiming to give expression to an experience with ultimate reality. One must ask critically whether behind this there are in fact different experiences. Does there exist a conflict of experiences or just a conflict of

---

28. The criterion of explanatory adequacy is a significant theme in the fundamental theology of David Tracy (*Blessed Rage for Order* [New York: Seabury, Crossroad, 1975], 9–10, 29, 44, 211). I work with the hermeneutical presupposition that explication begins with a pre-understanding already prethematically present in the metaphoric symbols and then moves through interpretation toward explanation. I also affirm that theological explanations make reference to God just as critical realism in science makes reference to the real world. Wentzel van Huyssteen similarly grants that the task of theologians is to explain reality by interpreting basic metaphors, and he also grants that critical realism provides a helpful guide to understanding the theological task: "The metaphoric language of theological models and theories can therefore be seen as referential and as reality depicting.... We can hope to speak realistically of God—in an explanatory and progressive way—through revisable metaphor and model" (*Theology and the Justification of Faith* [Grand Rapids, Mich.: Eerdmans, 1989], 161).

29. These criteria of adequacy emerge from Alfred North Whitehead's description of speculative philosophy in terms of logic, coherence, applicability, and adequacy (*Process and Reality*, corrected edition, ed. David Ray Griffin and Donald W. Sherburne [1929; reprint, New York: Free Press, 1978], 3–4). Differing from Whitehead, I make adequacy the inclusive concept and substitute comprehensiveness for his adequacy.

symbolizations of a common experience? This places the systematic theologian in a dilemma. On the one hand, the theologian recognizes that we humans thirst and desire for truth, that we press toward an understanding of a single whole of reality. On the other hand, the theologian must begin reflection with the given, which is a collection of primary symbolizations of human experience, and these symbolizations often conflict with one another. This makes the theological task infinitely more difficult, but intellectual honesty forbids changing the criterion simply because of the difficulty in meeting it.

By *logical* I mean that theology should seek to be consistent, to avoid self-contradiction. If reality presents itself in experience as mysterious or as paradoxical, then this mystery or paradox should be reflected by an appropriate timidity in the system, by a recognition of the metaxy of existence. Logic does not demand that all the bumps and wrinkles be ironed out. But it does require that what is argued avoid fallacious reasoning and that it draw only warranted conclusions. It further requires that what is asserted in one place not contradict and thereby nullify what is said elsewhere.

The term *coherent* refers to the intrasystematic criterion that various principles within the system complement one another. To cohere, they need to presuppose each other and to imply each other. One should be able to enter the system through any doctrinal door and be ushered gracefully throughout the entire conceptual house.

Note how these criteria for explanatory adequacy apply mainly to the constructive function of systematic theology. To measure the success of the expository function we would not turn primarily to explanatory adequacy but rather to the creedal ordering principle and especially to the ecumenical principle. Construction builds upon exposition yet goes beyond. The purpose of constructing systematic theological explanations while engaging the views of reality relevant to the contemporary context is to turn the switch on the originary symbols, so to speak, so that their light might burn brighter and illumine ever more of our contemporary experience and understanding.

The task of the systematic theologian is to try to understand more and more of contemporary life in terms of the ancient gospel. Like a stone generating ripples after being dropped into a still pond, systematic theology focuses its attention on the primal gospel experience and then seeks continually to widen the circumference of this understanding until the whole is encompassed. Because of the finite, contextual, perspectival, dialectical, and temporal character of all human knowing, theological construction is always in process. It is never final or fixed. Hence, the theologian must frequently go back to the beginning, drop the stone into the water again, and follow the ripples out anew.

THE POWER AND VALUE OF SYMBOLS

As mentioned above, more than the finitude of knowing humbles the theologian. The critical principle built into evangelical construction permits the event of Calvary itself to stand over against and in judgment of our interpretations and explanations. It draws the limit to what our speculative minds can accomplish by rendering our constructive thoughts provisional, not absolute. This means we need to recognize with critical consciousness the distinction between the provisional images of God that we construct and the reality of the actual God we imagine. This also means that the existential trust that is essential to Christian faith be directed beyond the world of meaning within which we live to the God who is not of this world. This means finally that the truest knowledge of God is found less in theoretical construction and more basically in the concrete personal act of obedience—that is, in the life of beatitude.

By wagering that life in the world can be colored with meaning if illumined through the symbolic prism of Jesus Christ, one begins to note how the "sun of righteousness" (Mal. 4:2) explodes like a supernova, engulfing us in the light spectrums of concomitant symbols such as God as loving Father, Christ as the saving messiah, the Spirit as living truth. Then we begin to see that our God is much more than vacuous transcendence. The divine comes to us as creator, sustainer, Lord, lover, liberator, deliverer, companion, friend, and everlasting destiny. The present chapter in the story of the existence of the cosmos becomes an indispensable chapter of the plot yet to be carried to its divinely authored climax. Our previously mundane daily world becomes reinterpreted within a cosmic-wide and history-long context of the broadest possible meaning. To have faith in the God of the future is to reorient one's life around the symbols associated with Jesus Christ.

The power and value of such religious symbols are that they illumine and make understandable our existence as human beings in a world we did not create. They provide a means for deciphering reality, for ordering our experience, for shedding light where before there was only darkness. If we enter honestly into the wager of faith, we will open ourselves to the possible truth of these symbols. Such truth will find confirmation when they prove capable of illuminating, ordering, and giving significance to the breadth and depth of our life—that is, when they construct again our world of meaning.

As I said in the first chapter, what distinguishes the reconstructive function of the postcritical appeal to religious symbols from that of the first naiveté is its hypothetical character. At the level of naive or compact consciousness the symbols are simply given. They are immediately present. But we become alienated from the symbols when in critical consciousness we objectify and doubt them. The distance this creates thrusts freedom upon us. There is no escape from this freedom and its concomitant responsibility. We are now compelled to choose either to reject or to accept the meaningfulness the symbols offer. The choice is inescapably our own. At the level of postcritical or integrative thinking, then, we enter into the world of the symbol willfully, freely, self-consciously. We try it on for size, so to speak. We take it out for a test drive.

We may not necessarily do this for the first time. If we ourselves have gone through the first two stages along faith's way, then the symbols on which we place our wager are the same ones that once belonged to our world of naive meaning prior to our critical distance from them. Hence, when we take them out for a test drive we may be discouraged at first, thinking of them as a used car without the attractiveness of a new one. Nevertheless, we soon find out that the old stand-bys have more than enough power to carry us into new worlds of meaning.

The hypothetical character of the symbol means that we choose to yield ourselves to this power tentatively at first, perhaps; but then as meaningfulness spreads and deepens we may gradually abandon our initial hesitancy. At any time in the process we are free to objectify and to doubt, to step back and out of its world and view it again critically and without active participation. We can put the prism back on the desk and satisfy ourselves with the white light that permits us to watch while others live out their roles of faith. But that freedom also means that we can a second time or a third time pick up the prism and view again the rainbow of meaning. We can enter once again into the Christian drama itself.

In summary, it has been my objective in this chapter on methodology to define systematic theology, identify its tasks, specify its functions, and outline its principles. I am defining systematic theology as the explication of the originary experience symbolized in the biblical gospel of Jesus Christ. Theology makes explicit what is already implicit. In saying this I have made certain assumptions. I have assumed, for example, that human experience as such is already meaningful—that is, the process of interpretation is equiprimordial with experiential understanding itself. This is indicated by the indelible presence of the symbol. Hence, to understand theology as explication is to understand its task as one of furthering an already existing interpretive process toward explanation. Theology seeks to explain the significance of the gospel.

PART TWO

THE FOUNTAIN
OF CREATION

INTRODUCTION

We believe in one God, the Father Almighty,
Maker of heaven and earth,
Of all that is, seen and unseen.

—Nicene Creed

The Apostles' and Nicene Creeds divide and order confessional commitments into three articles: first, the Father and creation; second, the Son and redemption; and third, the Spirit identified with sanctification and consummation. The systematic theology presented in this book follows this trinitarian pattern. Each of the three articles may be subdivided, and each subdivision becomes a topic, or locus, for theological explication.

Part Two opens the doctrinal content of systematic theology by examining the Christian understanding of God. This examination addresses various subdivisions or loci within the First Article such as God's attributes, the Trinity, and creation. Creation is further subdivided so as to focus on the nature of the cosmos as well as on the human being as a creature of creation with the accompanying problem of sin and evil that contaminate the creation.

In Part One on methodological foundations I discussed faith and revelation, which are prerequisites for the creedal introduction, "We believe." Now I turn to just what it is that "we believe."

3

GOD THE TRINITY

O infinite goodness of my God, for it seems to me I see that such is the way You are and the way I am! O delight of angels, when I see this I desire to be completely consumed in loving You!... Oh, what a good friend you make, my Lord!

—Saint Teresa of Avila

Theology's overriding question is this: who is God? Christians more specifically ask: what is the significance of the story of Jesus for understanding God? The attempt to answer this question leads to the Christian doctrine of the Trinity: God is the transcendent One who has become one with humanity in the person of Jesus Christ and through whose Spirit we and the whole cosmos are being brought to fulfillment. In Jesus the transcendent has become present; in the Spirit conflicting fragments are becoming integrated into a whole. The power and the heart behind and within this process are termed *God*.

When we use the word *God* we usually do so as if we knew what we were talking about. Upon close examination, however, we find that in the Christian vocabulary the word is ambiguous. On the one hand, God can refer to the first person of the Trinity, the Father. On the other hand, God can refer to the Trinity as a whole, inclusive of Son and Spirit. This ambiguity seems to bother very few people. For those who have a penchant for precision, the word *God* could be reserved for the first person of the Trinity, the Father, and the term *godhead* used to designate the Trinity proper. Such precision may be helpful for theological explication, but it is worth noting that the New Testament symbols lack this precision and speak of the divine in a much more ambiguous yet protean fashion.

The symbols for the divine in the Old Testament begin with the mysterious Tetragrammaton יהוה—designated now by the word *Yah-*

weh—revealed to Moses in the burning bush. The Old Testament also borrowed common Middle Eastern vocabulary to speak of the Holy One of Israel as simply God (*El* or *Elohim*), the Most High (*El-Elyon*), the covenanting God (*El-Berith*), or the God of the Mountain and Power (*El-Shaddai*). Yahweh of Israel is the creator and judge of the whole world. In the New Testament the God of Israel can be designated with the simple Greek word θεός, the generic term for the gods of Olympus. Familial connotations arise when speaking of God as Father, a counterpoint to speaking of Jesus as God's Son. What dominates scripture is the cluster of royal appellations such as king and Lord warranting the human response of praise. The term *Lord* is the most frequently used symbol in Christian liturgy. Yet the glory of the divine royalty is tied to its tensive opposite, humility and humiliation. The prince of peace is born in a stable, not a castle. The messianic king dies the death of a criminal on a cross. The good shepherd becomes the sacrificial lamb. Perhaps the built-in paradox is most succinctly expressed in the symbol of the lamb upon the throne.

These are symbols, not snapshots, that give us an image to which the divine reality conforms. God is not literally a king or a father or a lamb. Nor are symbols paradigms, depicting a divine model to which humans should conform their behavior. Rather than images or paradigms, symbols are markers that identify the experience of revelation. Symbols lie at the metaxy, at the edge, where mundane reality intersects with the transcendent reality of God. The theological task is to explicate these symbols so they construct a world of meaning that orients human life toward God.

AWARENESS OF GOD

Essential to every religious system is the belief that reality is more than what is perceived, that sensory experience communicates only a superficial appearance of what is really real. Behind, underneath, or above what we see and hear is a transcendent yet present reality that is suprasensory, supranatural, spiritual, divine, or all of these. What the religious mind does at this point is answer a question that derives from experience. The question: is reality more than what we perceive it to be?

This question explodes suddenly, in a flash, and many a poet or philosopher has been intellectually stunned by the flash. It is the sudden but stunning awareness of thereness, brute and indelible thereness. The experience may begin with a sense of the preciousness of the moment. Amid the hubbub of activity, the mind silently pauses and fixes on the sheer presence of what is there. Each individual item in the room or on the landscape is perceived with utmost clarity, with the awareness that it is what it is and not something else. Both persons and things exist, standing out in clear relief from the possibility that they might not have existed, or, because of their finitude, that they might not exist in the future. Life appears as a door to something profound. The door remains closed, but one senses that there behind it the whole meaning of existence—or nonexistence—is kept.

This experience is described by some philosophers as ontological shock. It gives rise to the ontological question: why is there something and not nothing? This is a question of profound depth and universal scope. It asks about the possibility of the nonexistence of everything. A close look, however, will reveal that it is derived from a more personal, more existential question, namely: why do I exist? Before we ask about the existence of the world, we want to know about our own existence. Whether in a dream or while awake, sooner or later each of us asks this question in various forms. For example, even if everything else in the world continued to exist as it is, what would it be like if I did not exist? Or, conversely, even if I should continue to exist as I am, what would it be like if all the persons and things I love would disappear in the next moment? Even if they do not disappear in the next moment, I know that they are ephemeral and mortal and will disappear in time. All will die; so will I. What then is the meaning of all this? If nothing but nonexistence is the future of all that I am and all that I love, then I ask: is everything ultimately meaningless? Is there a "more than" that transcends, supports, and gives meaning and perhaps even eternity to what I perceive as what is?

When confronted with the brute thereness of things and the accompanying awareness of possible nonbeing, we suddenly sense that what is is not just what is. Is there something more? But what is that something more? The answer can take us in one of two directions, either toward fulfillment of meaning or toward its annihilation. Like standing on the very edge of a high cliff, we can look back at the terra firma that lies behind us, or we can turn the other direction and look out into the abyss of nothingness. We can either affirm what is with some joy and appreciation or we can ponder with anxiety its possible if not inevitable loss into the meaningless pit of nonexistence.

The question arising from the experience of brute thereness is the question of God. It is not the answer. It is the question. The answer comes initially by an act of God that is a revelation of God. It is mediated to Christians through the house of faith in which they live—that is, through the symbols. Christian religious structures are built on these symbols as their foundation. What Christians need to do from time to time is return to the edge and from this vantage point reexamine their foundations. This is the task of the self-critical principle. If we find that our religious structures need renovation, then we may tear something down and rebuild. This is the task of constructive explication as a whole. When it comes to the doctrine of God, we employ the critical in behalf of the constructive:

The Beyond and the Intimate

The Apostles' Creed opens: "I believe in God, the Father Almighty, maker of heaven and earth." In his Small Catechism, Martin Luther asks, "What does this mean?" Then he answers, "I believe that God has created me and all that exists." Luther puts "me" first and then only subsequently mentions "all that exists." With subtle but dramatic impact he conveys a marvelous existential truth: the almighty designer and creator of galaxies and planets has me in mind. The totality of reality is not what it is without my place in it. I am not here by accident. I am an indispensable part of the grand whole, and God knows it. In fact, God actually cares for me. The juxtaposition of "all that exists" with what might otherwise be thought to be a person's relative insignificance gives voice to a necessary and healthy tension within our experience and understanding of God—the tension between the Beyond and the Intimate.

The Beyond draws our attention toward that which is radically transcendent. A translation of the Greek ἐπέκεινα, the Beyond is the ultimate and in itself indefinable reality that surpasses all categories of intracosmic thinking. Although indefinable and transcendent, it is not absent. It calls, and something within the human soul mumbles an answer. Or, perhaps better, it calls and we mumble a question, asking about the origin of the call. We can know about the Beyond only through revelation.

But the Beyond stands in dialectical tension with the Intimate. Whereas the Beyond is the absolute, the Intimate is the relative. Down at the deepest level of our personal being, we do not want to be alone. Yet, because we are finite and apparently discrete persons, the best we can do is live side by side with other people and things. Getting next to someone else through friendship is a gain, but it is not enough. No one can overcome the barriers and bounds that separate our inner soul from the world around, so no matter how deep the love or how many the shared interests, in the last analysis we are left alone at the bottom of our ephemeral being. Therefore, when we listen for the call of the Beyond, we listen with the silent and secret hope that the call comes from within as well as without. We want the Beyond and the Intimate to meet one another in the depths of our own person. The testimony of the biblical symbols such as Emmanuel—meaning "God with us"—is that they do.

Yahweh of Israel

In his great speech before all the tribes of Israel gathered at the city of Shechem, Joshua opens by acknowledging that "your ancestors . . . served other gods" (Josh. 24:2). He challenges the people to put away the gods of the Egyptians and the Amorites and concludes with the dramatic line, "As for me and my house, we will serve the Lord" (Josh. 24:15b). Joshua's Lord is the Holy God of Israel, the one who heard the cries of an oppressed people held captive in Egypt and who "with a mighty hand and an outstretched arm" reached into the course of human history, rescued what would become his people, and gave them the promised land. The Lord Joshua serves is the one who was revealed to Moses.

Exodus 3 portrays Moses at the foot of Mount Sinai inquiring about a bush that he sees burning but not being consumed. Out of the bush comes a voice commissioning Moses to become prophet and liberator of his people now captive in Egypt. Moses' task will be to return to Egypt and convince the Hebrews to strike out for freedom. At this point Moses asks the voice a crucial question: "If they ask me who sent me, what shall I reply? What is your name?"

This is a dramatic moment because of the function in this scene of natural literalism at the level of the first naiveté. It was assumed in the ancient world that a close relationship exists between a name and the object it names. Somehow the name of a thing is tied to the very essence of the thing. To know the name is to participate in the reality, to have some control over the thing named. In the case of the gods, knowing their names gives privileged access to them. We can invoke them in prayer or draw on their power through incantations.

So when Moses asks the voice for a name, much more is at stake than simply reporting the name of the divine commissioner. Should Moses learn the name, then he would possess access to the divine essence. He would be able to call upon the divine at will. To overstate the case a bit, Moses would gain a degree of control.

How does the voice answer? Very cleverly indeed! In Hebrew the response is: אהיה אשׁר אהיה, *'ehyeh asher 'ehyeh* (Exod. 3:14). We translate it: "I am who I am" or "I will be who I will be." We are working here with the first person of the verb "to be." When we stop quoting the voice and render what is said in the third person imperfect causative intensive, we get the Tetragrammaton, יהו, Yahweh, which is usually translated "he is," "he will be," or "he will cause to be." On strict grammatical grounds, the third person form of the "I am" can be rendered in either gender or in the neuter, he or she or it is.

Therefore, Moses is presented with a name that is not really a name.[1] On the one hand, the divine voice can say: "This is my name for ever, and this my title for all generations" (Exod. 3:15). On the other hand, this is not a name that presents a distinct essence over which anyone can gain any control. Yahweh is free, free to define the Godself. In fact, God has not fully defined the Godself as yet. That will come in the future. No essence is available to Moses at the moment. There is something blunt and

---

1. Terence E. Fretheim argues that the "name Yahweh" has a "more positive meaning." It means "God will be faithful." Yet he also grants with emphasis that knowledge of God only increases mystery and that this name is "never fully revealing of nature" (*Exodus*, a vol. of *Interpretation: A Bible Commentary for Teaching and Preaching* [Louisville: John Knox, 1991], 63–64).

intransigent about this revelation. It admits of no further penetration, no further interpretation. Yahweh is present but there remains an awesome sense of mystery, of transcendence, of anticipation. The text implies that the people will see who Yahweh is when they witness what Yahweh will do for Israel. There is a thrust toward the future. The prophet Ezekiel expresses this mood well with his often-repeated formula, "And they will know that I am Yahweh."

Second Isaiah develops this theme with an alpha-omega appellation: "I am the first, and I am the last" (Isa. 48:12b). Then the passage continues: "My hand laid the foundation of the earth, and my right hand spread out the heavens" (Isa. 48:13). This God who created the heavens is now enthroned in the heavens with the seraphim (Isa. 6:2-3), and from heaven Yahweh acts to bless earth (Ps. 8). The Christian creeds continue this theme by confessing that God is the "Father Almighty, who created heaven and earth." Hence, there is an interrelated double-sidedness to Israel's faith in the one God who is both immanent and transcendent.

On the one hand, Yahweh is Intimate. This God is the savior. Through Moses Yahweh becomes the liberator of the chosen people from bondage in Egypt and the provider of the promised land "flowing with milk and honey." The images of divine intimacy utilize both genders. As a parent would love a child, God calls Israel like a son (Hos. 11:1-4). God cherishes the people with a mother's love and comforts them as a mother comforts her child (Isa. 49:15; 66:13). As Israel's redeemer and provider, Yahweh is the Intimate one. Yahweh is close to the chosen people, caring for their daily needs.

On the other hand, Yahweh is Beyond. Yahweh is the heavenly originator of the cosmos, the author and creator of all things. The sublime mystery communicated in the voice from the burning bush in conjunction with the notion of divine creation points to the symbolism of transcendence. This is the contrast, the tension. God is both far and near, exalted and mundane, heavenly and earthly, a creator and a carer (Jer. 23:23-24).

Although historically Moses and Joshua may have been monolatrists or henotheists—worshiping one God while not denying the existence of other gods—the implications of the divine name, the divine creation, and the divine caring eventually led to Hebrew monotheism, to the belief in only one God who is both Beyond and Intimate. Through the mouth of Second Isaiah in the seventh century B.C., God says, "I am the Lord [Yahweh], and there is no other, besides me there is no god" (Isa. 45:5). Or, "Before me no god was formed, nor shall there be any after me. I, I am the Lord, and besides me there is no savior" (Isa. 43:10b-11). This divine singularity of Yahweh carries Isaiah still further. Israel has been privileged to receive the revelation of the one universal God. This means Israel has the inescapable mission of becoming the "light to the nations" (Isa. 42:6), the messenger of divine truth.

CLASSICAL THEISM AND GOD'S ATTRIBUTES

The oneness of Israel's God was explicated with great conceptual force as the Hebrew language gave way to Greek formulations during the Hellenistic period. This gave rise to what we now call classical theism, the formative influence on orthodox Christian theology. The heart of the synthesis between the Hebrew and Greek conceptualities is the identification of God with the source of being. The Jewish philosopher Philo of Alexandria identified the voice speaking to Moses in Exodus 3:14 as "he who is" (ὁ ὤν) or "that which is" (τὸ ὄν). Gregory of Nazianzus and John of Damascus followed by referring to God as "an infinite and unbounded ocean of being." This is appropriate because the God of Israel is the creator of all things, the "Maker of heaven and earth." God does not *have* being, say the theologians, but rather *is* being. Consequently, God is the origin of all other things insofar as God gives them being. Now that reality is cast in the categories of being, God begins to take on characteristics belonging to the ground of being. These characteristics are called the divine attributes.

Divine attributes are distinguishing qualities that are intrinsic to the divine being. A sample list of divine attributes can be found in the documents of the Fourth Lateran General Council of 1215, a list repeated by Vatican I in 1870: "We firmly believe and simply confess that there is only one true God, eternal, immense, unchangeable, incomprehensible, omnipotent, and ineffable." Similarly, the Westminster Shorter Catechism asks: what is God? It answers: "God is a Spirit, infinite, eternal, and unchangeable, in his being, wisdom, power, holiness, justice, goodness, and truth."

We may divide these divine attributes into two categories, the negative and the positive. Both categories represent divine characteristics analogous to human characteristics. The negative or apophatic statements (ἀπόφασις) about God are those in which human or creaturely limitations or imperfections are contrasted or negated, whereas the positive or kataphatic statements (κατάφασις) depict those perfections that are directly ascribable to God. Apophatic statements follow the negative path (*via negativa*) toward ascribing to God qualities such as incomprehensibility, infinity, and immutability. Whereas humans acknowledge that they have knowledge about the finite and changeable world in which they live, by negation they acknowledge that the Beyond that transcends their world is infinitely unknowable and unchangeable. God is, in the words of Karl Rahner, the "absolute mystery." Kataphatic statements, in complementary contrast, ascribe to God such qualities as life, holiness, goodness, lovingness, creativity, omniscience, and omnipotence. Humans know what life is on the terrestrial plane, so they can by analogy speak of eternal life on the heavenly plane. They have experienced goodness and lovingness in human affairs, so they can by analogy speak of that which is strictly good or totally loving. They understand their partial knowledge and limited power, so by extrapolation they can think of God's absolute knowledge and unlimited power.

To illustrate the process of moving from the historical experience of Israel to casting the divine attributes in Greek conceptuality, I will examine three in the long list of attributes: first, ineffability as it derives from the experience of God's holiness; second, eternity as it derives from the experience of God's faithfulness; and third, omnipotence as it derives from the experience of God's power. We might think of divine holiness, faithfulness, and power as metaphorical symbols found in scripture; and we might think of ineffability, eternity, and omnipotence as reflections upon these symbols leading to theological concepts.

The preeminent apophatic attribute of God is ineffability. The divine essence is unknowable. The Greek mind, in the tradition of Plato and Plotinus, attributed this unknowability to the problem of divine unity in contrast to the dualism of human thinking. For us to think, we must think in terms of contrasts and multiplicity. God, the ultimate reality, must be simple, not complex. Thus, the most sublime reality, the divine One, cannot be thought. It is beyond human comprehension. If it can be experienced at all, it can be experienced only in ecstasy. This Greek argument parallels that of the Upanishadic philosophers of the Hindu tradition.

Yet the root of the Hebrew and Christian understanding of the divine ineffability lies in the experience of God's holiness, not in the contrast between dualistic human thinking and monistic divine ontology. The Greek concept of ineffability became the vehicle by which the early Christian apologists sought to explicate the God whom Moses confronted in the burning bush, the "Holy One of Israel" who speaks to Moses and denies Moses a name. "No one can utter the name of the ineffable God," wrote Justin Martyr, "and if any one dare to say that there is a name, he raves with a hopeless madness."[2] The otherness of Israel's God becomes explicated as the sublime and simple One. Irenaeus says God is "a simple, uncompounded Being, without diverse members," and as such is "therefore indescribable."[3]

In scripture, God's holiness is associated with two things: God's future action and name. According to Ezekiel, Yahweh will demonstrate divine holiness by action: Yahweh will rescue the people of the covenant from their desperation in captivity and reestablish them in their land (Ezek. 20:41; 28:25; 39:27; see Hos. 11:9). "Thus says the Lord God: It is not for your sake, O house of Israel, that I am about to act, but for the sake of my holy name, which you have profaned among the nations to which you

2. Justin Martyr *Apology* 1.61.
3. Irenaeus *Against Heresies* 2.13.3, 4.

came.... The nations will know that I am the Lord, says the Lord God, when through you I display my holiness before their eyes. I will take you from the nations, and gather you from all the countries, and bring you into your own land" (Ezek. 36:22-24).

It is for the sake of the "holy name" that Yahweh plans to execute the plan of deliverance (Ezek. 36:22). Yahweh's name, which identifies the God of Israel but hides the divine nature, allows Israel to exist in covenantal relationship with God; but there is something about God that continues to remain separate and inscrutable. "Truly, you are a God who hides himself," says Deutero-Isaiah (Isa. 45:15), a God whose "understanding is unsearchable" (Isa. 40:28). That there could not be such a thing as an analogy of being—that we need to think of holiness apophatically—seems to be implied by the rhetorical repudiation of comparisons: "To whom then will you compare me, or who is my equal? says the Holy One" (Isa. 40:25). In sum, we have symbols that we can employ like names—that is, Yahweh, God, the Lord, and such—but they only point toward a divine reality that remains holy and beyond understanding.

With classical theists, Christians also say God is eternal. The idea of eternity employed here probably begins with Plato's definition of what is everlasting, unchanging, and perfect. It develops in the thought of Plotinus and Augustine until Boethius writes in his *The Consolation of Philosophy* in the sixth century, "Eternity is the whole, perfect, and simultaneous possession of endless life." In common parlance, eternity has come to mean God's timelessness. Humans are temporal and changeable and, hence, corruptible. As temporal, they die. God, in contrast, is unchanging and perfect. God as eternal is not subject to temporal decay.

However, to be precise, the biblical symbols do not themselves speak of eternity as simple timelessness. Rather, they indicate the Hebrew experience of God's faithfulness over time. Like grass, people may whither and die; but the word of God endures forever, says Isaiah 40:8. Or, in the words of the psalmist, "From everlasting to everlasting you are God" (Ps. 90:2). The God of Israel is not undone by time. Yahweh makes promises and keeps them. Yahweh remains faithful, even when humans suffer destruction and death. Time cannot destroy God, because God is everlasting.

What can eternity mean today? In our own modern and postmodern context, we cannot sensibly conceive of timelessness ontologically as a static state of being with no succession of events. For us in the modern world, the dynamic of events constitutes reality. An eternal state of existence without the succession of events would constitute eternal death, not the eternal life of the Christian promise. Therefore, when we use a term such as *eternal* it would be better to think of God as perduring through time, as everlasting, as employing the course of events in the history of creation and redemption.

This has an impact on how Christians use the terms *unchangingness* or *immutability* when referring to God. They do not refer to static immobility, to metaphysical inertness. The God of Israel is a God of action, not inaction. Yet this God is faithful. Divine promises can be trusted. God's promise for the future transformation of the world, the resurrection of the dead, and the advent of the new creation is reliable. What is unchangeable is God's trustworthiness over time.

One of the most controversial attributes has been God's omnipotence. The creed opens: "We believe in one God, the Father Almighty." "Almighty" means God is all-powerful. According to classical theism, God exercises almighty power in two ways: mediated intervention via secondary causes within the created order (*potentia ordinata*), or unmediated intervention, which is what brought the created order into existence in the first place and what today results in miracles (*potentia absoluta* or *extraordinaria*). Because divine power is ordinarily mediated to the world through the causal nexus, humans are not overwhelmed by God's absolute power. The actual course of individual events is not predetermined. Free choice among possibilities exists. In a sense, God decides to limit the direct exercise of divine power so as to make room for the exercise of creaturely power. Everything is dependent upon God, but not everything is precisely determined by God.

This self-limitation of God has led classical theists to speculate regarding logical qualifications to God's power. It is widely agreed, for example, that God can accomplish anything that is possible as long as it does not involve a contradiction. God is free to be God, to express the divine essence. But there are some things God cannot do. For example, God is said to be unable to suffer violence, repent of evil, steal, die, or make contradictory opposites exist. Nor can the omnipotent God create another God who also is omnipotent. This would contradict the very nature of omnipotence. So Thomas Aquinas says that "whatever implies a contradiction does not come within the scope of divine omnipotence."[4]

Hence, to the rhetorical question that I raised in the Preface ("Can God make a stone so heavy even he can't lift it?"), I may now have an answer. The answer is in the negative. The law of noncontradiction is the final court of appeal. Nevertheless, if God be the measure of all things within the present world that God created, and if God be omnipotent, then we could affirm that God is free to create another world operating according to other principles, a world in which it would be possible to make a stone that heavy.

What is it in the biblical symbols that is coming to philosophical formulation in the classical concept of omnipotence? It is not an interest in blind power. Rather, the Bible begins by reporting the experience in

---

4. Thomas Aquinas, *Summa Theologica*, I, q. 25, a. 5.

which Yahweh rescued the people from slavery in Egypt and established a covenant with them. In order for the God of Israel to accomplish this, it is observed, Yahweh must have had sufficient might to overcome the hegemony of the pharaoh. More than that, Yahweh must have been able to rule over the forces of nature to be able to part the waters of the Red Sea and to provide smoke and fire as beacons. Finally, the covenant is established at Sinai, which is a mountain. *Shaddai*, the Hebrew word for mountain, is also the word for power.

The biblical symbols indicating divine power cluster around the idea of royal sovereignty. This includes such things as kingship, lordship, the crown, the throne, and when it comes to nature it includes symbolism such as the heavens and thunder. "The God of glory thunders," writes the psalmist, after asking all heavenly beings to "ascribe to the Lord glory and strength.... The Lord sits enthroned as king forever" (Ps. 29). "Our God is in the heavens; he does whatever he pleases" (Ps. 115:3). Because God has such power, humans can consider God their protector and can find refuge within the divine presence. Knowledge of God's might is comforting:

> God is our refuge and strength,
> a very present help in trouble.
> Therefore we will not fear,
> though the earth should change,
> though the mountains shake in the
> heart of the sea. (Ps. 46:1-2)

What is revealed in the biblical symbols is not the simple existence of great power, but rather the God of grace who uses and shares divine power in order to make that grace effective.

In the New Testament the power of the true king becomes manifest under the humility of the true messiah, Jesus the Christ, who was crucified in weakness. God's weakness is stronger than human strength (1 Cor. 1:25-27; 2 Cor. 13:4). The true king, "though he was in the form of God, did not regard equality with God as something to be exploited, but emptied himself, taking the form of a slave." Having become obedient unto death, "God also highly exalted him and gave him the name that is above every name, so that at the name of Jesus every knee should bend, in heaven and on earth and under the earth, and every tongue should confess that Jesus Christ is Lord, to the glory of God the Father" (Phil. 2:6, 7, 9). Through weakness God's power is at work to accomplish salvation, and in accomplishing this Christ becomes the true king.[5]

---

5. It is fashionable these days for theologians to attack Christian conceptuality and symbolism for their alleged triumphalism. The attack has been launched not only against the concept of omnipotence but also against its originary symbols such as king, Lord, sovereign, and resurrection. Sallie McFague, for example, objects to the image of a divine monarch

Classical theism has used the concept of omnipotence to attempt to explicate the biblical symbols of divine sovereignty within the conceptuality of ontological speculation. For this there ought to be no complaint. But there is. In our own era process philosophers and theologians following in the train of Alfred North Whitehead and Charles Hartshorne attack the concept of omnipotence on the ground that it eliminates such things as chance and freedom from the cosmic order. They call their own position neoclassical so as to distinguish themselves sharply from the classical position they purportedly oppose.

What exactly is the position they oppose? Hartshorne describes the classical theists as believing that God has "the power to determine every detail of what happens in the world." He says that Christian thinkers followed the "tyrant ideal," picturing God not as a king who rescues, saves, and establishes, but as one who pinches out every possibility of creaturely freedom in order for divine rule to be total and complete.[6] Then Hartshorne puts the challenge: "Can we worship a God so devoid of generosity as to deny us a share, however humble, in determining the details of the world, as minor participants in the creative process that is reality?"[7] By the time Hartshorne is done describing the position of classical theism it appears so contaminated with divine tyranny that no rational person would want to touch it.

But is this a fair description of what Christian theologians have been saying? No, it is not fair. The purpose of the concept of omnipotence is to depict a God who rescues humankind from tyranny rather than imposing it. Through the idea of omnipotence theologians attempted to explicate conceptually images such as "a mighty hand and an outstretched arm" used by God to rescue the Hebrews from Egyptian slavery. The power to save seemed to be rooted in the power to create. So omnipotence became a vehicle for thinking through the creation account in Genesis where God brings the world into existence by simply speaking the divine word. As an explication of prior symbols, the doctrine of omnipotence contends that the whole world is dependent upon God while contending

---

ruling the world with domination and benevolence (*Models of God* [Philadelphia: Fortress, 1987], 64–65). Gordon Kaufman similarly objects to the symbol of the resurrection because it lays the foundation for Christian imperialism. He applauds the cross, however, because it signifies self-giving, suffering, and self-sacrifice (*Theology for a Nuclear Age* [Philadelphia: Westminster, 1985], 49–54). But McFague is suspicious even of self-sacrifice, preferring rather a model of interdependence for understanding God and the world (*Models of God*, 56). It seems to me that the royal symbols are inextricably tied to our experience of God in Jesus Christ, and that we cannot in cavalier fashion dispense with those that do not fit our current mood. What critics such as McFague and Kaufman fail to appreciate is the abiding tensive paradox of power-within-weakness inherent in the symbols of the humiliated king, the lamb upon the throne.

6. Charles Hartshorne, *Omnipotence and Other Theological Mistakes* (Albany: State University of New York Press, 1984), 11.

7. Ibid., 16.

as well that human decision making is undeniably essential. This is the point eventually made by the classical distinction between God's absolute power, which God exercises in the creation of the world from nothing, and God's ordinary power, which operates daily through secondary causation. Through this distinction traditional theologians found a way to affirm that everything is universally dependent upon God but that human beings still have an influence on determining the shape of particular events. Omnipotence does not mean omnicausality. Theologians did not for the most part confuse omnipotence with blind power, with a lifeless force.[8]

The Christian commitment is to God's commitment to keep the divine promise of a new creation. This means an affirmation of eschatological power. It took power for God to raise the dead Jesus on Easter, and it will take like power to transform the present aeon into the everlasting kingdom of God. Because the power of God in scripture has been so closely tied to the divine work of salvation, Christians need confidence in the divine power to accomplish the redemption that is yet to come.

To conclude this discussion, my exposition of ineffability, eternity, and omnipotence has sought to demonstrate that speculation on the divine attributes represents a process of theological explication of the compact meaning of the scriptural witness in light of the worldview of ancient Rome and medieval Europe, a worldview heavily influenced by Greek metaphysics. That process of explication is ongoing, and continues today. It would be a mistake for theologians today simply to accept as definitive the concepts bequeathed to them by Greek-speaking apologetic theologians. To do so would be to reify the concepts, to allow the Greek metaphysics of being to define reality today. The way to avoid such reification is to apply the principles of contextualization and criticism, to remind ourselves that the familiar list of classical attributes comes from a process of explicating the biblical symbols. The resulting classical formulations are indispensable as theological data, but in themselves they are means to a contemporary theological end. The goal today is to go behind these classical formulations and to explicate the originary biblical symbols while engaging the worldview of the modern and emerging postmodern context. I will attempt to demonstrate this in part by addressing the relevant divine attributes in discussions of the trinitarian life of God and the doctrine of creation in light of contemporary natural science.

GOD AS TRINITY

The Christian commitment is to understand God as Trinity, an understanding that developed during the rise of classical theism. Unfortunately, there seems to be considerable misunderstanding of what is at stake in

---

8. See Barth, *CD*, 2/1:527, 587.

trinitarian thinking. Too frequently Christian educators confuse students with misleading inanities such as this: the mystery of the Trinity is how God can be both one and three at the same time. Then they appeal to divine ineffability, claiming that this mysterious mathematical trick belongs to the realm of divine incomprehensibility. I have two problems with this approach. First, this trivializes the concept of ineffability. In order to cover over our own fuzzy thinking, we ascribe it to the divine mystery. God should not be blamed for confused theology. Second, this approach to the Trinity devolves into a problem of arithmetic. What is at stake in the doctrine of the Trinity has little or nothing to do with arithmetic. What is at issue is whether or not God can define the Godself by becoming human, whether the Beyond can become Intimate, whether the infinite can become finite, and whether all of creation can be redeemed and taken up into the divine life.

The New Testament's Proto-trinitarianism

The idea of the Trinity is a clear case of theological construction. As a symbol it lies initially at the secondary level, at the level of reflection upon more primary biblical utterances. The proto-trinitarian trajectory in the New Testament begins with the logic of Paul, who presumes that God the Father raised his Son, Jesus, on Easter. "If the Spirit of him who raised Jesus from the dead dwells in you, he who raised Christ from the dead will give life to your mortal bodies also through his Spirit that dwells in you" (Rom. 8:11). Paul has also bequeathed to us the benediction, "The grace of the Lord Jesus Christ, the love of God, and the communion of the Holy Spirit be with all of you" (2 Cor. 13:13). Although other trinitarian passages in the New Testament play a part (2 Peter 1:2; Jude 20-21), perhaps the best recognized is the Matthean baptismal formula in the mouth of Jesus: "All authority in heaven and on earth has been given to me. Go therefore and make disciples of all nations, baptizing them in the name of the Father and of the Son and of the Holy Spirit" (Matt. 28:18-19).

The key to the trinitarian doctrine is the Father-Son relationship. In Christian theology, God is symbolized as a divine Father primarily because Christ is symbolized as the divine Son. Not the other way around. Prior to the New Testament there had been no serious Hebrew investment in the Father symbol for God. The biblical writers did not understand the God of Israel to be the progenitor of humanity; there was no commitment to viewing the gods, whether male or female, as having given birth to the human race. If there was any parental relation, it was adoptive rather than generative. Through the covenant God adopts Israel (Hos. 9:10). It is more a legal matter than a biological one. Thus, the term *Father* designating God appears only fourteen times in the Old Testament, whereas there are 170 such references in the New Testament.

Jesus and His Father

The Christian use of the Father symbol to designate the first person of the Trinity derives initially from Jesus. The Gospel of Mark describes Jesus as the Son of man and the Son of God. The contrast and connection are dramatically portrayed in the anguish of the Gethsemane prayer where Jesus begins: "ἀββα ὁ πατήρ..." (Mark 14:36). The untranslated Aramaic address to the heavenly Father, Abba, seems important. It marks a special relationship between Jesus and the Holy One of Israel. When Jesus' contemporaries would address God as Father in prayer, the address was combined with royal imagery such as "Our Father and Our King." They appealed to God as Beyond. But Jesus' use here communicates the Intimate. From the Talmud and writings from first-century Antioch we learn that *abba* meaning "daddy" and *imma* meaning "mommy" were terms used by small children when speaking to their parents. They connote close family relations and familiarity. "To a Jewish mind," writes Joachim Jeremias, "it would have been irreverent and therefore unthinkable to call God by this familiar word."[9] Jesus, this indicates, enjoyed the kind of intimacy with God that a child would have with a loving parent.

Jesus sought to pass this intimate relationship with God on to his followers via the medium of prayer. Jesus teaches the disciples the Lord's Prayer (Luke 11:2-4; Matt. 6:9-13). Does Jesus authorize them to use the term *Abba* in addressing God? The Greek is not clear. But it would seem that what we translate as "Our Father, who art in heaven," most likely began in the original Aramaic with "Abba." Jesus is inviting his followers to share in his own intimate communion with God. Christians do this when they worship. There is a certain boldness implied in the use of this prayer, a boldness that Christians shoulder because it is Jesus' gift to them. The ancient liturgy of St. John Chrysostom reflects the significance of this when prefacing the Lord's Prayer with the phrase: "With boldness and without condemnation we may dare to call on Thee, the heavenly God, as Father, and to say, Our Father, who art in heaven."

The third person of the Trinity, the Holy Spirit, is significant here. The Holy Spirit empowers Christians to pray like Jesus and effects the same

---

9. Jeremias, *The Central Message of the New Testament* (New York: Charles Scribner's Sons, 1965), 21. An *ad hominem* dispute has broken out regarding the credibility of Jeremias's scholarship. See Ben F. Meyer, "A Caricature of Joachim Jeremias and His Work," *Journal of Biblical Literature* 110, no. 3 (Fall 1991): 451–62; and E. P. Sanders, "Defending the Indefensible," *Journal of Biblical Literature* 110, no. 3 (Fall 1991): 463–77. What seems beyond dispute is Jesus' claim to an intimate relationship with God. James Barr believes the evidence validates Jeremias's approach in general, but he is critical about certain aspects. "Abba" was not limited to the speech of children, argues Barr; adults—grown-up children—used it too. In addition, there is insufficient evidence to conclude that Jesus used "abba" exclusively when referring to God. Other expressions were probably available and utilized. In sum, Barr argues that we should not try to build a theological point on a single word ("'Abba Father' and the Familiarity of Jesus' Speech," *Theology* 91, no. 741 [May 1988]: 173–79).

intimate communion in their lives. "When we cry, 'Abba! Father!' it is that very Spirit bearing witness with our spirit that we are children of God" (Rom. 8:15; see Gal. 4:6). The Father-Son relationship between God and Jesus becomes through the Spirit inclusive of those who through faith are reconciled to God. As Jesus was a child of God, so also are his followers. As Jesus became heir to resurrection and new life, so also will they.

Alternative Ways of Viewing Jesus and His Father

If one asks the New Testament to clarify conceptually just how Jesus and the God of Israel are related, an array of possibilities emerges.[10] First, some texts are outright adoptionistic, such as "God made him both Lord and Messiah" (Acts 2:36). In the centuries that followed the New Testament, the Ebionites followed this adoptionistic trajectory, arguing that Jesus became adopted into messiahship at baptism (Luke 3:22). Second, other passages identify Jesus with God, for example, "The Father and I are one" (John 10:30). The theme of identity between Jesus and God was a favorite among the modalists such as Sabellius. As strict monotheists, the modalists posited one divine being who appears at different times, first as Father, then as Son, and finally as Spirit. Third, in contrast, other passages sharply distinguish, so that Jesus must pray to the Father (Matt. 6:9) because the Father is greater than the Son (John 14:28). Theologians such as Justin Martyr appreciated such passages because they communicated the distance between humankind and the ineffable or transcendent Father, a distance bridged by the mediator, the Son. Fourth, some passages see Christ as a derivative or extension of God—for example, they see Christ as God's angel (Rev. 12:7); as Spirit (Rom. 1:3-5); as Logos (John 1:1-14); and as the Son of God (Matt. 27:54; John 1:14). The symbols in the context of the New Testament stories and reflections leave four possible directions for reflection: adoption, identity, distinction, and derivation. Which direction should we go?

During the first four centuries of the Christian era, theological reflection went in many directions. Many proposals for evangelical explication were offered, considered, then rejected or revised until the orthodox doctrine of the Trinity took shape. Among the significant proposals that were eventually rejected were modalism and subordinationism.

---

10. The strict logic of the parent-child image does not itself warrant the use of "Father" instead of "Mother." In principle, either parental gender would do. The use of the Father symbol is based on other associations such as the abba prayers of Jesus and Paul. Sandra Schneiders suggests that Jesus addressed God as Father because he was in a patriarchal culture wherein the mother-son relationship would have carried less weight (*Women and the Word* [New York: Paulist, 1986], 43). This is a circumstantial argument. Perhaps this is right. Yet Jesus freely employed feminine imagery for God in his teachings, for example, the parable of the woman with the lost coin (Luke 15). Jesus was not intimidated by his patriarchal culture. Could Jesus' use of "Father" simply be a contingency of history?

According to modalism, the divine reality is timeless and unitary, thereby making the distinctions of Father, Son, and Holy Spirit refer to three successive modes of divine expression in the temporal world—that is, creator, redeemer, and sanctifier. No one of the three persons alone is God. Rather, the ineffable godhead finds partial expression in each of the persons. Sabellius in the third century argued that God is one individual being and that the appellations of Father, Son, and Spirit designate the different forms or modes of action in the world. They do not designate eternal or intrinsic distinctions within the divine being itself. Unity is permanent, whereas distinction is transitory. Divine oneness is thus preserved through positing a supratemporal, self-existent God. This position in effect denies full divinity to the modes of temporal expression, to the three contingent persons.

In the case of subordinationism, divine unity is preserved by identifying the full godhead with just one of the three persons, the first. This contrasts with the modalists, who deny full godhead to any one of the three persons. Because the Father generates the Son and because the Spirit proceeds from the Father (and proceeds from the Son as well, according to the later Latin theologians), the subordinationists argue that there is a certain sense in which one could say the first person is the cause of the other two. They describe the Father as the sole eternal and infinite God, thereby consigning God's two self-expressions in the Logos (Christ) and in the Spirit to underling status.

Origen, for example, depicted the three persons of the Trinity as three concentric circles, according to which God the Father, the most comprehensive circle, bestows existence on all things. The Son as the Logos is the second circle, organizing the created order and endowing rational beings with the ability to understand the principles of the organized order. The Holy Spirit, the innermost circle, participates in the lives of the faithful, bringing them into personal holiness.[11] Starting from the outside and moving inward, the Father is the most comprehensive, including the other two persons while neither of the other two includes the Father. They are subordinate to the Father. If one reverses the direction, then, one moves from a center of relatedness established by the Holy Spirit outward toward absoluteness, a quality belonging solely to the Father, passing through the Son, who is somewhere between. Although Origen wrestled with the possibility of the Son being without beginning, he finally took what would become the subordinationist and derivationist position, following Proverbs 8:22-31 in describing the Son as "the firstborn of all creation, a thing created, wisdom."[12]

---

11. Origen *First Principles* 1.3.8.
12. Ibid., 4.4.1.

In those early and formative centuries it was more or less assumed without question that God as heavenly Father should be equated with the eternal and ineffable One, with the absolute. The context seemed to make this mandatory. Plato had long before described the world's creator as the ineffable Father.[13] Neoplatonism and Gnosticism could use the term *Father* to designate the supreme reality above and beyond being itself. It was inevitable that the Abba of Jesus would be similarly identified with the absolute. Otherwise the dimension of the Beyond would be lost.

The issue for Christian theologians became whether or not they should place Christ and the Holy Spirit in the absolute as well. This was exacerbated by the influence of Greek thought that was stretching the distance between heaven and earth. The working assumption endemic to the framework of Gnostic and Neoplatonist ontology was that there is an immense distance between the eternal realm and the human plane of temporal reality. There can be no direct connection between the two extremes of absolute transcendence and mundane relatedness. So reality as a whole was conceived as a hierarchy with mediating levels of being that span the distance. The chief candidate for playing this mediating role was the Logos—which is both a philosophical and a biblical concept—because the Logos is sublime yet shares the structure of the ordinary world. One of the inclinations of the pre-Nicene apologetic theologians was to place Christ as the Logos in this mediating role, to make him the kite string connecting heaven and earth.

As long as one did not press the issue regarding the precise altitude at which the line could be drawn between what is divine and what is mundane, the concerns that led to the doctrine of the Trinity would not surface. But the question was asked. Attempts were made to draw a line, and this produced a squabble: on which side of the line is Jesus Christ? If he is placed too low, at the level of mundane existence, then there is a risk of his losing his saving power. If he is placed too high into the realm of divine transcendence, then there is a risk of compromising the oneness, eternity, and simplicity of the divine being.

The difficulties revealed themselves as Arius of Alexandria drew the line with Jesus Christ on the under side of it. He was refining the subordinationist position by extending the thought of the Origenist school. The Son must be subordinate to the Father, who is the sole God, he argued, otherwise we would have two co-gods. If it is the case that God as Father, the transcendent and unoriginate source of all reality (ἀγέννητος ἀρχή), is absolutely simple, without internal differentiation, and unique, then his being (οὐσια) cannot be shared or communicated. If God as Father could impart his essence to other things, then he himself would be divisible and, hence, subject to change. But this is inconceivable because

---

13. Plato *Timaeus* 28c.

God is simple. God the Father is a monad (μόνας), and there had always been a divine monad. But a dyad came into being with the generation of the Son, and then a triad with the production of the Spirit of wisdom. All of this took place prior to the creation of the mundane world.

It follows from this that the Logos or Son must be a subordinate creature made by the Father. The Logos must have had a beginning. This beginning, however, is "before the time of the ages." In a sense the Logos is not contingent upon time because, as the instrument of creation, he is the creator of time as well as space and the material world. Thus, although Arius can say of the Christ that "there was when he was not" (ἦν ποτε ὅτε οὐκ ἦν), the status of even this subordinated Christ is supramundane, supratemporal, exalted above the temporal world in which we creatures live. He is an angel, although certainly preeminent among the angels. He holds a position comparable to the creator god or demiurge in Plato's *Timaeus* and in Gnosticism. He is antecedent to the creation of the world yet still not equated with the supreme reality. So, as Christians look up toward the celestial vault and the realm of the high God, certainly they can see that Christ is above them and hence representing God for them. But he is not fully God in Godself. The Father is still higher. The net product was the Arian triad consisting of three divine persons (τρεῖς ὑπόστασες). But these were three different beings, utterly distinct, only one of which, the Father, was ungenerate (ἀγέννητος) and, hence, truly God for Arius.

Athanasius challenged Arius and in doing so paved the road from Nicea in 325 through Alexandria in 362 to Constantinople in 381 and to affirmation of the full consubstantiality of the Son and the Spirit with the Father. The Son is begotten, not made, "of one essence with the Father" (ὁμοούσιον τῷ πατρί). It was Athanasius's thesis that the Father is fully God, the Son is fully God, and that there is only one God. The supreme divinity at the top of the sublime ladder in gnostic and Neoplatonist thought is the same divinity that created—and loves—the world, that became incarnate in Jesus, and that dwells as spiritual presence in Christian faith.

Athanasius agreed with Arius that we should distinguish between the ungenerate Father and the generated Son, but he denied that the term *God* must refer to something simple. God is not a simple monad. God is complex and trinitarian. There is differentiation and dynamism within the divine life. Movement and relationality are not inimical to God. They belong to God proper. This led to the subsequent application of the term *God* to the Trinity as a whole and not just to the Father alone.

According to Athanasius and the resulting creedal position, the Father eternally generates the Son. There never was a time before which the Father existed alone. The Son and Father have always coexisted in a continuing and mutually identifying relationship. Arian poems had forced the issue by taunting: "Once God was alone, and not yet a father, but afterwards he became a father." Athanasius took issue with this. He attacked as inconsistent Arius's concept of generation prior to the time of creation, because the very notion of generation implies time. He accused Arius of trying to deceive the simple-minded by eliminating the word *time* from his slogan, "There was when he was not." Athanasius's position was that if generation did not take place in time, then the generated one must be coeternal with the generator. Thus, by removing the time factor within the godhead, Athanasius removed the temporal priority of the Father.

But much more is at stake here than just the issue of temporality. It has to do with the nature of God proper. Is God in essence fatherly? Or, to put it another way, is the Godself relational? To this Athanasius gave a positive answer. If being fatherly is fundamental to the essence of God, as an explication of the gospel seems to require, then God cannot be God without the Son any more than a light can be a light without its shining. The very being of the Father as Father would be incomplete without the Son.[14] Fatherliness and Sonship are not simply ways in which God relates to the creation *ad extra*. Rather, they belong to the eternal essence of deity itself *ad intra*. The relationship between the divine persons is internal and constitutive of their respective identities.

Now at first this may appear to be a real triumph for the God of intimacy. But upon closer examination, we find that although divine relatedness has been affirmed, curiously enough, it has been affirmed as unrelated to us. In principle, the Trinity as conceived by Athanasius could go sailing along its merry way even if there never had been a world to relate to or a sinful humanity that needed saving. This is because in the Nicean discussion the eternal Logos could be distinguished from the historical Jesus. Athanasius could say that Jesus, amid the greatest pain and suffering while hanging on the cross, had no effect on the indwelling divine Logos. "He himself was in no way injured," writes Athanasius, because he is the "impassible and incorruptible and very Word and God."[15] Athanasius has placed the eternal Logos up into the heavenly altitudes, even higher than Arius had placed him. There is risk here. Once the Son of God is catapulted into the lofty realms of perfection and unchangeableness he might no longer be able to mediate between the changeable and the unchangeable, between the impassible Father and the suffering of the human race. The result could be a Trinity of unrelated relatedness.

For the Nicene Creed writers, God is a being that exists in relationship, but it is an internal or immanent relationship. Within the divine reality itself there are sociality and community. The Father is ever generating the Son, and the Spirit is ever proceeding in a never-ending

---

14. Athanasius *Discourse against Arius* 1.13.14; see Robert W. Jenson, *The Triune Identity* (Philadelphia: Fortress, 1982), 83.
15. Athanasius *Incarnation of the Word* 54.

perichoresis (περικώρησις, *circumincessio*).[16] While sharing and expressing the same essence, the three persons condition and permeate one another in a dynamic mutuality. The inner being of God—the immanent Trinity—has a life of its own prior to and independent of the creation of the world.

So it was believed at Nicea that the divine life exists primarily in eternity, prior to creation, transcendent to our temporal existence. We must still ask: what about God's relationship to the world? This was by no means forgotten. The creed goes on to say that this eternal Son was made flesh (σαρκωθέντα) and became a human being (ἐνανθρωπήσαντα). The impact of this is that the ineffable and mysterious God of the Beyond does not remain in the state of beyondness. It is not enough to send an intermediary into the world. It is not enough to connect heaven and earth with a kite string called the Logos. God in God's own self is present in the incarnation. The relationality within the divine life opens out into a full relationality with the cosmos. Just how we should understand the incarnation was not yet clear at Nicea, however. The christological controversies culminating at Chalcedon in 451 continued the discussion and eventually added further clarification on the quality of divine relatedness to the world through Jesus Christ.

Now, as I mentioned earlier, the issue that drives Christian thought in the direction of the Trinity is not at root a matter of arithmetic, of relating one and three. Nor is it a matter of trying to find a middle ground between monotheism and polytheism. Rather, as I have tried to show, what is coming to articulation here is an awareness of the tension between the absoluteness and the relatedness of God. Even though the creed writers of the fourth century were tempted to raise the Logos to a heavenly high altitude, they never forgot completely its tie with earth. In fact, it was divine relatedness that spurred them on. With Augustine, writing at the end of the fourth century, the church could admire the Platonists who would agree that "in the beginning was the word." But what could not be found anywhere in sublime philosophy is that "the Word became flesh and dwelt among us" (John 1:14).[17] This is Emmanuelism, God with us even in the flesh. This commitment to God's incarnate involvement in the world eventually prevented Christian speculation from allowing the divine Son to soar up and completely out of sight. In addition, the Holy Spirit represented an Emmanuelism in another form: the continuing presence of the divine in the community of the church and especially in the sanctified life of the believer.

---

16. The term *perichoresis* was given us by John of Damascus (*Exposition of the Orthodox Faith* 1.8).

17. Augustine *Confessions* 7.9.

One God with Three Personal Identities

This concern for relationality within the absolute has driven evangelical explication in the direction of its customary description of the Trinity as one God in three persons. But this neat formulation does not in itself settle all matters. The logical hurdles confronted by the Nicene framers required bending the language and stipulating definitions in an attempt to arrive at clarity and eliminate ambiguity. But the elimination of ambiguity is difficult to accomplish, and much of it remains, especially regarding the understanding of God as person.

Risking a bit of oversimplification, we might describe this ambiguity in terms of the differing emphases of Athanasius and the Cappadocian theologians in the years between Nicea in 325 and Constantinople in 381. Although the Cappadocians—Basil, Gregory of Nyssa, and Gregory of Nazianzus—sided with Athanasius against Arius, they too had differing emphases. Whereas for Athanasius there is primarily one God whose mystery lies in the threeness of the Trinity, for the Cappadocians there are the three persons whose mystery lies in their unity. Whereas for Athanasius God is personal in God's unity and there is some blurring of the distinctions between the persons, for the Cappadocians each of the three hypostases is personal and their unity is found in a suprapersonal, sublime relationship. Athanasius says that everything said of the Father can also be said of the Son, except that the Son is Son and not Father. One of the Cappadocians, Gregory of Nyssa, says that the godhead signifies an operation and not a nature (φύσις), and that operation is relational in character.

The Council at Constantinople in 381 produced a bit of a compromise and ended up positing a single being in three hypostases (μία οὐσία, τρεῖς ὑπόστασεις), wherein the former denoted the divine nature (φύσις) and the latter a principle of genuine distinction or identity within that divine nature. When it came to render into Latin the creedal statement, first written in Greek, however, it risked reintroducing ambiguity. Ordinarily the Latin equivalent to ὑπόστασις is *substantia;* yet Tertullian had already in the previous century introduced the phrase *una substantia, tres personae.* Tertullian's term *person*, which did not appear in the Niceno-Constantinopolitan Creed, appeared later in the Athanasian Creed as a rendering of ὑπόστασις. The meanings are not equivalent. While the Greek ὑπόστασις (substantial being) tends to stress the distinctiveness of Father, Son, and Spirit, the use of the Latin *persona* (face) tends to stress the unity of the one God behind the various faces. Eventually through stipulation and convention, trinitarian vocabulary settled on referring to the one divine nature as οὐσία, φύσις (*natura, essentia,* and *substantia*), and on referring to the threefoldness as ὑπόστασις, πρόσωπον (*persona* and *subsistence*). Nevertheless, even the agreed-upon vocabulary seems to bear with it the tension between Athanasius and the

Cappadocians that was not fully resolved; and this has contributed some-what to the ambiguity today regarding Christian understanding of divine personhood.

How to understand the concept of person is crucial here. Coming from the Greek πρόσωπον through the Latin *persona*, the term *person* originally meant "mask" or "face," connoting the role played by an actor or actors in the theater. In late Hellenistic culture as πρόσωπον and *persona* became associated less with the mask covering the face and more with the face itself, the terms came to refer to the person as an individual. We can identify an individual by his or her face.

In the New Testament the term *face* is tied to the truth embedded in glory, for Paul can speak eschatologically about the time when Christians will no longer see through a mirror dimly but come to know God "face to face" (πρόσωπον πρὸς πρόσωπον) (1 Cor. 13:12). Or, they can anticipate that future truth ahead of time when they realize that already God's glory has shined "in the face [πρόσωπον] of Christ" (2 Cor. 4:6; see 3:18). The face of Christ not only identifies Jesus as the carpenter from Nazareth; it also shows forth the fullness of God's truth that lies beyond him.

It should be obvious to all that the New Testament and the fourth-century theologians did not have in mind the modern notion of person with its strong emphasis on individual autonomy and self-consciousness. We today tend to underscore the word *person*, thinking of a unique, dis-crete, self-initiating, and self-determining subject. Neither the Athanasian nor Cappadocian school had such a concept in mind. Nor did they have in mind the intermediate definition of "person" that marks the transi-tion from premodern to modern times, namely, the one formulated by Boethius: a person is a single, rational, individual substance. Although Boethius's definition could still be used by medieval theologians to refer to the three hypostases because reason could be shared, the trend in the morphology of nontheological vocabulary was definitely toward individ-ualized reason that eventually produced the contemporary concept of the unique personality.

Theologically, however, we must say that Father, Son, and Holy Spirit are not three distinct, divine, rational beings, three subjects, or three sep-arate selves. Nor are they distinct parts of a single divine self, which, in its oneness, hovers unseen behind or above the separate faces. There are not three personalities in God, although we certainly might speak of a personality of God. The one God is fully present and active in each and all modes of being and action; yet God is not distinguishable except in one or another of these modes of being and action. One or another of the faces is required to identify the one God.

If in our emerging postmodern context we try to iron out some of the ambiguities by extending the emphasis of Athanasius, we could speak of one God with one personality but with three faces. At first glance this might appear to be a form of modalism, according to which the divine essence is really transcendent and simple even though in its outward manifestation it appears multiple. But, if we try to keep the Cappadocian corrective in mind, we can avoid modalism by asserting that the persons face inward as well as outward. Each person faces the other two, and hence each is identifiable even within the divine life proper.

It is to this problematic that Robert Jenson offers a most helpful suggestion, namely, that we translate ὑπόστασις or *persona* with the English word *identity*.[18] This term is helpful because it avoids the link to independent selfhood or initiating subject that comes with the modern word *person*, yet it permits distinguishing the three faces of the Trinity in terms of their relation to one another and to humankind. In sum, we might say there is only one divine reality, but it has three distinguishable and interrelatable identities.

This does not mean, as some have suggested, that we must eliminate the use of the word *person* entirely when referring to the three hypostases. In our context as in any context we will have to stipulate what we mean when we use theological vocabulary. With the term *person* having itself gained some symbolic meaning through its use in hymns and customary liturgical formulas, it would be best to complement—not replace—it with terms such as *face* and *identity*.

With this in mind, we might develop this understanding of facing inward by recognizing that the identity of each person is dependent upon its relationship to the others. The originary symbols seem to contain their own relational logic. The Father is fatherly only because there is a Son to whom he is so related. Without a child there can be no parent. Hence, the first person of the Trinity becomes what he is due to his relationship to the second person. The converse is true regarding the Son. The Son's identity and divinity are dependent upon his being sent by the Father. These two persons are united with one another in a community of love. This communal relationship of love is the presence of the Holy Spirit—that is, the Spirit gains its identity because of the relationship between the first two. By designating the Spirit as the principle of unity, we can maintain a tight reign on the threeness of the Trinity. It is easy to fall into the trap of thinking there are three persons plus a unity, thereby hinting that the unity is itself a fourth quality that transcends the other three. What I am saying here is that the unity is itself one of the three. Thus, there is no so-called divine nature or substance that is passed around and shared by the three persons. Nor is there any room for the Trinity to be transcended by some higher or supratrinitarian realm of ineffable being.

This leads contemporary followers of Luther such as Karl Barth and Wolfhart Pannenberg to affirm that the divinity of each of the three per-

---

18. Jenson, *Triune Identity*, 108; idem, "The Triune God," in *Chr.D.*, 1:138.

sons is a dependent divinity. Divinity comes to each as the result of personhood in relationship. To the Son, divinity manifests itself in the form of the Father, as the ultimate and sublime creator of all things. The Son, in turn, cedes divinity to the Father through total obedience. Only total obedience can grant to the divine king a kingdom in which the king's will is done. As the universal Logos incarnate, the Son hands the creation over to the Father so that God can be "all in all." The Son knows himself as Son of the Father through participation in the Holy Spirit, and in the Spirit the Father finds his unity with the Son and therewith the certainty of his own divinity. Finally, the Spirit finds its own personhood and divinity in the community of Father and Son.[19]

Hence, the unity of the godhead is a unity of integrating love. It is not the primordial unity of some simple substance of which each of the three persons represents a different expression. It is rather a dynamic unity, a personal unity, an achieved wholeness. Tipping a bit closer to the Cappadocians than to Athanasius, Wolfhart Pannenberg stresses that God is not personal except in one or another of the three persons. When God confronts the world through personal relationship, it will be as the Father, as the Son, or as the Spirit, not as an abstract unity. God is personal only through one or another of the three persons, not as a single ineffable entity. We assume that the notion of person is a relational concept, and that the net effect of the doctrine of the Trinity is to understand the divine reality as a unity in relation.

But to posit a relational unity of three identities is still to posit a unity. This is no concession to tritheism. I believe we can employ Jenson's rendering of "person" as "identity" and a concept of intratrinitarian relation and still affirm as the church since Nicea has always affirmed that the works of the Trinity that are directed outward toward the creation are undivided. There is no act of God that is not the act of all three persons—that is, the act of the one God. If we work with the general idea that creation is the province of the Father, redemption that of the Son, and sanctification that of the Spirit, we do not mean that each activity has a separate agent.

The identifiable persons share fully in all of the divine works— creation, incarnation, effusion of grace, and so forth—in everything except the relations that constitute and identify each person. Here, with some modification, we might follow John Calvin, who already follows Augustine in thinking this way: Christ with respect to us is called God; with respect to the Father, Son. Again, the Father with respect to us is called God; with respect to the Son, Father. Finally, the Spirit in respect

19. Cf. Barth, *CD*, 1/1:419; Wolfhart Pannenberg, "Die Subjektivität Gottes und die Trinitätslehre," in *Grundfragen Systematischer Theologie* (Göttingen: Vandenhoeck & Ruprecht, 1980), 2:110–11, and *Systematische Theologie* (Göttingen: Vandenhoeck & Ruprecht, 1988), 1:340–47.

to us is called God; with respect to the other two persons, Spirit.[20] What this means for our worship and prayer life, then, is that we treat each of the three persons as fully God. We do not direct our religious affections toward the allegedly ineffable divine nature, which these identifiable persons allegedly hold in common. Rather, when our thoughts, feelings, and actions are directed toward the Father, the Son, or the Spirit, we can assume they are directed toward God proper.

The Immanent and Economic Trinity

Thus far I have been talking mainly about the immanent Trinity (sometimes called the "essential" or "ontological" Trinity). The immanent Trinity has to do with the eternal perichoresis between Father, Son, and Spirit that some believe would continue unabated even if the cosmos had not come into existence. However, by extending the notion of οἰκονομία introduced earlier by Tertullian, post-Nicene theologians began to speak of an economic Trinity (or "Trinity of manifestation"). This is the Trinity as manifested externally in the world through creation, redemption, and sanctification. The two can be distinguished when, for example, one looks at the way the second person is understood by the Nicene theologians. The cross of Jesus occurring within the stream of temporal history belongs to the economy of God's saving work but not within the eternal immanent Trinity. To that belongs only the eternal Logos. This Nicene scheme incorporates a partially absolute Son who mediates between two spheres, one an eternal sphere to which the immanent Trinity belongs and the other a temporal sphere of human need.

There is a gain here. The concept of the economic Trinity allows us to reaffirm the biblical insight that the entire godhead—even God as Father—is related to the world. This is a necessary extension of Christian understanding if we are to mark faithfully the watershed achievement of Nicea—namely, that it is the Trinity as such, not just the Father, whom Christians call God. Yet, I ask: is the addition of the economic Trinity enough? Is it not in effect merely a temporal image of a much more real and hence much more important eternal and unrelated Trinity? Is this not a subtle return of subordinationism? Now the related economic Trinity seems to be subordinated to the immutable immanent Trinity. The temporal Trinity seems to be subordinated to the eternal Trinity. Is this not another defense of the absolute Beyond at the cost of the related Intimate?

Recent theological discussions have led scholars such as Karl Rahner, Eberhard Jüngel, and Jürgen Moltmann to make a radical affirmation—namely, the economic Trinity is the immanent Trinity, and vice versa.[21]

---

20. Calvin, *Inst.*, 1.13.

21. This is best known as "Rahner's Rule" because Karl Rahner makes it plain: the economic Trinity is the immanent Trinity and the immanent Trinity is the economic Trinity (*The Trinity* [New York: Herder and Herder, 1970], 21–22).

This affirmation emerges from explication of the profound and thorough-going relatedness of God to the world apparently required by the gospel message. Jürgen Moltmann argues that we could not say that "God is love" and mean it unless God is actually engaged in the activity of loving, and such activity implies a world that is the object of this love. Love in the face of suffering causes pain, pain even for God as Father. The work of redemption becomes part of the very life of God.[22] This has led Moltmann to designate the Trinity as "open" in order to connote the essential relatedness of God to the creation.

I wish to applaud this line of development. It says something decisively important about relationality in God—namely, God's relationship to the world is internal to the divine life. God's relation to the world in redemption and consummation is not merely external, not merely an add-on to a God whose being is already intact. God is not a simple monad existing somewhere in eternal isolation who occasionally turns on a celestial television news show to observe what is happening on earth. Rather, God's involvement in the course of world affairs is so intimate that the character of divinity itself is shaped by it. The trinitarian understanding of God is that God's full self-investment in the incarnation redefines divinity to include humanity, the humanity of the historical Jesus. God's full self-investment in the Holy Spirit binds believers to Christ, so that in faith they are at one with Christ and, hence, at one with God. This means that for God to be God now includes divine diremption in Jesus Christ and return to unity through the Holy Spirit, a return that will ultimately include the consummate salvation of the world. The identity of God does not come predetermined in some timeless eternity that lies beyond and divorced from everything else; rather, the identity of God is shaped by the economy of the divine-human relationship taking place within time and history.

Before proceeding further along this line of reasoning, I should note one valuable contribution made by the immanent-economic distinction— namely, it protects the freedom of God. Does the total collapse of the immanent Trinity into the economic Trinity result in a finite God who is dependent for divine definition upon the world? Do we want to affirm divine relatedness to the world at the cost of surrendering God's absoluteness? Hardly. Therefore it appears that we have arrived at a dilemma. On the one hand, to affirm the immanent-economic distinction risks subordinating the economic Trinity and hence protecting transcendent absoluteness at the cost of genuine relatedness to the world. On the other hand, to collapse the two together risks producing a God so dependent

---

22. Jürgen Moltmann, *The Trinity and the Kingdom* (San Francisco: Harper & Row, 1981), 160–61. Moltmann tries to lead us into a social doctrine of the Trinity. I do not follow that far. Nevertheless, Moltmann makes a valuable contribution by stressing that God's relation to the world is internal to the trinitarian life.

upon the world for self-definition that divine freedom and independence are lost.

The solution to the dilemma, I believe, is to think of the identity of the immanent and economic Trinity as eschatological. This would require a modification in the commonly accepted understanding of eternity as timelessness. Rather than timelessness, I suggest that eternity be understood as everlastingness that takes up into itself the course of temporal history. What happens in time contributes to the content of what is eternal. This applies to God as well as to the world. God's trinitarian activity in temporal history becomes constitutive of the divine eternity. The redeemed creation is drawn up into the eternal life of God through the eschatological consummation. This is what salvation means.

Eschatological eternity is genuine eternity; but it is an eternity related to, rather than divorced from, time. From our point of view within the as yet uncompleted course of history it may appear that God is in the process of becoming a Trinity over time. Relationality requires becoming, and becoming requires time. God as Trinity requires time. Yet, from the point of view of eschatological fulfillment, there is one God temporally constituted of three persons.

Robert Jenson puts it this way: "This 'economic' Trinity is *eschatologically* God 'himself,' an 'immanent' Trinity. And that assertion is no problem, for God is himself only eschatologically, since he is Spirit. . . . As for God's freedom, only our proposal fully asserts it. The immanent Trinity of previous Western interpretation had but the spurious freedom of unaffectedness. Genuine freedom is the reality of possibility, is openness to the future."[23] In similar fashion Moltmann exclaims: "The economic Trinity completes and perfects itself to immanent Trinity when the history and experience of salvation are completed and perfected. When everything is 'in God' and 'God is all in all,' then the economic Trinity is raised into and transcended in the immanent Trinity."[24] Rahner's Rule— the immanent Trinity is the economic Trinity and the economic Trinity is the immanent Trinity—applies eschatologically to the one God, the future of the one world.

GOD AS FATHER AND FEMINIST CONSCIOUSNESS

Although post-Nicene precision would require that the term *God* refer to the entire godhead inclusive of Father, Son, and Holy Spirit, Christian piety often lacks that theological precision. But, then, so did Saint Paul, who, as I mentioned earlier, did not have the benefit of Nicea and so could use "God" and "Father" interchangeably. This is by no means to

---

23. Jenson, "The Triune God," 1:155–56; see also idem, *Triune Identity*, 141.
24. Moltmann, *Trinity and Kingdom*, 161.

suggest that the Niceans or Saint Paul made a mistake. It is to suggest rather that the theological explication during the period of trinitarian formulation attained a high degree of theological differentiation and that piety, especially at the level of the first naiveté, never ceases to respond to the symbols in their compact form. This leaves open the possibility that at any time the symbols may—due perhaps to differing contextual stimuli—differentiate in a direction differing from that taken by Nicea. This in part is what is happening in the current debate over speaking of God as "Father."

The heavenly Father worshiped at the level of the first naiveté is part of a Christian's world (of meaning) even if, theologically speaking, he transcends the world (the created order). He combines fully the qualities of the Beyond and the Intimate. He is considered the head of the cosmic household, and human beings are his family. God is acknowledged to be the creator and sustainer of humanity and, hence, is overseer of the world. "The earth is my footstool" (Isa. 66:1). It is with great respect and comfort that congregations can sing Maltbie D. Babcock's well-known hymn:

> This is my father's world;
> I rest me in the thought
> of rocks and trees, of skies and seas,
> His hands the wonders wrought.

In the strong hands of the Father—the hands that fashioned the world in the first place—Christians find understanding, refuge, and safety. This is by no means the utterly transcendent absolute One who resides in the heavens so far above mundane existence that he is immune from temporal influence. At this level of symbolization the creator cares. "Children of the heavenly Father," opens the hymn by Caroline V. Sandell Berg, "Safely in his bosom gather."

But things have changed in the era of modern awareness and the hermeneutic of suspicion. As I mentioned in my earlier discussion of the hermeneutic of suspicion, the linguistic symbol system within which we live and move is now undergoing critical analysis from the perspective of feminist consciousness. Feminist analysis reveals a preponderance of grammatical forms and images that presuppose male dominance. Women who have been living much of their lives at the level of the first naiveté suddenly discover that they have been co-opted, that for generation after generation the self-understanding of women has been directed by a linguistic system that presumes for them a subordinate role. Our linguistically formed world of meaning serves to deny women the equality and freedom envisioned by Enlightenment ideals. The attainment of such equality and freedom requires among other things a process of cultural and psychological consciousness raising.

Out of this emerges a major premise of feminist theology: symbolization of God as Father leads to the social oppression of women. The symbol of divine fatherhood is said to be the source of a cultural neurosis that has rape, genocide, and war as its symptoms. Feminist theologian Mary Daly, for example, contends that the image of the Father-God makes the "mechanisms for the oppression of women appear right and fitting. If God in 'his' heaven is a father ruling 'his' people, then it is in the 'nature' of things and according to divine plan and the order of the universe that society be male dominated."[25] Or, much more tersely, "If God is male, then male is God."[26] The problem begins already with the compact symbolism of scripture. Rosemary Ruether argues:

> Most images of God in religions are modeled after the ruling class of society. In biblical religion the image of God is that of a patriarchal Father above the visible created world, who relates to Israel as his "wife" and "children" in the sense of creatures totally dependent on his will, owing him unquestioning obedience. This image allows the king and patriarchal class to relate to women, children, and servants through the same model of domination and dependency.[27]

The argument of Daly and Ruether brings to light a serious matter, because there are examples within the history of the Christian church where just this kind of perversion of power seeks theological justification for the imposition of hierarchical rule. For example, despite all of its flowery language regarding "the unity of the family of God," chapter 3 of the Dogmatic Constitution on the Church at Vatican II continues the long tradition of contriving a hierarchy of fathers leading from the local priest up to the bishop then to the Holy Father in Rome, who is the Vicar of Christ, the Son of the heavenly Father. There are no women in this chain of command. Nor does this form of explicating the symbols seem to permit it. In the mid-1970s in order to repel growing interest on the part of women religious to celebrate the mass, the Congregation for the Doctrine of the Faith denied that women could preside at the eucharist in its document *Inter insignores* ("Declaration on the Question of the Admission of Women to the Ministerial Priesthood"). The denial was based on an argument of likeness. Men can pray the eucharistic prayer because men are physical representatives of Jesus.[28] Women cannot because they are not.

---

25. Mary Daly, "After the Death of God the Father," in Carol P. Christ and Judith Plaskow, eds., *Womanspirit Rising* (San Francisco: Harper & Row, 1979), 54.

26. Mary Daly, *Beyond God the Father* (Boston: Beacon, 1973), 19.

27. Rosemary Radford Ruether, *New Woman New Earth* (New York: Seabury, Crossroad, 1975), 74.

28. Sandra M. Schneiders is sharply critical of *Inter insignores* on two grounds. First, the argument from likeness has no precedent in tradition. Second and more important, it raises doubt regarding salvation. Since Gregory of Nazianzus, theologians have maintained that "what is not assumed is not redeemed." Does this Vatican document implicitly argue that Jesus assumed the likeness of men and not women, thereby, failing to redeem women? This would be absurd, says Schneiders (*Women and the Word*, 4).

This stimulated immense speculation around the world as people began to ask in jest: if Jesus had long hair and weighed 130 pounds, and the local short-haired priest weighs 240 while a long-haired nun weighs 130, would then the nun's words of institution be preferable? Would this principle make a thirty-year-old woman a better representative of Jesus than a sixty-year-old man? Of course not. So then why is gender the decisive factor?

It appears that this amounts to a case of sheer gender discrimination with an overlay of theological gobbledegook. The feminist critique has legitimacy: religious symbolism is being used to sanctify a patriarchal power structure. This exclusively male hierarchy is offensive to many because it runs counter to key tenets of modernity. The modern revolution in consciousness with its reverence for such things as equality and dignity applied to all people regardless of gender is essentially antihierarchical. Be that as it may, what is important for our theological discussion here is that the feminist critique assumes that the cause of this discrimination can be traced to the symbolism of the divine Father. We need to ask: granting that divine Father symbolism has been used to buttress human patriarchy, is it the case that divine Father symbolism is the source of this patriarchy?

Daly and Ruether see divine Father symbolism as the source of oppression. When they critique the term *Father*, they do not wish to explicate the sense of father as creator or carer. Rather they seek to describe a relationship between God and the world understood in terms of the relationship between the ruler and the ruled, between master and slave, between lord and subject, between boss and secretary, between oppressor and oppressed. The argument assumes a paradigmatic theory of human behavior—that is, the theory that people behave in accordance with their understanding of how the gods behave. Following a divine model, people allegedly copy God. With this assumption the argument seems to take the following form: if God behaves like a ruler over the ruled, and if God is male and not female, then it follows that there is an apparent divine justification for men to rule over women. But, these feminists charge, this is only apparent justification. Assuming that women have rights equal to men, it follows that such patriarchal rule is illegitimate and, further, that its theological justification must similarly be illegitimate. The final conclusion, then, is that humans—especially women—can no longer feel at home in a naively constructed premodern world with its heavenly Father.

This loss of one's world of meaning can be good for theology, say the feminists. It can help us distinguish idols from the true God. "Religious symbols die when the cultural situation that supported them ceases to give them plausibility," writes Daly. "This should pose no problem to authentic faith, which accepts the relativity of all symbols and recognizes

that fixation upon any one of them as absolute in itself is idolatrous."[29]
Feminist theology, operating at the level of critical consciousness, helps
Christians to avoid idolatry. But it also signals a temporary loss of their
symbolic home.

Revolutionary and Reformist Feminisms

Some feminist theologians have taken up the task of world-reconstruction
by developing an alternative symbol system, one that may be polytheistic
and may include worship of one or more goddesses. Other feminists have
sought reconstruction but also have sought to remain within the fold of
Christian monotheism. The former are sometimes dubbed "revolutionary" or "post-Christian" while the latter are thought to be "reformist"
and within the Christian tradition.

The revolutionary position is the more virulent and more logical of
the two when it comes to drawing conclusions from feminist premises. Its
major premise is that divine Father symbolism leads to the social oppression of women. This premise has a corollary: whoever names the world
controls the world. We must surmise, therefore, that the divine Father
symbolism of scripture is the invention of men for the purpose of controlling women. To attain liberation such control must be arrested from
men and placed in the hands of women. The theological task becomes
one of using our imaginations to construct paradigms of gender equality
in heaven that we may copy here on earth. Women then can and should
rename and hence re-create a just social world.

The revolutionary implications for Christianity are clear. If it is true
that Christian symbolism at the compact level is in fact the invention
of men and is inherently and forcefully oppressive to women, then no
amount of evangelical explication could ever rid it of its dark spot. Because religious people actually live most of their lives at the prereflective
level—that is, at the level of compact symbolization—any modification
of that symbol system at the level of critical consciousness will accomplish
only a modest change in behavior at best. Consequently, full liberation
would seem to require an entirely new religious gestalt. The proposal:
worship of the goddess. To this end feminist theologians see their task
as one of producing a symbol system wherein women get to name the
ultimate realities. This will bring the dignity and respect to women that
worship of the heavenly Father could not bring, and, of course, it need not
be exclusivist. If we are not asking for female superiority—if all we want
is parity or equality between women and men—then we could live out
of a bi-gender, divine symbol system while simply making sure the maleness of deity is not given dominance. The revolutionary or post-Christian

---

29. Daly, "After the Death of God the Father," 56.

position consciously counts the cost: the abandonment of the revelation and norm embodied in the compact symbolization of scripture.

The reformist position is less radical. As a consequence it must be more subtle. It seeks to affirm the tenets of the Christian faith, and, to do so, it must affirm the symbolization of this faith at its most compact level, the scriptural witness. However, this means among other things that worshiping God through the symbol of the Father is inescapable. Thus the reformists find themselves in the delicate dilemma of both affirming the feminist premise—that divine Father symbolization leads to the oppression of women—yet, at the same time, seeking to retain divine Father symbolization while liberating women. The proposed solution to this dilemma is to keep but to weaken divine Father symbolization.

The weakening of divine Father symbolization involves two steps, both taken at the level of critical consciousness. The first step is to put distance between the symbol and its referent, between language about God and the being of God. Following a variant of the apophatic method, it deliteralizes speech about divine things. God in God's own being is said to be ineffable, infinite, indefinable, mysterious, not subject to univocal statements. Therefore, God is not literally "our Father." The term *Father* is just a metaphor or symbol. The reality of God is posited as independent of this and of any other such metaphor or symbol. The second step follows closely. It involves the manipulation and interchanging of symbols and metaphors for God. It involves especially the demoting of the Father image and the promoting of nonpatriarchal images. It is, in short, a divide-and-conquer method.

Making Metaphors and Models of God

The thought of Sallie McFague provides the best example. The essential problem, as she sees it, is the literalism "rampant in our time." She objects to people for whom "if the Bible says that God is 'father' then God is literally, really, 'father.' "[30] Literalism is a problem because "no finite thought, product, or creature can be identified with God."[31] She responds to this rampant literalism by exacting her metaphorical version of the Protestant principle drawn from Luther and Tillich, what I earlier identified as the apophatic principle. According to this principle the bond between symbol and referent is so loosened that when Christians say loudly "God

---

30. McFague, *Metaphorical Theology* (Philadelphia: Fortress, 1982), 5. That McFague in this book is committed to doing theology at the level of modern critical consciousness is clearly stated when she says of her work: "It comes out of a post-Enlightenment, Protestant, feminist perspective which I would characterize as skeptical, relativistic, prophetic, and iconoclastic. It is more aware of the discontinuities between God and the world than of the continuities. It seeks a way of believing in a nonbelieving time by asserting no more than the evidence supports rather than what the tradition has proclaimed" (ibid., x).

31. Ibid., 19. Schneiders's analysis is different: no one in the Christian tradition would ever posit that God is literally male. The problem is not divine ontology. The problem is spirituality (*Women and the Word*, 6–7).

is Father" they may simultaneously whisper "he is not." Her key term is *metaphor*, and by its use she means to emphasize the dissimilarity between the word *Father* and the ineffable reality of God. Step one has been taken.

Step two—the divide-and-conquer step—is accomplished by piling up metaphors. It involves the following argument: McFague says that divine Father symbolization is idolatrous because it is taken literally; and the reason it is taken literally is that it so dominates Christian language that no other symbols can carry any religious freight. The way to deliteralize and hence to deidolatrize the heavenly Father and hence finally to liberate women socially is to relativize the Father symbol by employing it side by side with nonpatriarchal symbols. McFague nominates alternative metaphors as symbols: God as mother, God as lover, and God as friend. "A metaphorical theology will insist that many metaphors and models are necessary, that a piling up of images is essential, both to avoid idolatry and to attempt to express the richness and variety of the divine-human relationship."[32]

McFague recognizes that by applying critical analysis to compact symbols the risk of denying their validity is high. In her book *Metaphorical Theology*, she entertains and rejects the possibility of exchanging the root metaphor of the Christian system for another one, and in doing so recognizes that this would mean a new religion. But McFague is a Christian. She can justify remaining within the Christian fold because she does not have to give up Christianity's root metaphor. What is that root metaphor? It is the kingdom or rule of God. "The root metaphor of Christianity is not God the father but the kingdom or rule of God."[33] This observation extends step two by knocking the metaphor of the Father out of the center and making it contingent upon the primary and central symbol, the kingdom or rule of God. She can in good conscience remain Christian if she can think of God as her king or ruler and if she is not dependent upon thinking of God as her Father.

The impact such modern feminist consciousness has had on piety at the level of the first naiveté is not yet clear; however, at the level of critical consciousness it has compelled a thorough reassessment of theological methodology and of the Christian concept of God. Its long-range implications for the doctrine of the Trinity have yet to be explored. That exploration lies beyond the scope of the present work. What can be explored here even if briefly, however, is the validity of the premises and hence the soundness of the feminist argument against God as Father.

God the Father and Sexist Oppression

The initial premise, recall, is that divine Father symbolization leads to the social oppression of women. This premise entails two implications that

---

32. McFague, *Metaphorical Theology*, 20.
33. Ibid., 146.

are often articulated by feminist theologians. The first is that symbols or metaphors function paradigmatically—that is, that human behavior consists in copying what the gods do. The second is that to understand God as Father is to understand God as oppressor. Because men oppress women, and if men are fulfilling the paradigm of the divine Patriarch, then the divine Father worshiped by Christians must be the oppressor of the human race.

This leads to a number of observations. First, if the above is true, then invoking an apophatic principle to stress the ineffability of God will in no way help solve the problem. If it is in fact true that human behavior consists in copying the divine paradigm, and if the paradigm promulgated at the level of critical theology is the divine ineffability, one has the right to ask: how can one copy ineffability? How can the mystery and incomprehensibility of God actually affect our lives if we assume that the way the divine affects our lives is through mimetic repetition? The fact is—and McFague recognizes this—that the power exerted on us through awareness of the divine indefinability is the human power to define, the power to create. Rather than leading us to copy preset patterns, the divine mystery leads us forward to create new things, our lives and our responsibilities included. Spiritual apprehension of God's transcendence is liberating. What this means for us theologically, I would recommend, is that we should drop the whole notion of paradigmatic thinking and proceed creatively in the task of liberation. The symbol and concept of the divine Father need not inhibit us.

It is worth noting that the notion of divine ineffability has never been stressed more strongly than it was by the theologians of the pre-Nicene period under the influence of Hellenism; and these theologians never questioned giving a name to sublime ineffable reality, the name Father. The symbol of the Father, so prevalent during this early period of theological differentiation, points to the very truth that Daly and McFague wish to use to weaken it. This in no way invalidates McFague's use of the Protestant (or apophatic) principle, but it does raise the prospect that she may be unnecessarily negating a notion that is at the heart of much of her thought.

A second important observation is this: McFague's method in particular seems to presuppose that one can have access to absolute reality apart from the related symbol.[34] But, as I have argued earlier, access to such transcendence is necessarily through the symbol. Feminist theologians are

---

34. In her more recent book, *Models of God*, McFague indirectly rejects the hermeneutical task of theology—that is, she rejects the necessity of interpreting the biblical and traditional symbols. She says they are outmoded, and what we need are metaphors that express the experience of our own time. Hence, the theological task is a constructive and heuristic one: we construct new metaphors that are suggestive of new meaning. Such a procedure seems to presuppose access to God apart from the originary symbols.

fond of employing the Buddhist finger-moon lesson. When someone's finger points out the moon, you then look directly at the moon and no longer at the finger. It allegedly follows that once a religious symbol points out the divine, you look directly at the divine and abandon the symbol. Now this argument may have some significance for an Asian religious philosophy that posits an ineffable ultimate such as nirvana that is solely transtemporal, solely absolute, and solely unrelated. But the argument does not work in the case of Christianity, which holds that the ultimate reality is related to us through events in temporal history. To abandon the Father symbol to embrace pure ineffability—as an act parallel to abandoning the finger to embrace the moon—is to abandon symbolic access to whoever was incarnate in the Son.

Which leads to a third observation. Here we may ask: is the feminist explication of what the symbol "God the Father" means exegetically accurate? Is it in fact the case that the understanding of God as Father at the level of compact symbolization communicates that God is an oppressor? Feminists are rightly struggling against the subordination of women to men through the equivalent of a massive social, economic, political, and cultural conspiracy. The power to maintain this conspiracy must come from somewhere. Does it come from the biblical picture of God as Father?

In light of what we found in the proto-trinitarian thinking of the New Testament, it does not seem that the God whom Jesus addressed as Abba could rightly be invoked to endorse sexist oppression. Rosemary Ruether explicates Jesus' teachings (esp. Matt. 23:8-11) in order to make this very point:

Traditional theological images of God as father have been the sanctification of sexism and hierarchicalism.... Jesus, however, refers to God as father in such a way as to overthrow this hierarchical relationship of the rulers to the ruled.... The fatherhood of God could not have been understood as establishing male-ruling class power over subjugated groups in the Church or Christian society, but as that equal fatherhood that makes all Christians equals, brothers and sisters.[35]

In other words, the "traditional theological images of God as father" that Ruether blames have nothing to do with the Father-God of Jesus. An evangelical-critical explication of God as Father in the New Testament shows a symbol that holds together the two poles of divinity—

---

35. Ruether, *New Woman New Earth*, 65–66. Ruether is referring specifically to Jesus here, not to Saint Paul or other biblical writers. See McFague, *Metaphorical Theology*, 151. Paul Ricoeur explicates the biblical notion of the divine Father by exploring the penumbra of connotations of the symbol to draw out further richness of meaning. He sees a divine Father who suffers and, hence, can no longer be conceived as "an enemy to his sons; [so it is better to say that] love, solicitude and pity carry him beyond dominion and severity" ("Fatherhood: From Phantasm to Symbol," in Don Ihde, ed., *The Conflict of Interpretations: Essays in Hermeneutics* [Evanston, Ill.: Northwestern University Press, 1974], 467–97). This means that the nonoppressive meaning of "God the Father" is already present in the symbol and can be drawn out through evangelical explication.

absoluteness and relatedness, creativity and caring. These are not the seeds of oppression. The heavenly Father of the earthly Jesus is simply not to blame.

What then can explain this theological broadside attack against the heavenly Father? Recall that the experience to which feminist theology is applicable is the modern experience of alienation and the rising to awareness of a previous false consciousness. This experience is authentic. It is no mirage. It requires reflection. It is my thesis here that feminist liberation is a further chapter in the story of liberation that began with the egalitarianism of the Enlightenment. As such the target of its attack is not the loving Father of Jesus, nor the male gender per se, nor the progeneration of children through fatherhood. The quality of patriarchy that is so detestable is the cultural force it exerts when defining human relationships in the hierarchical terms of ruler-ruled, governor-governed, king-subject, lord-servant, master-slave. It is the culturally determined tendency for a man to believe "his home is his castle and his wife is his vassal." The Enlightenment was a rebellion against such authority. It rebelled against the authority of the king to tell us what to do and against the authority of the church to tell us what to think. The liberation of women is a further development and a culturewide radicalizing of this principle of liberation.

Thus one wonders if feminist theology, given its concern for the rulers' oppression of the ruled, might have targeted a more appropriate symbol. Instead of targeting God as Father, its hermeneutic of suspicion and critical analysis should have been turned loose on the most salient ruler symbol of all—God as king, and its partner, Jesus as Lord. The Enlightenment philosophers understood this as they began to draft theories of political organization that excluded kings, lords, and other royalty. They bitterly attacked Renaissance doctrines such as the divine right of kings, which was the alleged theological sanction for monarchy, and they supported nationalism and the breaking up the Holy Roman Empire. They attacked the great chain of being as the metaphysical justification for the great chain of command, according to which God ruled from heaven and the king ruled from the throne and the rest of humanity took orders. In its place the Enlightenment put a society made up of equal citizens—building on the Reformation priesthood of all believers—each with his or her own dignity and the right to govern his or her own life.

The symbolism of God as king underwent overt and covert attack in some quarters. In a time of rising optimism regarding human potential and affirmation of human dignity and independence, the Christian notion of a God-king appeared at first blush to be inhibitory. A heavenly ruler who promulgated moral laws to which his terrestrial subjects were obliged to conform their lives appeared as a celestial despot (on the order of terrestrial kings George III and Louis XIV) prohibiting the advance of human freedom and autonomy. In fact for some, the very existence of such a

God represented an insult to human dignity. Deism, humanism, agnosticism, and eventually atheism were the products of rebellion against the heavenly king.

But history shows that not every modern person became an atheist. In fact, very few did. The symbol of God as king not only survived but continued to carry religious meaning in egalitarian societies that had outlawed royalty. It continued to live for generations of people who never experienced political royalty. The ability of the symbol to illumine and edify life was not destroyed by this very violent outbreak of critical consciousness. This may be so in part because we have returned to the biblical understanding of kingship voiced by Samuel: if God is king then no human is king. This means, then, that the paradigm theory of human behavior, even if valid in part, is not exhaustive. It is possible to live out of a symbol's meaning without mimicking on earth what we believe to be the case in heaven.

With this chapter of the story of modernity in mind, one might ask how Sallie McFague could hold the premises she does yet still affirm positively that the root metaphor of the Christian faith is "the kingdom or rule of God." It is just that quality of patriarchy—the ruling—that has been identified as so oppressive. If the paradigmatic theory of human behavior were valid, then, rather than offset the male dominance allegedly reinforced by the idea of a heavenly Father, McFague's idea of the heavenly king would only buttress and strengthen an already intolerable situation. Or at least one would surmise that any criticisms of the divine Father would apply as well if not more to the heavenly king. In short, McFague's argument is inconsistent.

McFague herself has come to realize this. In a subsequent book, *Models of God*, she offers a critique of the monarchical model for God that parallels her earlier critique of the patriarchal model.[36] But now, of course, she is left bereft of the Bible's root metaphor, the kingdom of God. Having cut what she believes to be the root of symbolic meaning with the sharp blade of criticism, she is left with nothing in the tradition that can grow in meaning. So she virtually starts over. She cultivates new metaphors: God as mother, God as lover, and God as friend. In doing so she tries to get beyond critical consciousness and attempts to reenter the realm of theological meaning in a positive way.[37] She argues that these

---

36. McFague attacks the idea of God as a king ruling over a kingdom because (1) it fosters distance between God and the world; (2) it assumes God relates only to humans and not to nature as a whole; and (3) it depicts God in terms of dominance and benevolence. McFague wants to eliminate domination and substitute egalitarianism for benevolence. The traditional picture of the heavenly king who sacrifices his Son to atone for our sins and give us salvation is out-of-date, she argues, and should be replaced (*Models of God*, 65–67, 93).

37. This almost marks a move from modernity to postmodernity on McFague's part. In *Models of God* (4, 14, 51) she acknowledges that hers is a postmodern agenda that focuses on holism.

constructed metaphors need not replace but rather complement the traditional patriarchal and monarchical symbols. As she interprets her own metaphors she does so in a healthy way by emphasizing God (as mother) loving the creation, God (as lover) healing brokenness and overcoming hierarchical divisions, and God (as friend) befriending the stranger and creating cosmic community. McFague's reconstructive work is courageous and appropriate, but I doubt if it requires us to dismiss the yet to be explicated meaning already within the biblical symbols of God as Father and as king.

In sum, I must conclude that the feminist argument against divine Father symbolism is weak. Its major premise is doubtful. It does not appear that the compact symbolism of the New Testament presents a heavenly Father who is oppressive, and evangelical explication can make this clear. In addition, feminists such as Rosemary Radford Ruether even depend upon such explication of the biblical symbol of Father in order to depict God as loving and caring. Nevertheless, feminist theology performs a valuable service. As critical theology, it invokes the apophatic principle and performs the service of idol analysis. Its value is that it loosens the tie between symbol and referent so as to help avoid the naive literalism that leads to the worship of the finger instead of the moon. It reminds us of the transcendent absoluteness of the divine and, correspondingly, the responsibility we have for critically assessing the role that symbols of God play in our lives. Most importantly, it inspires critical and constructive action toward restructuring social relations so as to embody justice more fully. But should we wish to proceed beyond critical consciousness to a postcritical naiveté, then more factors than feminism will have to be taken into account.

TRINITARIAN LIBERATION

I have said that the word *God* when used by Christians need not refer to the Father alone but may refer to the entire life of the divine Trinity. It need not be consigned to an image of a heavenly despot who oppresses his angels and provides the paradigm and validation of all human despotism and oppression. Rather, the God whom Christians worship as the sovereign king is he who, upon hearing the cries of the oppressed in bondage to the ancient Egyptians and in bondage to contemporary sin, leaves his throne of grace in heaven and enters the struggle here on earth. When the Son proclaims liberty to the captives, it is the Father who is making the promise. When Jesus suffers at the hands of earthly rulers who misuse their power, it is heaven that suffers. When Christ rises from the dead on Easter, it is God who is victorious. When the Spirit becomes poured out onto all flesh, the life of the world becomes freed from its corruption and is taken up into the life of the Holy Trinity.

There is no way that an honest explication of the trinitarian symbols, including God as Father, can be used to ratify the social oppression of women or any other group of people. The power of raising our consciousness toward affirming dignity for women and striving for liberation is already nascent in the compact symbols of the gospel. The problem of social oppression does not originate in the existence of Christian symbols. Nor is the solution to this problem to be found either in abandoning these symbols or in diluting them by inventing parallel symbols. The contribution of Christian theologians is found rather through a liberating explication of the existing symbols, recognizing the dynamic of the divine life revealed in the gospel.

In her review of and response to the feminist rethinking of the doctrine of God, Anne E. Carr remarks that the very understanding of God as liberator is liberating in itself. Liberation requires an open future where new ways can replace old ways. *"The God who is future* is the God of resurrection faith," says Carr. Then she adds, "To envision God as future, as ahead, rather than above and over against the human and natural world, is a reorientation that helps women to see the feminist dilemma in the church as a temporary one."[38] The liberating power of God the world's future begins with the divine relatedness that is coming to articulation in the doctrine of the Trinity. The ineffable God cannot tolerate human oppression and suffering and thus leaves (so to speak) the realm of ineffability to become one force among others working toward redemption and reconciliation. God enters the struggle as a concrete identity, Jesus the Son. As a concrete identity the Son can be distinguished conceptually from the ineffable source out of which the Son derived. This gives the ineffable an identity it would not otherwise have had, namely, the face or *persona* of the Father. In addition, the Spirit of conviction working within us is the identifiable divine *persona* that opens our eyes to perceive the presence of the divine and that emboldens us to act courageously. All this belongs to the one divine life.

Hence, the rise of critical consciousness among women in our time is not external or extrinsic to the relationship God shares with the world. We must consider the possibility that our awareness of human dignity and equality is itself an expression of the divine Spirit that is seeking to elicit conviction within our hearts and minds because it is part of the larger drama of the godhead's redeeming and reconciling work within and for the created world.

---

38. Anne E. Carr, *Transforming Grace: Christian Tradition and Women's Experience* (San Francisco: Harper and Row, 1988), 153.

4

GOD AND
THE CONTINUING CREATION

God who stretched the spangled heavens infinite in time and place,
Flung the suns in burning radiance through the silent fields of space;
We, your children in your likeness, share inventive powers with you;
Great Creator, still creating, show us what we yet may do.
—Catherine Cameron (b. 1927)

To think of the world as a creation implies belief in a creator who is the "maker of heaven and earth, and of all things visible and invisible." This raises the question: how does God make heaven and earth and everything else? Although no easy answer can be given, explicating the symbols relating to the gospel provides a response. Just as the experience of the gospel with the Son of God led to the understanding of God as Father, so also the experience of new creation in the gospel will have an impact on our understanding of newness regarding the creative process.

Should we speak of creation only in the past tense? Are we tied down to thinking of the creative event as having happened only once at a single point of time in the past? Might God still be at work making things? In fact, this is what I will argue in this chapter: God creates continually and will not finish this creative work until the creation is consummated in the eschaton. The destiny of all things determines what they are.

HOW GOD RELATES TO THE WORLD

The first question we need to consider has been asked by Christian thinkers since the close of New Testament times: how does God relate to the world? Numerous responses are logical possibilities. We can think of God and the world as the same thing—which is *pantheism*. We can think of God as separated from and uninvolved in the world—which is *deism*. We can think of God as separated from the world yet involved in it—which is *theism*. Or we can posit God as including the world in the divine being but without exhausting this being—which is *panentheism*. By following the method of explicating the fundamental Christian symbols in order to make rational sense out of the gospel presented in scripture, the deciding criterion will be which of the logical possibilities best bears the message of God's saving action.

Pantheism, which means literally "all is divine," posits the identity of God with the world of nature. All things, beings, and persons are modes or appearances of the one single divine reality or divine being. Pantheism is the religion of total divine immanence. Types of pantheism range from polytheism to monism. Polytheists believe in many gods, but the various divine beings usually represent what moderns call natural entities or forces. Polytheist pantheons normally include a sun god, moon goddess, earth goddess, master of the animals, and such. The multiplicity of divine beings does not in itself indicate a multiplicity of realities; rather, one reality is shot through and through with divinity. This makes polytheism quite compatible with its apparent opposite, monism, which is the belief that all things are at bottom just one thing, namely, a divine thing. Hinduism provides an excellent example of this combination of polytheism and monism. Every individual Hindu may choose a single god, an *ecca deva*, or a variety of gods to worship, while still recognizing that all gods are but expressions of the one encompassing reality, Brahman.

The logical opposite of pantheism is deism, the view that God is to be distinguished from the world and that the world operates independently of God. According to deism, God is the creator of the cosmos. In the words of Freemasonry, God is the "supreme architect." Creation took place once, at the beginning of all things, and now it winds its way down the corridors of temporal history operating according to its own principles—that is, according to the laws of nature. God does not intervene in the course of events. God does not do miracles. Humans are on their own. Through the scrupulous study of nature they can discern its laws, gain some degree of mastery over natural forces, and in retrospect understand something of the mind of God that constructed the world in the first place. Deism is the religion of total divine transcendence.

Theism, sometimes called monotheism, is the option most frequently advocated by Christian theologians. Theists contend that there is one single divine reality that is distinguishable from the cosmos yet involved in the continued processes of the cosmos. The God of theism created the world in the beginning and continues to act within the world through providence and governance, through incarnation and redemption, through grace and inspiration. Theism affirms both the immanence and transcendence of God. Theists usually take a strong stand against pantheism, arguing that unless God be transcendent to the world, God would be incapable of bringing salvation to it; and against deism, arguing that unless God be involved in the world, God could not bring salvation to it.

Panentheism attempts to reconcile the insights of both pantheism and deism. With sympathies leaning toward pantheism, panentheists argue that the world is included in God's being. God and the world are ontologically one. This makes the world divine and the divine worldly. The world does not exhaust the being of God, however. There is more to God. Something of God transcends the world. With sympathies leaning toward deism, panentheists argue that God as transcendent offers guidance or direction but does not exert the divine will over against the world. The world is free to operate according to its own designs. God will not intervene to save us if we decide to set a course toward self-destruction. By combining ontological immanence and transcendence, panentheists can affirm the presence of God in all things while affirming the freedom of all things to operate independently.

Pantheism and its variant, panentheism, are alive and well in postmodern scientific thinking. Revisionist physicists such as David Bohm and Fritjof Capra are taking scientific speculations beyond the laboratory into philosophical considerations of an all-pervasive divine reality. Bohm is very reluctant to make explicitly theological commitments, but he clearly says he sees all atomic processes as expressions of a single comprehensive "holomovement" that derives from the all-encompassing "multi-dimensional ground."[1] Capra is reconsidering the validity of Asian mysticism and speaks of all of nature as the "dance of Shiva."[2] The doctrines of the new religious cults along with transpersonal psychology and revived spiritualism have filled the media with the idea that each human person has a built-in divine potential, a divine spark, that awaits some psychotechnology to foster the actualization of one's innate divinity in daily life.

In addition, process theologians following in the train of Alfred North Whitehead believe that their own version of panentheism offers for our time the most adequate understanding of God's relation to the world. According to the Whiteheadians, the world exists in relation to God somewhat like the body relates to the mind. God is more than the world, to be sure, but God is dependent upon the world for God's very existence and life. Consequently, God cannot exist apart from a world of one kind or another. This means *creatio ex nihilo* would be simply impossible. There could be no beginning to the world that is preceded by the reality of God; nor could there be an end to the world that would be superseded

---

1. David Bohm, *Wholeness and the Implicate Order* (London: Routledge & Kegan Paul, 1980).

2. Fritjof Capra, *The Tao of Physics* (New York: Bantam, 1975).

by a new reality. God and world are co-primal and co-everlasting. It is important to process theists to promulgate such a doctrine because they believe that it makes more sense to the modern scientific mind than do other Christian perspectives.

In complementary contrast to the above, the position I plan to develop here might be referred to as proleptic theism or *prolepticism*. It is a proleptic view in that it depicts God as constantly engaged in drawing the world out of nonbeing and into existence with the aim of consummating this creative work in the future. God's present work in and for the world anticipates the final work. This view is also theistic in that it affirms that God is active in, yet transcendent to, the work. It is not pantheistic or panentheistic because it does not grant that God's presence in the world is ontological in character—that is, there is no continuity of being between the nature of God and the nature of the world. God is not stuck in the world. God is *a se*. God is not dependent upon the world for God's own being. This is true save in one respect. The full realization of God's power is dependent upon the cooperation of the cosmos. By imparting chance and freedom to the world processes, God has jeopardized the possibility that God's "will be done on earth as it is in heaven." So God is dependent upon the world in one respect—namely, God will not be fully God until the kingdom comes in its fullest and God's will for the creation is fulfilled.

There are also some overtly anti-Christian options, which first appeared in ancient Greco-Roman times and which are appearing again amid modern critical consciousness. Advocates of atheism or naturalism, for example, answer the question of how God relates to the world by denying that there is a God who can relate to the world. Nature is all there is, and it is self-existent, self-directing, self-explanatory, and exhausts the whole of reality. There is no room for a supranatural divine reality. Agnostics are people who have heard the arguments of the naturalists, take them seriously, but are not yet convinced. So they take the position of "I don't know." They await proof. Modern theologians have from time to time sought to offer evidence drawn from an examination of the natural world that God exists and is worthy of belief, but this evidence has frequently been unconvincing to atheists and agnostics. A study of nature by itself is usually ambiguous. It does not necessarily reveal the presence of God in an indubitable fashion. Some sort of special revelation from God seems to be necessary if persons are to understand that nature is more than natural—that is, if they are to understand the cosmos as God's creation.

THE GOSPEL AND CREATION

That special revelation that provides the symbolic lenses through which Christians view nature and see creation is the gospel of Jesus Christ. The gospel begins with the story of Jesus told with its significance—that in this historical person, Jesus, the eternal God who is the creator of all things has acted in the course of temporal events to bring salvation to what has been created. Salvation for humans consists in the forgiveness of sins and the promise of a final redemption for the dead. This resurrection coincides with the advent of the new creation. For God to fulfill this promise, God must have the power to bring new creation to pass. If God has this transformatory power, then God must have had the power to bring creation into existence in the first place. The logic is this: the God who saves must also be the God who creates. Nothing less will do.[3]

The Tie between Redemption and Creation

Creation and redemption are tied together. What is the nature of the tie? Old Testament scholars in our era are divided into two schools of thought: the redemption-first school and the creation-first school. Gerhard von Rad, for example, begins with Israel's experience of redemption and works backward to creation. His point of departure is the *credo*, a brief confessional statement that recites the history of the redemption—and, thereby, the creation—of Israel.

A wandering Aramean was my ancestor; he went down into Egypt and lived there as an alien, few in number, and there he became a great nation, mighty and populous. When the Egyptians treated us harshly and afflicted us, by imposing hard labor on us, we cried to the Lord, the God of our ancestors; the Lord heard our voice and saw our affliction, our toil, and our oppression. The Lord brought us out of Egypt with a mighty hand and an outstretched arm, with a terrifying display of power, and with signs and wonders; and he brought us into this place and gave us this land, a land flowing with milk and honey. (Deut. 26:5-9)

The *credo* depicts the creation of Israel but does not mention the creation of the world. Thinking theologically about cosmic creation came later, says von Rad. A theology of creation probably first appeared with the Jahwist at the dawn of kingship in Israel about the eleventh century B.C. and was further developed by Second Isaiah and the Priestly writer in later periods. Until this relationship between the Exodus and creation could be worked out in some detail, the Hebrews probably accepted the picture of the cosmos that was shared by their non-Hebrew, myth-oriented neighbors such as the Canaanites, Egyptians, and Babylonians. They shared the generic genesis common to the ancient Near East. The Hebrews began to develop their own particular creation theology only as the significance and implications of God's saving acts became clear, and what they had to say about creation was an extension of their experience of the Exodus redemption.

---

3. The theme of this chapter can be summarized in the words of Karl Barth: "The end is also the goal; the Redeemer is also the Creator" (*The Epistle to the Romans*, 3d ed. [London: Oxford, 1977], 77).

Terence E. Fretheim, in contrast, puts creation first. He contends that Israel interpreted its experience of redemption within a wider vision of creation. Key is Exodus 9:16, where the rescue from Egypt has as its purpose the resounding of God's name "through all the earth." Fretheim argues that there is a cosmic purpose behind God's redemptive activity on Israel's behalf, that salvation for the covenant people is not an end in itself but a means toward an end that is cosmic in scope. "Redemption is for the purpose of creation, a new life within the larger creation, a return to the world as God intended it to be."[4]

These two positions may not be irreconcilable. We might think of von Rad as taking a phenomenological or historical approach, noting that Israel began with the experience of redemption and then, in the process of reflection, began to recognize its significance for creation. We might think of Fretheim as beginning immediately with a theological approach, recognizing with the ancient Hebrews the logical priority of creation. Regardless, it is obvious that Old Testament theology as a whole requires an inextricable tie between creation and redemption. This is clear in Isaiah:

> Thus says the Lord, your Redeemer,
>   who formed you in the womb:
> I am the Lord, who made all things,
>   who alone stretched out the heavens,
>   who by myself stretched out the earth.
>   (Isa. 44:24)

Similarly, Psalm 136 opens by offering praise to the creator who "made the heavens" and who "spread out the earth upon the waters" before making "the sun to rule over the day" and "the moon and stars to rule over the night." It then follows with the story of the Exodus and describes God as the one who "with a strong hand and an outstretched arm ... divided the Red Sea" and "overthrew Pharaoh" to "rescue us from our foes." Thus, creation, even if added later, becomes the first chapter in the story of salvation. The sequence of chapters in the story of salvation becomes important in retrospect because it marks the rise of historical consciousness. The Exodus is something later Hebrews and Jews still today can look back to and remember. It was a once-for-all temporal event that occurred at a particular point in the past. The creation of the world, then, must have occurred prior to that. It too occurred only once. Time runs in one direction, thought the Hebrews, from the past to the present. Events may be remembered, even remembered vividly, but they do not repeat

---

4. Terence E. Fretheim, *Exodus*, a vol. of *Interpretation: A Bible Commentary for Teaching and Preaching* (Louisville: John Knox, 1991), 14; see also 124–25. Many ecologically minded critics in our era attack the Hebrew-Christian concern for redemption, arguing that this demotes creation and encourages the brutal exploitation of nature. Such criticism is aimed at the wrong target, in my judgment, as the subsequent explication of the tie between redemption and creation will show.

themselves. This is true of creation as well. Once created, the world has continued down to the present time.

This temporal move from creation to salvation and the sense of historical time are key to understanding the prophets, especially when they introduce a new and dynamic element, namely, eschatology. With the prophets, the future begins to take precedence over the past. The sins of Israel, the violation of the covenant and the refusal to repent, bring the previous history of Yahweh with Israel to an end. Yahweh is about to start something new: a new Exodus, a new covenant, a new Moses. Yahweh is about to act in a fashion that will be understandable in light of the old history, but Yahweh's future saving acts will be even more splendid.

This prophetic period marks an early stage in the development of the idea of eschatology. It is not yet eschatology in the more recent sense of positing a final end to all things. At this early phase of differentiation in Hebrew consciousness it represents a shift from past-dependence to future-dependence, even though the future is thought to be open. In the prophetic message we are drawn toward a "break which goes so deep that the new state beyond it cannot be understood as the continuation of what went before."[5] The significance of this is that reality is not dependent upon its past. It is cut free from the principles established at the point of origin. All ties with mythological conceptions of the cosmos are severed. The God of future salvation—the God beyond the present state of reality—is not restricted by what already exists. Therefore, the door is open to conceiving of salvation itself as an act of creation.

When we allow our thoughts to carry us speculatively backward in time toward the point of origin, then, we can think of the beginning as the advent of something absolutely new, as creation from nothing. The original creation of the world as depicted in the opening chapters of Genesis is not simply the making of order out of a previously existing chaos. It is a coming into being for the first time. Certainly this was the assumption of the author of 2 Maccabees 7:28, who emphasizes that God did not create heaven and earth out of anything that was already in existence. It was also the assumption of Paul, who describes God as calling "into existence the things that do not exist" (Rom. 4:17b). This leads toward an eschatological view of creation.

Creation out of Nothing

Some would criticize the approach that begins with redemption and works backward to creation, suggesting that this reduces creation to a mere stage on which the real drama, the drama of salvation, takes place. Such critics fear it demotes creation. But the approach I am proposing here by no

---

5. Gerhard von Rad, *Old Testament Theology*, 2 vols. (Edinburgh: Oliver & Boyd; New York: Harper & Row, 1962–65), 2:115; see also 2:127–28.

means sidetracks creation. Rather, it seeks to understand God's creative work in light of what we know about the work of redemption. The two belong together.

Thus far we know this: the Bible depicts historical time, the unrepeatability of events, the eschatological power of creating new things, and the gospel of salvation. These lead to the idea of a finite beginning and the doctrine of *creatio ex nihilo*, creation out of nothing. The seeds are in the Bible. What brought the seeds to full flower in classical theism was engagement with an alternative viewpoint, the challenge of the belief that the material of the universe has always existed. This challenge came from two competitors to the Christian view in the early centuries of the church, from dualism and pantheism.

Against the dualists, the post–New Testament apologists argued that God is the sole source of all finite existence, of matter as well as form. Whether via myth or via philosophy, the dualists had been assuming that the world was created out of preexisting matter, that creation consists in ordering a preexisting chaos. This meant there were two ultimate principles for reality, God and the world. The Christians, in contrast, argued that there is no preexisting matter that is coeternal with, and separate from, the ordering God. If the God of salvation is truly the Lord of all, then this God must also be the source of all. Theophilus of Antioch in the middle of the second century, for example, praised Plato for acknowledging that God is uncreated. But then he criticized Plato for holding that matter is coeval with God. This would make matter equal to God. "But the power of God is manifested in this, that out of things that are not He makes whatever he pleases."[6] Irenaeus makes the same point emphasizing that God "called into being the substance of His creation when previously it had no existence."[7]

Against the pantheists, Christians contended that the world is not divine by nature. It is a creation, brought into existence by God but something distinct from and over against God. The world is not equaeternal with God, because the world has a temporal beginning. Irenaeus contended that God is eternal and uncreated, and this distinguishes God from the world that is temporal and created.[8]

---

6. Theophilus *Autolycus* 2.4. The concept of creation out of nothing already appears in the Shepherd of Hermas 2:1. See Tatian *Address to the Greeks* 5; and Philo *On the Account of the World's Creation Given by Moses* 26.

7. Irenaeus *Against Heresies* 2.10.4. Although Justin Martyr may have still assumed a Platonic notion of creation as ordering preexisting matter (*First Apology* 1.59), creation from nothing was firmly established by the time of Origen (*On First Principles* 1.3.3; 2.1.4). See Olaf Pederson, "The God of Space and Time," in David Tracy and Nicholas Lash, eds., *Cosmology and Theology* (Edinburgh: T. & T. Clark; and New York: Seabury, 1983), 15.

8. Irenaeus *Against Heresies* 3.10.3. See Philo *On the Account of the World's Creation Given by Moses* 26; Augustine *Confessions* 12.7; and Langdon Gilkey, *Maker of Heaven and Earth* (Garden City, N.Y.: Doubleday, Anchor, 1959), 44–66.

This distinction between the eternal creator and the temporal creation led to a concomitant distinction between generation (or emanation) and creation. *Generation*, coming from the root meaning "to give birth," suggests that the begetter produces out of its essence an offspring that shares that essence. But terms such as *creating* or *making* mean that the creator produces something that is extraessential, a creature that is dissimilar in nature. The creature may bear the "image" of God, but its essence or nature is that of a creature. The patristic theologians applied the term *generation* to perichoresis within the life of the divine Trinity, but not to the way God relates to the world. Hence, John of Damascus could state emphatically that the creation is not derived from the essence of God, but is rather brought into existence out of nothing.[9]

These commitments make it difficult for Christians in our own time to embrace the recent retrieval of the birth metaphor in feminist and neopagan theology. When Sallie McFague calls God "mother," she is saying that the divine mother gives birth to the world and, further, that the world is physically God's body.[10] In her attempt to revive witchcraft, Starhawk says, "The Goddess is not separate from the world—she *is* the world." This is important, argues Starhawk, if women are "to see ourselves as divine."[11] The problem with these monistic models is that they render the promise of new creation null and void. For God to be able to deliver transformation of the present world, God must be transcendent to it. In addition, the birth model and its accompanying pantheism render the love of God a mere matter of extended self-love—that is, the goddess loves herself through her children. This results in a cosmic narcissism. Genuine love, or ἀγάπη, in contrast, is the love of what is other. The Christian commitment is that God loves the world as other.

Thus, to affirm *creatio ex nihilo* is to affirm that God is creator, that humans are creatures, and that it is possible for God to keep the divine promise to transform humankind and the rest of creation into something new.

One more observation. We can see that arguments in behalf of *creatio ex nihilo* do not rest simply upon an exegesis of Genesis 1:1—2:4a or upon a word study of the Priestly writer's use of the Hebrew word ברא, *bara*. Yes, there is some ambiguity to phrases such as "in the beginning God created" (RSV) versus "when God began to create" (Moffat). Was there anything prior to God's initial creative act? Or, consider the description of God's Spirit moving "over the face of the waters." Are

---

9. John of Damascus *Exposition of the Orthodox Faith* 1.7. In the twentieth century, Russian Orthodox theologian Nicolas Berdyaev puts it this way, "Birth implies a unity of nature, consubstantiality—ὁμοούσια, while creation means similarity, ὁμοιούσιας, with difference in nature" (*The Destiny of Man* [London: Geoffrey Bles, 1937], 33).

10. McFague, *Models of God* (Philadelphia: Fortress, 1987), 69–78; 105–9.

11. Starhawk, *The Spiral Dance* (San Francisco: Harper & Row, 1979), 8–9.

these preexistent waters? Exegetes debate. Be that as it may, such textual ambiguity is insufficient grounds for returning to an affirmation of some sort of eternal material chaos and abandoning *ex nihilo*. As I have shown, the weight of the argument for a creation with a finite beginning rests upon more wide-ranging theological concerns. Specifically, it rests upon the process of evangelical explication—that is, it rests upon interpreting the biblical material and constructing a picture of reality based on an apprehension of the saving message of the gospel. The eschatological promise of a new creation seems to warrant worship of the creator and Lord of the first creation.

As I proceed in my discussion of the doctrine of creation, the reader will see that the view developed here stands between two polar extremes. At one extreme is process theology with its panentheism that virtually rejects *creatio ex nihilo* and embraces only the idea of continuing creation, *creatio continua*.[12] In my judgment, process theologians so strip God of divine power that God will be unable to deliver the salvation God has promised. At the other extreme is scientific creationism, which embraces *creatio ex nihilo* and virtually rejects *creatio continua*.[13] In my judgment, scientific creationists fall victim to the archonic fallacy and inadvertently leave no room for God to act creatively, and hence redemptively, in the future. I will argue here that in our own context—a context heavily influenced by modern science—it makes eminent sense to speak of both creation out of nothing and continuing creation.

BIG BANG, ENTROPY, EVOLUTION, AND ECOLOGY

The contemporary context has changed since the classical theists confronted the task of bridging the gap between the Bible and Greek metaphysics. Certainly, pantheism and panentheism are making a return bid for theological attention. But the most formidable challenge to theological thinking comes from the scientific community because modern science has produced staggeringly significant knowledge regarding the nature of nature. This knowledge is so vast and multiplying so quickly that libraries and laboratories cannot keep up. Here I will mention all too briefly four contemporary scientific concepts that are pertinent for under-

---

12. "Process theology rejects the notion of *creatio ex nihilo*, if that means creation out of absolute nothingness" (John B. Cobb, Jr., and David Ray Griffin, *Process Theology: An Introductory Exposition* [Philadelphia: Westminster, 1976], 65). Schubert Ogden is a bit more nuanced, wishing to keep the phrase *creatio ex nihilo* while rejecting the idea that it refers to a first stage in the temporal world process (*The Reality of God* [New York: Harper & Row, 1966], 213).

13. Duane T. Gish of the Institute for Creation Research in San Diego, for example, contends that according to the opening chapters of Genesis God created all the "kinds" of animals and plants we now have; there was no evolution from species to species (*Evolution: The Fossils Say No!* [San Diego: Creation-Life Publishers, 1973]).

standing nature as God's creation: the big bang, entropy, evolution, and ecology.

The first concept is the big-bang theory of the origin of the cosmos. According to this cosmogony as it comes to us from George Gamow and other researchers, everything—all the material in all the galaxies— was originally concentrated at a single point in a single undifferentiated reality of incalculable density and heat. Then at a point some fifteen or twenty billion years ago, something happened: the single bit of reality began to expand at lightning speed. The entire cosmos as viewed today through telescopes consists of fragments still flying through space. We on planet earth are riding away from the point of origin on one of those fragments. For all practical purposes, we can say time began when the big bang first began its bang. It will end—if we have an open universe with insufficient matter to cause its recollapse—when the explosion has exhausted its energy, when the dissipation of heat is complete, when all matter has been reduced to inert components. The cosmos began with a bang, but we can expect it to end with a forlorn and frozen fizzle.[14]

This movement from a hot beginning to a frozen end brings us to the second significant scientific concept—entropy. Also known as the second law of thermodynamics, the law of entropy can be stated this way: in a closed system heat flows from the hot source to the cold, not vice versa. Once heat has dissipated and the system has attained equilibrium, the original heat energy is no longer available to do work. Entropy increases as the system moves closer to equilibrium. If entropy can be applied to the cosmos as a whole, then the ever-increasing entropy requires that we think of the whole universe as walking a one-way street toward complete dissipation, toward complete equilibrium, toward complete loss of energy, toward a frozen death. Among other things, entropy has enormous implications for our understanding of time.

Ilya Prigogine, who won a Nobel Prize in 1977 for his research on the thermodynamics of nonequilibrium systems, argues convincingly that on the macro scale time is monodirectional and irreversible. This makes the universe finite in time. It had a beginning and it will have an end. The idea that time moves from past through the present and toward the future is not just a product of human subjectivity. Nature itself reveals this fact. *"Science is rediscovering time,"* he writes.[15]

---

14. James Trefil, *The Moment of Creation* (New York: Scribners, 1983). Recent discoveries and criticisms continue to make modifications in big-bang thinking, but the theory to date provides the most comprehensive framework for cosmological creation research. For the theological implications of big-bang cosmology, see Ted Peters, ed., *Cosmos as Creation: Theology and Science in Consonance* (Nashville: Abingdon, 1989); and Robert John Russell, William R. Stoeger, and George V. Coyne, eds., *Physics, Philosophy, and Theology* (Vatican City: Vatican Observatory; and Notre Dame, Ind.: University of Notre Dame Press, 1988).

15. Ilya Prigogine and Isabelle Stengers, *Order Out of Chaos* (New York: Bantam, 1984), xxviii; Prigogine's italics. Some debate is taking place regarding a boundary of time at the

Of course the movement of the universe is not a simple or undifferentiated movement toward deterioration. There are pockets or regions or subsystems that have increased energy, and this combined with the interplay of randomness and chance provide the continuing creativity of the dynamic universe. The open or far-from-equilibrium subsystems are continually fluctuating, and this fluctuation (randomness, chance) leads to a bifurcation point, the moment when change can take place. At this moment it is inherently impossible to determine in advance which direction a change will take, whether it will disintegrate into further chaos or leap to a new and higher level of order. These fluctuations become the chaos out of which order emerges. Prigogine calls this "order through fluctuation." But the scale here is important. The creation of new order through fluctuation occurs at the meso or subsystem level of the universe. At the macro or most-inclusive level, there is only the relentless march toward ever-increasing entropy, toward the final dissipation of all energy.

This leads to our third and fourth scientific concepts—evolution and ecology. The planet earth represents one of these open subsystems at the meso level. Earth is constantly receiving energy input from the sun. Its own system—its ecology—is for the time being exempt from falling victim to entropy. Hence, the interplay of randomness and chance makes possible leaps in creativity, fluctuations out of which new and higher forms of order can emerge. The fact that earth is an open system has made possible the evolution of life.

By *evolution* I mean here essentially what Charles Darwin in 1859 meant, namely, the gradual epigenetic appearance of new species due to mutations and natural selection. The chronology looks something like this: point zero (t = 0 or time = zero) in time and the onset of the big bang began perhaps 20 billion years ago; the earth's crust congealed about 4 billion years ago; dinosaurs roamed the planet from 180 million to 63 million years ago; and the proto-human *homo erectus* flourished between 600,000 and 350,000 years ago. It took considerable time and creativity to produce the human race.

Note the overriding significance of time in evolutionary theory. Creativity is epigenetic, not archonic. Nothing was created all at once. Everything, including human beings, is on the way, so to speak. Furthermore, as earth's system continues to take in energy, we can expect still more creative activity in the future. Creation is ongoing.

---

point of origin, at t = 0. Physicist Stephen Hawking, for example, argues for a quantum theory of gravity that would eliminate the need for a singularity at the point of origin. This, in Hawking's judgment, would eliminate the idea of a time-space boundary as well as the need for a God to create out of nothing at the absolute beginning (*A Brief History of Time: From the Big Bang to Black Holes* [New York: Bantam, 1988], 139–43). What I find significant for contemporary theology is that arguments regarding the relevance of the doctrine of God are occurring within science proper over the issue of a temporal beginning to the universe.

This observation leads Philip Hefner to describe the human being as a "created co-creator."[16] To say we are created reminds us that we are dependent creatures. We depend for our very existence on our cosmic and biological prehistory. Yet we are also creators. Each human being is an open system, so to speak. We use our personal freedom and cultural power to alter the course of historical events. We may even find ourselves altering the course of evolutionary events. Theologically speaking, we participate with God in the ongoing creative advance.

The concept of ecology refers to the system itself that sustains and enhances life on our planet. It refers to the delicate network of physical and biological relationships that maintain life while gradually permitting evolutionary change. Humans are factors in this delicate network. Our creative potential brings with it destructive potential. The result is a scientifically based ethic that says that if we are to affirm life we must care for the environment. It recognizes that the human race is part of something larger and that our ethical responsibility extends beyond our own species to the whole of creation.[17]

A PROLEPTIC CONCEPT OF CREATION

In light of the current scientific milieu, I wish to now engage in some constructive explication of basic Christian faith commitments regarding the nature of God's creative work. We have already seen the reasons for the classical Christian commitment to *creatio ex nihilo*. In light of the big-bang cosmogony and its concept of finite time beginning at $t = 0$, there may be some consonance between natural science and this Christian commitment. In addition, however, non-equilibrium thermodynamics and the theory of evolution clearly indicate epigenetic or ongoing creative activity. Time means new things can appear. It makes sense, then, to speak as well of *creatio continua*. Therefore, we need not have to choose between creation out of nothing and continuing creation. We need both.

More needs to be said, however, if we are to understand God's creation in light of the gospel promise of a new creation. There must be an eschatological component.[18] My hypothesis, then, is the following principle of proleptic creation: God creates from the future, not the past.

16. Philip Hefner, "The Evolution of the Created Co-creator," in Peters, ed., *Cosmos as Creation*, 225–26; and idem, "The Creation," in *Chr.D.*, 1:325–28. See also the pioneering work of Arthur R. Peacocke, *Creation and the World of Science* (Oxford: Clarendon Press, 1979); and idem, *God and the New Biology* (San Francisco: Harper & Row, 1986).

17. See H. Paul Santmire, "The Future of the Cosmos and the Renewal of the Church's Life with Nature," in Peters, ed., *Cosmos as Creation*, chap. 9; and Ian G. Barbour, *Technology, Environment, and Human Values* (New York: Praeger, 1980).

18. Here I am led by the early work of Carl Braaten, who said, "The new place to start in theology is at the end—eschatology" (*The Future of God: The Revolutionary Dynamics of Hope* [New York: Harper & Row, 1969], 9). Braaten's eschatological approach to ontology

Such a principle may seem to fly in the face of the commonly accepted Christian view—perhaps even the common-sense view—of causality. This common view of time and causality—at least in Western culture with its historical consciousness—is that time consists of a linear, one-way passage from the past, through the present, toward the future. The power of being in this scheme is usually thought of as a push coming from the past—that is, a past cause and a present effect. We assume the state of affairs today is the result of yesterday's causes, which in turn are the result of the previous day's causes, on back to the divine first cause at the beginning. I nickname this the "bowling-ball" theory of creation. The image here is that of a divine bowler providing the power of being by hurling the creation down the alley of time. We assume we presently are rolling somewhere down that temporal alley. The hand of the divine bowler is behind us. There may be a strike yet ahead of us. Our task, to the extent that we can make a contribution to our direction, is to keep ourselves in line with God's original aim so as to avoid a gutter ball.

But does this image of a push from the past adequately describe how we actually experience time and the power of being? I suggest not. Although we certainly do experience some current effects due to past causes, we implicitly recognize a certain priority given to those things that have the power of creativity for the future. Without a future, things drop into non-existence. Without a future, the present moment becomes a death trap. And because we accept as axiomatic that all things are always in the process of changing, the future that sustains existence must be thought of as a creative future. I believe we know this implicitly. The power of being is preconsciously apprehended as that which can overcome anxiety by assuring the future, especially a future that is not stuck by the precedents of the past. To be is to have a future. To lose one's future and to have only a past is to die. Deep down we know this. The dynamic perdurability of the present moment is contingent upon the power of the future to draw us into it.

According to the principle enunciated above, the first thing God did for the world was to give it a future. Without a future it would be nothing. Referring to the finite beginning with the phrase *creatio ex nihilo*, then, means referring to God's first gracious gift of futurity. When thinking about the unfathomably dense ball of proto-matter and energy at $t = 0$, we could think of God's first act as bestowing upon it an open future. God bestows the future by opening up the possibility of its becoming

---

and ethics influenced the title of the present work. "That future" in which the human race places its hopes, he said, "we call 'God'" (ibid., 17). I must admit, however, that this eschatological starting point lacks consonance with the prevailing big-bang cosmology and the law of entropy, which make room for local creativity but only dissipation and death on the macro scale. If there be an eschatological consummation, it must come as an act of God that cannot be foreseen by current natural processes.

something it never had been before and by supplying it with the power to change. The big-bang cosmogony suggests that everything we know in nature—from the existence of matter to the natural forces and laws that structure matter—is contingent and finite, having come into existence at a particular point in time and without any previous precedent. Not only does God release the exploding energy that drives the universe, but God also opens up the future so that new things can occur. This gift of the future is the very condition for the coming into existence and the sustaining of any present reality. From our perspective today, of course, we have the sense that we are looking back upon this first divine act. It seems now to be a part of the dead past. But we need to be careful because God is continuing to bestow upon us a future, even at this very moment. It is the continuing divine work of future-giving that is the source of life and being.

The power of the future is the source of contingency or chance in nature and the source of freedom in human consciousness. When in the present moment we feel overwhelmed by trends set in motion by past causes, we feel cramped, contained, and constrained. To look at a future we believe to be predetermined is to feel that life has been lost. The bowling-ball theory of time places all power in the past, which cannot help but result in a determinism regarding the present. The power of God, however, comes to us not as a brute determination from the past but as that which counters such determinations. Each moment God exerts divine power to relieve us from past constraints so as to open up a field for free action, for responsible living.[19]

Hence, I suggest we think of God's creative activity as a pull from the future rather than a push from the past. This leads us to the next principle of a proleptic theory of creation: God's creative activity within nature and history derives from God's redemptive work of drawing free and contingent beings into a harmonious whole. Here the postmodern notion of holism helps us to grasp what is going on. Recall that the chief tenet of holism is that the whole is greater than the sum of the parts. It is this "greater than" that distinguishes a whole from a simple totality or agglomeration of otherwise individual things.[20] A corollary is that the

---

19. Many philosophical theologians mistakenly presume that divine power limits or eliminates human freedom. The reverse is the case. God's future-oriented power comes as grace that makes human freedom possible. Wolfhart Pannenberg says that "the experience of the God who is the power of an ever-renewed future" makes us "free for a truly personal life" (*Theology and the Kingdom of God* [Philadelphia: Westminster, 1969], 69). Karl Rahner says forcefully: "Grace and freedom do not rule one another out, since freedom, a God-given capability and act, must itself be looked upon as grace" (*TI*, 21:240).

20. Although the field of quantum physics was not mentioned above, it is significant for increased interest in the concept of holism. After noting how an electron has to be considered as a state of the whole atom and not as a separate entity, Ian Barbour writes, "There seem to be *system laws* that cannot be derived from the laws of the components.... The being of any entity is constituted by its relationships and its participation in more inclusive

parts are defined by their relationship to one another and by the whole that frames that relationship. These insights help illumine the divine destiny that determines God's past and present activity.

This principle helps us to avoid two reductionistic fallacies. The first is the fallacy of reduction to origin, the archonic fallacy, where all of reality is thought to be determined by what happened at the point of origin in the past. The problem with this archonic view is that it precludes the coming into being of anything fundamentally new, most importantly, the new creation. When imported into Christian theology the archonic view leads inevitably to deism, not to theism.

The second fallacy is atomic reductionism, a fallacy afoot in modern academia. It assumes that the macrocosm is simply a composite of much more fundamental building blocks at the microcosmic level. The problem with this assumption is that it fails to recognize as ontologically significant the patterns and interactions that exist only at more complex and comprehensive levels of reality. If incorporated into theology, atomism would produce only naturalism.

The holistic vision helps us to answer the question of how God acts vis-à-vis nature and history. The reductionism of the modern mind has painted us into a corner, into a deterministic model of a world in which God's actions cannot be made intelligible. The mechanistic worldview emerging from eighteenth-century science saw all events as inextricably linked together by a single chain of cause and effect. Because all events have finite causes, adequate explanations consisted in identifying these finite causes. But this way of thinking offers no way to understand how God, an infinite being, could be one finite factor among others in the already determined causal nexus. The focus for a time centered on miracles. Some thought that God would have to intervene directly into world affairs every so often to keep the machine of creation running properly. Others thought that an occasional miracle would remind us that God still exists. Still others argued that there could be no such thing as miracles, because direct interventions by God would upset the causal chain. The working assumption was that a miracle consists in a direct act of God within the world's nexus of events, making God in effect one causal agent among others. The correlate assumption was that for normal day to day activities the world machine operates on its own without any need of divine input. At least a partial deism seemed to be presupposed, so that reference to divine action became superfluous.

The proleptic theism I propose here, however, is unwilling to grant that God's action is superfluous to the course of natural events. What

---

patterns. Without such holistic quantum phenomena we would not have chemical properties, transistors, superconductors, nuclear power, or indeed life itself. Such holism contrasts with the reductionism of Newtonian physics" (*Religion in an Age of Science* [San Francisco: Harper and Row, 1990], 105–6).

we need now is a concept of God's relation to the creation that will allow us to understand that every divine action within the world, miracles included, is performed in, with, and under the things of the created world. God's activity is not an intervention from the outside that interferes with the natural course of events; nevertheless, it imparts the divine will to what happens. Holism can aid us in this conceptual construction.

Holism helps us first to untie the knotty relationship between freedom and natural causation. The mechanistic model of Enlightenment physics could not account for human freedom, or even randomness in nature. Free human acts cannot be exhaustively explained by their antecedent causes. Because holism avoids atomic reduction, it helps affirm equal reality to complex forms of interrelationship where freedom is exercised; and it does so without denying efficient causation at relatively simpler levels.

If we apply this line of thinking to God's work of creating the world, we can describe the whole of cosmic and human history in terms of a single, creative, divine work. We might borrow Gordon Kaufman's term here, "master act."[21] God's primary action is the divine master act by which God creates and consummates the whole cosmos. En route to the completion of this work God engages in many subacts, of course. A homemaker, for example, may bake a lemon meringue pie. The baked pie is the master act. But en route to completion the baker must perform certain subacts such as gathering the ingredients, stirring together the lemon juice with the sugar and cornstarch in a double boiler, pouring the resulting custard into the baked pie shell, adding the meringue, baking, removing the pie from the oven at the proper time, cleaning up, and so forth. There is one master act, but it incorporates numerous subacts, all of which can be identified by their contribution to the purpose of bringing a delicious pie into existence.

There is no lemon meringue pie—no whole—until the creative work is completed. So also, God's act consists in a purposive event of creation that will not become an event of its own until its completion, until the eschatological consummation. Viewed strictly from our present perspective, there is no whole of all things. The uniting and determining whole is yet to come. This leads into a curious paradox: knowledge of God's subacts depends upon prior knowledge of God's master act, but the master act is not yet complete. To be able to discern an event to be a subact within the divine master act would require having the eschatological completion in sight. Is it possible to have the end revealed ahead of time? Yes, the creator of the world has revealed to us that there is a purpose that is being brought toward fulfillment. This purpose can be discerned in the ministry,

---

21. Gordon Kaufman, *God the Problem* (Cambridge, Mass.: Harvard University Press, 1972), 137. For a similar position see Wolfhart Pannenberg, "Gott und die Natur," *Theologie und Philosophie* 58, no. 4 (1983): 481–500.

death, and resurrection of Jesus Christ. In Jesus Christ we see proleptically God's intention for the whole, God's single purpose that runs from alpha to omega, from beginning to end. "For in him all things in heaven and on earth were created, things visible and invisible.... He himself is before all things, and in him all things hold together" (Col. 1:16-17).

Hence, we may think of the whole of cosmic history as a single divine act of creation, and our own personal histories are minute but indispensable parts of that whole. Just as the operations of the human heart are drawn up into the decisions and purposes of the human personality as a whole, individuals' personal lives will be drawn up into and find their proper definition through their relationship to the whole of God's creative work. But because God's creative history has not yet come to its completion, it is not yet whole. The future is still open. Reality is on the way to being determined and defined in mutual reciprocity between the actual course of finite events and the overall divine design. The promise of the future completion of God's master act permits us to think holistically. In the meantime, we find ourselves within the creative work of God, a work yet to be completed, and hence appropriately called from our point of view "continuing creation."

5

BECOMING HUMAN
AND UNBECOMING EVIL

Life can only be understood backward, but it must be lived forward.
—Søren Kierkegaard, *Journals*

The whole of creation history includes, among other things, human history. After all, humans are creatures. Systematic theologians commonly include an anthropology—an explication of what is human—in their explication of Christian doctrine. Sometimes the anthropology appears between expositions of the First and Second Articles of the creeds—that is, between explications of God as Father and God as Son. The sorry state of the human condition explains why the good creation is in need of redemption. So it fits in the crack between the first two persons of the Trinity, so to speak.

BECOMING HUMAN

Anthropology normally focuses on two things: the image of God and the fall into sin. In the proleptic framework I am developing here I will view the image of God in humans as the call forward, as the divine draw toward future reality. We are becoming. Sin and its fruit—evil—retard this becoming. We sin by trying to fixate ourselves in present reality, thereby diverting or blocking God's call forward toward the new creation. Evil is unbecoming.

So we will now turn to the question: what does it mean to be human? I will begin with the observation that humans live in the metaxy, the tension between what is and what is beyond.

140

The Tension between Soil and Spirit

The constant tension between soil and spirit is metaxic. We find ourselves between earth and heaven, between the past and the future, between the knowable and the mysterious. The writer of the Adam and Eve story in Genesis establishes the metaxy from the start: "Then God the Sovereign One formed a human creature of dust from the ground, and breathed into the creature's nostrils the breath of life; and the human creature became a living being" (Gen. 2:7; *ILL*). The first human being created here is a combination of soil and spirit. The Hebrew word for "human creature" (*ILL*) or "man" (NRSV) in this passage is אדם (*adam*). The Hebrew word for earth or ground is אדמה (*adamah*). Although we have become accustomed to referring to the first human being with a personal name belonging to the male gender, Adam, in this key passage the term *adam* is inclusive of all humankind: men, women, and children. The term chosen here is not איש (*ish*), referring to man as the male gender in contrast to the female gender, אשה (*ishah*). Inclusivity is not the point here, however. What is decisive is the virtual identity of the human with the earthly, the physical, the material, the finite, the created. We are totally dependent upon the soil. Not only do vegetables and fruits come directly from seeds sown in the ground, but even such products as milk and hamburger begin as grass that is transmuted by bovine digestive processes. We come from the soil, and when we die and are buried, we return to it. We come from dust and shall return to dust. We are soil. The symbol of the soil emphasizes how much we are a part—a fleeting part—of this world. The modern physical and biological sciences depict life as an instance of negative entropy, as a time and place where order is on the increase. As the above example of eating demonstrates, an essential feature of living systems is that they are open to the world. We humans are examples of open living systems, and we are not sealed off from what surrounds us. We can survive only by exchanging energy and material with our environment. The energy of the cosmos flows through us, so to speak. In this flow, to use the words of physicist Erwin Schrödinger, we concentrate the energy in the order of life and temporarily escape the decay into atomic chaos. The cosmos as an entirety may be winding down according to the second law of thermodynamics, but as a far-from-equilibrium subsystem within the cosmos we, as living things, are experiencing a temporary but exciting advance in the order of things. Eventually, of course, as individuals and as parts of the whole cosmos, we will experience the final triumph of entropy, the dissipation of all energy into equilibrium and the demise of all life. We are, after all, soil.

But soil is not all. The breath of God is added in the book of Genesis. We become a living being, נפש (*nephesh*), only after the creator breathes into our nostrils the power of life, the נשׁמה (*neshamah*). It is curious that in many ancient languages the word for breath or wind is the same as that for spirit: in Sanskrit *atman*, in Chinese *chi*, in Greek πνεῦμα, in Hebrew רוח (*ruach*). This may be due to the basic experience of noting that when a baby is born life begins with breathing, and when a person dies the lungs stop moving. Yet breath, which is so life-giving, is itself elusive and uncontrollable. It is invisible, yet we know it is there and we know that without it we are dead.

These combined qualities of being life-giving yet uncontrollable have led us to use the term *spirit* to refer to the dynamism of human life, to our freedom and our ability to transcend our physical situation. Negative entropy can be experienced in human consciousness, so to speak. We can order and reorder ourselves through decision making and commitment. We can bind ourselves to one another in community through love. Our imaginations free us from the restrictions of what is immediately given and open doors to new and different possibilities. We can create. We may have begun as soil alone but we need not stay that way when we inhale the Spirit of God and gain the freedom to transcend ourselves. Thus as soil inspired by spirit, we recognize that our life is radically contingent on something bigger and external to us, something that invades and enlivens us, something that by nature is gracious.

Sometimes instead of *spirit* we use the word *soul* to indicate the animating power of human life that distinguishes life from inert matter. The word *soul* comes from the Greek ψυχή, and we have come to associate the soul with the human mind, the seat of consciousness and willing, and that which makes an individual a subject, a personality. We can say we have a mind or we are a person.

To be a person even in the modern sense is to stand at the metaxy between part and whole. The classical understanding of the human person comes from Boethius, who defined the human being as an individual substance possessing a rational nature (*naturae rationalis individua substantia*). This applies both individually and universally. On the one hand, each of us is a particular individual. We differ from one another. On the other hand, our soul or mind is attuned to the rational structure of the cosmos. Therefore, the whole of reality is in a way present in the individual. So Aristotle and Thomas Aquinas could speak of the human mind as "in a way all things" (*quodammodo omnia*). The whole of reality is, curiously enough, somehow present to each of us individually, at least as a quest. Each of us, although unique, seems to be programmed from within to seek reality in its entirety.

This is the source of the modern concept of dignity. To be a person is more than just to be an individual. To be a person is to exhibit the truth of the whole of reality in, with, and under our individuality. It is this that leads us to think of each person as an end and not a means to any further end. According to the modern mind, personhood could be sacrificed to no higher value or goal.

The metaxic tension we experience is due to the elusive presence of spirit or soul. The tension is due to our thirst for supraindividual reality that goes unquenched. It is due to our hunger for wholeness that goes unsatisfied. We yearn to meet the fulfilled person, the one in whom the infinite has made peace with the finite, the one in whom the eternal dwells amid the temporal, the one in whom the whole is present in the part, the one in whom the divine has become human. Only such a fulfilled personhood can resolve the metaxy and quench the human thirst for wholeness.

Thus, the spirit cannot be identical to or limited to the human individual. Rather it comes from without. It invades us or, perhaps better, draws us beyond ourselves into a transcendent order of reality. Spirit is present to us, but it is not ours to keep. If there were to be such a thing as human nature, spirit would not be part of it. Spirit is the condition for human life, but in itself it does not belong to what is human. In its origin and in its destiny, it is divine.

The Word

Sometimes the concept of the word is closely identified with that of the spirit. It should be. In the opening chapter of Genesis the Spirit of God and the word of God are identified with the creation of the cosmos. At Pentecost it is the Spirit who gives the apostles utterance, who enables their tongues to speak and their divine message to be understood.

When it comes to the human condition, we can almost draw a parallel between breath in our lungs and words in our mouths and minds. As the surrounding atmosphere gives us life that we internalize and then feel we possess, so also are we born into a culture with an already structured language system without which we could not express ourselves. The words first spoken to us by parents and other significant people stimulate and evoke over time our own self-consciousness, our own sense of autonomy, and our ability to think and act independently. Language is the decisive power that catapults us up and out of mere biological existence and into the realm of culture, history, value, meaning, and intense relationships.

Speaking and listening signify presence and transcendence. To carry on a conversation with anybody means, among other things, that we are not alone. Someone else is present. Someone stands over against me not just as an object of my perception or manipulation, but as a subject, as a person. The other party is present but transcendent in the sense that he or she remains beyond my control, inviolable, mysterious, a force that could in time provoke a change in me.

Conversation, then, opens us out toward the future. To enter into any interpersonal relationship through genuine dialogue is to open oneself to learning something new, to establishing a new relationship that may follow in an unforeseen direction. One could, of course, refuse to engage in dialogue either by not talking at all or by simply dominating a conversation so that no real interchange can take place. But even if one does this, it may not be enough to escape the spirit of the future. The very givenness of the language (*langue*) within which one is immersed makes talking (*parole*) possible, almost necessary. Hence, it even makes dialogue within one's own mind possible. Even within the privacy of our own minds we need the vocabulary and grammatical logic of the language we inherit in order to construct alternatives and then deliberate over them. This possibility is something given the individual from without, from growing up in culture. Through such inner dialogue, realities that do not now exist can be imagined, changes in the present state of affairs can be pictured, and alternative futures can be projected. It is no accident that people with particularly creative minds speak of inspiration in their thoughts.

All of this means that we are not imprisoned in the soil. We cannot be reduced or confined to our physical makeup. The spirit through language liberates us from any solipsism of the soil. It frees us to enter into profound relationships and to be open toward what transcends us.

There is a flip side to self-transcendence, however. It makes us aware of our limits, of our finitude. The presence of spirit reminds us of our contingency, of our dependence upon our physical situation in contrast to that which transcends us. This prompts our imaginations and desires to press beyond the limits of soil, beyond the bounds of our bodies and our personalities, beyond the borders of our earthly life at present to envision heavenly life in the future. "In my quality of earth, I am attached to life here below," writes Gregory of Nazianzus, "but being also a divine particle, I bear in my breast the desire for a future life." Gregory may have been mistaken to think that he himself was a divine particle, but there is no doubt that he experienced the presence of spirit, and this spirit was responsible for that pressure in the breast to press beyond the limitations of the cycle of soil. From dust to dust is not enough.

Hence we are not simply products of the soil as are dirt clumps and maple trees. Nor are we so free from the soil as to fly like angels unencumbered through the heavenly realms. We are in between, embodying both soil and spirit. We are creatures but with a divine presence. Although mortal we dream of immortality. Although we are finite and limited our desires and imaginations soar to the infinite and the boundless. We live at the inbetween, at the point of tension between soil and spirit. This is the human reality. To deny it makes us ripe for tragedy. The tragedy comes when we try to eliminate the metaxy by resolving the tension prematurely.

The New Adam

The new Adam is calling us. Our restlessness is a sign that we are not now what we will yet be. The metaxic tension is a sign of our continuing creation, the draw forward toward what we will finally become. The Adam of Genesis, to whom we are presently heir, was subject to tragedy in a way that the new Adam, who participates in the resurrection of Jesus Christ, will not be. Saint Paul struggles to paint a picture of who we will be:

Thus it is written, "The first man Adam became a living being"; the last Adam became a life-giving spirit. But it is not the spiritual that is first but the physical, and then the spiritual. The first man was from the earth, a man of dust; the second man is from heaven. As was the man of dust, so are those who are of the dust; and as is the man of heaven, so are those who are of heaven. Just as we have borne the image of the man of dust, we will also bear the image of the man of heaven. (1 Cor. 15:45-49)

In commenting on this Pauline interpretation of Genesis 2:7, Luther advocates a doctrine of immortality of the soul, saying that "the last Adam was made a quickening spirit, that is, such a life as has no need for those animal requirements of life."[1] There is a contrast here. The contrast that should be made, Luther says, is not the one between people and animals such as donkeys, with whom we share the combined soil-breath nature. The contrast is one between the present and the future, between life headed for mere death and life headed for resurrection. We have a destiny. Our destiny as resurrected and eternally living creatures in the kingdom of God defines who we are as human beings. This is what "life-giving spirit" means.

I believe we should reinterpret Irenaeus's theory of recapitulation along these lines. Irenaeus argues that in Christ we recover what we had lost in Adam, namely, "to be according to the image and likeness of God." Irenaeus believes that in order to restore our original true humanity Jesus Christ must have embodied it, and he did so by recapitulating the whole human life cycle, living it as it ought to be lived. "Wherefore also He passed through every stage of life, restoring to all communion with God."[2] This is how he became the second Adam. But because we who through faith are united with Christ still live with the old Adam very much alive within us, I wonder if Irenaeus's theory is precise enough. Instead of recapitulation I suggest we think of Christ's work as *pre*capitulation. Christ establishes ahead of time what it is that will define who we as humans shall be.

In his own destiny the Son of God accomplishes the resurrection from the dead and a life purged of the blemishes of sin, and it is that which accrues to the definition of who we as humans will become. Irenaeus

1. Luther, *LW*, 1:86.
2. Irenaeus *Against Heresies* 3.18.1, 7.

says Christ has done what he has done "so that the corruptible might be swallowed up by incorruptibility, and that the mortal by immortality, that we might receive the adoption of heirs."[3] Christ has gone ahead of us like a scout through the jungle, and his salvific work like a machete has cut away the strangling vines of death. He has opened a path that we could not have cleared on our own. Who we are and will be has been precapitulated at Easter, as Carl Braaten makes clear: "In raising Jesus from the dead, God incorporated the dimension of eschatological fulfillment into the definition of human being."[4]

Hence the notion of the spiritual body that Saint Paul develops in 1 Corinthians 15 should be thought of not so much as a way of divorcing us from the physical realm so that we no longer have to eat the fruit of the soil. Even the resurrected Jesus ate fish for breakfast (John 21:12-14). The importance of the spiritual body is that it is who we will be. It is our future. It marks the contrast or tension between the present and the fulfillment that is to come. It is the future spirit in metaxic relation to our present soil. We live constantly between future and present when we live proleptically.

The Imago Dei

Some would like to say that the spirit that God breathed into Adam's nostrils constitutes the *imago Dei*, the image of God stamped upon human nature. Saying this immediately raises questions, however. Just what is it in or about humans that constitutes the mark of the divine? Is it enough to talk about spirit in terms of the air we breathe? Luther pointed out that like us the donkey breathes air. So what is the difference? What is it that distinguishes us from the animals and places us in the metaxy between soil and spirit?

Different theories have been suggested. Each theory seems to find some aspect of our being that exhibits continuity between human existence and the divine nature. The first and most prominent is the rational theory. Some, as I mentioned earlier in my discussion of the soul, have believed that the human intellect reflects the divine reality. The Logos connects us to God, said Athanasius, John of Damascus, and Vladimir Soloviev. They define the human being as a rational animal (*zoon logikon, animal rationale*) and then posit that our rational capacity corresponds to or participates in the divine mind. Augustine, for example, thought the three mental functions of remembering, understanding, and loving correspond to the divine Trinity.

A second theory links us to God morally. John Wesley, for example, says that humans were created in God's "natural image," meaning that

---

3. Ibid., 2.19.1.
4. Braaten, "The Person of Jesus Christ," in *Chr.D.*, 1:524.

we are spiritual beings with free will, and that we were created in God's "political image," meaning that we share in the governance over nature. But most importantly we were created in God's "moral image." Prior to the fall we humans were filled with love, justice, mercy, and truth. When we first came from the hand of our creator we were pure and spotless. "God is love," and we, created originally in God's moral image, were also loving. We "knew not evil in any kind or degree."[5]

This moral image seems to require ignorance of evil. This reminds us of a caution. We ought not suggest that our ability to discriminate between good and evil constitutes the *imago Dei* within us. To say that the moral image consists in the ability to discern good and evil is to give credence to the serpent in the Garden of Eden. If the serpent would be right on this score—that disobedience would give us the moral knowledge that God has—then we would attain the image of God only after the fall into sin. Yet Genesis, and even Wesley too, seem to assume that the divine image was present in us prior to the fall.

Third, a cluster of *imago Dei* theories emphasize a shared dynamism between the human and divine life—that is, some sort of relationality. Karl Barth, for example, interprets the *imago Dei* passage of Genesis 1:26-29 to mean that we humans exist in relationship, that we have the capacity for an I-Thou encounter. This reflects the divine reality because relationality is internal to the Trinity. Gordon Kaufman argues that the *imago Dei* in us is historicity. God is historical. So are we, he says. God is a being who acts freely and creatively to produce the world. Correspondingly, we are beings who act freely and creatively to transform our world. The *imago Dei* is not then a quality that we humans possess by nature; it is rather an ongoing interaction between God and the human project. Jürgen Moltmann extends this a bit by saying that the *imago Dei* is a democratic society. It consists of human beings in relationship to one another—economically, socially, politically, and personally—and in relationship to the earth. God is relational and social. So are we.

This relational understanding of the *imago Dei* is reflected in the work of the Reformers. Luther, for example, understands the *imago Dei* in terms of our ongoing relationship with God. Luther says that the image of God indicative of Adam and Eve prior to the fall consisted of faith, a faith according to which they so trusted God that they had no fear of harm or death.[6] For Philip Melanchthon the image of God is the knowledge of God, righteousness, and truth.[7] John Calvin along with Luther and Melanchthon argues that although this intimate relationship with God

---

5. Wesley, *WW*, 6:66; see Charles W. Carter, "Anthropology," in Carter, ed., *A Contemporary Wesleyan Theology*, 2 vols. (Grand Rapids, Mich.: Zondervan, 1983), 1:205, 224.

6. Luther, *LW*, 1:62–63.

7. Philip Melanchthon, "Apology of the Augsburg Confession," Art. 2, *BC*, 103.

was lost with the fall into sin, it will be restored through Jesus Christ. This is what salvation means. Christ "is also called the Second Adam for the reason that he restores us to true and complete integrity." This complete integrity can be manifest now as we are "reborn in the spirit; but it will attain its full splendor in heaven."[8] In sum, the *imago Dei* for the Reformers is a dynamic principle by which we understand our past, present, and future relationships with God. Most importantly, this relationship will come to fulfillment in the future when we share the image of God as fully as Christ does.

That human integrity is already embodied in Christ and will attain its full splendor in the eschaton is important. The proleptic position I am developing here seeks the *imago Dei* not in the old Adam but in the new Adam, not in the old creation but in the new one. With obvious excitement Paul can proclaim "the gospel of the glory of Christ, who is the image of God" (εἰκών τοῦ Θεοῦ; 2 Cor. 4:4b). The term εἰκών is used both of Christ and of the person who has faith in Christ, and Paul describes us as "being transformed into the same image" (2 Cor. 3:18; see Rom. 8:29). The Christ of whom he speaks is the Easter Christ, the risen Christ, the first fruits of those having fallen asleep (1 Cor. 15:20, 48), the advent of the new creation. Christ as the divine image is our prototype. We live now as the *imago Dei* insofar as we live in him, insofar as we participate in the reality of the resurrection.

When it comes to the numeration of possible ways to identify that elusive *imago Dei* within us, we may add one more to the traditional list: creativity. It is our creative propensity that demonstrates the image of God at work in the human phenomenon. Philip Hefner, as mentioned above, describes the human being as a "created co-creator." What makes us co-creators with God is our self-awareness combined with our ability to make assessments in light of values and purposes, criticize those assessments, make decisions, and then act on those decisions. We can conceive of actions and then carry them out. We are *homo faber*. We make things; and the ability to make things compounds from generation to generation, so that the products of our creative design carry us farther and farther into a technological world we have created and into more complex relationships with the natural environment. Creativity and its resultant culture constitute an expression of our freedom.

But at the same time, this freedom to create does not make us independent. As *homo sapiens* we are as dependent upon the health of the ecosystem as are all other forms of life. We constantly interact with it. No matter how masterful we judge the products of our creative hand, we have but transformed the basic resources that we found around us.

---

8. Calvin, *Inst.*, 1.15.4; see Luther, *LW*, 34:139–40.

We create nothing *de novo*, nothing that is totally new. *Creatio ex nihilo* is still solely God's province.

Proleptic Humanity

Irenaeus offers two important contributions to this discussion, one that is a diversion and one that helps to keep the discussion on track. The diversion is the result of the misleading contrast he draws between the image of God (צלם [*zelem*], εἰκών [*imago*]) and the likeness of God (דמות [*demut*], ὁμοίωσις [*similitudo*]) based on Genesis 1:26, where men and women are said to be created in the "image and likeness" of God. With this distinction Irenaeus seeks to identify εἰκών with our inborn or latent potential for reason and the ὁμοίωσις with our actualization of this potential through living a Godlike life. Exegetically, however, Irenaeus's distinction is faulty. He does not recognize the literary form of the doublet that appears in Genesis 1:26. Modern exegetes would contend that doublets seek to say basically the same thing in two different ways, allowing the nuances of the different terms to complement one another. Therefore, it is clear that, exegetically speaking, *zelem* and *demut* refer to essentially the same quality of human existing.

In addition to this diversion, however, Irenaeus helps to keep us on track by identifying Jesus Christ with the true image of God. He proffers almost a developmental or evolutionary theory, according to which we become more and more human as we become more and more identified with Christ. Christ makes us truly human. We are not fully at present the *imago* and *similitudo* of God. Only the Son of God is that because only he possesses the whole of God's fullness in himself. We humans were created for the Son and will attain our perfection and hence our divine *imago* in him.[9] Irenaeus compares us to children who have yet to grow. We will in time grow into and participate in the image of God that is Christ. In other words, when applied to the incarnate Christ the *imago Dei* is past and present but when applied to us it is still future. We get a taste of this future ahead of time, however, with the indwelling of the Holy Spirit and in becoming Christlike in our love for one another.

Becoming human, in the last analysis then, is not really a restoration to a prefallen state of grace that humans once possessed and then lost. It is not a return to the old creation. It is rather a future arrival for the first time. It is participation in the new creation.

Irenaeus's influence on subsequent generations has been curious. The diversionary and misleading contrast caught on. Following its further development in Gregory of Nyssa, Eastern Orthodox theologians have to the present day identified the εἰκών of God with our personal freedom and the ὁμοίωσις with that deified human being that we are yet to become.

---

9. Irenaeus *Against Heresies* 5.16.

The medieval Latins followed this train by distinguishing the *imago*, referring to intellectual powers, from the *similitudo*, referring to the human capacity for willing to do what is moral. Fortunately, for the most part Protestants have ignored these misleading distinctions.

In contrast, Irenaeus's future-oriented anthropology—which I believe to be the most valuable contribution—seems to have been overlooked. Most of Christendom has held to some sort of restoration theory. Even Luther and Calvin followed the path of least resistance and conceived of salvation as a return to a primeval state of blessedness.

Once we have seen how the New Testament identifies the εἰκὼν τοῦ Θεοῦ with Jesus Christ, however, it seems clear that our being created in the image of God should be conceived as part of the work of new creation. True humanity is an eschatological concept. Hence Wolfhart Pannenberg, who follows in the footsteps of Irenaeus on this point, describes the development of human identity by using the term *Bestimmung* with its multiple meanings of "destiny," "destination," "determination," and "definition."[10] Who we are now is retroactively determined by who we will be in the future kingdom of God when we will be fully Christlike. To approximate living in a Christlike manner now is to anticipate that future reality and to draw upon its power ahead of time.

Hence the *imago Dei* is essentially future. But it has a proleptic quality as well. Our created humanity is our eschatological humanity. Who we are is determined by who we will be. To think of ourselves as created in the image of God is to think backward from the fulfillment to the present, from the final creation to the present process of creating. To the extent that the *imago Dei* is present now it is present proleptically—that is, it is an anticipation of a reality yet to be fully realized. It is present as spirit—as the Holy Spirit—and therefore stands in some tension with present reality. The tension between soil and spirit is the tension between present and future. The *imago Dei* is the divine call forward, a call we hear now and respond to now but a call that is drawing us toward transformation into a future reality.

Divinization

Such transformation is sometimes called "divinization." This description of our transformation into the new Adam is found primarily in Eastern Orthodox theology, and it has provoked considerable opposition in the West. The probable cause for this opposition is found in what appears to be a most scandalous term, *theosis* (θέωσις). In its equivalent English translations, "divinization" or "deification," *theosis* sounds to Western ears like an attempt to deny creaturely finitude and elevate what is human

---

10. Wolfhart Pannenberg, *What Is Man?* (Philadelphia: Fortress, 1962), 140–41; idem, *Anthropology in Theological Perspective* (Philadelphia: Westminster, 1985), 514–32; see also James M. Childs, Jr., *Christian Anthropology and Ethics* (Philadelphia: Fortress, 1978), 119.

into the sphere of the divine, as if Prometheus were seeking permanent residence with Zeus atop Mount Olympus. If this is what *theosis* means, then of course we have a case of outrageous human pride, the nonacceptance of our divinely given role as creatures within the creation, the presumptuous denial of the essential goodness of our humanness. It may even mean a return to polytheism if heaven is filled with former human beings now become gods.

In their own defense, however, the Eastern theologians claim that *theosis* has been misunderstood. They say it ought not to be confused with a form of *theopoiesis* (Θεοποίησις)—that is, with the human being actually becoming a god. It is not the mystical translation or transmogrification of the human into the suprahuman realm. *Theosis* rather refers to the indwelling of the Holy Spirit, to the penetration of the human condition by the divine energies (ἐνέργια). Based upon 2 Peter 1:4—which says that we may escape corruption and become "participants of the divine nature" (θείας κοινωνοὶ φύσεως)—*theosis* is said to refer to this participation, to our synergistic participation in God's grace. It is the process whereby the blessings of incorruptibility and immortality wrought by Christ's saving work are experienced by the person who has faith. The complete realization of this divinization process occurs only at the eschatological consummation with its resurrection from the dead. Salvation, for the Eastern Orthodox, is more than a restoration of what Adam had before the fall. It includes incorporation into the divine life of the new Adam, the risen Christ.

Thus, divinization is the process of achieving a union of the human and the divine. What is important here according to the Eastern point of view is the hypostatic union, the term *hypostasis* referring to the union of two different things. In other words, the human remains human and its humanity is fulfilled in divinity.

The model is Christ. In the Son become incarnate, Christ was the hypostasis who united the two natures, the human and the divine. This hypostatic bond accomplished in the incarnation makes human *theosis* possible. "God became human so that humans could become God" is the motto bequeathed to the Orthodox by Athanasius. Humans become Christlike when rising up from their humanity, and they can do so only because Christ became human when descending from his divinity. Hence, divinization is the result of divine grace and not an autonomous human achievement.

Despite this defense, Roman Catholics and Protestants are still a bit nervous about the idea of deification. Their nervousness is quickened by people such as Dionysius the Aeropagite, who, taking a position quite close to Plotinus, describes deification as a renunciation of the realm of the created in order to obtain union with the uncreated and unknowable deity. Or by Maximus the Confessor, who startles especially Protestant sensibilities by saying that the deified humanity becomes "by grace all that God is by nature," save only identity of nature; Maximus also states that "whole people might participate in the whole God."[11] To Western ears this sounds like a denial of our created humanity, like a Promethean attempt to leave earthly existence behind and soar straight for divinity in the heavenly pantheon. Eastern theologians today insist, however, that this is not what is meant. They employ the term *hypostasis* to reaffirm that humans remain creatures while becoming divine through the energy of divine grace, just as Christ remained divine when becoming human through the incarnation.[12] Thus, humans become God in *theosis* in parallel but reverse fashion to God becoming human in Christ.

In sum, humanity will remain human even after its glorification. In glorification it will then be the truly human humanity that God is in the process of creating. Thus, soil is not fully replaced by spirit. Through divinization humanity as the *imago Dei* becomes fulfilled in us. If this is what is meant by *theosis*, then it expresses in other language what I have here been referring to as the call forward to true humanity.

TWO SEXES AND ONE JESUS

The acute gender consciousness pervading theological scholarship in our time raises another question: if the historical Jesus was only of the male gender, can he function as the new Adam for both women and men? Do we need a new Eve who is distinguishable from the new Adam to provide the paradigm for woman's renewal? Should we think in terms of two parallel forms of humanity and not just one?[13]

Eastern Orthodox piety has long utilized the image of Mary, the Mother of God, as the model for true femininity. She has even been designated the new Eve on occasion, giving us two prototypes of human perfection, Jesus and Mary. This goes back at least as far as Irenaeus, who viewed Mary as the obedient virgin who reverses the disobedience of the original mother of our race. Thus, Mary makes possible the birth of the new Adam.[14] In Eastern Orthodoxy and in Roman Catholicism as well,

---

11. Maximus the Confessor *Book of Ambiguities*, in J. P. Migne, ed., *Patrologia Graeca* (Paris, 1857–66), 91:1308B.

12. Vladimir Lossky, *The Mystical Theology of the Eastern Church* (London: James Clarke, 1957), 87; see John Meyendorff, "Christ as Savior in the East," in Bernard McGinn and John Meyendorff, eds., *Christian Spirituality* (New York: Crossroad, 1985), 241.

13. The maleness of Jesus is, theologically speaking, independent of the divine nature. Ambrose said that Jesus' "sex is attributed to human nature, but never to the Godhead" (*Of the Christian Faith* 3.10.63). Hence, Sandra Schneiders argues that the maleness of Jesus is irrelevant to systematic theology. Yet it is very relevant to spirituality, to the daily experience of the faith. The relationship women have to Jesus must not so exalt masculinity that their femininity becomes degraded (Schneiders, *Women and the Word* [New York: Paulist, 1986], 56–67).

14. Irenaeus *Against Heresies* 19.1.1.

Mary comes to represent both the individual human soul and the Christian church that are morally pure and spiritually open to the presence of God. She is honored in Christian art with countless paintings of the annunciation in which she responds to the angel Gabriel saying, "Let it be to me according to your word." She is totally open, totally receptive to God's will. In this way, Mary signifies not just perfected femininity but the new humanity itself. In extreme cases she is dubbed the "queen of heaven"; she is said to have been resurrected from the dead; and she serves as mediatrix for the prayers of sinners. (She is not mediatrix for the justifying grace of God that comes from the merits of Christ alone, but rather she mediates other grace and blessings.) Protestants have objected to this mediating role not because Mary is of the female gender, but because Mary is still a human being of the old aeon and, like us, is awaiting final resurrection into the new age. Christ alone to this point has fully embodied the new Adam.

In our own period, the maleness of Jesus has come under attack. Some feminists charge that this image—especially the Protestant male-dominated image—of human fulfillment in Christ is exclusively androcentric and that its exposition of what the new Adam means represents a one-sided and biased male perspective.[15] What men would find fulfilling is not necessarily what women would find fulfilling, and up until now it has been primarily men who have defined the field. In fact, to interpret everyone's future according to the image of the man Jesus would appear to some women as frustrating and oppressive. Consequently, some feminist theologians are seeking to construct models and images of female fulfillment that are clearly distinguishable from parallel male models.

With this in mind we must ask if the symbol of the new Adam necessarily excludes the female gender. We can get at this question by asking some corollary questions: is it significant for the symbol of the new Adam that Jesus was about thirty years old when he was crucified? Does this disqualify him for serving in a representative role for senior citizens or for very young children? We do not know exactly how tall Jesus was or how much he weighed, but if we did have such information would it disqualify him from representing people who are taller or shorter, heavier or lighter? Jesus was unjustly treated by the religious leaders and governmental agencies of his time, so we must ask: can only those who are similarly oppressed identify with him? Can those who seem to slip through life with health and affluence also see in him their own future? All of these physical and situational factors could be considered relevant for asking just what fulfillment for Jesus would constitute. Does this mean that Jesus is

---

15. "The son, as a model for all human behavior, no matter how prophetic, feminist, or androgynous, cannot include women" (Rita Nakashima Brock, *Journeys by Heart: A Christology of Erotic Power* [New York: Crossroad, 1988], xiii). Only some feminists take this extreme position, as we will see.

disqualified from representing other people who do not share the same physical makeup or whose contingent social situations are quite different?

Just what is it that constitutes the *imago Dei* and the fulfillment of the human project? Is it physical characteristics? Not likely. Augustine thought that in the eschatological resurrection we would probably find that our renewed bodies will be tall or short, depending on their size at death. Yet our physical vigor will be that of a person about thirty years old. He believed this not because Jesus was this age when he died but because this is the age, so Augustine thought, when each of us is at our physical and mental peak. The point is that even for Augustine our bodily conformity or nonconformity to the bodily Jesus is not at stake. No one, it seems, would argue that it is our physical or even historical particularities that determine the makeup of the *imago Dei*. This includes Jesus' gender right along with his age, height, weight, race, nationality, and such. We need not imitate any of these to participate in the destiny of the new Adam.[16] What is at stake is a more universal quality of being human, something we can all share while still maintaining distinctive identities.

This is quite relevant to the current agenda being set by feminist theologians. In her book on Christology, Patricia Wilson-Kastner argues rightly that our common humanity comes prior to our division into male and female.[17] Similarly, Letty Russell asks women to take their stand with Christ, "the Representative," and "to make clear that Christ's work was not first of all that of being a male but that of being the new human." She then explores the qualities of humanness possessed by Jesus that apply to women today. The most important one is personhood. Jesus reveals true personhood, and he helped both men and women to understand their own total personhood. She continues, "The life of Jesus displays characteristics of love, compassion, and caring often considered to be cultural characteristics of women. In his own life he was a 'feminist' in the sense that he considered men and women equal. . . . The most important affirmation of ourselves and of Jesus is that we want to be accepted as subjects and persons, within whom biological differentiation is a secondary aspect."[18] I believe Russell is right in saying that by treating people with dignity Jesus was indirectly edifying each of us—women, men, children—as a person.

---

16. Augustine *City of God* 22.15. Augustine says both sexes will rise, women as women and men as men (ibid., 22.17). Yet, somewhat inconsistently, Augustine associates the *imago Dei* with the man and woman together or with the man alone but not with the woman alone (*On the Trinity* 22.7.10).

17. Patricia Wilson-Kastner, *Faith, Feminism, and the Christ* (Philadelphia: Fortress, 1983), 56.

18. Letty M. Russell, *Human Liberation in a Feminist Perspective* (Philadelphia: Westminster, 1974), 138–39; see Rosemary Radford Ruether, *Sexism and God-Talk* (Boston: Beacon, 1983), 137–38. Anne E. Carr says that "sexuality has nothing to do with saviorhood" (*Transforming Grace: Christian Tradition and Women's Experience* [San Francisco: Harper and Row, 1988], 187).

The feminist critics of Christian anthropology want to emphasize more than the physical difference between the two sexes. They wish to emphasize that the historical experience of repression on the basis of physical difference is what makes women distinct; and fulfillment for women must include a liberation from such repression. Thus the significance of Letty Russell's point is that Jesus Christ as the new Adam imputes and thereby educes dignity and personhood in women. This is redemptive and liberating. This is the process by which women become more fully human, and when women follow the example of Jesus and continue to impute and educe authentic personhood in others, the fulfillment of our own humanity is coming to expression. This is the dynamic of the Christian life by which gender difference is transcended and true humanity is discovered if not created. Whenever we gain a sense of our value as persons and participate in the person-making or person-liberating process, we are hearing the call toward future fulfillment of the image of God.

UNBECOMING EVIL

Despite God's gracious call to fulfillment, however, there seems to be a proclivity in human thought and action that resists God's intention. Instead of answering the call forward, we choose to fixate ourselves in an unchanging present. Instead of answering the call to wholeness, we choose partiality. Fixation and partiality cannot help but produce destruction. To choose fixation and partiality is to choose sin; and the result is evil. Instead of becoming human, we find ourselves awash in unbecoming evil.

Sin produces evil.[19] Evil is the destruction and suffering that result from sin. The evil produced may be direct or indirect, causing suffering either to the sinner or to someone who is innocent or to both. Our lives are part of a wide web of connections that link us across time and across space with so many other people, creatures, and things that evil spreads and infects like a disease. It is almost impossible to retrace the chain of infection so that each event of suffering can be traced to a specific act of sin. When we first become conscious of the human condition, we find ourselves already knee deep in the currents of unbecoming evil.

When it comes to actual sins, they can be listed in different ways. The classic list of seven deadly sins—actually vices—included (1) pride, (2) covetousness, (3) lust, (4) envy, (5) gluttony, (6) anger, and (7) sloth. Here, I will utilize the number seven; but instead of listing vices I will

---

19. Here I contend that evil—at least moral evil—refers to the suffering produced by sin. Not every theologian uses the terms this way. Karl Barth, for example, distinguishes the two by saying that evil attacks the creature whereas sin attacks God. But then Barth turns around and defines evil as that which "is alien and adverse" to God's grace (*CD*, 3/3:311, 353). Because the meanings overlap so extensively, such attempts at fine distinctions between sin and evil are worth only modest effort at best.

anatomize the single phenomenon of the sinful act that yields these and other vices. In seven steps I will show the development of sin from anxiety to blasphemy, passing through unfaith, pride, concupiscence, self-justification, and cruelty. Although my picture here is that of a step by step descent, in daily life we probably do not experience these steps in sequence. Typically they rush upon us all at once. In what follows, I will attempt to analyze the experience of sin in order to delineate its component parts, noting a kind of dependence of each step on the previous one.

1. Anxiety

Anxiety is the prelude to sin. In itself, anxiety is not sin; but it stands before us like fruit on the tree of knowledge, tempting us toward aggression.

The metaxy of human finitude produces the tension of anxiety, a tension that does not exist in quite the same way for other animals or for plants. When other animals find themselves in immediate danger, they fear death just as we do, to be sure; but the imaginative power of our spiritual capacity adds something more fearsome. We can imagine possibilities not immediate to hand. We can anticipate perils. Even when our immediate situation seems secure and we have every right to be content, we can conceive of contingencies wherein that security would be taken away. So, we become tempted to overstretch our limits with a preemptive strike. We dump excessive amounts of DDT into the environment, and that poisons our water. Storing becomes hoarding. The investments of insurance companies include stocks in multinational corporations that support oppressive political regimes. We bomb those we consider our enemies before they can bomb us. We seek our own security at the expense of other life.

This is a denial of communal wholeness. By defending the survival and the edification of one's self at the cost of destroying others, the harmony of the whole undergoes relentless disruption. We sin when we magnify the self by exerting destructive power, by trying to establish the self in its own righteousness over against the alleged evil of the surrounding world. Deep down we have the inchoate sense that we are but part of a larger whole, yet due to our failure to trust God to maintain the health of the whole we assert our own self as if it were the whole, as if all the other parts should serve us. We end up treating ourselves as if we were the whole rather than one of the complementary parts.

All this is a response to anxiety. Paul Tillich defines anxiety as the awareness of a finite being that he or she might become nonbeing. It is the amorphous and as yet inchoate fear of loss, total loss. It is the anticipation of death, meaninglessness, and oblivion. As such, anxiety is a significant breeding ground for sin. Reinhold Niebuhr sees it as the internal state of temptation. Here he follows Søren Kierkegaard, who describes anxiety as the psychological condition that precedes sin.[20] It is the soil in which sin grows.

2. *Unfaith*

"Adam would never have dared oppose God's authority unless he had disbelieved in God's Word," contends John Calvin. Or, in the words of Martin Luther, "The root and source of sin is unbelief."[21] God is faithful and trustworthy. The problem is that we do not believe it. Unbelief produces distrust. The inability to trust God for all things opens the door for anxiety to do some damage. Once challenged by anxiety, we work diligently to protect ourselves and even to expand ourselves.

In itself anxiety is not sin, because there is the possibility that an anxious person could live in faith. Faith includes trust in the God of the future. Such trust disarms anxiety before it can inflict the damage wrought by self-assertion. If anxiety is the fertile soil, then the root of sin is unfaith—that is, untrust. By this I mean the lack of trust in God when we are confronted by our anxiety.

If we lack trust in the everlasting God we are tempted to seek escape from the metaxic tension. We will try to establish immortality within the confines of mortality. The press toward immortality expresses itself in the lust for power and perfection. Even though we realize that we must die physically, we pursue with relentless passion every means for substitute immortality. We may try to accumulate as much money as possible and bequeath it to our heirs, so that we leave a legacy of ourselves to go on having an influence beyond our grave. Ideologies such as nationalism or Marxism become means whereby we can meld our personal existence with a supraindividual power, and the stronger the nation or the political movement the greater will be our legacy after we are gone. This striving to get some grip on our immortality through "righteous self-expansion and perpetuation" is the root of all evil, says social theorist Ernest Becker. This author of *The Denial of Death* and *Escape from Evil* believes that all the wars and massacres of history derive ultimately from the hideous illusion that we humans can successfully deny our animal nature and attain eternal life on our own power. Becker in effect is speaking about anxiety and unfaith, our refusal to put our trust in the only source for eternal life, God.[22]

To trust something or somebody other than God is the essence of idolatry. It is "trust and faith of the heart alone that make both God

---

20. Reinhold Niebuhr, *The Nature and Destiny of Man*, 2 vols. (New York: Charles Scribner's Sons, 1941), 1:182. See Paul Tillich, *The Courage to Be* (New Haven: Yale University Press, 1952), 35.

21. Calvin, *Inst.*, 2.1.4; Luther, *LW*, 1:162, 34:155.

22. Ernest Becker, *The Denial of Death* (New York: Macmillan, Free Press, 1973); and idem, *Escape from Evil* (New York: Macmillan, Free Press, 1975), esp. 135, 163.

and idol," contends Luther in the Large Catechism. This is true whether what we trust is our nation's military might, the capitalist economic system, communist ideology, our own intelligence and get-up-and-go, the mystical insight of Krishna, or the fertility of an earth goddess. Idolatry consists in missing the mark, in failing to accept and trust in the will and promise of the God of Israel.

Unfaith and idolatry through ego-aggrandizement go together. This recalls John Calvin, for whom "unfaithfulness" was the root of the fall, "but thereafter ambition and pride, together with ungratefulness, arose."[23] This mention of egocentricity and ambition leads to the next characteristic of human sin, pride.

3. Pride

Pride appears prominently in the list of the seven deadly sins and has long been considered the seed that comes to bloom in all the others. In recommending humility to the citizens of the City of God while it sojourns in this world, Augustine contends that "pride is the beginning of sin."[24] By pride he means the self-exaltation that results from centering our attention upon ourselves when pursuing satisfaction of temporary or ephemeral desires rather than the long-range purposes of God. It refuses to allow God to be God. It tries to co-opt divinity for itself. This is symbolized by the manner in which the serpent tempted Eve in the Garden of Eden: should she eat from the tree of the knowledge of good and evil she would become like God. This is the attempt at human self-divinization. Although Paul Tillich prefers the untranslated Greek term hubris (ὕβρις) to the English pride, he is clear that this amounts to the human denial of soil in behalf of spirit. He calls it "spiritual sin," saying that its main symptom is that we do not acknowledge our finitude; it is the self-elevation of oneself into "the sphere of the divine."[25]

In individuals pride manifests itself as narcissism.[26] The narcissist organizes all his or her psychic concerns around a single center, his or her own self. Other persons are treated as things or objects to be manipulated, even if that manipulation is subtle. As a group phenomenon, pride manifests itself as family pride or clan revenge. It is the willingness to

---

23. Calvin, Inst., 1.1.4.
24. Augustine City of God 14.13.
25. Tillich, Systematic Theology, 3 vols. (Chicago: University of Chicago Press, 1951–63), 2:50–51.
26. Beginning with the pioneering work of Valerie Saiving ("The Human Situation: A Feminine View," in Carol P. Christ and Judith Plaskow, eds., Womanspirit Rising [San Francisco: Harper and Row, 1979], 37), many feminists have suggested that pride applies to men, not women. Sin for a woman is not the proud push for power but rather underdevelopment or negation of self. After numerous interviews and conversations with women who have reflected on their experience in this regard, it seems clear to me that pride is manifest in both women and men even if in slightly different ways. If pride does not take the form of group identity or command of social power, it manifests itself in women as narcissism.

sacrifice other groups for the aggrandizement of the group to which the proud belong. Group pride is the origin of the "isms" so destructive to the structures of justice in the modern world: ethnocentrism, nationalism, chauvinism, racism, sexism, and so on.

One of the problems with pride is the truth of the oft-repeated proverb, "Pride goes before destruction" (Prov. 16:18). This produces a haunting anxiety during our time of nuclear standoff. If we think on a global scale we find ourselves today amid a giant form of the ancient feud between clans with the threat that blood revenge will do away with the human community entirely. In a time of global consciousness we live with the frustrating paradox of being able to conceive of a single worldwide human community, while at the same time living within one or another sovereign state. The stockpiling of nearly fifty thousand nuclear weapons at a recent count in a proliferating number of sovereign countries risks bringing our world to a state of critical mass, where the detonation of one bomb might precipitate a chain reaction of destruction that could spell the end of the human race and much of nature as well. Through this balance of terror we find ourselves in the position of holding a knife at the throat of those on the other side of the brink, while ironically holding the same threat of death against ourselves and against all whom we love. We do not need to go to the theologians to find an interpretation of our situation since 1945 as sin. The scientists do it for us. According to the director of the Manhattan Project, Robert Oppenheimer, the bombings of Hiroshima and Nagasaki mark the fall from innocence of the modern age. Oppenheimer's words will be long remembered: "Physicists have known sin." Physicist Freeman Dyson describes the possession of our nuclear arsenal as "a manifestly evil institution deeply imbedded in the structure of our society." We have become servants to this evil. We have sold ourselves into atomic slavery.[27]

Here, completely outside conventional theological circles, our experience with the human predicament is rising to articulation; and those who wish to give it voice find they must use the symbols of sin in order to express the depth of the despair we are experiencing. It is the self-assertion, the *hubris*, of autonomous nations that threatens the health if not the very existence of the global community. Yet once the original sin has been committed, what can a single nation choose to do? If the human race were capable of acting as a whole in the best interest of itself as a whole, then single decisions of global consequence could be made that would reduce and eventually eliminate the peril. But in our world where individual nations are sovereign and have the initiative—where the ancient system of clan revenge is now writ large—there is no

---

27. Freeman Dyson, *Weapons and Hope* (San Francisco: Harper & Row, 1984); see Jonathan Schell, *The Fate of the Earth* (New York: Knopf, 1982); and idem, *The Abolition* (New York: Knopf, 1984).

way that one can act directly in behalf of the good of the whole. Augustine was right: in our present situation we cannot not sin, *non posse non peccare.*

4. Concupiscence

If in unfaith we find ourselves unable to trust in God and then allow our lives to be dominated by *hubris*, the result is what we call "sensuality" or, better, "concupiscence" (ἐπιθυμία in Col. 3:5; 1 Thess. 4:5). Concupiscence is the form of sensual desire leading to lust, envy, greed, avarice, and covetousness. Concupiscence consists primarily in the attempt to become solely soil while denying the spiritual dimension of consciousness. Although originally identified with sexual lust or with giving in to one's animal appetites in general, in our own time concupiscence is expressed most saliently in the consumer mentality. It is the assumption that we should be engaged constantly in buying and having. It is an effort to escape the metaxic tension and the infinite possibilities of the spirit by overindulging in the details of ordinary daily life and its activities. The result is what Reinhold Niebuhr calls "unlimited devotion to limited values" or what Thomas Aquinas refers to as "turning inordinately to mutable good."[28]

Concupiscence is perverted love. "I just love to go shopping!" we say, meaning that shopping is an enjoyable pastime. We handle and manipulate newly manufactured products that we can imagine possessing. We get a feeling of power as sales clerks beckon to our wishes. For Augustine a transitory enjoyment could find its proper place amid a complex of loves that are ultimately ordered toward love of the everlasting God. But when love for God is sacrificed or pressed into the service of more mundane desires, the result is concupiscence and a life dominated by mimetic desire, envy, and consumption. Worse, it is a life that lives off the death of others.

Borrowing some Marxist categories for a moment can help clarify the fundamentally concupiscent structure of economics in the modern industrial world. Capitalism depends upon the production of what Marx called "surplus value," the excess value or profit that results from the mass production of goods. The ability to control and reinvest surplus value is the index of a given people's freedom. Marx identified the primary source of friction between classes and between nations as the desire to appropriate the surplus of others. Since the industrial revolution the European and North American nations along with Japan have gained control of much of the world's surplus value. They have placed themselves at the center of the global economic system. By establishing a periphery

---

28. Niebuhr, *Nature and Destiny of Man,* 1:185; Thomas Aquinas, *Summa Theologica,* I/III, q. 77, a. 4; see Luke 12:20; Rom. 8:6; Gal. 5:16; Plato *Timaeus* 90.

of underdeveloped economic colonies around the globe, the developed nations have assured that raw materials and export crops flow cheaply to the center and that manufactured goods flow back to the peripheral markets. The surplus value, in turn, flows back to the center and accumulates. In the Third World where cash crops for export replace local food production, this is more than just a case of taking merely the surplus. The very livelihood of millions of people becomes drained off into the luxuries of the First World. It is more than money. It is life that is at stake.

Thus, the essence and bane of concupiscence are finally the consumption of someone else's life-giving power. Like vampires we thrive on the blood of our victims. That we have similarities to vampires may not be immediately obvious in our daily routine as we cash our paychecks and head for the shopping center. Yet our whole economy is based upon this more basic human structure: the desire to consume someone else's life-giving power. It began in our prehistory with the ceremonious eating of the heart of the strong animal that the hunters had slain. The strength of the animal was assumed to be somehow transmuted into increased strength for the hunters. It continued with the systematic slaying of those captured in war. The kings of the African Dahomey captured members of inland tribes to sell to slave traders. But not all the captured were sold. Once a year hundreds would be lined up and the Dahomey would cut off their heads. They would give up financial profit for the exhilaration of demonstrating their power over weaker peoples. Ernest Becker says the public display, humiliation, and execution of prisoners are psychologically very important because they affirm: "They are weak and die; we are strong and live." The killing of others affirms our own power over life. Worldwide economic structures maintained to enhance the profit of select societies today reaffirm the power of life consumed by the few at the expense of the many. What is visible is the shopping center. What is invisible is the misery.

I have begun by describing concupiscence as the desire to consume material things, as seeking to avoid the metaxy by losing ourselves in things of the soil. But there is more to it than this. Below the obvious pattern of consuming material things lies the illusory consumption of life-power through vampirism. This represents an attempt to escape anxiety, to escape our inevitable destiny of being buried in the soil.

5. Self-justification

None of us wants to be blamed for the loss of someone else's livelihood or life. None of us wants our pride and concupiscence advertised or our public image tarnished. We wish to be considered innocent, righteous, good, just. If things go wrong, it must be somebody else's fault. This brings us to the hidden force in sin: the illusion, the lie.

Unless we understand the secret dynamics of self-justification, we cannot understand why the New Testament would depict Jesus attacking the most pious and powerful people of his society. Instead of prophesying against corrupt tax collectors or thieves or murderers or traitors, Jesus concentrated his ire on the Pharisees and the scribes. These were the upright citizens and the religious leaders of the day. They commanded respect, and for good reason. Yet Jesus minced no words in criticizing them as hypocrites: "Beware of the yeast of the Pharisees, which is hypocrisy" (Luke 12:1b). Jesus likened them to the death hidden within whitewashed tombs: "Woe to you, scribes and Pharisees, hypocrites! For you are like whitewashed tombs, which on the outside look beautiful, but inside they are full of the bones of the dead and of all kinds of filth" (Matt. 23:27). With this Jesus accused them of exhibiting a beautiful exterior that hid an inner decay. Why? Because they were legalists? Because they sought scrupulously to learn God's law and to live according to that law? Because Jesus was trying to teach a higher or more abstract understanding of the law as the law of love? No, not exactly. It was because a mechanism of self-justification had come to dominate their religious minds. They were assuming that if they could orient their lives according to God's will, then God would approve and favor them. In concentrating on this task of conformity to their perception of the divine will, they had become blind to their own contribution to the aggression in the world about them. Whereas they thought themselves to be just, their attitude in fact spawned injustice. Whereas they thought themselves to be loyal to the teachings of the prophets, they belonged in the league with those who murdered the prophets (Matt. 23:31-32).

Sometimes self-justification is called legalism. With this label our attention is drawn to the law plus the justice achieved in abiding by the law. What is rendered invisible, however, is an insidious mechanism that nearly always structures self-justification, namely, scapegoating. Scapegoating is invisible because it requires a lie—what Jesus called hypocrisy—to be effective.

People in all societies are constantly threatened with aggression and the unleashing of uncontrollable violence. Adherence to the law is ostensibly the way in which societies protect themselves from this threat. Obedience to the law is ostensibly the way in which justice and peace are maintained. The struggle to maintain the law and its just order, however, frequently requires a sacrifice. The sacrificial victim is the scapegoat.

René Girard argues that each society engages in some form of sacrifice that is aimed at stemming the tide of violence and establishing social order. People believe that the flood of uncontrolled violence—whether subtle or overt—can be dammed up and its destructive force averted through a controlled act of ritual violence. "If left unappeased, violence will accumulate until it overflows its confines and floods the surrounding area. The role of sacrifice is to stem this rising tide of indiscriminate substitutions and redirect violence into proper channels."[29] Thus the purpose of sacrifice is to restore harmony to the community, to reinforce the social fabric.

Girard believes that we can better understand the madness of collective violence in our era if we pay attention to the archetype of the scapegoat.[30] The scapegoat mechanism is likely to function when (1) we are confronted by a cultural crisis, such as a plague or a war, which obliterates stable social differences; (2) we are able to make a symbolic accusation—that is, when we can identify the cause of the crisis with some representatives of moral breakdown; and (3) certain victims are selected who allegedly embody this moral breakdown, usually people belonging to a minority and having characteristics that distinguish them from the majority—these might include a different skin color, religious affiliation, or class status, and might even include sickness or madness. The line between good and evil is drawn. The just can now be distinguished from the unjust. The result is mob action in an attempt to purge the atmosphere of the evil that precipitated the crisis. The purge may take the form of slander, discrimination, persecution, or war. Once the purge has been successful, peace is established and law-abiding citizens are affirmed as just.

To make scapegoating work all of the accusers must agree on where to draw the line between good and evil. They must also agree that the potential scapegoat falls on the evil side of the line. Then, in the name of the good, aggression and violence may be inflicted on the victim with full self-justification. What dare not be missed in examining this structure is the way the lie functions: in the name of what is good or right or just the scapegoat is victimized and those engaged in victimizing feel justified in doing it.

This is the way family, racial, or national pride can justify discrimination, exploitation, and even persecution of so-called outsiders. The outsiders are depicted as lacking in morality, goodness, and humanness, and thereby are seen as a threat to the establishment of insiders. The values, loyalties, and laws of the insiders justify aggression against the outsiders. People with AIDS and welfare mothers in ghettos can be justly denied dignity in middle-class North America because they are allegedly sexually immoral. Marxists make scapegoats out of the middle-class and multinational corporations because they allegedly oppress people with AIDS and the welfare mothers in the ghettos. A crisis could suddenly turn these temptations into the sin of which Girard speaks, and mob chaos would be the result.

---

29. René Girard, *Violence and the Sacred* (Baltimore: Johns Hopkins University Press, 1977), 10.
30. René Girard, *The Scapegoat* (Baltimore: Johns Hopkins University Press, 1986).

The structure of self-justification and scapegoating, like that of any lie, is fragile. Truth is a threat. The truth revealed in the crucifixion of Jesus Christ is a threat in this sense: it reveals the lie to be a lie. The martyrdom of the innocent one from Nazareth reveals the oppressiveness of the scapegoat system and the fruitlessness of seeking self-justification through persecution of others. Christ as the lamb of God exposes the hypocrisy of the scapegoat mechanism. He destroys the mob's self-justifying belief in the guilt of the victim. Scapegoats can no longer save because witch-hunts, pogroms, and persecutions have been demystified. Christ is the final scapegoat, the sacrificial lamb of God who puts a theoretical end to all other sacrifices.

Theologically, the important point here is that, according to the gospel, our justification comes to us as a free gift of God's grace. We receive this justification through faith, not as the result of works of the law. This is the point Paul drives home. All people, whether Jews or Greeks or anybody else, are subject to sin. Citing Psalms 14 and 53, he says, "There is no one who is righteous, not even one" (Rom. 3:10b). To think that we have the power of righteousness within ourselves or in our works is to delude ourselves, and this delusion leads to deception and finally to violence. Alluding to the vitriolic mood of Jesus as well as Psalms 5, 10, and 140, Paul writes,

> "Their throats are opened graves,
>   they use their tongues to deceive."
> "The venom of vipers is under their lips."
>   "Their mouths are full of cursing and bitterness."
> "Their feet are swift to shed blood;
>   ruin and misery are in their paths,
> and the way of peace they have not known."
> (Rom. 3:13-17)

Self-justification, says Paul, leads finally to the disruption of peace and the shedding of blood.

The concupiscent person wants to hide his or her anxiety, and this is an integral part of sin itself. Self-justification is the mask behind which we hide. This hiding in turn exacerbates the problem. Like a hurricane lurking at sea until it builds up power and then slams against the coast with increased fury, the masking of our sin increases the damage it can do. Down deep we may hate what we are tempted to do. In order to divert this hatred away from ourselves, we project it outward. We project our own temptation toward sin onto someone else. We point the finger away from ourselves, making us look good and someone else look evil. We create a scapegoat, someone who will appear unjust so that we can appear just. If the projection gets out of hand, we may engage in violence to rid the earth of the unjust enemy we have pointed out. The result is the shedding of innocent blood.

6. Cruelty

We treat our scapegoats cruelly. All the hatred we have toward ourselves and hidden from ourselves comes to expression in acts of cruelty, which I will here define as the inflicting of physical or emotional pain on another person in order to cause anguish or fear. A nation may ask its police force or the military to inflict torture on its enemies, or a narcissistic parent may overpower and abuse a child. The self-deceit requisite for self-justification and scapegoating makes it possible to define the victim as the evil one and, hence, deserving of the pain we intend to inflict.

Cruelty comes in passive and active forms. Passive cruelty is the result of a lack of care. The narcissistic parent, for example, may seal himself or herself off into a private emotional world, leaving the child to wander alone in the chaos of uncontrolled feelings and fears. One of the products of the world economic order, to cite another example, is the passive cruelty experienced by impoverished peasants who are removed from their land to make way for mechanized farms growing export crops. They wander to the outskirts of large cities, settle in barrios, and suffer the humiliation of scavenging for food they could have grown for themselves.

Active cruelty is the deliberate infliction of pain, usually as physical or psychological torture. Most active cruelty is partially protected under the umbrella of self-justification. The narcissistic parent, to return to a previous example, may in frustration over difficulties in earning a living scapegoat the child with beating or other forms of abuse. Such child abuse is frequently justified as rightful parental discipline. Systematic torture, to add an additional example, is occasionally legitimated by political ideologies that justify scapegoating for ethnic, national, or class purposes. Enemies or suspected enemies of the body politic in many parts of the world are imprisoned in secret, mentally harangued, physically abused, and occasionally murdered in their cells.

Cruelty in the form of torture marks a transition from the lie to blasphemy. With one foot in scapegoating, cruelty refers to what proud and concupiscent persons engaged in self-justification do to their sacrificial victims. Yet, insofar as the lie remains intact, it is done blindly. The blindness is due to the belief that the victim deserves the suffering. Any sympathetic feeling of the scapegoat's pain is cushioned by the multiple levels of self-justifying legalism. With the other foot in blasphemy, however, awareness of the victim's pain becomes a desired commodity. Cruelty in the form of torture and sacrifice consciously becomes food for feeding the insatiable appetite of the proud for power.

7. Blasphemy

At the bottom of our descent into the pit of sin and evil is blasphemy. Coming from the Greek Βλασφημία, this term has traditionally referred to profaning or slandering God's holy name. Here, I would like to assert that blasphemy consists of the attempt to steal power from divine symbols.

There are two forms of blasphemy. The first is subtle. It is the use of God's name hypocritically to justify scapegoating. It is the use of sacred symbols to incite prejudice against outsiders or to inspire soldiers to go off to war. It is the identification of one's own tribal or nationalistic interests with the providence of God. This first form of blasphemy is the attempt to steal the power of religious symbols for selfish purposes. It purportedly honors God's name in the very misuse of God's name.

The second form of blasphemy is not subtle. It is the overt manipulation of divine symbols for the purpose of profaning the God of grace and for obtaining power from lesser spiritual forces. Overt blasphemy occurs in satanic and similar pagan rituals that seek supranatural power for engaging in vengeful or criminal enterprises. It is the attempt through a theft of symbolic power to employ divine might in one's own behalf against others, something intrinsically inimical to the God of grace.

A controversy is currently raging between three competing groups: Satanists, anti-Satanists, and anti-anti-Satanists. The Satanists make positive use of symbols for evil through worship. I will examine this shortly. The anti-Satanists fear that worshipers of Satan in large numbers are threatening the security of society. The anti-Satanists consist of a confederation of parents of children in preschools, law enforcement officers, fundamentalist and evangelical clergy, and other anticult organizations. The anti-anti-Satanists, in curious contrast, contend that Satanism does not exist and that the real enemies to society are the anti-Satanists. The anti-anti-Satanists include academic social scientists, secular humanists, and philosophical atheists who fear that if the claims of the anti-Satanists are well founded, then belief in Satan could indirectly lead to belief in God. Of the three competing groups, the Satanists are those relevant to my concern with blasphemy.

The worship rituals of satanic cults include the reading of pseudoscriptures that slander God and praise the devil. Animals such as dogs, cats, chickens, squirrels, and goats are tortured and sacrificed during worship. The extremities of these animals are amputated so that the blood flows and fills up waiting drinking cups. When an animal is not used, young children or grown women may be stretched nude on the altar. The priest's dagger is used to draw blood for the chalice and scrapings of skin are taken to be used in the very literalized eucharistic ritual. Whipped up into a frenzy by taking drugs and alcohol, the participants drink animal or human blood and eat flesh in a mockery of the Christian sacrament.

On some occasions, even the human victim on the altar is put to death so that the devil worshipers may eat and drink the life-forces of the sacrificed one. In her book tracing the life of a little girl who grew up with a mother who was a member of such a satanic cult, Judith Spencer records the devil's priest saying to the child, "Suffer the children to come unto him, for of such is the kingdom of hell."[31]

The accompanying blasphemy makes cruelty in the context of satanic religion doubly evil. Such religions use Christian symbols in inverted form: the upside down cross, the Lord's Prayer said backward, the black mass, the literal consumption of body and blood, and the renunciation of baptism. This twisting of the symbols results in a loss of spiritual access to divine grace. Satanists recognize the tremendous power of symbolism and employ it to their own ends. They employ a profaning hermeneutic. What is so heinous is that victims of ritual abuse are robbed of the symbolic meaning that might give mental comfort amid physical pain. The very symbols of God that could otherwise give them courage in the face of suffering are stolen and perverted, leaving them with mental as well as physical agony. The victim's consciousness is spiritually raped along with the physical body.

One might at this point ask: when, if at all, should we consider the role of Satan in human evil? Is sin simply one social or psychological function among others, or is there an extrasubjective spiritual force involved?[32]

The question of whether radical evil should be personified in a metaphysical entity such as Satan is potentially diversionary.[33] At issue is the experience at some times and some places of a suprapersonal force that seeks to drive either a group or an individual toward destruction. An *agent provocateur* does exist. This is Walter Wink's term. Unable to decide whether the Devil is a person or not, Wink says, "Satan is the real interiority of a society that idolatrously pursues its own enhancement as the highest good. Satan is the spirituality of an epoch, the peculiar constellation of alienation, greed, inhumanity, oppression, and entropy that

31. Judith Spencer, *Suffer the Child* (New York: Pocket Books, 1989). My own study of the phenomenon of Satanism is reported in "Satan's Friends and Enemies," *Dialog* 30, no. 4 (Fall 1991): 303–13.
32. John Newport puts the challenge: "Can one adequately explain the genocidal campaigns of Adolf Hitler or Idi Amin, the murder sprees of Charles Manson or Ted Bundy, the suicide/murder of Jim Jones and his cult followers in Guyana, or the success of the kiddie-porn industry without at least considering the possibility of a personal power of evil in the universe?" (*Life's Ultimate Questions: A Contemporary Philosophy of Religion* [Dallas: Word, 1989], 186–87). Newport's conclusion is that "Satan really exists, and he wants to destroy us" (ibid., 211).
33. Newport would be sympathetic here. "Some Christians have come to regard highly emotional and dramatic cases of possession as the primary manifestation of the forces of evil. In actuality, Satan, the great deceiver, may be encouraging interest in outwardly dramatic cases in hopes that Christians will become careless about other more subtle forms of influence by the powers of evil. . . . Satan also works through groups of people and organizational structures—political, social, even religious" (*Life's Ultimate Questions*, 204).

characterizes a specific period of history as a consequence of human decisions to tolerate and even further such a state of affairs."[34] Wink may be saying too much. The term *Satan* here seems to apply to everything. I would like to narrow the scope and say that what is distinctively satanic is the call to shed innocent blood. This is my criterion: the force of Satan is present when we hear the call to shed innocent blood. Self-justification and yielding to the temptation to create a scapegoat open the door through which Satan can enter and begin to control things with a spirit radically opposed to the will of God. The result is cruelty. When cruelty is inflicted in behalf of God's name or in profaning God's name, it is blasphemy.

Having begun with anxiety, we have ended up with cruelty, especially blasphemous cruelty. On the way we followed the steps of unfaith, pride, concupiscence, self-justification, and scapegoating. It is a descent we may follow whether the first step begins with national pride, racial arrogance, ideological commitment, or uncontrolled appetites within the individual soul. In all cases, it is a downward spiral, at the bottom of which is the pit of evil.

ORIGINAL SIN

Symbols such as Satan and demonic forces give expression to something endemic to human experience—namely, sin comes from the outside as well as the inside. Evil is larger than we are. It comes to us just as we go to it. If any of us initiates evil through a sinful act, we then discover evil. We find it already present when we are born. It will continue after we are gone. The serpent's tempting of Eve in the Garden of Eden symbolizes the truth we know by experience. Paul Ricoeur states: "I do not begin evil; I continue it."[35]

The Christian tradition, especially since Augustine, has accustomed itself to using the term *original sin* to refer to the sin that is outside of us. This controversial term can mean at least two things. On the one hand, it may refer to the first sin (Latin: *peccatum originale originans;* German: *Ursünde*) committed by Adam and Eve in Eden. On the other hand, it may refer to inherited sin (Latin: *peccatum originale originatum;* German: *Erbsünde*). The image at work here is that of Adam and Eve committing the first sin and then passing the propensity for sin to us on the analogy of an inherited disease. The first parents have infected the whole human race down to the present time. Critics have objected to the idea of original sin because (1) the story of a first sin in a primeval garden sounds mythical rather than historical; (2) it is unjust for the

---

34. Walter Wink, *Unmasking the Powers* (Philadelphia: Fortress, 1986), 25.
35. See Ricoeur, in Don Ihde, ed., *Conflict of Interpretations: Essays in Hermeneutics* (Evanston, Ill.: Northwestern University Press, 1974), 284.

present generation to suffer because of the sin of its ancestors; and (3) too frequently the sexual intercourse necessary for procreation has become the target of those who wish to point to the precise moment at which the disease is passed on. Despite these criticisms, I believe theologians need a concept such as original sin to account for the human experience it articulates. Evil comes to us and we sin—these are basic elements of human experience and are symbolized in the story of Adam and Eve, who represent everyone. Sin is universally human. The idea of original sin is an attempt to provide a workable concept of this universal phenomenon.

The metaphor of disease and the story of sin's history from Eden to the present are theological constructs that create a problem only when one takes them more literally than they are intended. The idea of original sin is already an attempt to explicate something more basic. The first task of the systematic theologian today is to attend to this more basic phenomenon and then try to bring it to conceptual explication. In my judgment, the term *original sin* should not be forgotten as constructive efforts proceed. The neoorthodox term *state of sin* avoids the traditional trappings; however, it connotes a static reality. My proposal to speak of evil as unbecoming—as resisting the becoming creation—is intended to connote the appropriate dynamism and to hint at the universality of the human experience with sin and evil.

GOD, SIN, AND THE FUTURE WHOLE

The connectedness of all things over the globe and over time and the sense of sharing a single destiny underscore the universality of sin and the universality of our need for God's saving activity. The nuclear sword of Damocles that now dangles over our own heads represents the worst conceivable case in which the pride of the part threatens the health and harmony of the whole, in this case the whole of planetary life. With these things in mind, and given the growing postmodern consciousness that partially constitutes the current context, we can think of sin as the assertion of the part against the whole and as the assertion of the present against the future.

It is common to think that self-centeredness on the part of any of us constitutes sin, because it is God and God's whole that belong in the center of our lives. Yet we ought not let this notion lead us to degrade the concept of finite selfhood per se. The coming into existence of human selves is part of the overall divine plan to create a unity that is in essence a community of selves. We find our fulfillment not in destroying ourselves but in sharing the respective goodness that belongs to the whole of God's creative process. The epigenetic understanding of God's creative process is one of complementarity, synthesis, and renewal. Our aim, as Augustine makes clear, is to center our lives on God and, in turn, center ourselves in the whole. Such is the fulfillment of human destiny. To assert one's self in resistance against this destiny constitutes sin and produces evil. "Evil arises," writes Reinhold Niebuhr, "when the fragment seeks by its own wisdom to comprehend the whole or attempts by its own power to realize it."[36]

The difficulty in this matter, as Augustine warned, is that we cannot by our own power center our individual existence in the whole. Once we have placed ourselves and defined ourselves as individual centers of self-hood, we are unable on our own to defend ourselves against the threat of anxiety. We are unable to extricate ourselves from our state of estrangement. Any attempt to center one's self outside the self is, by definition, a self-constituting act. This is a paradox. As long as the self retains the initiative it can only fix upon itself and further establish itself as the center. Yet, somehow it must be uprooted from this center and be drawn to find its center in that which is beyond itself, in the Spirit of the whole. One cannot even say that the true aim of the self is its own salvation, for even the pursuit of salvation only further establishes the self as center and ensures its own perdition. Salvation is experienced only by those who have ceased to be interested in whether or not they personally are saved, because these have given themselves over completely to the Spirit of the whole.

We find ourselves in an impossible position. We need the whole to take the initiative. We need God to act. We need the transforming power of divine grace.

In this book I have been arguing that at present there is no genuine whole in anything but a formal sense. For material wholeness in the sense of the whole-centeredness and communion of all things we must await the finishing of the old creation at the point where the new creation is established. In short, we do not have a whole until the eschaton. Yet the power of the eschatological whole is effective in the present. It is effective proleptically. It is the power of God's grace calling us forward and empowering us to center our existence through trust in the future that will be God's.

---

36. Niebuhr, *Nature and Destiny of Man*, 1:168. Most helpful in this regard is pioneer theologian William Temple, for whom God is "the Spirit of the whole" (*Nature, Man and God* [London: Macmillan, 1934], 376, 390). The human predicament, he said, is that we find ourselves unable by our own power to center ourselves in the whole that is God. It takes the transforming power of the whole itself to accomplish this—that is, it takes grace.

PART THREE

THE FORETASTE
OF NEW CREATION

INTRODUCTION

We believe in one Lord, Jesus Christ,
  the only Son of God, eternally begotten of the Father,
  God from God, Light from Light, true God from true God,
  begotten not made, of one Being with the Father.
Through him all things were made.
For us and for our salvation he came down from heaven;
  by the power of the Holy Spirit he became incarnate from the virgin Mary
  and was made man.
For our sake he was crucified under Pontius Pilate;
  he suffered death and was buried.
On the third day he rose again, in accordance with the Scriptures;
  he ascended into heaven and is seated at the right hand of the Father.
He will come again in glory to judge the living and the dead,
  and his kingdom will have no end.

—The Nicene Creed

Part Three examines the creed's Second Article, which deals with the story of Jesus (the person) and its significance for the redemption of creation (the work).

Jesus Christ brings the forgiveness of sin and a proleptic foretaste of new creation. Attention is directed toward the conflict between the new creation and the old because this conflict resulted in the crucifixion of Jesus and led to the resurrection to new life on Easter. On the basis of this Easter victory Jesus becomes the Christ, the bringer of the new aeon in his role as the final prophet, the final priest, and the final king.

6

THE PERSON AND WORK
OF JESUS CHRIST

Oh, come, oh, come, Emmanuel,
and ransom captive Israel,
That mourns in lonely exile here
until the Son of God appear.
Rejoice! Rejoice! Emmanuel shall come to you, O Israel.
—*Psalteriolum Cantionium Catholicarum*, Cologne 1710

The story of Jesus is significant because of who Jesus was and because of what he accomplished. Ordinarily the word *Christology* refers to who he was and is, and the word *soteriology* refers to what he did and does. Sometimes the word *Christology* refers to both.

Christology is the church's doctrinal conversation regarding the person of Jesus Christ. The focus of discussion has traditionally been the incarnation—that is, reflection upon the affirmation of the divine presence in the human person of Jesus. Coming from the Greek term σώζειν, meaning to save, soteriology is the doctrine of salvation accomplished by Jesus Christ. It normally presupposes the doctrine of the incarnation. It then proceeds to focus on the atoning work of Christ. Generally, soteriology concerns itself more with the means of accomplishing salvation than with the nature or content of salvation itself.

For centuries theologians have distinguished Christology, dealing with the person of Christ, from soteriology, dealing with the work of Christ to accomplish salvation. Many modern theologians are uneasy with this distinction, however, saying that the work depends on the person or vice versa. That there is a close relationship nobody would deny. Friedrich Schleiermacher puts it well when he says that even though the theological

174

propositions put forth in each of the two doctrines are different, they both deal with one and the same content. Philip Melanchthon puts it still better: "Hoc est Christum cognoscere, eius beneficia cognoscere" (that is, to know Christ is to know his benefits). Hence, we may use one term, "Christology," inclusively to refer to both topics.

My plan here is to outline briefly the concept of the threefold office of Christ, called the *triplex munus*, as a framework for an exposition of christological development. The *triplex munus* is a traditional way for explicating the significance of the story of Jesus in terms of his three offices: the prophet, the king, and the priest. Let me note in passing that this procedure deviates somewhat from the classical approach, wherein the topic of the person Christ (*de persona Christi*) typically dealt with the union of the divine and human natures, and this was followed by a separate discussion on the office of Christ (*de officio Christi*). I treat these together on the grounds that the three offices—prophet, king, priest—are inherent to the originary symbolization and that theories of the two natures and of atonement are explications of these prior symbols.

It is often overlooked that there is no dogma of the incarnation as such in the New Testament. Incarnation theory is the product of theological development, of evangelical explication. The scriptural witness contains a number of symbols drawn from the linguistic and cultural context of first-century Palestine that were used to convey the conviction that the God of Israel had acted decisively and uniquely in the life, death, and resurrection of Jesus of Nazareth. Symbolic appellations such as messiah, Son of David, Son of man, Son of God, and Emmanuel were rooted in the Hebrew tradition. As the church began to branch out into the wider Greco-Roman world, these symbols began to require further clarification, interpretation, and development. The dominant light source shining on the intellectual horizon was late Platonic philosophy, and so the early apologists began to think through the biblical symbols in the categories of Greek metaphysics. The contextualization and engagement principles employed by the patristics in large part led to the great debates between the Council of Nicea in 325 and the Council of Chalcedon in 451 and the fixing of the main creedal formulations that have been handed down to the present day. These formulations continue to give shape to Christology across the spectrum of Christianity, including the Eastern Orthodox, Roman Catholic, and Protestant communions. The agreements were reached before any of these great divisions arose.

The issue that prompted the original christological controversies and that continues to energize discussion down to this day is the Emmanuel question: just how is God with us in Jesus Christ? Just how does the Beyond become Intimate in this person? I call this the Emmanuel question because it is rooted in the biblical symbol of Emmanuel (meaning "God with us"), the title given the infant Jesus when being conceived by his virgin mother (Isa. 6:14; Matt. 1:23). The christological concern is to explicate the meaning of Emmanuel.

JESUS CHRIST AS PROPHET, KING, AND PRIEST

The seed for the *triplex munus* or threefold office of Christ was growing slowly for a millennium and a half until harvested during the period of the Reformation. The honorific titles of prophet, king, and priest were first grafted together during intertestamental times by the Testament of Levi 8:14 and applied to John Hyrcanus (134–104 B.C.) to signify Yahweh's approval of his leadership. Philo gathered up all three offices into the person of Moses, even employing a bit of Platonic thought by dubbing Israel's founding prophet a philosopher-king. The threefold office was pruned for Christ in Eusebius's *Church History* of the fourth century.[1] It sprouted occasionally in the work of John Chrysostom, Augustine, and Thomas and appeared in the Catechism of the Council of Trent. Luther seemed to focus only on two offices, priest and king, although in his *Christian Liberty* Christ as priest seems to include much of what we think of as prophet. The seeds of the *triplex munus* were resown in Protestant soil by Andreas Osiander about 1530, followed by Martin Bucer in 1536. Then it was John Calvin who cultivated it for eventual harvest by seventeenth-century Protestant orthodoxy.

Because the words *messiah* and *Christ* mean "anointed one," Calvin argues that they should apply to the three offices of prophet, priest, and king. Why? Because each of these biblical roles is identified with an anointing and because Jesus as mediator between God and the human race has fulfilled them. Christ is the eschatological prophet, and "the perfect doctrine he has brought has made an end to all prophecies." Christ is the eternal and spiritual king who "arms and equips us with his power, adorns us with his beauty and magnificence, enriches us with his wealth." Christ is the great high priest "because by the sacrifice of his death he blotted out our own guilt and made satisfaction for our sins."[2]

Calvin's approach to the three offices is an attempt to draw out the salvific implications of the two-natures doctrine.[3] He understands Christ as the mediator who bridges the gulf between God and humankind, and this mediation absolutely requires that Christ be both divine and human. That he be Emmanuel and that he share "our common nature" are requisite to making his salvation effective for us. Therefore, Calvin asks of

---

1. Eusebius *Church History* 1.3.
2. Calvin, *Inst.*, 2.15.1–6.
3. Perhaps I should note in passing that my method is the reverse of Calvin's. Calvin took the Chalcedonian formulation of the two natures as axiomatic and then explicated it with the biblical symbols, which was typical of the loci method of systematic theology in times past. My method grants priority to the biblical symbols and then critically reassesses the way they have been explicated at various points in the history of the church.

each office: what is its meaning or benefit "for us"? Because the mediator is prophet we now know the truth about the Father's grace. Because the mediator is king he could be victorious over death and the devil; and now through the indwelling of the Holy Spirit he empowers us to overcome temptation and attends to our spiritual destiny in heaven. Because the mediator is priest he can render expiation for our sins and present us blameless before the throne of grace. It is because Christ is who he is that his work accrues to our benefit. The Westminster Shorter Catechism explicates the *triplex munus* this way:

Question 24: How doth Christ execute the office of Prophet?
Answer: Christ executeth the office of a Prophet in revealing to us by his Word and Spirit the will of God for our salvation.

Question 25: How doth Christ execute the office of Priest?
Answer: Christ executeth the office of Priest in his once offering up of himself a sacrifice to satisfy divine justice, and reconcile us to God, and in making continual intercession for us.

Question 26: How doth Christ execute the office of King?
Answer: Christ executeth the office of a King in subduing us to himself, in ruling and defending us, and in restraining and conquering all his and our enemies.

John Wesley employs the *triplex munus* to describe the work of Christ in the life of the believer. The work of Christ is not simply a once for all accomplishment resting already completed at some time in the past. In each of his three offices, Christ is at work today.

The holiest of men still need Christ as their Prophet, as "the light of the world." For He does not give them light but from moment to moment: the instant He withdraws, all is darkness. They still need Christ as their King; for God does not give them a stock of holiness. But unless they receive a supply every moment, nothing but unholiness would remain. They still need Christ as their Priest, to make atonement for their holy things. Even perfect holiness is acceptable to God only through Jesus Christ.[4]

The concept of the *triplex munus* has found wide usage, but it does have its critics. Albrecht Ritschl says the doctrine is inconsistent because the office of king belongs to Christ strictly in his exalted state, whereas the roles of prophet and priest belong to the historical Jesus during his earthly humiliation.[5] Wolfhart Pannenberg similarly rejects any application of the *triplex munus* to the pre-Easter Jesus, and will not grant that the offices of prophet and priest accurately apply to Jesus in the state of earthly

---

4. John Wesley, *A Plain Account of Christian Perfection* (1767; reprint, London: Epworth, 1952), 72–73.
5. Albrecht Ritschl, *The Christian Doctrine of Justification and Reconciliation* (Clifton, N.J.: Reference Book Publishers, 1966), 3:422–31.

humiliation. The pre-Easter Jesus did not hold any offices, he argues.[6] The criticisms offered by Ritschl and Pannenberg will not inhibit my use of the *triplex munus* here because I treat the biblical references to prophet, king, and priest as metaphorical symbols that are equiprimordial with the biblical picture of Jesus; and I conceive of systematic theology as a second-order reflection upon these symbols. The primary symbols themselves do not make this distinction between the pre-Easter Jesus and the exalted Christ, as 1 Corinthians 15:3b makes clear: "Christ died for our sins." The text does not say "Jesus died for our sins." Thus, the earliest proclamation of the gospel starts with Jesus as the Christ of God. To speak of the historical Jesus as if he were not yet the Christ—not yet God's prophet, king, or priest—is to offer a historical reconstruction. It is to abstract the historical Jesus from the actual symbols with which we have to work. It is to pursue speculation. We start from New Testament symbols that depict Jesus as the Christ. Going behind the text to the pre-Christ Jesus is a form of critical analysis of the symbols themselves. But such critical analysis does not automatically forbid reference to the symbols when organizing evangelical explication. Thus, I feel justified here to treat the threefold office as a point of departure for theological reflection.

Jesus, the Prophesied King

We apply the title of Christ to Jesus of Nazareth in large part because we understand his birth, life, teachings, ministry, passion, death, and resurrection as the fulfillment of certain prophecies (Luke 24:25-27). The title Christ is a Greek translation, Χριστός, of the Hebrew מָשִׁיחַ (messiah). It literally means "anointed one" and refers to the person anointed by the prophet to be king over Israel. The first messiah was the first king, Saul (1 Sam. 24:6). Samuel was reluctant to anoint Saul because in the prophet's mind Yahweh alone was king. The significance of Saul's anointing despite Samuel's better judgment is that the messiah is clearly understood as an extension of God's rule, but in no way is the messiah to be confused with God.

The seed that eventually sprouts as the expectation of an eschatological messiah who will come at the end of time to establish the eternal reign of God is sown by Nathan the prophet when he announces to King David that his dynasty will endure. "Your throne shall be established forever," he tells David (2 Sam. 7:16). Nathan, like Samuel before him, was worried that the terrestrial king might usurp powers and prerogatives belonging only to the heavenly king. Nathan's fear proved justified, just as Samuel's had. Saul, David, and even Solomon overstepped the boundary of representing the true king, Yahweh, and used their power

---

6. Wolfhart Pannenberg, *Jesus—God and Man*, 2d ed. (Philadelphia: Westminster, 1977), 212–25.

for self-advancement. This resulted in the gradual and violent loss of the kingdom and the repeated threat that Nathan's prophecy was subject to nullification by the events of history. With no kingdom how could David's throne endure?

While the prophets were announcing the doom of the kingdom because of repeated sins of pretentiousness on the part of kings of dwindling stature, a desire began to grow to have Yahweh act unilaterally and decisively to establish God's reign. Instead of dallying with one corrupt monarch after another, what was needed was a special heaven-sent messiah—but still a descendant of David—who would be immune to sin and who would reestablish the nation of Israel. Thus there is an ambivalence. On the one hand, Yahweh is declared the only true king, which seems to exclude an overlap of authority with the province of a human messiah (Isa. 24:23; Obad. 21; Zeph. 3:15; Zech. 14:9). On the other hand, the corruptibility of human nature even if anointed seems to doom Israel to apostasy, sin, warranted judgment, and destruction. What is needed, therefore, is for Yahweh to supply a messiah through whom God can rule without impediment—a messiah through whom Yahweh can become Emmanuel, God with us.

This brings us to the Emmanuel prophecy in Isaiah. The context is that Isaiah is counseling King Ahaz in 734 B.C. regarding his possible alliance with or opposition to Assyria's Tiglath-Pileser. He announces that the Lord will give Ahaz a sign: "Look, the young woman is with child and shall bear a son, and shall name him Immanuel" (Isa. 7:14b). Although the context could possibly indicate that the sign was to appear within Ahaz's own generation, the title Emmanuel becomes applied to Jesus in Matthew 1:23. The Hebrew word עַלְמָה (*almah*), denoting a young woman of marriageable age who has most likely not known a man, is rendered παρθένος, specifying her virginity, in the Septuagint and in the New Testament. Although some have sought to exploit the element of ambiguity in the translation from the Hebrew to the Greek, there is no doubt that the author of Matthew intended to say "virgin." The verses immediately preceding describe her conception as due to the Holy Spirit, not Joseph. That virginity may or may not be important in the Isaiah passage is beside the point. Perhaps even the original context at the time of Ahaz is irrelevant. The real force of Matthew's description of Jesus as born of a celestial Father and a terrestrial mother is to dramatize the significance of the term *Emmanuel*. God is really with us.

Isaiah proceeds to develop further the messianic expectation with the visionary passages in chapters 9 and 11. He says the people will see a great light, and knowledge of God will spread throughout the land. A shoot from the stump of Jesse, David's father, will grow and branch out. His delight will be in the Lord. He will rule the people with justice; he will give dignity to the meek; and he will rescue the poor from their oppression. The whole of nature will rejoice in his rule: leopards and goats, lions and calves will lie down in the presence of a small child.

> For a child has been born for us,
>   a son given to us;
> authority rests upon his shoulders;
>   and he is named
> Wonderful Counselor, Mighty God,
>   Everlasting Father, Prince of Peace. (Isa. 9:6)

In Deutero-Isaiah, as in Amos and other prophets, we find no expectation of a figure corresponding to the messiah. This is due most likely to the assumption that Yahweh will be king at the time of salvation (Isa. 52:7). Many are the instruments that Yahweh can employ to execute the divine reign, including Cyrus of Persia, whom Yahweh refers to as an "anointed" one (Isa. 45:1). What will eventually become important, however, is Deutero-Isaiah's description of the suffering servant. It is definitely not a typical reference to the messiah such as we have found in the other prophets. But that it might possibly refer to the fulfillment of Nathan's promise is found in a slight hint: the servant is a young plant growing like a root out of dry ground (Isa. 53:2). Could this have been designed to connote the shoot from Jesse's stump? Whether this harks back to the prophecy of First Isaiah or not, it is clear that the servant of the Lord here takes over the messianic function of establishing justice. Yahweh will put the Spirit upon him; he will bring the prisoners out of their dungeons, give light to the blind, and bring forth justice to the ends of the earth (Isa. 42:1-7). The servant accomplishes this through suffering, an efficacious suffering in the form of a sacrifice that atones for humanity's sin.

> He was despised and rejected by others;
>   a man of suffering and acquainted with infirmity;
> and as one from whom others hide their faces
>   he was despised, and we held him of no account.
> Surely he has borne our infirmities
>   and carried our diseases;
> yet we accounted him stricken,
>   struck down by God, and afflicted.
> But he was wounded for our transgressions,
>   crushed for our iniquities;
> upon him was the punishment that made us whole. (Isa. 53:3-5a)

Some mystery remains regarding Isaiah 53. About whom is it written? Is the servant the nation of Israel as a whole? Or is it an individual representing the nation? And if it is an individual, is it a prophet, a priest, or a king? Although some Jews in the time of Jesus were willing to transform the notion of the messiah to include the notion of suffering, many simply assumed the two figures were different. Deutero-Isaiah's original intent is not clear.

What is clear is that the New Testament understands the mission of Christ in terms of the suffering servant and synthesizes it with that of the messiah. The messiah accomplishes his work through suffering. Jesus speaks of his own sufferings as having been written of in advance (Mark 9:12). He describes his own ministry and passion as that of a servant who gives his life as a ransom for many (Matt. 20:28). Paul, reiterating that "all have sinned," understands the redemptive work of Christ as an "atonement by his blood" on account of which God passes over our sins and renders us just (Rom. 3:23-26). The net effect is that Deutero-Isaiah's suffering servant becomes a prophecy fulfilled by Jesus the Christ.

The figure of the Son of man found in apocalyptic literature plays a role somewhat parallel to the suffering servant. Although mentioned briefly in Daniel 7:13, the image of the Son of man is most fully developed in the Similitudes of Enoch (Enoch 37–71), probably written in Hebrew and Aramaic about two centuries prior to the time of Jesus. Sometimes called the Elect One, he possesses the spirit of wisdom, understanding, and power. He sits on the throne of glory as the judge, and at the resurrection he elects those deemed righteous and holy. God has been keeping the Elect One hidden up until now, but soon he will be revealed in all his majesty. Thus, although not specifically designated the messiah, the Son of man takes over some of the messianic duties such as sitting on the throne and establishing justice.

According to Mark and the other Synoptic Gospels, Jesus refers to himself as the Son of man. In fact, it is his most frequent title. The Son of man has the power to forgive sins (Mark 2:10), is lord over the Sabbath (Mark 2:28), is betrayed into the hands of sinners (Mark 14:41), and will be seen coming on the clouds in great power and glory (Mark 13:26; 14:62). Combining allusions to the suffering servant as well as Hosea 6:2, the Synoptics have Jesus predict that "the Son of man is to be betrayed into human hands, and they will kill him, and three days after being killed, he will rise again" (Mark 9:31).

The Gospel of Mark also contains a clever play on the ambiguity of the phrase "Son of man" (ὁ υἱὸς τοῦ ἀνθρώπου, also translated "Human One"); on the one hand, this play on words emphasizes the Son of man's humanity in contrast to animals and angels while, on the other hand, connoting the heavenly champion expected by Enoch. The theme of the gospel as a whole is not ambiguous, however. It is the assertion that Jesus, the Son of man, is really the Son of God (ὁ υἱὸς τοῦ Θεοῦ) (Mark 1:1; 15:39).

There is some debate as to just how closely Jesus identified himself with the Son of man figure. On occasion he speaks of the Son of man in the third person, as if he were speaking about someone entirely different

(Matt. 24:27, 44). This has led some scholars to posit that Jesus did not claim to be the Son of man, and that the reasons the Synoptics (and even John 1:51) depict Jesus calling himself such are the theological agenda of the early church and the work of the Synoptic redactors. These scholars claim the primitive church developed a "Son of man Christology" that it read back into Jesus' teachings regarding himself.

However, there is a weakness in this argument. In general, early Christology did not develop the Son of man theme very far. That Jesus came to be thought of in post–New Testament times as the messiah, the Christ, and the Son of God indicates the direction the Christology of the early church actually followed. The Son of man designation seems to hit a virtual dead end with the New Testament evangelists. These facts indicate it is very likely that Jesus called himself the Son of man, but his followers got only minimal use out of the term. Nevertheless, I grant that this counter-argument is less than fully decisive.[7] No argument to date is. That someone found it necessary to understand what Jesus was doing in terms of this apocalyptic image is clear. What is less than fully clear is whether it was first done by Jesus himself or by his followers.

It is fully clear, however, that the New Testament story of Jesus incorporates the notion that this man from Nazareth is the anointed one, the messiah whom God sent to fulfill the promises of old. Jesus is the true king because he fully represents God; and, because of his sacrificial suffering, he does not corrupt his kingly power in the name of his own personal pretentiousness.

Jesus, the Prophesier of the Kingdom

A prophet lives in the present and announces the kingdom of God coming in the future. This is what Jesus did too. But the way Jesus did it is more complicated. Somehow Jesus himself belonged to that future kingdom in such a way that the kingly rule of God was already present in Jesus' announcing it. We saw this in the last section—Jesus Christ is understood as the prophesied messiah, God's king who lets God rule, but he also prophesies the coming kingdom. He is both fulfillment and promise.

The sense of urgency and ultimacy that characterized the prophetic attitude is conveyed as well in the teachings of Jesus. "The time is fulfilled, and the kingdom of God has come near," Jesus tells the people of first-century Palestine; "repent, and believe in the good news" (Mark 1:15). He also commits the same message to his disciples, asking them to tell others that the kingdom of God has come near (Matt. 10:7; Luke 10:9). What does "come near" mean? It means that something is within reach for those who repent and believe the gospel. In short, Jesus prophesied and subsequently became thought of as a prophet.

---

7. See James M. Robinson, *A New Quest of the Historical Jesus* (London: SCM, 1959), 101–4.

What has come near? The kingdom of God, the Βασιλεία τοῦ Θεοῦ. The Old Testament prophets had said that God's self-manifestation would be as the sovereign king and Lord. Such prophecy could presuppose, of course, that the Adonai of Israel is already king, the eternal king whose reign will last forever and ever (Exod. 15:18; Ps. 145:11-13). But this eternal reign will become visibly and undeniably manifest in the future eschatological event.

During Jesus' century, what the prophets had previously said was viewed through apocalyptic lenses. When Jesus spoke of the kingdom of God he evoked in his listeners images of the heavenly champion coming on the clouds with great power and glory to defeat the children of darkness and to raise the faithful children of light from death to new life. Regardless of what Jesus himself meant to say, it was simply necessary to employ apocalyptic language and imagery to convey the message.

The teaching and ministry of Jesus both affirm and modify the prophetic and apocalyptic understandings. This happens in a most dramatic way. Jesus creates and conveys a new and elusive relationship between the future and the present. I have been calling it prolepsis, referring to the appearance of the yet outstanding kingdom of God ahead of time, to the presence of the new aeon amid the old aeon.

That the future is arriving ahead of time with Jesus is what is important in his miracles. On one occasion John the Baptist, also a prophet foretelling the coming kingdom of God, sends two of his disciples to Jesus with a question: "Are you the one who is to come, or are we to wait for another?" Jesus gives what seems an evasive answer: "Go and tell John what you have seen and heard: the blind receive their sight, the lame walk, lepers are cleansed, the deaf hear, the dead are raised, the poor have good news brought to them" (Luke 7:19, 22; see Matt. 11:2-6). This apparently roundabout answer is in fact to the point. Jesus is the fulfillment of Isaiah's prophecy (Isa. 35:5-6; 61:1). Jesus is not simply the prophet. He is the prophesied. He is the kingdom come.

This can be further illustrated in his miracles of exorcism. In the case of the dumb demoniac, for example, Jesus casts out the demon so the man could speak again (Matt. 12:22-23; Luke 11:14-15). Skeptics among those watching try to stir things up by murmuring that Jesus is using the power of Beelzebul, the prince of demons, to perform his public magic. But Jesus perceives what they are thinking and then launches into a little speech about kingdoms divided against themselves being subject to collapse. Then he adds, "If it is by the finger of God that I cast out demons, then the kingdom of God has come to you." This miracle is a sign of victory not simply over the demoniac's loss of speech but over the arch-enemy, Satan himself (Luke 10:18). What apocalypticists envisioned as a holy war is taking place here in the life of an individual; and Jesus is the heavenly champion. This is the new note being sounded by Jesus that distinguishes his work from apocalyptic visions in general: the experience of the individual has become the arena of eschatological conflict.[8] What was thought to be future and cosmic has become in Jesus present and individual.

Our relationship to the cosmic future will be determined by our relationship in the present to this one person. A saying usually ascribed to the Q source (Luke 12:8; see Matt. 10:32) makes this clear: "Everyone who acknowledges me before others, the Son of Man also will acknowledge before the angels of God; but whoever denies me before others will be denied before the angels of God."[9] The title Son of man belongs to apocalyptic literature and refers to the heavenly being who at the end of time will separate the righteous from the unrighteous, those destined for salvation from those consigned to damnation. It may not be clear whether or not Jesus is actually asserting that he is the Son of man, but what is unmistakable is the correspondence between one's confession of Jesus in the present and one's relationship to God's kingdom when it comes in its fullness. In Jesus the eschatological fulfillment is appearing ahead of time.

Because Jesus embodies the kingdom in his person he can speak with an authority that is usually reserved for God alone, something only prophets are in the habit of doing. When at Capernaum four men lowered a paralytic through the roof of the house in which he was teaching, Jesus said to the man in need of healing, "Son, your sins are forgiven" (Mark 2:5). Some of the scribes were overheard to say that the forgiveness of sins is something only God can do. The evangelist who wrote the book of Mark reports that "he taught them as one who had authority, and not as the scribes" (Mark 1:22).

The clearest claim to such authority is found in the Sermon on the Mount. In a series of aphorisms Jesus contrasts accepted teaching with his own teaching, linking the two with "but I say," ἐγὼ δὲ λέγω. For example, with obvious reference to the Ten Commandments, Jesus says: "You have heard that it was said to those of ancient times, 'You shall not murder'; and 'whoever murders shall be liable to judgment.' But I say to you that if you are angry with a brother or sister, you will be liable to judgment" (Matt. 5:21-22; see Exod. 20:13; Deut. 5:17; 16:18). Apart from the content of what Jesus is saying, the way he says it makes him supersede Moses, and Moses had hitherto been the prime authority for Jewish piety. In fact, the very setting of this teaching, which calls to mind Mount Sinai and the revelation of the divine Torah, makes clear what the author of Matthew wants to say—namely, Jesus is the new Moses. He speaks for God.

---

8. Norman Perrin, *The Kingdom of God in the Teachings of Jesus* (Philadelphia: Westminster, 1963), 171.

9. Matt. 10:32 puts "I also" (κἀγώ) where Luke 12:8 puts "the Son of Man" (υἱὸς τοῦ ἀνθρώπου).

Taking into consideration the criticism of the *triplex munus* raised by Ritschl and Pannenberg, it is important to note the thesis of the New Quest for the Historical Jesus school that there is some kind of recognizable continuity between the actual life of Jesus and what the apostles and evangelists later report, a bridge between Jesus of Nazareth and the exalted Lord. The basis for that continuity is Jesus' teachings and miracles. The continuity between Jesus and the apostolic preaching consists in a development, a bringing to further expression, of the significance of Jesus' ministry in the only way possible within the prophetic-apocalyptic horizon. This means confessing him as the messianic king and as the prophet of God.

THE CROSS AND THE RESURRECTION

Before examining the third office, that of priest, it is necessary to explore how the crucifixion seemed to demolish hopes that Jesus might be the long-awaited king and prophet, and to see how the Easter resurrection constitutes God's confirmation.

The Need for Confirmation

Two elements in Jesus' teaching make it open to the future, his announcement of the coming kingdom and his claim to divine authority. There is no reason to believe what the carpenter from Nazareth says simply because he says it. What if he is deluded? What if he is just another megalomaniac who only thinks he is God? Those of us who live in modern democracies are used to campaigns wherein political candidates make promises for the future and hire advertising agencies to create an image that rivals divinity. We have learned how to take all this with considerable skepticism. Why not be skeptical of Jesus too? The Sanhedrin who tried Jesus were certainly skeptical. They sought the death penalty on the grounds that he was a blasphemer.

How can we corroborate or refute Jesus' teachings? When we want to know if a prophet is authentic or not we ask if his or her prophecies come true. Each January the *National Enquirer* publishes the predictions for the year made by ten or so self-proclaimed psychic prophets. Occasionally the *Skeptical Inquirer* gathers together the relevant statistics to compare these predictions with the actual course of events. The percentage of accuracy is uninspiringly low. So also the Old Testament recognized that prophets could be victims of misleading and deceptive visions, making the distinction between false and true prophets important (Lam. 2:14). It is not unreasonable then to ask about Jesus' prophecies regarding the coming of God's kingdom. Should the course of history roll on everlastingly without the kingdom ever coming, then we surely would agree that this prophet ought not be honored in his own country, or any other for that matter (Matt. 13:57). Jesus' teaching requires confirmation from the future.

This has a direct bearing on Jesus' claim to authority as well. He more or less assumes he is speaking directly for God. What does God think? Does God agree? This question is on the mind of the Pharisees who demand a sign from heaven (Mark 8:11-12; Matt. 12:38-42; Luke 11:16, 29-32). Jesus indicates he does not like the attitude of the questioners, calling them an "adulterous generation" because they cannot see the presence of God standing before their very eyes. In apocalyptic language, the Elect One remains hidden beneath the vicissitudes of history, and the Pharisees' vision fails to perceive this presence because they lack faith. So Jesus says he denies them the privilege of seeing a sign. But this is not quite true. Jesus is exaggerating. The signs are there, as Jesus himself affirms in the case of John the Baptist mentioned above. But they are ambiguous. It is not crystal clear that they portend the kingdom of God. To be certain we must await the arrival of the kingdom for their confirmation as such.

The Disappointment of the Cross

Churches today prominently display the cross above the altar, on the rooftop, emblazoned on books and vestments, and wherever else something needs decorating. The cross has become a favorite form of jewelry, sparkling beneath a pierced ear or purveying masculinity while nestled in chest hair and hanging from a neckchain. But this represents a change in symbolic meaning from that first experienced by Jesus and his followers. The cross originally meant death, disappointment, and dashed hopes. The hoped-for divine confirmation of Jesus' ministry appeared to disintegrate amid the political intrigue and jeering crowds of Jerusalem at Passover time. The messianic champion was reduced to a bruised corpse of a failed seditionist. Instead of the expected divine confirmation of the Nazarene's ministry and authority, it appeared that history had disconfirmed in a most drastic way all hope for salvation through Jesus Christ. In the words of Origen's *Commentary on Matthew*, instead of our salvation coming on the clouds with great power and glory what we got was *mors turpissima crucis*, "the utterly vile death of the cross."

In first-century Palestine the cross was a symbol of failure, shame, and utmost humiliation. The Jews were conscious of the statement in the Torah that "anyone hung on a tree is under God's curse" (Deut. 21:23). Therefore death by crucifixion was avoided except in the most extreme cases, such as high treason. Only someone who would betray his or her own people to a foreign power could warrant being subjected to this utmost dishonor, to the curse of God. Thus, despite the political difficulties of God's chosen people through history, the cross could never become a symbol of Jewish suffering. A crucified messiah would be unthinkable. No wonder the preaching of the early Christians was so offensive to Judaism. Hence, Paul's description of the gospel as a "stumbling block to Jews" (1 Cor. 1:23; see Gal. 5:11).

Outside Judaism crucifixion was widely practiced in the ancient world as punishment for the most heinous of crimes and as an opportunity to release the forces of sadism lurking within the human soul. We know from the writings of Cicero that crucifixion was for the Romans the supreme penalty, considered worse than burning (*crematio*), decapitation (*decollatio*), or being eaten by wild beasts (*damnatio ad bestias*). The list of crimes punishable by crucifixion included desertion to the enemy, the betraying of secrets, incitement to rebellion, murder, prophecy about the welfare of rulers, nocturnal impiety, and magic. Because of the shamefulness and humiliation associated with the cross, crucifixion was almost always inflicted on the lower classes. The upper classes were given more humane punishments. It was inflicted especially on slaves as a way of keeping other slaves in line.[10]

In his study of this dismal background of the cross, Martin Hengel asks if there is any evidence in the ancient Roman world for a non-Christian, positive interpretation of death by crucifixion, perhaps in the manner of the death of a philosopher or national martyr. He answers in the negative: "I have not been able to discover a single historical instance."[11] There is no precedent for using the cross to symbolize triumph or victory. Its only possible meanings were shame and humiliation. This is possibly why Jesus' enemies pressed for his crucifixion. It would be the most obvious way to refute any messianic claims. In light of that Hengel comments on what must have been the impression made on first-century listeners to Paul's preaching about the messiah on the cross. That this crucified Jew could truly be a divine being sent to earth, God's Son, the Lord of all and coming judge of the world, must inevitably have been thought by any educated person to be "utter madness and presumptuousness."[12]

Certainly this is how it must have looked to the followers of the Nazarene on Good Friday. That the messiah was not supposed to die, especially in this fashion, was the point of Peter's rebuke at Caesarea Philippi (Mark 8:32). The two men walking toward Emmaus make it clear that they had hoped the man from Nazareth would be the one to redeem Israel, but that hope was frustrated at the crucifixion (Luke 24:20-21). Thus, the death of Jesus on the cross was a grave disappointment because it appeared that the open future was suddenly closed. All possibility of divine confirmation of Jesus' messiahship and prophecy regarding the coming salvation seemed dashed on the rocks of Golgotha. Was God's kingdom

---

10. See Martin Hengel, *Crucifixion* (Philadelphia: Fortress, 1977), 33–34, 59.
11. Ibid., 64.
12. Ibid., 83; see also Hengel, *The Atonement* (Philadelphia: Fortress, 1981), 43.

really coming? Had this potential messiah been anointed only to die? With the loss of Jesus' blood came the loss of hope.

The Significance of the Resurrection

The apocalyptic horizon that provided the context for Jesus' ministry included among other things a concept of the resurrection of the dead, ἀνάστασις ἐκ νεκρῶν. The judgment rendered by the Son of man in Daniel 12:2, for example, presupposed that the dead would rise to face their destiny (see 1 Enoch 51:1; 62:15; 91:10; 92:3; 103:4; Jubilees 23:30). The New Testament's report that the Sadducees did not believe in the resurrection indicates that the matter was under debate and that someone was advocating such a doctrine (Matt. 22:23; Acts 23:8). Jesus seems to have presupposed it when he asserted forcefully but perhaps a bit ambiguously, "He is God not of the dead, but of the living" (Matt. 22:32). Jesus is here employing a concept of a general resurrection that would come at the end of history and initiate the establishment of God's everlasting kingdom. Resurrection was associated with the transformation of the world, with the eschatological and salvific act of God. It was universal in scope. We know of no expectation of an individual resurrection slated for a slain messiah other than the predictive words of Jesus at Caesarea Philippi, which exegetes such as Rudolf Bultmann and Gunter Bornkamm believe were *vaticinia ex eventu*—that is, read back into the text following the experience of Easter (Mark 8:31). Thus, what happened to Jesus on Easter—the resurrection of the crucified one—came as a bit of a surprise. The question became: what does this mean? How should we interpret what has happened?

These questions have been the focus of Wolfhart Pannenberg's illuminating work in Christology. Following Pannenberg's analysis of the significance of Easter, we see, first, that if Jesus has been raised, then the end of the world has begun. His prophetic message has been met with divine fulfillment. This is certainly how Paul interprets it when he describes Jesus as "the first-born within a large family" (Rom. 8:29) and the "first fruits of those who have died" (1 Cor. 15:20; see Col. 1:18; Rev. 1:5). Jesus is the first. The rest of us will follow. The general resurrection of the dead has begun. Jesus leads the way and prefigures what will become universally the case in the future.

The expectation of the end to history was certainly not fulfilled in the world as a whole. It was fulfilled in this one person. The person of Jesus became a microcosm revealing what would happen to the whole, to the macrocosm, or perhaps affirming what was previously thought. As Jesus' destiny led to his demise and resurrection, so also can we expect the world to hit its end and become subject to renewal by God. It was the expectation of the latter that makes sense out of the former. It was the former that confirms belief in the latter.

Second, Easter means, then, that God has confirmed the pre-Easter authority of Jesus. After Jesus' ignominious death on the cross, we could not really justify belief in him without a rather dramatic confirmation by God. This is what happens in the resurrection. In this event God has ratified his Son's claims. Without Easter his accusers would stand correct: Jesus was a blasphemer. He claimed more authority than he had. His prophecies came to naught. But the resounding note of triumph that rang out in early Christian evangelism was that this very Jesus who suffered the curse of the cross was vindicated and even exalted by God through his resurrection from the grave.[13]

Easter does not establish Jesus' divinity for the first time, as if he becomes something he had not been previously. It is confirmation, meaning that God had been fully present and fully at work all along. Nevertheless, the event of the resurrection is decisive regarding Jesus' relation to God, just as our relation to the eschatological future is decisive for determining who we are. This leads Pannenberg to describe God's confirmation of Jesus as a retroactive force. The essence of this man was determined by his future. Easter determines what had been true all along.

Third, it follows from this that the resurrection justifies applying to Jesus titles such as Christ, Son of man, Lord, and Son of God. As suggested earlier, it is possible that Jesus either did not directly claim such titles or, if he did, it was in a muted and contingent form. Jesus certainly did place himself in the position of determining our eschatological destinies. To encounter Christ was to encounter God. To decide for Jesus was to decide for the kingdom of God. That Jesus was justified in doing so is confirmed by his Easter resurrection. The interpretive move to these salvific titles was virtually unavoidable. They were embedded in the experience with Jesus itself.

The title of messiah or Christ was appropriate and perhaps could not be avoided because of the political consequences of Jesus' activity. He was executed under a Roman law designated for punishing agitators and seditionists. The sign nailed to the top of the cross makes clear why he was executed: he wanted to be "king of the Jews" (Mark 15:26). This is misleading in the sense that Jesus did not seek a terrestrial monarchy. "My kingdom is not from this world," he is reported to have told Pi-

---

13. Acts 2:36; 3:25; 5:30; 1 Tim. 3:16. See Pannenberg, *Jesus—God and Man*, 67–73, 135–41, 362–63; Hengel, *Atonement*, 65–66. Hans Dieter Betz complains that there is no textual basis for the thesis that the resurrection of Jesus was primarily understood to be God's authentication of Jesus' expectation or that it was the beginning of the eschatological resurrection of the dead. But Betz offers no counter-analysis of the passages (those in Acts listed above or 1 Cor. 15:20) that seem to demonstrate the thesis (Betz, "The Concept of Apocalyptic in the Theology of the Pannenberg Group," in Robert W. Funk, ed., *Journal for Theology and the Church* [New York: Herder & Herder, 1969], 204). See also Ulrich Wilkens, *Resurrection* (Atlanta: John Knox, 1978), 125, which seems to confirm Pannenberg's notion of confirmation.

late (John 18:36). But the title of messiah still applies because in light of the resurrection there is no longer room for any other bringer of salvation apart from or in addition to Jesus, whose second coming the biblical writers now await. But the nature of the messianic hope becomes transformed. Rather than consisting in a hope for fulfillment through the reestablishment of David's throne in this world of political competition, Jesus' salvation consists in a reconciliation with God that overcomes death and promises life in a divine kingdom that transcends the present aeon. When we add to this transcendent and eschatological notion the idea that Jesus is the criterion—the judge who determines the destiny of the saved and the damned—then the title Son of man applies as well. These two titles become combined with the suffering servant of Isaiah 53 in a new synthesis that affirms the previous prophetic expectation while reinterpreting all three titles in light of the events of Good Friday and Easter.

Fourth, the resurrection signifies the definitive revelation of God. Pannenberg argues that if Jesus, having been raised from the dead, is ascended to God and if thereby the end of the world has begun, then God is ultimately revealed in Jesus. Only at the conclusion of the course of historical events can God be revealed in full divinity as the one who works all things, who has power over all things. Now the end has appeared in advance at Easter. In Jesus the end of all things, which for us has not yet happened, has already occurred. So it can be said of Jesus that ultimate reality is already present in him. Therefore, God in God's glory has made a definitive appearance in the Christ in a way that cannot be surpassed.

We might modify this argument a bit by observing that Pannenberg begins with a quantitative assumption and moves to a qualitative conclusion. He says that it is because all things, quantitatively speaking, have not yet occurred that God is unable to reveal the full divinity. In order to see full divinity we evidently need to be able to see all things, the totality of what is real. How is it possible, though, that in this one person we see this large number of things? It is neither possible nor necessary. I contend rather that it is the qualitative identity of Jesus with the consummate whole of reality that marks him off as definitively revelatory. Here we might distinguish between the totality of individual things and the whole of reality, wholeness being a quality of all things taken together, a quality granted by their consummate relationship with God.

Hence, a better way to express what Pannenberg wishes to say, in my judgment, is to employ the microcosm-macrocosm correlation. The person of Jesus embodies yet represents the history of creation in its entirety. What is true of Jesus is true of God's relationship to history, and vice versa. There is a correlation between his death and resurrection and the eschatological conclusion and transformation of the created order. The renewal of Jesus' life at Easter participates in the same power and the same reality that will transform the mundane order. In Jesus it has happened ahead of time, proleptically. In saying this, I must acknowledge that there is very little here that is quantitatively conceived. We do not now or in the future need to know all of the details of all of the events to appreciate God's creative and redemptive activity. Nor need we know with precision exactly what transformation and renewal mean. To know Christ as the prolepsis is to know that God's glory is revealed, even if we cannot know exactly of what that glory consists.

When this notion of temporal prolepsis becomes interpreted within the horizon of Hellenistic conceptuality, it yields the doctrine of the incarnation. In the child born at Bethlehem and in the man crucified on Golgotha, God is present. The proleptic principle embodying the whole of future reality can be understood as the divine Logos, the word by which creation becomes created. It is the rational principle of cosmic organization taking flesh in this solitary figure. The truth of the whole—even if the truth is not fully understood—becomes present in the part, in the individual person of Jesus.

Fifth, the eschatological and transcendental dimensions of the Easter experience establish the universal significance of the event, a significance that spills well beyond the borders of Israel to include all Gentiles. Although the dominant Hebrew belief was nationalistic and regarded the Gentiles as simply godless and dispensable at the arrival of the messianic kingdom, the Hebrew tradition already harbored signs of a universalistic thrust. Israel was slated to be "a light to the nations" (Isa. 42:6; 49:6). In the latter days all the peoples of the world will flow toward Mount Zion (Mic. 4:1). But these prophetic charges are not enough to establish a Gentile mission. What establishes it theologically is the universality built into the notion of the resurrection as anticipation of the consummate totality of reality. Resurrection applies to everybody, not just Jews.

Historically speaking, however, this is probably not how it went. Jesus (or the Matthean redactor or both) had given a certain priority to his mission within Judaism (Matt. 15:24), and Peter persisted in Jewish exclusivism to the point of arguing with Paul over the matter (Gal. 2:11). The Gentiles of the Gate, lurking near the synagogues of the Diaspora, overheard the Jewish evangelists preaching the gospel to Jewish listeners, and they were the ones who began to ask questions and open up dialogue between Jews and non-Jews. Then it became obvious that the resurrection of Jesus had implications for non-Jews too. The resurrection will be inclusive because God's saving work will be inclusive of the whole of creation.

We need now, in a brief excursus, to draw out the significance of Jesus' resurrection from the dead. We need to ask: can the resurrection of Jesus be considered historical? And if it is historical, what does it mean?

The Historicity of the Resurrection

To ask whether or not the resurrection of Jesus is historical is in fact to ask three questions, not one. The first question is: did anything happen to which we may ascribe the term "resurrection from the dead"? Assuming a positive answer to this, the second question would be: did it happen to Jesus or to the followers of Jesus? And third: what is the relationship between the historical and eschatological dimensions of the event?

The answer to the first question is clearly yes. Even the most skeptical historian must account for the amazing behavior of Jesus' disciples. In the wake of Good Friday, when they saw all their hopes for messianic victory dashed on Calvary, the disciples became frightened and disoriented and wandered back to their homes depressed and disappointed. Yet in a matter of days they were back in the streets boldly proclaiming Jesus' resurrection to many of the same people who had sought to eliminate the influence of the Nazarene through execution. The question is: just what was it that precipitated this dramatic change in the disciples' behavior? It seems clear that something must have happened to cause such a transformation. Jesus' followers claim, of course, that they witnessed the risen one and this refired their hope and enthusiasm. Although their faith died with the crucified one on Good Friday, it too was resurrected with Jesus on Easter Sunday.

In observing this renewed spirit among Jesus' followers, exegetes such as Rudolf Bultmann, Willi Marxsen, and Norman Perrin have argued in answer to our second question that the term *resurrection* actually refers to the rise of faith in the disciples. They claim it does not refer to something that happened to Jesus. Rather than an objective event occurring to the body of the dead rabbi, it is a subjective or existential event occurring to his students who come to faith in the saving efficacy of the cross. Jesus himself remains dead, but his followers proclaim the kerygma that celebrates new life. This proclamation constitutes the birth of the church; and the presence of the kerygma constitutes the presence of the risen Christ in the church. It is this presence that has the power to transform the life of the believer.[14]

Not every contemporary exegete or systematician would agree. The opposing position holds that the term *resurrection* applies primarily and objectively to what happened to Jesus. These exegetes argue that the rise of faith on the part of the disciples and the creation of the church were responses to the resurrection. They were not the resurrection itself. The existential or subjective dimension of faith is a personal appropriation of the significance or meaning of the event. We have previously affirmed

14. Rudolf Bultmann, "New Testament and Mythology," in Hans Werner Bartsch, ed., *Kerygma and Myth* (New York: Harper, 1961), 41; Willi Marxsen, *The Resurrection of Jesus of Nazareth* (Philadelphia: Fortress, 1970), 126–28, 147; Norman Perrin, *The Resurrection* (Philadelphia: Fortress, 1977), 58, 77.

the inextricable presence of such meaning belonging to the event proper. But this does not warrant extricating completely the objective element, according to which we reduce an event to its subjective significance.

Pannenberg, for example, opposes the identification of the Christian faith with a merely subjective conviction, because that would make it indistinguishable from self-delusion. Faith is a response to the knowledge that something happened to Jesus, namely, knowledge that he rose from the dead.[15] Or, as Reginald Fuller puts it, faith is always a response to revelation. It does not create the revelation, and it is not equated with the revelation itself.[16] Against Marxsen and Bultmann, Ulrich Wilkens contends that the resurrection is an actual event that occurred to Jesus. God elevated Jesus out of death, thereby making God's creative omnipotence effective.[17] We may say in sum, then, that the position of Bultmann and Marxsen, according to which the term *resurrection* refers to the rise of faith into the church, begs the question. We need to find and affirm the cause of this rise in faith.

It seems to me that the weight of the evidence and strength of argument fall in favor of the objectivists. One needs to account for the dramatic change in the disposition of the disciples that took place between their disappointment on Good Friday and their subsequent proclamation of the resurrection. To assert as the Bultmannians do that Jesus' body might as well deteriorate in the tomb while the disciples experience a rising of spirits and a new enthusiasm only serves to reask the question. It does not answer it. We still need to know why faith rose and what precipitated it. If there was no external provocation, no objective stimulus such as that supplied by a resurrection that happened to Jesus, then what resources did the disciples find within themselves after Easter that were not there prior to Easter? One searches in vain in Bultmann's theory for an answer to this. It seems much more reasonable to think that the rise of the resurrection faith was a response to just what those who experienced it said it was, namely, the resurrection of Jesus.

This raises the third question regarding the historicity of the resurrection of Jesus: what is the relationship between history and eschatology? Wolfhart Pannenberg and Ulrich Wilkens contend that what happened to Jesus on Easter Sunday morning was a historical event.

On this point Bultmann and Fuller stand together against the historicity school. Their argument is primarily theological: because the resurrection of Jesus is an eschatological event, which signifies the transcendence

---

15. Wolfhart Pannenberg, "The Revelation of God in Jesus of Nazareth," in James M. Robinson and John B. Cobb, Jr., eds., *Theology as History* (New York: Harper & Row, 1967), 128–31.

16. Reginald H. Fuller, *The Formation of the Resurrection Narratives* (Philadelphia: Fortress, 1980), vii, 169.

17. Wilkens, *Resurrection*, 122–24.

of history, it is improper to refer to Easter as historical. Within history, Bultmann argues, dead people do not rise. This includes Jesus. Within history everything is subject to the closed causal nexus of natural law. This means dead people stay dead. If we wish to talk about resurrection, we must talk eschatologically.[18]

Being eschatological, then, resurrection occurs at the end of history, the point of exit from the course of events. What comes at the end of history is not open to direct observation because of its transcendent character. Ordinary methods of historical research cannot check up on reports of eschatological activity. The resurrection is other-worldly, not this-worldly. Hence, Fuller places Easter at the boundary between history and metahistory, between this age and the age to come.[19] It seems to me that Fuller overstates his own case when he so flatly denies the historicity of the resurrection, because consistent with his own understanding he can make the following statement: "The eschatological future . . . cannot happen until the End. What can happen within this age is a certain event which is perfectly explicable as a historical event, yet is a disclosure of the transcendent and eschatological to the eye of faith." Fuller needs to decide the matter one way or the other. If the resurrection is nonhistorical, then it cannot be called an event. Events are historical by definition. If Fuller thinks of the resurrection as an event, then it should follow that it is (at least in some sense) historical.[20] Evidently, for Fuller to stand at the boundary between history and metahistory means to cross it and cease to be historical at all.

It seems to me that the weight of conjecture here falls on the side of supporting Pannenberg with Wilkens. I wholeheartedly grant and affirm the theological point made by Bultmann and Fuller that the resurrection of Jesus is eschatological in character. This is essential to the concept of prolepsis with which I am working: the future consummation of all things has appeared ahead of time in the Christ-event. But it is also true that since the time of the original Easter, history has rolled on for two millennia. During this time the Easter-event has become one force among others influencing the course of subsequent events. We can observe this historically. If it were not for Easter, the church would not have come into existence, and the story of the last twenty centuries would be very different.

To press the challenge of historicity: if what happened on that first Easter was not a historical event, then how do we account for its subsequent cultural, social, political, and ecclesiastical influence? How could

---

18. Bultmann, "New Testament and Theology," 38–40.
19. Fuller, *Formation of the Resurrection Narratives*, x, 22–23. This is the position of neoorthodoxy in general, and Karl Barth in particular (*Word of God and Word of Man* [1924; reprint, New York: Harper, 1957], 90).
20. Fuller, *Formation of the Resurrection Narratives*, 181.

a nonhistorical nonevent have such an influence? There must be a historical dimension to Jesus' resurrection, even if in saying so we do not mean its historicity exhausts its eschatological significance. It seems we must conceive of God's action in raising Jesus to be an intervention into history as well as a form of ending history. Therefore, even though in one sense the resurrection is definitely eschatological in character, it is also inescapably historical. It is this that we affirm when using the concept of prolepsis: the eschatological new reality has entered the flow of historical events in the person of Jesus. Even though the fullness of its transforming power remains outstanding, it has come to authentic expression in the person of Jesus as one event among others within finite history.

Now in saying this I am not suggesting that historical argument is a substitute for theological interpretation. What we can say historically is that something dramatic happened that transformed Jesus' disciples, but exactly what that event was is somewhat open. To affirm that the risen Jesus is the Christ of God and "my Lord" requires an act of faith and involves a theological interpretation as well as a historical judgment.

Finally, the words reported to have been said by the resurrected Jesus to his disciples serve to interpret the resurrection itself. They explicate the significance inherent in the event proper. Jesus' words to Mary Magdalene, to the two men along the road to Emmaus, to his disciples in the upper room, or to doubting Thomas add nothing different. They serve to draw out and make sense of the event while still being a part of the event and, hence, belong to the actual resurrection experience itself. As we look back on things through the eyes of scripture, the records of these incidents and of what Jesus said all belong to the single symbol complex that we know as Easter.

ONE EMMANUEL WITH TWO NATURES

The historicity of the whole event of salvation—resurrection included— has led Christology down the path it has taken. Once the significance of the resurrection began to settle in, a retroactive interpretation of the events of Jesus' birth and career as a teacher, miracle worker, and victim of crucifixion began. The presence and saving activity of God could now be seen more clearly than before. What had previously been merely a series of incidents in the unwritten biography of the carpenter's son from Nazareth could now be assessed as a totality. Jesus' life could be viewed as a whole, and something awesomely dramatic was perceived. The creator had become the created. The eternal had entered time. The future had become present. The infinite had become finite. The impassible had become subject to suffering. The immortal had become subject to death. The king had become servant. The affirmation of Christ's full historicity became necessary if we were to take seriously the presence of Emmanuel and the effectiveness of his saving work.

The Tension in Emmanuel

Just as there is an ongoing tension in the human metaxy between soil and spirit, a healthy Christology maintains a parallel tension between the divinity and humanity of Jesus Christ. Never absent is the temptation to relieve the tension by weakening or eliminating one of the poles. Should we ever yield to the temptation we would lose the concept of Emmanuel, God with us.

That such a tension should be vigorously maintained was not immediately obvious to the first Christian thinkers. It developed over time due to controversy. Trains of christological thought followed different tracks in different times and places, and occasionally these tracks crossed. Where they crossed collisions took place. What followed was reconstruction—that is, evangelical explication at a more conscious level. We have already seen how conflicting explications produced the trinitarian controversy with its climax at Nicea in 325. But a climax is not necessarily a conclusion, and the controversy broke out in new form. This led to a second climax at Chalcedon in 451, which made clear to the church for the subsequent millennium and a half that "Emmanuel" means God and humanity are united in the one person, Jesus Christ. The theme at Nicea was life within the divine, the relation of God to God. Now the theme had shifted to the dwelling of God within our life, to the relation of God to humanity in Jesus Christ. After reaffirming as confessional the Niceno-Constantinopolitan Creed, the theologians meeting at Chalcedon affirmed

one and the same Son, our Lord Jesus Christ, at once complete in manhood, truly God and truly man, consisting also of a reasonable soul and body; of one substance [ὁμοούσιος] with the Father as regards his godhead, and at the same time of one substance [ὁμοούσιος] with us as regards his manhood, ... recognized in two natures [ἐν δύο φύσεσιν], without confusion, without change, without division, without separation, the distinction of natures being in no way annulled by the union, but rather the characteristics of each nature being preserved and coming together to form one person and one hypostasis [ἓν πρόσωπον καὶ μίαν ὑπόστασιν].

The concept of nature (φύσις) here refers to a general or universal quality, the quality of divinity shared with each member of the Trinity and the quality of humanity shared with the rest of us terrestrial mortals. The concept of hypostasis refers to what is individual, to the particular person of Jesus. The position taken by Chalcedon has been called "dyophysite," because united in this person yet unmixed and unconfused we find two natures.

Why explicate the incarnation in dyophysite fashion? Chalcedon here was seeking to maintain the tensive difference between the absoluteness and relatedness of God, between the high God, the Beyond, which the preexistent Logos was rapidly becoming, and the lamb, the Intimate one, who is the vehicle of grace. On the one hand, it would take a God who is eternal and impassible to provide the gift of eternal life; but on the other hand, it would take a historical person subject to suffering and death to deliver the saving gift. This polar tension is reflected in the repeated and generally agreed upon concept of the two natures in one person, according to which Jesus Christ is impassible in his divine nature and susceptible to suffering in his human nature. He is at once both the eternal Logos and the carpenter from Nazareth. He is at once both the Son of God and the new Adam. He is a single person with two natures, one divine and one human. This is the point of the incarnation. This doubleness and singleness are required to explicate the significance of Emmanuel, God with us. The Chalcedonian formula keeps both poles together in a single unity while maintaining for all time the tension between them.

The Chalcedonian formula, interestingly enough, paralleled but reversed the trinitarian formula. In the case of the Trinity, Nicea had acknowledged three persons (πρόσωποι) with one common essence (οὐσία). Chalcedon was now acknowledging that Jesus Christ is one person (πρόσωπον) understood as one hypostasis (ὑπόστασις), but with two natures. He shares one essence (ὁμοούσια) with God and one essence (ὁμοούσια) with humanity.

Subsequent centuries have shown, of course, that not everyone has wanted to follow the track laid out by Chalcedon. For example, very quickly two alternative Christologies became especially important, the Nestorian and the monophysite. All agreed that there is one person Jesus Christ. Yet that one person represents the unity of one nature and one hypostasis for the monophysites, two natures and one hypostasis for the Chalcedonians, and two natures and two hypostases for the Nestorians. Such differences of theological opinion in the days of heresies, anathemas, and excommunication meant a fracturing of the body of Christ. The irony is that while the unity of the person of Christ was being affirmed the church was becoming permanently divided.[21]

This brings us back to the ecumenical principle. We can say that at the time of the Niceno-Constantinopolitan Creed there existed a virtual churchwide orthodoxy—that is, what comes close to a pan-Christian unity. Even today we refer to the Nicene confession as an "ecumenical creed" because it is next to impossible to find a Christian who disagrees with what it says. But this is not the case with the Chalcedonian formulation. It is quite possible to be pro-Nicea yet anti-Chalcedon.

---

21. *CT*, 2:37.

Emmanuel during the Reformation

Although all parties during the Reformation of the sixteenth century accepted without question the Chalcedonian formula, the christological problem made its appearance in debates over the communication of attributes (*communicatio idiomatum*). Can the human Jesus take on the attributes of God and remain human? Can God take on human attributes and remain divine? Ignatius had already implicitly answered in the affirmative when writing against the Gnostics. He would speak of "the blood of God" or use antinomies such as "God existing in the flesh; true life in death; both of Mary and of God."[22] The idea of the *communicatio idiomatum* was further developed by the Alexandrian theologians, according to whom the flesh of Jesus shares in the properties of the Logos while remaining flesh. Conversely, the Logos shares in the properties of the flesh while remaining Logos.

The Lutherans took with utmost seriousness this concept of the communication of attributes. Luther himself explicated the incarnation in these terms. He understood the *kenosis* (Phil. 2:6-7: "He emptied himself...") as descriptive of Jesus' continuing attitude of self-sacrifice, of his willingness to allow the pangs and pains of human despair to have an impact on his divine nature. Luther did not interpret Christ's self-emptying in an ontological sense as did some kenotic theologians, according to whom the incarnation signified the abandoning of the divine nature in favor of a strictly human one. For Luther the divine nature was present throughout the earthly life of Jesus, suffering the slings and arrows of human fortune.

This led the Lutherans to affirm theopassianism—that is, the notion that God genuinely suffers. This is not the same as patripassianism, according to which God as Father suffers. Rather, it affirms that due to the communication of attributes in the person of Christ, Jesus' experience of suffering as a human being is simultaneously a divine experience. Ulrich Zwingli could not accept this, arguing with considerable historical precedent that "strictly speaking, the suffering appertains only to the humanity."[23] Zwingli dubbed *alloeosis* any statement that ascribed to the deity a quality belonging to the humanity, or vice versa. But the Formula of Concord, while admitting that "the deity surely cannot suffer and die," went on to quote Luther to the effect that "since the divinity and humanity are one person in Christ, the Scriptures ascribe to the deity, because of this personal union, all that happens to the humanity, and vice versa.... [Therefore] it is correct to talk about God's death." This is

---

22. Ignatius *Ephesians* 1; 7.
23. Ulrich Zwingli, *On the Lord's Supper*, The Library of Christian Classics, vol. 24 (Philadelphia: Westminster, 1953), 213.

important because our salvation depends on it. "If it is not true that God died for us, but only a man died, we are lost."[24]

The Reformed tradition has been reluctant to follow the Lutheran track in this matter. Zwingli thought of the communication of attributes as a mere figure of speech because, as we saw earlier, for him there could not be, strictly speaking, any such communication. But John Calvin did not reject the *communicatio idiomatum* outright. He approved of it. Nevertheless, comparing his enthusiasm for the doctrine to that of the Lutherans would be like comparing a candle to a forest fire. He finds examples of the communication of attributes in various scriptural passages, noting that they would be "quite unconvincing" if the Bible did not have divine authority standing behind it. As with the bulk of theologians in Chalcedonian times, Calvin could not conceive of the possibility that God could really suffer and experience crucifixion. He acknowledges New Testament passages such as "God purchased the church with his blood" (Acts 20:28) and "the Lord of glory was crucified" (1 Cor. 2:8), but then he asserts: "Surely God does not have blood, does not suffer, cannot be touched with human hands."[25] It follows that the dirty work was borne by Christ, but God was able to maintain pristine divinity untouched by the whole affair of the incarnation.

This led Lutherans in the heat of battle to accuse the Reformed churches of Nestorianism. The Reformed theologians in turn leveled the charge of monophysitism against the Lutherans. In reality, of course, the theological troops on both sides belonged well within the Chalcedonian camp. But they were battling for slightly different territory. The driving direction of the Lutheran theology of the cross was toward the revelation of the sublime godhead in the humble and humiliated humanity of Jesus. Reformed thought was advancing toward a slightly different objective, namely, an emphasis on the sovereignty of God acting in free grace through the incarnation. This is something the Lutherans would never deny, of course; but the difference lies primarily in the relentless concern of the Reformed thinkers to assert divine sovereignty and independence and to stand against the threat of those qualities being merged and dissolved in the humanity that God assumes in Jesus Christ. Thus, the Reformed thinkers looked with suspicion on the Lutheran proposal, seeing a tendency toward the divinization of Jesus' humanity along with the de-divinization of his divinity.

---

24. The words of Luther quoted in "The Formula of Concord," Solid Declaration Article 8, *BC*, 599.

25. Calvin, *Inst.*, 2.14.2; see François Wendel, *Calvin* (New York: Harper, 1963), 220–24. The Acts 20:28 passage is ambiguous, ending in αἵματος τοῦ ἰδίου, which could refer reflexively to God's blood or, if the noun *Son* is implied, then the blood of God's Son. The NRSV opts to translate it "the blood of his [God's] own Son."

The Calvinists found that the sovereignty of God could be protected with an Antiochene emphasis on the incarnation as indwelling, according to which God is genuinely incarnate in Christ but not exhaustively so. Even though God is present in Jesus Christ, God does not cease to dwell in heaven as well. God's divinity does not leave its eternal and immutable habitat to become enclosed within the flesh as in a cell. This doctrine, known as the *extra Calvinisticum*, served to defuse the impact of Lutheran phrases that implied that "God suffered" or "God died." Such phrases, the Reformed thinkers held, refer to the man Jesus who, united with God, suffered and died. Reformed theologians could use such phrases, but in doing so they would take them in a nonliteral sense. In general, it was tenacious loyalty to the Platonized God of the ancient apologists—complete with eternal ineffability and immunity to influence by the course of historical events—that pulled Reformed theology along the track of the *extra Calvinisticum*.

The Crucified God in Current Reformed Theology

Among twentieth-century theologians of the Reformed tradition, a half century ago Karl Barth clearly identified with Zwingli and Calvin over against the Lutherans on this matter.[26] The current Tübingen school of Reformed theology, however, is much more sympathetic to Luther's theology of the cross and is even quite willing to employ Tertullian's ancient phrase "the crucified God." Eberhard Jüngel and Jürgen Moltmann both seek to knock Platonized monotheism off its throne in the courts of Christian theology, saying that belief in God's eternal immutability prevents us from apprehending what is truly revealed in the cross. What is truly revealed in the cross? That God has become Emmanuel and genuinely shares in the suffering of humanity. The safeguards of the *extra Calvinisticum* are thrown away, so that God's heavenly divinity cannot escape being tainted by its involvement in the course of historical events. What is true of Jesus Christ is true of God. That is it, pure and simple. Jüngel goes so far as to contend that God's existence and essence are undifferentiable; therefore, the event of Christ's self-sacrificing love is in fact the essence of God. God's very being, God's essence, is found in this coming into the human sphere. Who God is is the result of what God does, and what God does is act humanly and lovingly.[27]

Moltmann, in his book with the revealing title *The Crucified God*, links the incarnation with the cross in a most dramatic fashion. "When the crucified Jesus is called the 'image of the invisible God,' the meaning is that *this* is God, and God is like *this*. God is not greater than he

---

26. Barth, *CD*, 4/2:66–69, 104–5.
27. Eberhard Jüngel, *God as the Mystery of the World* (Grand Rapids, Mich.: Eerdmans, 1983), 300, 343, 379–80.

is in this humiliation. God is not more glorious than he is in this self-surrender. God is not more powerful than he is in this helplessness. God is not more divine than he is in this humanity."[28]

Where are the safeguards against monophysitism here? Where is the *extra Calvinisticum*? Where is the everlasting divine nature that is not subject to suffering and death? Like Luther, Moltmann does not want to limit suffering and death to the man in Jesus. They apply to God proper, and this is what gives the incarnation its power. Although Moltmann is reluctant to identify his position as theopaschite and would prefer to speak of "death in God" rather than "the death of God," we certainly have here a courageous reaffirmation of Emmanuel that does not shrink from its most dramatic implications.

INCARNATION AND TRINITY

At stake here is our understanding of God. Must we begin with a philosophically produced concept of an immutable spiritual essence that dwells ineffably and eternally in metaphysical isolation from the physical world? Must we then pin that on the divine symbols whenever they appear in New Testament discourse? Or, is God free to define divinity? Is God permitted to be the author of who God is and what God does? Can we take seriously what the voice uttered to Moses from the burning bush: "I will be who I will be"?

The two-natures discussion is a response to an event in which God altered our definition of what constitutes divinity. In the incarnation God ceases to be God in a previously stereotypical sense and enters fully into the plight of human suffering. The history of Jesus is divine history. Through the resurrection of Jesus—and eventually the eschatological consummation wherein the Spirit unites all of creation to its Lord, Jesus Christ—God sweeps the human reality up into the divine life proper. What appears at first to be alien to God is, in fact, God. God defines the Godself through historical action. Our interpretation of this action reveals to us that God is a Trinity.

---

28. Jürgen Moltmann, *The Crucified God* (San Francisco: Harper & Row, 1974), 205; Moltmann's italics.

7

THE WORK AND PERSON
OF JESUS CHRIST

The edges of God are tragedy;
the depths of God are joy, beauty, resurrection, life.
Resurrection answers crucifixion; life answers death.
—Marjorie Hewitt Suchocki, *God, Christ, Church*

Soteriology is a continuation of the discussion begun in Christology. It presupposes what I have already said about becoming human, unbecoming evil, and the person of Christ. It then proceeds to focus discussion on the atoning work of Christ, the concept of justification, and the outcome of human destiny in the kingdom of God. Generally soteriology concerns itself more with the means of accomplishing salvation than with the nature or content of salvation itself. The content of salvation will be addressed here, of course, but it will extend to the loci on eschatology and ethics that explicate further the symbol of the new creation.

Thought about the work of Christ might be organized by making reconciliation the most inclusive category. Paul presents the gospel using this key term, "In Christ God was reconciling the world to himself" (2 Cor. 5:19a). The good news is that the events of Good Friday and Easter Sunday have accomplished reconciliation between God and the apostate creation. Within this inclusive category we deal with the question: just how does reconciliation through Jesus Christ take place? The answer is explored through discussion of topics such as atonement, justification, regeneration, and sanctification. Atonement, the work of Jesus Christ in the office of priest, is the starting point.

ATONEMENT

The word *atonement* is one of the few theological terms whose etymological meaning can be discerned almost within the bounds of the English language alone. We break it down into three words belonging together, "at-one-ment." It probably originated in the Anglo-French usage by the Normans after their conquest of the Anglo-Saxons in 1066: *etre a un*, meaning "to agree." Thomas More (1478–1535) is the first we know to use it in its modern form. In his *The History of Richard III* it means reconciliation, especially between disputing political powers. Anglican Bibles of the sixteenth and seventeenth centuries began using "atonement" to translate the Hebrew כפר (*kaphar*) and the Greek ἱλασμός and καταλλαγή, meaning expiation and reconciliation. In the developing theological vocabulary the term has come to refer to the state of reconciliation between our gracious God and the estranged human race, the state of at-one-ment, accomplished through the work of the savior, Jesus Christ. What makes atonement a theological issue is the question: how is such reconciliation accomplished? The New Testament answer is: the blood sacrifice of Jesus Christ results in the forgiveness of sins and the justified status of otherwise ungodly people.

Jesus, the Atoning Priest

Although in his office as king Christ is often pictured as the rescuer and in the office of prophet he is often depicted as the revealer of truth, the concept of atonement is most frequently—although not exclusively—tied to Christ's office of the priest. The author of Hebrews dubs him "a priest forever, according to the order of Melchizedek" (Heb. 5:6). Professionally, of course, Jesus was never a priest. He was a carpenter and a teacher. He did not lead anybody in public sacrifice. He is designated priest, however, because he "became the source of eternal salvation" (Heb. 5:9). The symbol of the priest overlaps considerably with an equally primary symbol that conveys essentially the same thing, namely, the sacrificial lamb. Jesus' sacrifice of himself was efficacious for our justification and gift of everlasting life.

The relationship between Jesus' death and the remission of sins is so close in the New Testament writings that for us to separate them would constitute an abstraction at the level of critical consciousness. In the Pauline literature the atoning significance of Jesus' death is found in two oft-repeated formulations, the surrender and death formulas. According to the surrender formula, Jesus is "given up." In some cases God is the subject who gives up the Son: "He who did not withhold his own Son but gave him up for all of us" (Rom. 8:32). Jesus "was handed over to death for our trespasses and raised for our justification" (Rom. 4:25). In some of the Deutero-Pauline texts it is Jesus himself who is the subject, who "gave himself up for us, a fragrant offering and sacrifice to God" (Eph. 5:2; see 1 Tim. 2:6; Titus 2:14). That there is an implied reference to the suffering servant of Isaiah 53:6, 12 seems clear from the frequent use of παραδιδόναι or διδόναι, the verb employed by the Septuagint.

The death formula is best exemplified by 1 Corinthians 15:3b: "Christ died for our sins." It is frequently found in various shorter forms such as "Christ died for us" (Rom. 5:8; 1 Thess. 5:9-10). There are three indispensable elements: (1) Christ is the subject who dies; (2) the word *died* comes in the form ἀπέθανεν, which indicates a single and unrepeatable past event; and (3) the preposition ὑπέρ with the genitive makes the saving work apply to us. It might also be worth mentioning that the death formula's being placed in these opening verses of 1 Corinthians 15 may make it part of the παράδοσις, the tradition handed down to and by Paul. If so, this formulation probably goes back to a pre-Pauline time before the Damascus Road conversion, to Jerusalem immediately in the wake of the saving events themselves.[1]

Sacrificial Lamb as Atonement Symbol

The need for reconciliation carries the assumption that a rift exists between God in God's absolute justice, on the one hand, and humanity in its impure and sinful state, on the other. Humanity needs to be purged of its impurities and cleansed from its sin (Lev. 16:16). Ancient Israel and other ancient cultures seemed to assume that ritual washing and the shedding of sacrificial blood could accomplish the remission of sins and establish atonement. Ritual bathing in conjunction with the sacrifice of bulls and lambs on the Day of Atonement (Yom Kippur) was performed for the purpose of cleansing the sanctuary, priesthood, and all the people from their sins (Lev. 16:23-32; Num. 29:7-11). The rite included the sacrifice of a goat and the sprinkling of its blood seven times on the mercy seat. The actual slaughtering of the animal was not the central event. The killing was done to obtain the sacrificial blood. The slaughter and sprinkling were followed by attending to a second and living goat. The priest would then list and confess Israel's sins, ritually heaping them upon the goat's head. This animal was then driven out into the wilderness, bearing Israel's iniquities as the scapegoat. The result was a cleansed and reconciled Israel. This scapegoat imagery is recalled by the prophet Isaiah when using the image of the suffering servant who was "crushed for our iniquities," who "bore the sin of many" (Isa. 53:5, 12). The reconciled state to which all this leads could be described as a "new covenant" (Jer. 31:31-34).

The ever-critical prophets later began to insist that without true repentance and righteous living the offering of animal sacrifice for remission

---

1. Martin Hengel, *The Atonement* (Philadelphia: Fortress, 1981), 34–49.

of sins was futile. The nation could not drown out the cries of the oppressed with the noise of hymns, nor legitimate exploitation through increased offerings (Isa. 1:10-17; Amos 5:21-24). John the Baptist reiterated the prophetic theme of heartfelt repentance while adding ritual bathing—baptism—for the forgiveness of sins (Mark 1:4).

Like John the Baptist, Jesus stressed repentance but added such an emphasis on God's mercy that it made sacrifice unnecessary (Matt. 9:13). Perhaps such sacrifice would henceforth be unnecessary because Jesus himself was preparing to "give his life as a ransom for many" (Mark 10:45). The shedding of Jesus' blood would result in the forgiveness of sins (Matt. 26:28) and the establishment of the new covenant (Luke 22:20; 1 Cor. 11:25). Because of this the author of Hebrews could declare that the one final and eternal sacrifice—the sacrifice of God's only Son—has rendered all subsequent sacrifices unnecessary and superfluous (Heb. 6:27).[2]

Thus Christ replaces the Temple. The ongoing sin offerings and atonement rituals performed by the Temple priests on Mount Zion are rendered superfluous by the single act of everlasting atonement on Calvary. The saving power of Christ's blood emerges from God's own sanctuary. It does not just lay on the altar of the Holy of Holies awaiting divine acceptance. But just because the Temple ceases to serve as a place of sacrificial atonement does not render it functionless. For Jesus and later for James and the other apostles headquartered in Jerusalem, the Temple becomes a "house of prayer for all the nations" (Mark 11:17; Isa. 56:7).

The sacrifice to end all sacrifices is symbolized in various New Testament traditions by the lamb without blemish. In 1 Peter 1:19 it comes in the form of a simile: "the precious blood of Christ, like that of a lamb without defect or blemish." For Paul in 1 Corinthians 5:7 it becomes a metaphor: "Our paschal lamb, Christ, has been sacrificed." In the Gospel of John, Jesus' death is more subtly juxtaposed with the paschal lamb of the Passover ritual (John 19:14-16) so that the sacrificial quality of Jesus' death can be sensed. The liturgical chanting of the Agnus Dei over the centuries repeats the Johannine words of the Baptist when he saw Jesus approaching: "Here is the Lamb of God, who takes away the sin of the world" (John 1:29). In today's worship hymnity we sing:

> My faith looks up to thee,
> Thou lamb of Calvary,
>   Savior divine!
> Now hear me while I pray,

---

2. René Girard argues that Jesus Christ was a scapegoat but not a sacrifice. Sacrifice would imply that God, who receives the offering, is bloodthirsty and violent. Sacrifice implies appeasing divine wrath (*Things Hidden since the Foundation of the World* [Stanford, Calif.: Stanford University Press, 1987]). Girard does not see clearly enough that in the New Testament God is the agent who offers the sacrifice for us. This declares that God wants an end to all sacrificing as well as all scapegoating.

Take all my guilt away,
Oh, let me from this day,
Be wholly thine!

The graphic symbol of the *agnus Dei* or lamb of God is a familiar one in the art of Christian churches. When the lamb is pictured lying down, the emphasis is on the suffering of Jesus who "bore the sin of many" (Isa. 53:12). When the lamb is depicted standing, the sacrificial theme of Good Friday is maintained but the victory of Easter is added. Sometimes the standing lamb is pictured prancing with a raised right foreleg and carrying a resurrection banner, a white pennant with a red cross hanging on a cruciform standard. The cruciform standard represents the cross, of course. The white pennant is the body of Christ hanging on it. The clean white brilliance of the banner along with the lamb's wool is a clear testimony to the triumph of Easter. Just as the book of Revelation can place the once sacrificed yet now triumphant lamb on the throne with myriads of angels and elders and animals all singing Te Deums (Rev. 5:6-14), so also in our worship hymnity we sing:

Crown him with many crowns, The Lamb upon his throne;
Hark, how the heavenly anthem drowns all music but its own.
Awake, my soul, and sing of him who died for thee,
And hail him as thy matchless king through all eternity.

The continuing symbol for this event of atonement is the lamb, the innocent one whose blood is shed on Good Friday and whose Easter victory bequeaths to us joy for forgiveness and participation in the eternal divine glory.

HOW ATONEMENT WORKS

How does atonement work? Just how is it that what has happened in Jesus Christ is redemptively efficacious? There is no officially established dogma that answers this question, but there has been considerable theological speculation that has resulted in a variety of opinions and options.[3] The structure of each option is determined in part by its assumptions regarding the nature of the human condition—that is, regarding just what it is that constitutes human estrangement from God. The nature of the estrangement then determines the nature of Christ's work in overcoming

---

3. The two-natures doctrine is dogma because the Council of Chalcedon said so. No council has fixed an atonement dogma. Different models for explicating it have appeared. Arland Hultgren offers four types or variant models of how Jesus' atonement works within the New Testament (*Christ and His Benefits: Christology and Redemption in the New Testament* [Philadelphia: Fortress, 1987]). The variants I will look at here are based upon the New Testament but come from the history of theology.

it. Let us look briefly at six conceptual models that appear in the history of systematic theology. All make a contribution to the explication of atonement, yet I recommend the fifth and sixth as the most fruitful for future discussion.

Jesus as Teacher of True Knowledge

The first model for understanding the work of Christ is that of the premier example of true knowledge or gnostic revealer. The framework is one of education, and the picture is that of Jesus as the teacher of the way to salvation. Although what Jesus actually taught verbally is valuable, the kind of life he led is more valuable for teaching because it provides a pattern for us to follow. Jesus is the premier example not because he is the first in history to teach the path to salvation, but because he most fully embodies that teaching. There is a fullness of God's truth in Jesus, a fullness that all humankind can and should enjoy. This makes Jesus first and foremost among mortals and warrants our emulation. In addition, the presence of this fullness of true humanity emits a drawing strength, a power of influence that inspires and enables others to follow the path Jesus has blazed. The unmistakable axis around which the model of the true teacher turns is this: Jesus shows us the way, but salvation does not occur until we follow it.

"I am the way, and the truth, and the life," says Jesus (John 14:6). To be at one with Jesus is to be at one with the sublime and ultimate reality of God. Symbolized on liturgical vestments as a burning oil lamp representing wisdom, Christ is depicted in the Bible as the "light of the world" (John 8:12) or the psalmist's "lamp to my feet" (Ps. 119:105).

If one conceives of the fundamental problem of the human condition in terms of ignorance, then atonement would be achieved through proper knowledge. If we are estranged from God because we live in a terrestrial world of darkness, and in this darkness we overindulge in materiality and war against one another because we cannot see the truth, then we would need a celestial teacher who descends from the realm of light to show us the proper way. We would need someone who would do such things as present clearly the divine law, provide an example of how we should live, lead us into philosophical truth, or introduce us to mystical insights into transcendental realities. With such assumptions Jesus would be understood as the prophet: the great teacher, the gnostic revealer, who saves us through delivering heavenly knowledge.

This emphasis on Christ as the revealer of transcendental truth energized the work of the early Greek apologists. The gospel is said to answer the questions posed by sublime philosophy. The Logos of the second person of the Trinity is affirmed to be the same Logos that inspired the rational thought of Socrates and Heraclitus. Justin Martyr goes so far as to call these Greeks *Christians* because they "lived reasonably."[4] The gospel revelation contains the same eternal truth but manifests it more fully in Christ. There is here no sharp division between faith and philosophy. In fact, the apprehension of the significance of Christ's work yields a Christian philosophy.

Christ as the premier teacher characterizes Nestorian soteriology and distinguishes it from that of Chalcedon. Babai the Great says that the Logos clothed itself in human flesh "in order by his word to instruct us about the matters of the age to come." Jesus Christ teaches us "perfect knowledge," and it is our charge to imitate the pattern set by the Logos in the man from Nazareth. What happens when we imitate the pattern? We become deified. Our bodies become the temple of God, just as Jesus' body played host to the indwelling Logos. The Nestorians caution us, however, by adding that our deification does not put us in a position of being worshiped. Worship still belongs only to God.[5]

The revealer of truth model is also the pattern of atonement followed by ancient Gnosticism and, in those cases where Jesus is factored in, by postmodern religiosity today. In the new age version of this soteriology such as one might find in transpersonal psychology, the concept of human potential is added. This corresponds to the notion of the divine spark in ancient Gnosticism. According to the ancient gnostic scheme, the spark of the divine light lies deep within the soul of each of us. But it cannot shine because it is covered over with layers of darkness, with misleading ignorance. According to the new age version of the gnostic scheme, unlimited human potential lies deep within us just waiting to burst forth. What inhibits it from doing so is ignorance in the form of a false consciousness that causes us to think in terms of categories, stereotypes, and dichotomies. To free this potential we need to raise our consciousness by thinking holistically. Atonement here consists in gaining true knowledge of at-one-ment with one's true self and with the whole cosmos. This raising of our consciousness can be facilitated by a teacher who has already attained true knowledge. This teaching combined with our following constitutes the soteriological work. The teacher of saving knowledge followed by new age religionists could be Jesus Christ or perhaps some other guru who possesses transcendental insight.

Jesus as Moral Example and Influence

Closely related to the idea of Jesus as the teacher of truth through example is the moral-influence theory of atonement. This theory assumes that humans need to be enabled to engage in sacrificial love. Usually identified with Peter Abelard (1079–1142), the theory presupposes something less

4. Justin Martyr *Apology I* 46.
5. *CT*, 2:46.

than a full-blown doctrine of original sin. In his ethical treatise, *Know Thyself*, Abelard argues that the human race as a whole does not share in the guilt of Adam's sin. Through the use of natural reason we are capable of deciding what is good. We need knowledge of what is good and the strength of resolve to do it. This is what we get through the work of Christ. Thus, the moral-influence theory contends that the atoning significance of Jesus' death is that it provides us with a compelling example to follow. Jesus, in persevering through humiliation and the cross, fully embodies God's own self-sacrificial love. So dramatic are the life and passion of Jesus that they grasp the human imagination and move the heart so that we are empowered to re-embody that same self-sacrificing love in our own lives. Once we have followed suit, reconciliation has taken place.

Some liberal Protestants have developed variants of the moral-influence position in the wake of Immanuel Kant's understanding of Jesus as the moral ideal. It is our duty, Kant writes, "to elevate ourselves to this ideal of moral perfection, that is, to this archetype of the moral disposition in all its purity—and for this the idea itself, which reason presents to us for our zealous emulation, can give us power." Note, first, how Jesus as the moral example provides the ideal we should emulate and, second, how the very reasonableness of the ideal provides the power to emulate it. Once we voluntarily engage in moral activity that copies Christ then we may "hope to become acceptable to God (and so be saved)."[6] According to the moral-influence theory, reconciliation comes as the result of our own efforts at following Jesus' example, efforts that are aided by the compelling power of that very example.

Currently the British myth-of-God-incarnate theologians such as John Hick and Michael Goulder tend toward the moral-influence theory. The overall objective of their project is the abandonment of making metaphysical claims about the person of Jesus while still affirming that Jesus provides the premier example of God's self-giving love. He is described as the "archetypal believer" whose self-sacrificing life makes him "the man of universal destiny." Jesus belongs on a continuum with other great leaders such as Churchill, Mao Tse-tung, Gandhi, and Martin Luther King, Jr., who were people of great destiny. The Christian church is founded on the moral influence of Jesus. The existence of the church is testimony to the tremendous influence he has had in human history. We are enjoined to follow his example and live a life of love. This is what salvation is. "To be saved is to love," writes Michael Goulder, who attacks the *Christus Victor* theory of atonement as an example of "empty speculations" and the satisfaction theory for making "Christ a whipping boy" in the face of a "faceless justice." Then Goulder goes on, "So we do not need an

---

6. Immanuel Kant, *Religion within the Limits of Reason Alone* (1934; reprint, New York: Harper & Row, 1960), 54–55.

atonement theory to explain what is already explained. We are saved into the community of love, the church, which Jesus founded by a life of love that inexorably ended on the cross. . . . He gives the responsibility of our world, including our church, to us."[7]

At first glance this position appears to be a form of the gnostic-revealer model mentioned above. In fact Abelard was criticized during the Middle Ages for reducing the work of Christ to that of a mere teacher. But there is an element in the moral-influence theory that goes beyond teaching by example. It is the compelling power inherent in the example. Not only does Jesus teach us through word and example, writes Abelard in his *Commentary on Romans*, but "he has very strongly drawn us to himself through love, so that, inflamed by this great benefaction of divine grace, true love now shrinks not from the endurance of anything whatsoever." There is more to Christ's atoning work than mere moral example. It is also moral influence.

Jesus as Victorious Champion

The third form of atonement explication treats Jesus as a victorious champion. Known widely as the *Christus Victor* theory, it describes our rescue from distress by Christ who, like a brave and victorious knight, has been able to defeat the prince of darkness and free us from enslavement to death. The symbolism here is rich and exciting. Its most vivid biblical image is that of Saint Michael engaged in the great war in heaven with the devil, whom he is able to defeat and throw down to earth (Rev. 12:7-12; Dan. 12:1). He comes on a white horse, being called "Faithful and True," leading a great army by which he will rule the nations. On his thigh he has a name inscribed, "King of kings and Lord of lords" (Rev. 19:11-16).

The patristics employed a much less elegant figure that was picked up by Luther, namely, that of the worm on a hook. The innocent Jesus is the bait that the devil, like a hungry fish, devours. But the devil is supposed to devour only those whose souls have already been given over to evil. By eating the innocent Jesus, the devil has overreached himself and thereby disqualifies himself as the rightful heir to the booty of sin. The divine innocence of the incarnate one was the hook whereby the devil was outsmarted and brought to defeat.

The *Christus Victor* theory has been proffered primarily by Gustaf Aulén (1879–1977). In claiming that this is the so-called classic theory and reading it back into the works of the ancient fathers such as Irenaeus as well as Reformers such as Luther, Aulén argues that the fundamental problem of the human condition is enslavement. We are enslaved to the

---

7. Michael Goulder, "Jesus, the Man of Universal Destiny," in John Hick, ed., *The Myth of God Incarnate* (Philadelphia: Westminster, 1977), 58–59, see also 9, 36, 54, 127, 163; and John Hick, "Evil and Incarnation," in Michael Goulder, ed., *Incarnation and Myth* (Grand Rapids, Mich.: Eerdmans, 1979), 79–80.

powers of sin, death, and the devil. God working through Christ does battle with these powers, defeats them, and the spoils of Christ's victory accrue to our advantage. God is the chief actor in the whole drama, so that reconciliation is achieved apart from human contribution. This stands in sharp contrast to the gnostic-revealer and moral-influence theories, wherein atonement is something we accomplish ourselves under the guidance of Jesus' teaching or influence. The overriding emphasis of Aulén's theory is that God and God alone accomplishes the victory. Therefore, we can and must think of our salvation as a gift bestowed through grace alone, *sola gratia*.

In very recent times a variant on the *Christus Victor* motif—Jesus as the liberator—has been proffered by the current generation of liberation theologians. The symbol of the liberator takes its inspiration from such passages as Galatians 5:1, "For freedom Christ has set us free; stand fast, therefore, and do not submit again to a yoke of slavery." There is a shift here, however, in the understanding of what binds us and what freedom means. Whereas concomitant with the *Christus Victor* symbolism we become liberated from sin, death, and the power of the devil, liberation theologians picture the savior freeing us from political, social, and economic oppression. Whereas Saint Paul in Galatians may have thought of the "yoke of slavery" metaphorically as referring to the law that keeps us in sin, liberation theologians take the idea of slavery as referring metaphorically to economic or political bondage to which the First World subjects the Third World. No one treats slavery literally.

Theologians working in the Third World are reluctant to adopt the *Christus Victor* model in its traditional form, suggesting that the image of Jesus as liberator should replace it. They question the desirability of the warrior imagery in hymns with lines such as "onward Christian soldiers, marching as to war" or "stand up, stand up for Jesus, ye soldiers of the cross." The problem is the soldiers, in this case the average Christians, may identify too closely with the victory of their champion. "Be we Christ's, in him forever we have triumphed over all." Historically, Christian crusaders actually marched to war under the banner *Christus est Dominus*, Christ is Lord. Thus, the military and triumphal imagery comes under suspicion here. Although its avowed reference is to the victory of Christ over sin and in our behalf, the rhetoric of victory can too easily be used to support the coercive conquest of pagan nations by Christian civilization. Hermeneuts of suspicion seem unconcerned about worms on hooks, but they worry that military metaphors may risk contributing to oppression rather than liberation.

Thinking of Jesus as liberator is better than considering Jesus as victor, say some liberation advocates, because it avoids this problem. Whereas "victory" would have as its object the enemy that has been conquered, "liberation" refers us to those set free. The emphasis is on the act of freeing rather than on crushing the enemy. It appears that *Christus Victor* and Jesus as liberator share the same deep structure, although the symbols are lifted up and interpreted in slightly different directions.

Yet there is another significant difference that is worth noting. We can get at this difference by asking: just how does the liberation take place? Whereas Aulén emphasizes that the *Christus Victor* motif requires that we understand the work of salvation as solely God's work, liberation theologians add the motif of moral example and influence. According to Jon Sobrino, for example, the historical Jesus favored the poor against their rich oppressors. We should follow Jesus in this regard and carry on the work of liberation. Similarly, Leonardo Boff sees Jesus as liberator because he taught "loving all as sisters and brothers," which includes liberating the human person "in body, soul, and all secular dimensions as well." Boff believes Jesus actualized this potential for freedom that lies in every human being, and so Jesus calls us into the freedom of becoming our true selves. J. Severino Croatto argues for a revolutionary form of Christianity on the grounds that Jesus Christ "has proclaimed the values of justice and freedom that are the basis of socio-political liberation movements." Jesus is more than an example. Through his teachings he is also an influence that goads us into pursuing the task of social transformation, and because of this influence we can think of him as our liberator.[8] The result, perhaps, is a merging of moral-influence and *Christus Victor* models in liberation theology.

Jesus as Our Satisfaction

The fourth interpretation, the satisfaction theory, assumes that the basic problem is one of disorder. The order of divine justice that governs the cosmos has been disturbed by the introduction of human sin. Consequently, God must perform an act whereby the just order is fulfilled—that is, is satisfied. This theory is most articulately presented by Anselm of Canterbury (1033–1109), according to whom the merciful God became incarnate and suffered the cross in order to reestablish the cosmic harmony requisite for human salvation.

Anselm's work *Cur Deus Homo?* raised the question of the incarnation: why did God become human? In this work Anselm sought to pursue theology as he had formulated the task of theology, namely, as faith seeking understanding (*fides quaerens intellectum*). He wanted to understand the why of the incarnation. He also had in mind an apologetic mission: to demonstrate convincingly to nonbelievers that the doctrine of the atone-

8. Jon Sobrino, *Christology at the Crossroads* (Maryknoll, N.Y.: Orbis, 1978), 60, 105, 305, 395; Leonardo Boff, "Images of Jesus in Brazilian Liberal Christianity," in José Míguez Bonino, ed., *Faces of Jesus: Latin American Christologies* (Maryknoll, N.Y.: Orbis, 1984), 19–21; J. Severino Croatto, "The Political Dimension of Christ the Liberator," in Míguez Bonino, ed., *Faces of Jesus*, 96.

ment makes sense. So he set out to prove the necessity of the incarnation by the use of reasoning alone apart from any prior historical knowledge regarding the work of Christ (*remoto Christo*). Let us briefly review the essential stages of Anselm's argument.

God's purpose for creating the human race emerges out of God's infinite love and compassion. So, from the beginning God planned for us to enjoy perfect blessedness and happiness. This blessedness requires the total and voluntary harmony of our own will with the divine will; for it is upon God's will that the very harmony and beauty of the universe rest. But through an act of defiant willing the human race has chosen disobedience, and this has fractured the cosmic harmony and frustrated God's plan for our happiness. Any deviation of our will must be balanced by a deprivation of blessedness. The imbalance can be righted in one of two ways: either through punishment and denial of blessedness or through an act of satisfaction whereby an offering is rendered up that is greater than the act of disobedience. God does not want to follow the road of punishment because God's purpose is to bestow blessedness. Therefore, satisfaction becomes the preferable solution.

But this leads to a dilemma. On the one hand, unconditional forgiveness is not an alternative, according to Anselm, because such an act would introduce further irregularity into God's universe. On the other hand, no member of the human race can offer any satisfaction to God because each human is already under the obligation of total obedience. If total obedience is already required, then there is no extra moral or spiritual capital available with which we can redeem ourselves from our past or future sins. Therefore, unless something drastic is done about it, the whole human race must suffer the punishment produced by a disharmonious universe and forfeit the blessedness for which we were created.

Up until this point we have been working on the premise of divine love, a love that purposed human happiness and that seeks a solution to the problem created by human sin. But now Anselm moves to a second phase in the argument and introduces another premising factor, God's omnipotence. It would appear that God's purpose for the creation has been frustrated. But this is impossible if God is omnipotent. Therefore, a means of redemption must exist. The offering for satisfaction ought to be made from the human side, but since we have nothing to offer, it cannot be made by us. But God is capable of making such an offering. Because only God is able to make the offering that we ought to make, it must be made by a combination of the divine and the human. Therefore, concludes Anselm, the incarnation is necessary. We know why God became human.

Anselm proceeds then to tell the gospel story. The incarnate Son of God freely offers up his sinless life to death in honor of God. But death is a form of punishment to be incurred only as a result of sin. Therefore, because Jesus' self-sacrifice is an unwarranted deed that the Father cannot allow to go unrewarded, and because the Son needs nothing for himself, the reward accrues to the advantage of those for whom the Son dies.[9]

Gustaf Aulén finds this whole scheme objectionable. He centers his attack on Anselm's doctrine of *satisfactio* because it allegedly depends upon a legalistic structuring of God's relationship to the creation based on the idea of penance and because it is allegedly a human being and not God who accomplishes the atonement. But a closer look would show that Aulén is wrong when he says that the Latin idea of penance provides the sufficient explanation for Anselm's understanding of the atonement. If we grant that the root idea of penance is that we must make an offering or payment to satisfy the principles of justice, then it is certainly true that Anselm employs such imagery in his satisfaction motif. But at the absolutely crucial point Anselm deviates by saying that no human being can make such satisfaction. Only God can do it; and God does it through the incarnate God-man. Hence, the Latin theory of penance may be necessary to understand Anselm, but it is by no means a sufficient explanation. Anselm offers more.

Aulén's most forceful attack is a broadside bombardment of the role of Christ in Anselm's account of the atonement. Aulén wants the work of redemption limited to Christ as God, not Christ as human. "This is the decisive issue; and, therefore, the crucial question is really this: Does Anselm treat the atoning work of Christ as the work of God himself from start to finish? . . . The contrast between Anselm and the Fathers is as plain as daylight. They show how God became incarnate that he might redeem; he teaches a human work of satisfaction, accomplished by Christ."[10]

It is clear that the criterion by which Aulén assesses the various theories of atonement is his own particular atonement model, according to which the redemptive acts of the incarnate one were really acts solely of God. God acts in Christ in a way that excludes the thought of any atoning work done by Christ as a human. If by Christ we mean the incarnate one with the two natures and the two wills, the one who is fully human and fully divine, then who is Aulén talking about when he says "God" does

---

9. It is Hultgren's judgment that a satisfaction theory cannot be derived from the New Testament. He argues on the grounds that Christ does not "appease the wrath or justice of God" (*Christ and His Benefits*, 175). Like so many critics of Anselm, Hultgren assumes that the satisfaction theory belongs within the framework of appeasement. He fails to acknowledge that the framework for Anselm is not appeasement. It is order and the problem of restoring order once sin has brought disorder into the world. The most pertinent criticism of the satisfaction theory, in my judgment, is that offered by René Girard, who says: (1) it depends upon a sacrificial reading of the Christ-event in the New Testament, whereas there is no sacrificial component in Jesus' death; and (2) it founds the Christian social order on a ritual murder, and ritual murder is the core of evil (*Things Hidden*, 182). Yet, even Girard's criticism fails to hold because, as we have seen, sacrifice is built into the primitive New Testament symbolism of the lamb.

10. Gustaf Aulén, *Christus Victor* (New York: Macmillan, 1967), 86–88.

it? God as Father? God as Logos but just one half of Christ? Such an extreme emphasis places Aulén in the same camp with the monophysites. The problem with monophysitism (and other similar doctrines such as monergism, monotheletism, and docetism) is that it overemphasizes the role of divinity in Christ to the exclusion of the human. This means risking the loss of true Emmanuelism. Thus, the recoil from firing the cannons of criticism at Anselm throws Aulén farther and farther back on *sola gratia*, farther and farther back on divine initiative and divine responsibility for the atonement, so that eventually the human nature of Jesus becomes jettisoned and Aulén risks backing himself right off the deck of Chalcedonian orthodoxy.

Is it not the position of Chalcedon that it is the divine word that acts, but that this word has truly become flesh, so that Jesus Christ acts *divine et humane*—in a divine and a human manner? Is this not precisely what Anselm himself proposes?

> *Anselm:* Therefore none but God can make this satisfaction.
>
> *Boso:* So it appears.
>
> *Anselm:* But none but man ought to do this, otherwise man does not make this satisfaction.... [Therefore] it is necessary for the God-man to make it.... Now we must inquire how God can become man. The Divine and human natures cannot alternate, so that the Divine should become human or the human Divine; nor can they be so commingled as that a third should be produced from the two which is neither wholly Divine nor wholly human.... Since, then, it is necessary that the God-man preserve the completeness of each nature, it is no less necessary that these two natures be united in one person, ... for otherwise it is impossible that the same being should be very God and very man.[11]

What we have in Anselm's satisfaction theory of the atonement is a valiant attempt by faith to seek understanding, a significant attempt at evangelical explication of the biblical symbols. It is doubtful, however, given the hermeneutical question, that we would wish simply to repeat Anselm's formulation in our own day and expect it to be adequate to the intellectual context of the twentieth or twenty-first centuries. Nevertheless, we can learn from Anselm. If we can get beyond recent theologians' criticisms of Anselm, we can appreciate the seriousness with which he takes the human predicament and how he employs Chalcedonian Christology to demonstrate the depth and power of God's compassion expressed in the work of Emmanuel.

Jesus as the "Happy Exchange"

Sometimes called the penal substitution theory, the Reformation understanding of atonement through an exchange is in large part a further development of Anselm's notion of satisfaction. Here, Christ assumes

---

11. Anselm *Cur Deus Homo?* 2.6–7.

the penalty belonging to sinful humanity and in exchange bestows upon us his justice and his resurrected life. John Calvin, for example, holds that the God of righteousness cannot love iniquity. It must be punished. Christ the mediator steps in as our substitute and takes the pain and penalties of sin unto himself. God then transfers—imputes—Christ's righteousness to us. This, in Calvin's view, is how Jesus Christ performs his priestly office.[12]

Aulén does not include the happy exchange motif in his catalog of atonement theories, unfortunately, because he makes the mistake of saying that another Reformer, Martin Luther, flatly rejected the satisfaction theory and relied totally on the *Christus Victor* motif. The sources do not support Aulén, however. It is true that Luther employed the imagery of the victorious champion, but certainly not to the exclusion of satisfaction. Not only was Luther accustomed to using the term *satisfaction* and even *payment* and *punishment* when describing the work of Christ, but the notion of satisfactory atonement underlies his doctrine of justification by faith (just as it does for Calvin).

Note how Luther combines *Christus Victor* and satisfaction motifs, including the notion of payment, in his exposition of the creed's Second Article in the Large Catechism:

He has snatched us, poor lost creatures, from the jaws of hell, won us, made us free, and restored us to the Father's favor and grace.... The remaining parts of this article simply serve to clarify and express how and by what means this redemption was accomplished—that is, how much it cost Christ and what he paid and risked in order to win us.... He suffered, died, and was buried that he might make *satisfaction* for me and pay what I owed, not with silver and gold, but with his own precious blood.[13]

We can see here that Luther faced the same problem Anselm confronted—that is, what is the relationship between divine forgiveness and the sufferings of the incarnate Christ? The forgiveness does not consist in a simple nonimputing of sin, as though God could have simply signed a heavenly decree henceforth absolving everybody of everything. If this were possible, then the sufferings of Jesus Christ would become unnecessary and superfluous. God's struggle with the forces of estrangement and destruction would be a mere sham battle. What makes all this necessary, in Luther's mind, is the need for satisfaction of divine justice—that is, the fulfillment of the divine law.

The mode of satisfaction that Christ uses in behalf of sinners is twofold: (1) he fulfills the will of God expressed in the law; and (2) he suffers punishment for sin—that is, he becomes a victim of the wrath of God.

---

12. Calvin, *Inst.*, 2.16.3–6; 3.11.2.

13. *BC*, 414; my italics. John Calvin was even more Latin than Luther in affirming satisfaction "to appease God"; that satisfaction "derives from God's love; therefore it has not established the latter" (*Inst.*, 2.9.1, 4).

What Luther means by fulfilling the law is expressed in popular piety with the notion that Jesus was sinless. He loved God and neighbor. He obeyed when called to minister. He did not yield to temptation. His faith was true, and he remained loyal even amid great pain and loneliness. He served God completely, even to surrendering his life.

More than this: although he fulfilled the law, he still suffered the punishment that law ordinarily pronounces against transgressors. He was condemned to death as a law-breaker—as a blasphemer according to Jewish law and as a seditionist according to Roman law. He was innocent yet punished. It is interesting to note here that Luther goes farther than Anselm on this point. Anselm distinguished punishment from satisfaction. Luther conflates the two, saying that it is through the punishment of Christ that satisfaction is made.

Luther thinks this through while commenting on what Paul had said in Galatians 3:13: "Christ redeemed us from the curse of the law by becoming a curse for us—for it is written, 'Cursed is everyone who hangs on a tree.'" The curse of Deuteronomy 21:23 repeated by Paul is the punishment prescribed for someone who has committed a crime punishable by death. But Jesus Christ is innocent. How does this apply then to him? Luther's answer: he suffers the curse for us; he receives the punishment for our capital offenses; and by doing so he satisfies the law and frees us.

At first glance this may appear to stand in sharp contrast to Aulén's *Christus Victor* interpretation, according to which the atonement victory consists in a triumph over the enemies of God, namely, sin, death, and the devil. For Luther the contest seems to be less with outright enemies of heaven than with God's left hand, with the "strange work" (*opus alienum*) of law and wrath. God's "proper work" (*opus proprium*) is grace and forgiveness, and after all is said and done law and wrath are finally pressed into the service of salvation. The left hand ends up serving the right. Thus demonic powers of wrath such as sin, death, and Satan are not simply and everlastingly God's enemies. At some point they are taken up into another dimension of divine activity and made to serve, even if unwillingly, God's overall plan. Hence, Paul Althaus can say over against Aulén that for Luther "everything else depends on this satisfaction, including the destruction of the might and the authority of the demonic powers."[14]

The whole mood of Luther's understanding of Christ's work is extremely dramatic, emphasizing the tragic depth of Emmanuelism. Jesus experiences (and here we are reminded of Irenaeus's notion of recapitulation) all that humans experience: anxiety, fear, anger over injustice, loneliness, abandonment, God's wrath, death, and hell. How deeply this hurt Jesus is vividly expressed in the fourth word from the cross: "'Eli, Eli, lema sabachthani?' that is, 'My God, my God, why have you forsaken

---

14. Paul Althaus, *The Theology of Martin Luther* (Philadelphia: Fortress, 1966), 220.

me?'" (Matt. 27:46). This is what Luther means by the descent into hell. So deeply does Jesus enter the human predicament that he experiences forsakenness by God, the curse of hanging from a tree.

Luther is not timid when it comes to the participation in sin by the sinless one. Christ takes possession of our sins and bears them. "Whatever sins I, you, and all of us have committed or may commit in the future," he writes, "they are as much Christ's own as if He Himself had committed them. In short, our sin must be Christ's own sin, or we shall perish eternally."[15] The value of this is that an exchange takes place. In addition to Christ's bearing our sin, the righteousness and justice of Christ become transferred to us. Sometimes this is called the "wonderful exchange" or "happy exchange." Luther describes it with a metaphor of marriage that can apply to the individual through faith or to the church as the bride of Christ:

Faith . . . unites the soul with Christ as a bride is united with her bridegroom. By this mystery, as the Apostle teaches, Christ and the soul become one flesh (Eph. 5:31f). And if they are one flesh and there is between them a true marriage—indeed the most perfect of all marriages, since human marriages are but poor examples of this one true marriage—it follows that everything they have they hold in common, the good as well as the evil. . . . Christ is full of grace, life, and salvation. The soul is full of sins, death, and damnation. Now let faith come between them and sins, death, and damnation will be Christ's, while grace, life, and salvation will be the soul's.[16]

This is firm testimony to the mystery of Emmanuelism, to divine involvement in the human condition at the level of deepest intimacy. As God binds the Godself to us, we become unbound as we are born anew into the divine freedom. This is how atonement works for Luther. It is this happy exchange combined with the mysterious unity we share with Christ through faith that underlies the doctrine of justification. If Christ is just, and if his justice is exchanged for our injustice, then we become declared just on account of Christ. It is here that we find the heart that pumps life and new life throughout everything having to do with the Christian faith. It is the gospel. In the words of Philip Melanchthon, "The Gospel is, strictly speaking, the promise of the forgiveness of sins and justification because of Christ."[17]

Jesus as the Final Scapegoat

This emphasis on forgiveness and justification recalls my earlier discussion of unbecoming evil, especially the mechanism of self-justification and scapegoating. God justifies us; we do not justify ourselves. Jesus Christ

---

15. Luther, "Commentary on Galatians" (1535), *LW*, 26:278.
16. Luther, "The Freedom of a Christian," *LW*, 31:351, see also 31:190, and 26:129–31; see also Leo the Great *Sermons* 54.4.
17. Melanchthon, "Apology of the Augsburg Confession," in *BC*, 113.

is the means whereby we become justified. This act of divine grace is not something the human race can appreciate as long as it assumes that the sacrifice of scapegoats is an effective means for attaining self-justification. One way to conceptualize the work of atonement is to view it as a revelation of human sin and a revelation of the bankruptcy of the scapegoat mechanism. The Christ-event is an event of truth that disarms the lie. Once the human race discovers that self-justification is doomed to fail, then suddenly the gracious gift of divine justification becomes visible and attractive. With this in mind I propose a sixth model of atonement: Jesus as the final scapegoat.

René Girard helps here. According to Girard, what Jesus says and what happens to Jesus converge on a single message: no more scapegoats! Jesus says that the human race throughout history, beginning already with Cain's murder of Abel, has sought to establish a peaceful and just social order on the bodies of the slain. Prophets and wise counselors are routinely persecuted, some even "murdered between the sanctuary and the altar" (Matt. 23:35). Jesus' diatribes against broods of human vipers are revelations of a truth: human social structures are built to cover violence.[18] The word of God Jesus is delivering comes in the form of a revelation of hypocrisy and a command to stop the cycle of violence. "Turn the other [cheek]," says Jesus, and "love your enemies" (Matt. 5:39, 44). Do not repay evil for evil.

What Jesus says and what happens to Jesus make the same point. He becomes a scapegoat and is martyred. In order to prevent Jesus' words from shedding the kind of light that would expose the truth, the dark powers of violence rise up to put Jesus to death.[19] Jesus is nailed to the cross as an act of legal justice in conjunction with mob violence. Its single purpose: to maintain peace in the social order.

So the chief priests and the Pharisees called a meeting of the council, and said, "What are we to do? This man is performing many signs. If we let him go on like this, everyone will believe in him, and the Romans will come and destroy both our holy place and our nation." But one of them, Caiaphas, who was high priest that year, said to them, "You know nothing at all! You do not understand that it is better for you to have one man die for the people than to have the whole nation destroyed." He did not say this on his own, but being high priest that year he prophesied that Jesus was about to die for the nation, and not for the nation only, but to gather into one the dispersed children of God. So from that day on they planned to put him to death. (John 11:47-53)

---

18. See Girard, *Things Hidden*, 159–64.

19. Girard's theory suggests that the scapegoat is normally chosen randomly. Does that apply in this case? Not according to Raymund Schwager, who has attempted to apply Girard's theory to the biblical understanding of atonement. Schwager sees Jesus as the "necessary" scapegoat because the preaching of Jesus was the cause of his conflict (*Must There Be Scapegoats? Violence and Redemption in the Bible* [San Francisco: Harper & Row, 1987], 191). Girard's own argument seems to lead to Schwager's conclusion.

What irony! In order to prevent the portending disruption of the social order by Roman reprisals, Jesus must be put to death so that "the whole nation" might not be "destroyed." Also worthy of note is that after Jesus had been sent back and forth from Roman to Jewish tribunals: "That same day Herod and Pilate became friends" (Luke 23:12). In conclusion, the peace of the social arrangement is achieved and maintained through the death of the scapegoat.

What is revealed by the New Testament—and this is one reason the New Testament is such an important document—is the cruelty of the scapegoat mechanism and the hypocrisy of a self-justified social order. This is because the New Testament memorializes and celebrates the scapegoat, not the social order. The written account is there for everyone to read. The reading and resulting revelation help to unmask and thereby dismantle the scapegoat mechanism. Once the truth has exposed the lie, it becomes clear that God's will is that Jesus be the final scapegoat, that no more follow.

Treating Jesus as the final scapegoat has much in common with the first model, Jesus as the teacher of true knowledge. Yet there is a difference. Rather than revealing a sublime path to God that spiritual disciples should follow, Jesus here reveals to us our sin and the hopelessness of justifying ourselves by scapegoating others. This theory also shares something with the *Christus Victor* and happy exchange models—namely, it shows that God has been willing to suffer as the victim of human scapegoating, and, further, once the truth has liberated us from the need for scapegoating we can appreciate the gracious offer of God's justification.

Each of these six models has something to contribute to our understanding of the atoning work of Jesus Christ, the benefit of which is that sinners stand just before God. The process by which an unjust person is rendered just is called justification, the topic to which I now turn.

ATONEMENT AND JUSTIFICATION

The doctrine of justification is the result of theological reflection on the significance of the symbol of Christ as the lamb of God, who through sacrifice transfers the innocence of the lamb to us while shedding his blood in atonement for our sins. Our own deeds of justice, our own good works, do not make us just in the sight of God. Our justice is rather an alien justice, one that comes to us from without but one that becomes our own through an act of God's grace. The Reformers emphasize repeatedly that Christ and Christ alone gives us our state of redeemed justice as a gift by faith, not a human accomplishment. As we would put on a wool sweater to face a cold day, so also do we obtain justice before God by clothing ourselves with the righteousness of the lamb of God. John Calvin, describing justification as "the main hinge on which religion turns," says: "Justified by faith is he who, excluded from the righteousness of works, grasps the righteousness of Christ through faith, and clothed in it, appears in God's sight not as a sinner but as a righteous man."[20]

This union with Christ through faith that makes the happy exchange possible is the target at which the doctrine of justification aims its evangelical explication. But some interpreters miss this. Some miss by shooting too high and emphasize a strictly forensic or declarative understanding of justification. Here God simply announces our innocence in a purely formal manner. The tendency in this case is to return to the autocratic magician in heaven who simply waves a hand or mutters magical words to alter the cosmos. This risks missing the drama of atonement and Christ's indispensable role in it.

By far the more frequent and devastating error, however, is to aim too low and to fail to realize the completeness of God's work in Jesus Christ. This error is the form of works righteousness against which the Reformers railed. That Christ's work is insufficient or incomplete is the implicit assumption of the medieval theory of condign merit, according to which people of faith engage in a process of sanctification at the end of which they are rewarded with salvation. It is also the assumption of Protestant enthusiasts and revivalists who similarly contend that faith in Christ is not good enough, that each Christian must also engage in a disciplined life of self-denial and sincere prayer until visited by a supranatural experience of the Holy Spirit that alone grants the so-called full gospel. In sharp contrast we must affirm that Christ's work is enough. Faith in Christ consists primarily in saying thank you for the justness we have been given, not in seeking something further.

One might question here why I am considering the concept of justification within the doctrine of soteriology. Quite often one finds it in a systematic theology under pneumatology or the Christian life. In such cases it is associated with regeneration and sanctification. But the problem with such topical placement is that it tends to divorce justification from the work of Christ on Calvary. It tends to think in terms of multiple justifications, one for each person who comes to faith or who earns sufficient merit or to whom the work of salvation is applied. It risks making the event of justification dependent upon the Christian individual and his or her prior regeneration or conversion. In the present treatment I am operating with the assumption that "Christ died for the ungodly.... We have been justified by his blood" (Rom. 5:6, 9).

Justification is the work of Christ for the cosmos, for the whole. The appropriation of this work to the individual parts—that is, to the lives of particular people—is the work of the Holy Spirit, and it is done through the evocation of faith, hope, and love, which are the effects of sanctification. But we ought not to think of the work of the Spirit or of our

---

20. Calvin, *Inst.*, 3.11.2.

pursuing the sanctified life as necessities warranted by the insufficiency of Christ's accomplishment. Our relationship with God has been reestablished fully and completely by what Christ has done, so that we should understand our life in the Spirit as an expression of this already established relationship and not as the pursuance of the relationship. But obtaining clarity on this point has been quite difficult over the centuries. Perhaps this lack of clarity is itself due to the persistent human propensity to say no to God's grace, to pursue self-justification rather than accept it as an unconditional gift.

EMMANUEL AS PROLEPSIS

The problem with Chalcedonian incarnationalism is that it risks assuming it knows too much about God independently of the revelation in Jesus Christ. All through the patristic period it was taken for granted that such a thing as a divine nature exists. This divine nature can be predicated with such attributes as unity, eternity, omnipotence, immutability, and impassibility. If these concepts become reified, then the theologian begins to think of the divine nature as fixed, not subject to modification or change due to the course of historical events. It could also be considered to be very different from human nature, which is also assumed to be fixed for all time. Natures or substances are then thought to be ontologically prior to persons, so that a person can never act to change his or her nature. God gets stuck with divinity, and we are stuck with our humanity. Hence, never shall the twain meet. With assumptions such as these, it is no wonder the Chalcedonian formulation eventually met with problems.

I believe we should honor our patristic forebears with sympathetic understanding for the difficult task of apologetic engagement they undertook, namely, the task of rendering an intelligible theological explication of Emmanuel amid the Greco-Roman philosophical milieu. But in its understandable desire to protect the transcendence and independence of God through the use of the sublime categories supplied by Hellenistic thought, Chalcedon may have made the problem of relating God to the world more difficult than it might have been otherwise. The tortuous intricacies of combining and distinguishing such concepts as *ousias*, natures, and hypostases were taken so seriously that eventually those notions were thought to be literal designations of metaphysical actualities. I have sought here to relieve the pressure a bit with a theological method that begins with the symbolization concomitant with the originary experience of Jesus, and then proceed to understand the theological process as one that brings the symbol to further conceptualization. This method should prove less brutal in its treatment of those we have defined as heretics, because it could recognize the integrity of each theological position that sought to be faithful to the basic symbol of Emmanuel, God with us.

In addition to this methodological suggestion, I have proposed that christological discussion can be aided substantively by developing the notion of prolepsis. As should be clear from my discussion of Jesus as the prophesier and the one prophesied, there was an intense futuristic thrust to his life and teachings. He was anticipating something, namely, the kingdom of God. This anticipation appeared not only in his announcement that the kingdom would be coming, but it appeared also quite concretely in his deeds, in his miraculous healings, in his passion, and in his resurrection. Jesus preactualized in his person what will ultimately become reality for all of us and for all of creation. That ultimate reality, depicted with the metaphor kingdom of God, will be one characterized by unity and harmony with God. It is this very unity and harmony that existed in Jesus under the conditions of the old aeon, as an alien invader from the future coming into our era of time. The not-yet has become an already in the preactualization of it in the person of Jesus. The future unity of all things with God is proleptically anticipated in the man from Nazareth.

The doctrine of the incarnation sought to convey this. But the problem with incarnation as a concept is that it worked with misleading assumptions regarding the relationship of time and eternity. It assumed that like the two natures, time and eternity are mutually exclusive and self-contained realities. God is alleged to exist in eternity untouched by what happens in time, as immutable and impassible. If there were no such thing as temporal history, God would go on unchanged. Even with temporal history, God goes on unchanged, according to this scheme.

But if we assume a closer relationship between time and eternity, wherein there is a genuine dialectic between them, then God's involvement in the world becomes more intelligible. I contend that the nature of all things real is yet to be determined because the creative process is still ongoing. It is not done yet. Reality is not yet fixed. There is no eternal realm currently to which we may direct our attention to find unchanging forms or immutable realities, God included. God, like the course of history itself, is in the process of constituting Godself. This admission of change or becoming within the divine life in no way jeopardizes God's identity. The divine identity is maintained through change because God makes promises and keeps those promises. God is faithful to Godself and to God's word. The incorporation into the divine life of the event of Jesus Christ constitutes a move from temporality to eternity, a move on the part of the yet-to-be-eternal God to constitute and to express the trinitarian life. In Jesus, God was "adding humanity to his divinity,"[21] to borrow a phrase from Hilary of Poitiers that coheres with the doctrine of *communicatio idiomatum*.

---

21. Hilary of Poitiers *The Trinity* 11.40.

We today stand between the times. We live proleptically. Like Jesus delivering the Sermon on the Mount, we await the divine confirmation of our faith. We know that Jesus was God incarnate on the basis of what we in faith expect he will be in the future kingdom. In principle we must acknowledge that should that kingdom never come, then not only will our faith be in vain, but also the incarnation will turn out never to have happened.

Our retroactive ontology is at work here. We must go to the future before we can establish what was genuinely real today or yesterday. Creation is not done yet. The future can alter the past through redefinition. Our faith takes us initially to the ultimate future of all things—to the consummate fulfillment of all things promised by our faithful God—and then works backward to the proleptic reality of its anticipation in Jesus. On the basis of our belief in what God has promised we can think of Jesus' life in terms of divine incarnation.

THE LIFE OF
THE NEW CREATION

INTRODUCTION

We believe in the Holy Spirit, the Lord, the giver of life,
   who proceeds from the Father and the Son.
With the Father and the Son he is worshipped and glorified.
He has spoken by the prophets.
We believe in one holy catholic and apostolic Church.
We acknowledge one Baptism for the forgiveness of sins.
We look for the resurrection of the dead,
   and the life of the world to come.

—The Nicene Creed

Part Four takes up the Third Article of the creed, the locus associated with the third person of the Trinity, the Holy Spirit. The Spirit of God is the spirit of divine presence. It makes both the Christ of yesterday and the kingdom of tomorrow present today in the word of preaching and the celebration of the sacraments. As the incarnate Jesus was Emmanuel—God with us—through the second person of the Trinity, so also the Holy Spirit is Emmanuel through the third person.

Part Three explicated what God did in Jesus. Part Four begins with the locus on pneumatology, emphasizing what God is presently doing in the Spirit and will do tomorrow in the consummation. Today God's work is through the life of the church, which I explicate as the doctrine of ecclesiology. Tomorrow that work will be through new life in the resurrection, which I explicate as the doctrine of eschatology.

8

THE HOLY SPIRIT

You call from tomorrow, you break ancient schemes.
From the bondage of sorrow the captives dream dreams;
our women see visions, our men clear their eyes.
With bold new decisions your people arise.
  Spirit, spirit of gentleness,
  blow through the wilderness
    calling and free.
  Spirit, spirit of restlessness,
  stir me from placidness,
    wind, wind on the sea.

—James K. Manley, 1978

Pneumatology is the study of the Holy Spirit. It receives its name from the Greek term for spirit, πνεῦμα (*pneuma*), which can also mean breath or wind. What we today call "pneumatic" devices, such as pumps and air hammers, receive their names from the same root as our concept of spirit.

Air is a source of power. As I pointed out in the chapter on becoming human, this identification of spirit with air was widespread in the ancient world. Perhaps the phenomenological origin of such thinking is the observation that breath and life belong together. Just as the invisible wind activates fallen leaves by blowing them around, so also does air passing into our lungs animate human life. When someone dies, he or she stops breathing. The air leaves the lungs. The spirit departs. Our very life is apparently dependent upon a much bigger yet invisible force that surrounds us. By means of our spirit we humans share life with that which transcends us.

In the Old Testament this double reference is embodied in the word רוח (*ruach*), meaning both breath and spirit. The continuity between the human spirit and the divine Spirit is graphically portrayed in the creation account, according to which the Lord God formed the human being from the dust from the ground, and breathed into its nostrils the breath of life, and the result was living beings (Gen. 2:7). The life-giving quality of the breath of God is reflected in numerous Old Testament texts (Gen. 6:17; 7:15; Num. 16:22; Judg. 15:19; Ps. 104:29-30; Eccles. 3:1; 9:21; 12:7; Isa. 37:6, 8; Zech. 12:1). Just as the Old Testament depicts divine breathing creating life, the New Testament depicts it creating new life. The Gospel of John tells how the resurrected Jesus suddenly appeared in the room with the disciples, even though the doors were locked. After greeting them with "peace be with you," he "breathed on them and said to them, 'Receive the Holy Spirit'" (John 20:21-22). This symbol of divine breathing (Latin: *spiratio*) is employed today when congregations sing Edwin Hatch's hymn, "Breathe on Me, Breath of God."

The breath of the ever-living Christ continues to breathe within us in the form of the comforter or the paraclete, whom Gordon Kaufman calls "the companion." The companion is the counselor, the Spirit of truth (John 14:16). The power of the Holy Spirit makes the words of Jesus ("And remember, I am with you always" [Matt. 28:20]) and of Saint Paul (nothing "in all creation will be able to separate us from the love of God in Christ Jesus our Lord" [Rom. 8:39b]) effective in our lives. We identify the presence of God through the concept of the Spirit. Where the divine breath blows there is comfort, counsel, and truth.

To share in the single breath of God is to participate in the unifying work of the Holy Spirit. The Spirit unifies in that it ties us to the saving work of Christ and binds us to one another through membership in the one body of Christ, the church. The Spirit is the very life-giving and communion-making presence of God at work in our lives, a post-Easter form of Emmanuelism. The work of Christ for our justification becomes, through the Holy Spirit, the work of sanctification. When we inhale the divine breath within our souls, we exhale the three theological virtues: faith, hope, and love. The Spirit makes the past work of Jesus Christ present to faith, and it makes the future fulfillment of God's kingdom present to hope. It inspires and empowers love, a love prescinding from gratitude for grace in the past and anticipating the final oneness of all things in the future.

The specific channel for the Spirit's work is the church, which is created through the preaching of the gospel and the response of faith. Faithful people in the church in turn continue to re-present the gospel, so that the church becomes the means whereby more and more people hear the good news and are invited into the body of Christ. The word creates the church, but the church re-presents the word in a continuing march through history.

The most important theme of pneumatology has to do with the work of God's Spirit in the life of faith of the individual believer and in the Christian community. Faith is our first and foremost concern because in faith the Spirit makes the Christ of Calvary in the past as well as the new Adam of the future present to us now. It is this collapsing of time that affords to us personally the knowledge of forgiveness and the power of new creation. This dynamic of faith expresses itself in the freedom to hope and the freedom to love.

In addition, the Spirit is responsible for the distribution of gifts, talents, and fruits of the Spirit that characterize our lives as individuals and together as a community.

THE SPIRIT AND NEW LIFE

My overall plan here is to draw out some of the richness of the biblical symbols of the Holy Spirit. In doing so I will suggest that the Spirit, like the second person of the Trinity, has a proleptic task. The Spirit makes the future present, thus binding us to the new creation yet to come. The Spirit also makes the past present, especially the event that took place on Calvary many years ago. The Spirit of unity and wholeness works through collapsing time in order to grant us the proleptic foretaste of the salvation that awaits us.

Symbols of the Spirit

Of the three persons of the godhead, the Holy Spirit has the fewest symbols and images. But the symbols it does have are powerful, especially fire and water. Breath and the descending dove are perhaps less potent symbols, but they both say something about the Spirit. Together these symbols convey that in the Holy Spirit God is present, and this presence issues in new life, the life of beatitude.

The Holy Spirit is the source of revelation, truth, and wisdom. Here the symbols are fire and light. It was from a burning bush that the mysterious name of the divine was first revealed to the kneeling Moses. On the day of Pentecost the Holy Spirit arrived not only like a "violent wind" but with "tongues as of fire" (Acts 2:3). To illuminate things and to enable us to see during the dark of night have always been treasured properties of fire. They are also properties of the Holy Spirit.

Another symbol of the Spirit is water understood as that which nourishes life. The Spirit is "the Lord, the giver of life," we say in the creed, and we sometimes imagine regeneration and sanctification in terms of heavenly rains, water wells, or effervescing streams that quench our thirst and cause the crops to grow. Abraham made a covenant at Beersheba after digging a well (Gen. 21:30); when Moses struck the rock in the Meribah wilderness water welled out (Exod. 17); it was with joy that Isaiah could sing of the "wells of salvation" (Isa. 12:3); and it was at Jacob's well that Jesus offered the Samaritan woman "living water" (John 4:6). Alluding to the spring flood by which rich silt is deposited on the plain, a process that leads to a bountiful harvest, Ambrose of Milan describes the flow of the Spirit springing from the fount of life and carrying us toward eternal life in the New Jerusalem:

> For neither is that city, the heavenly Jerusalem, watered by the channel of any earthly river, but that Holy Spirit, proceeding from the Fount of Life, by a short draught of Whom we are satisfied, seems to flow more abundantly among those celestial thrones, dominions, and powers, angels and archangels, rushing in the full course of the seven virtues of the Spirit. For if a river rising above its banks overflows, how much more does the Spirit, rising above every creature, when he touches the as it were low-lying fields of our minds, make glad that heavenly nature of the creatures with the larger fertility of his sanctification.... Let, then, this water, O Lord Jesus, come into my soul, into my flesh, that through the moisture of this faith the valleys of our minds and the fields of our hearts may grow green.[1]

Ambrose goes on to delineate the gracious work of the Spirit within us in terms of gifts such as wisdom and understanding, counsel and strength, knowledge and godliness, and a genuine reverence for God. These are all different directions in which life can flow out from its single source. There is only one river, Ambrose says, but many are the channels of the gifts of the Spirit. John and Charles Wesley continue the water metaphor in a hymn of 1742:

> The sanctifying Spirit pour,
> To quench my thirst, and wash me clean;
> Now, Saviour, let the gracious shower
> Descend, and make me pure from sin.

In sum, we pray today for a repetition of what happened at Pentecost, namely, an "outpouring" of God's Spirit (Acts 2:17).

When it comes to Christian art and iconography, the Holy Spirit is seldom portrayed in human form, even though the Father and the Son frequently are. Most frequently the Holy Spirit is indicated by the presence of a dove. The dove had already been used to symbolize the soul by the Greeks. Exactly what it means to the Christian is less than fully clear. We may speculate a bit, however. A dove brought back an olive branch to Noah, signaling the reappearance of land after the flood (Gen. 8:11). But the natural association with wind might be more important here. Because the dove flies, soaring and gliding through the air, the avian dimension evokes a sense of the dynamism of the listing winds. Or, perhaps more abstractly yet more directly, the dove connotes communion. Recall from

---

1. Ambrose *Of the Holy Spirit* 1.16.178; 1.intro.16.

the above discussion of the Trinity that the special work of the Spirit is to establish communion between the Father and the Son within the immanent Trinity and to establish integrative wholeness between the divine life itself and the ongoing creation. The Spirit effects the integrating power of love both within the godhead and between God and the world. Perhaps in retrospect we can see why the descending dove image associated with Jesus' baptism (Matt. 3:16; Luke 3:21), which unites heaven and earth, the Father and the Son, has seemed to be the most fitting symbol for the communal work of the Spirit.

The Spirit and the Future

The Spirit has a special relationship to the future because the work of the Spirit is tied so closely to creation and new creation. The book of Genesis opens with the Spirit of God moving over the face of the deep. One gets the feeling that the Spirit is brooding, cogitating, contemplating, and planning what kind of order will be drawn from the chaos. The Spirit then sets fire to the divine dynamism that explodes with the words, "Let there be light." God's Spirit is creative. It presses on toward the new, toward fulfillment.

As the prophets began to announce the coming kingdom of God, they foresaw the anointing of a new messiah by the Spirit. "The Spirit of the Lord shall rest on him," wrote Isaiah (Isa. 11:2), endowing the promised king with extraordinary power, insight, and wisdom. Because "I have put my Spirit upon him," says the Lord, "he will bring forth justice to the nations" (Isa. 42:1).

In Ezekiel's vision of the dry bones we find the Spirit at work creating new life where previously there was only death. From the four winds Ezekiel draws the breath (*ruach*) of God, which enters into the reconstituted bodies of the slain. Just as in Genesis, the divine breath causes the lungs to flex and living souls to rise up from the dust of the ground. "And you shall know that I am the Lord, when I open your graves and bring you up from your graves," says God through the mouth of the prophet, "and I will put my Spirit within you, and you shall live" (Ezek. 37:13-14a).

This is just what happens at Easter. God puts the Spirit in the dead Jesus and life begins anew. The resurrection of Jesus is the eschatological act of the Holy Spirit whereby the promise is fulfilled in the person of Christ and made anew for the rest of the creation. With the coming of the Spirit the end-time has begun. As Christ has already been transformed, so also will the Spirit transform us. Saint Paul reinforces this vision when describing the resurrection of the faithful into their spiritual bodies. Although we may be buried as perishable beings, God will raise us to an imperishable existence. Although we may be buried in dishonor, we will be raised in glory (1 Cor. 15:42-43). The Holy Spirit has already begun this transformation process by raising Jesus, the first fruits of a yet outstanding harvest (Rom. 8:23; 1 Cor. 15:20). In sharp contrast with the first Adam who chose to bury himself in the soil, Christ as "the last Adam became a life-giving spirit" (1 Cor. 15:45).

Thus, the Spirit belongs to the future, to the transformed future. It will be through the power of the Spirit that new life will appear where old life had died, that justice and peace will finally be established and remain undisturbed, and that the law of God will be written on our hearts. The Spirit is the eschatological power by which the present age will be transformed into the kingdom of God.

The Spirit of Unity and Community

The Spirit integrates, unifies, and brings things into relationship. The Spirit does not simply demand conformity to an already existent or static state of oneness. Rather it engages in the dynamic process of integrating what is presently estranged or disintegrated. Unity in the Spirit is a reconciling unity, or better, a process of entering into unity, a holomovement.

This unity is not simply a matter of turning plurality into oneness, of eliminating every distinction by collapsing all things into a single, universal mass of undifferentiated being. It is rather a matter of coordination, cooperation, integration, and harmony. What prevents harmony is not difference but rather estrangement. The human problem comes from the ambition and competition that make people willing to inflict violence to succeed. Our problem is due to our willingness to accept the involuntary sacrifice of others for our own profit. It is the absolutizing of the part to the detriment of the whole, thereby making the choice of death over life.

The task of God's Spirit is reconciliation, restoring wholeness to a creation broken apart by self-absolutization and sin. The concept of reconciliation emerges out of scripture, where it means that God no longer remembers our sins (Jer. 31:34), but casts them behind our backs (Isa. 38:17) or sweeps them away like a cloud (Isa. 44:22). Forgiveness leads to blessedness (Ps. 32:1). Through Christ God forgives us our trespasses, and this becomes the act whereby the world is set on the path of reconciliation with its estranged creator (Rom. 5:10; 2 Cor. 5:18-19). Through Christ God seeks "to reconcile to himself all things, whether on earth or in heaven, by making peace through the blood of the cross" (Col. 1:20). The Holy Spirit proceeds from this work of the Father through the Son to effect this ministry of reconciliation within the world. Reconciliation is a process leading eventually to its consummate fulfillment in the unity of all things in their creative and redemptive ground, God.

THE LIFE OF FAITH, HOPE, AND LOVE

The process of reconciling us with God and with the world leads to the three theological virtues: faith, hope, and love. In faith the Holy Spirit

234 • THE LIFE OF THE NEW CREATION

makes Christ present to us; it unifies what is separated by time and space so that the happy exchange can actually take place in our lives. In hope, the Spirit illumines our consciousness with visions of God's future, with the freeing confidence that the divine promises will attain fulfillment. In love, the Spirit actually releases the power that bears effective witness to the ongoing work of divine reconciliation. These three magnificent virtues imbue the life of beatitude.

The Spirit and Faith

"Faith is the principal work of the Holy Spirit," writes John Calvin.[2] Saying it this way is important. Because faith is a work of the Holy Spirit, we ought not think of faith simply as a human achievement. Although in a sense faith is our response to God, we are not completely responsible for it. Like God in Godself, faith is not something completely at our disposal. There is an element over which we have no control, an element that makes Christian faith distinctively faith in Christ, namely, the presence of Christ himself. This presence of the Lord in the midst of human lives is the work of the Holy Spirit.

People in the church have always thought that faith involved more than giving intellectual assent to historical facts or doctrines about God. There is a deeper and more personal dimension as well. Calvin insisted that this "very assent itself . . . is more of the heart than of the brain."[3] Hence, many have come to emphasize that faith is a matter of heart-felt trust, a personal or existential disposition whereby one actually gives himself or herself over to God. In faith, we make our life decisions based upon what we believe to be God's will for us—that is, our vocation. We put our future in God's hands. When confronted with the mysteries and tragedies that occasionally beset us, we live out of the trust that God's faithfulness will see us through. Hence, belief and trust are indispensable to Christian faith.

They do not tell the whole story, however. Believing and trusting characterize human response to the grace of God. They are something we do. But there is more. There is something the Holy Spirit does too—it gives us the presence of Christ. It is this that saves. It is this that makes the gift of God our own. The work of the Holy Spirit appropriates and personalizes all that has been said here with regard to the work of Christ. "The Holy Spirit is the bond by which Christ effectually unites us to himself," says Calvin.[4] Only in faith can we receive this gift (Gal. 3:2). Only in faith can this union take place.

---

2. Calvin, *Inst.*, 3.1.4.
3. Ibid., 3.2.8.
4. Ibid., 3.1.1.

This presence of Christ wrought by the Holy Spirit produces the paradoxes of Christian faith. The first paradox is that new life stands amid old death. Because the Spirit brings the new life of resurrection to us amid our old life of despair and death, it cannot show itself as pure glory or grand unity. Its presence is first made known in those unutterable groanings deep within the despairing soul whereby the Spirit itself intercedes in our behalf (Rom. 8:26-27). The Spirit makes the suffering Christ present to our suffering soul. The Christ of Good Friday is present in our brokenness, and paradoxically in this shared brokenness lies the power of healing and salvation.

The second and parallel paradox, then, is that we are at one and the same time guilty yet forgiven, sinful yet just. The Reformers described this in terms of *simul justus et peccator*, simultaneously justified yet sinful. Such double realities can rise up to the level of consciousness when we feel simultaneously both embarrassment and relief, both anger and calm, both injustice and love, both dead and alive, both alone and in the company of God. Thus the climb leads to new life, to the life of beatitude. The struggle within the human soul does not end in the pit where we recapitulate Good Friday. The Christ present to faith is also the Easter Christ, the victorious Christ. The transforming power of Jesus' Easter resurrection lives on in us when present in faith. "It is no longer I who live," writes Saint Paul, "but it is Christ who lives in me" (Gal. 2:20).

There are a couple of important theological implications to be drawn from this understanding of the Holy Spirit working amid the paradoxes of faith. First, the presence of Christ is not simply a matter of experience, empirical or religious. Christ is present to faith even if we cannot hear, see, or touch him physically. Nor is it necessary to have an oceanic experience, the ecstasy of feeling at one with the whole unified cosmos. In fact, the inner conflict of faith has an indispensable element of brokenness, a recognition that reality is—at least at present—something less than a unified whole. Our actual experience is one of brokenness, while at the same time the presence of the risen Christ promises a healing wholeness.

Second, we do not have here a doctrine of the human spirit, according to which there is a built-in affinity between the human and the divine. Inspiration is not the actualization of a human potential. This is not a case wherein God has placed within our soul a little divine spark called the "pneuma," which we fan with trust and virtue until it burns more brightly. Justification by faith is not a process of actualizing an innate divine potential until it attains a Christlike mode of existence. Rather it is the actual presence of Christ with all his saving power. Our justness is his justness, pure and simple. The Holy Spirit, not our spirit, binds us to Christ.

In sum, the presence of Christ is absolutely crucial to an understanding of pneumatology and Christian faith.[5] So close is the identification of the resurrected Christ with the Holy Spirit that they are almost interchangeable in the New Testament. Whether it be the indwelling of the Spirit (Rom. 8:9) or the indwelling of Christ (Rom. 8:10), in faith we become united with God and receive new life.

The Spirit and Hope

Along with faith, the Spirit works to give us hope. Faith and hope are the first two of the theological virtues that adorn the Christian life, and both are the work of God's Spirit. "For through the Spirit," says Saint Paul, "by faith, we eagerly wait for the hope of righteousness" (Gal. 5:5). Whereas in faith the Spirit makes present the saving work of Christ in the past, *hope* is the term that describes how the future becomes present.

John Calvin was fond of demonstrating the distinction yet complementarity between these two virtues. He describes hope as the expectation of those things in which faith has already believed. Faith believes God to be true, while hope awaits the time when that truth will be fully manifested. Faith holds that eternal life has been given to us, while hope anticipates the time when it will be consummated. Faith is the foundation upon which hope rests, while hope nourishes and sustains faith. "Hope refreshes faith, that it may not become weary. It sustains faith to the final goal, that it may not fail in mid course, or even at the starting gate."[6]

This combination of faith and hope yields something else too—liberation. As the past and future become present through the Spirit, the net result is a burst of freedom, a liberation from the present order of things.

Nowhere is this put more forcefully than in the epistles of Saint Paul. "Where the Spirit of the Lord is," he writes, "there is freedom" (2 Cor. 3:17b). Why are we free? Because we are no longer bound to the old order of things. "If anyone is in Christ, there is a new creation: everything old has passed away; see, everything has become new!" (2 Cor. 5:17).

In Galatians the presence of the Holy Spirit is depicted as the power of the new to free us from the old. The work of Christ has delivered us "from the present evil age" (Gal. 1:4). In the present aeon we have lived in bondage to "the elemental spirits of the world," to "beings that by nature are not gods," and have been bullied to live "under the law" (Gal. 4:3, 8, 5). But God has acted to free us from all this. United with Christ through the work of the Holy Spirit, we like him have become children

---

5. "The Christian Faith says nothing more than that we have been called into the immediacy of the mystery of God himself and that this mystery gives itself to us in unspeakable nearness" (Rahner, *TI*, 5:21).

6. Calvin, *Inst.*, 3.2.42. Barth unjustly criticizes Calvin here for failing to posit that it is the presence of Christ in hope that gives it its expective power. Calvin, as mentioned, certainly affirmed Christ's presence (Barth, *CD*, 4/3:913-14).

of the new age. We have been adopted into the divine family and have become heirs to all the riches belonging to the Prince of Peace. Because we have been received by adoption, "God has sent the Spirit of his Son into our hearts, crying, 'Abba! Father!'" (Gal. 4:6). When the Spirit cries "Abba" from within our hearts, we know that we are experiencing ahead of time that state of close kinship with God that will be fully ours in the consummate kingdom.

Thus the first element of freedom in hope is gained through our citizenship in the new age to come and liberation from bondage to the structures of the present aeon. The second element follows closely. We become freed from ourselves. The reception of Christ's presence in faith and hope requires a decision on our part to move over and make room, to allow Christ the place of lordship within our innermost being. When we serve this Lord, we are no longer bound to serve ourselves as lord. Saint Paul writes: "We do not live to ourselves, and we do not die to ourselves. If we live, we live to the Lord, and if we die, we die to the Lord; so then, whether we live or whether we die, we are the Lord's" (Rom. 14:7-8). Another way of saying this is that we turn all care for ourselves over to divine grace, trusting our total existence to the hands of God. This results in another dimension of the happy exchange: we surrender to God all the loyalty we have for life in this present world, and Christ turns over to us his resurrection to new life in the new world. The result is liberation from the cares and demands made by an ego dedicated to securing its own safety, health, wealth, influence, power, and happiness.

The Spirit and Love

Love is the third theological virtue. Christ himself is present in each of the three virtues, thanks to the work of the Holy Spirit.

There is no question that the Bible calls us to manifest the love of God concretely in our daily lives. From Jesus' denunciation of the hypocrites who had right beliefs but lacked genuine compassion to the stinging words of James that "faith without works is also dead" (James 2:26b), the New Testament is unyielding in its demand that we obey the great law: love God and love neighbor (Matt. 22:37-40; Rom. 13:8-10).

But love in the Spirit as the New Testament describes it quickly goes well beyond our obedience to God's law. Because Jesus Christ has fulfilled the law of love, and because the Holy Spirit bestows that fulfillment upon us, the net impact on our lives is one of freedom, spontaneity, and creativity. In his magnificent little essay "The Freedom of the Christian," Luther puts it starkly:

> A Christian is a perfectly free lord of all,
>   subject to none.

A Christian is a perfectly dutiful servant of all,
subject to all.[7]

Because the gospel declares us fully holy on the basis of what Christ has done, the life of love we lead can add nothing to our status before heaven. We are already of infinite value in the eyes of God, so whatever good deeds we perform cannot increase our value. This sets our love free from any self-serving motives that would diminish its giving or sacrificial quality. Gone is the disabling intimidation of legalistic preachers who constantly ram moral judgment and pseudoguilt down the throats of their parishioners. Gone is the neurotic desire to paw through our innermost consciousness to see if we have tarnished our motives with tinges of selfishness. Gone are the hurdles and barriers that prevent direct movement out of the ego and into shared communion. We are free to tackle life once again with a nonchalance, with a second naiveté, with a spontaneous participation in the concrete needs and deeds of our community.

This freedom makes love creative. When we love we do not simply conform to some moral precept. Rather, we give our attention totally to the practical situation at hand, and the dynamic of the Spirit at work within us establishes a new and spontaneous relationship that lives in the present moment. It is truly a spiritual work. We do not contain in ourselves a great storehouse of a commodity of stuff called "love" that we can simply distribute when we are willing to reduce our inventory. Love is not a thing or a substance that can be possessed or given away. Rather, it is a quality of relationship and action that is created on the spot, in each separate situation, through the freedom given by the Spirit.

In this sense God's love in one's life is creative love. It is "love which does not ask or seek or demand or awaken and set in motion our love as though it were already present in us," writes Karl Barth, "but which creates it as something completely new, making us free for love as for an action which differs wholly and utterly from all that we have done hitherto.... The love of God is this liberation."[8]

The apostle Paul certainly had a high opinion of love. Of the three theological virtues he wrote, "Faith, hope, and love abide, these three; and the greatest of these is love" (1 Cor. 13:13). The Spirit of love frees us from anxiety and from the illusory need of self-centeredness and prompts in us a life of faith that is patient and kind, not jealous or boastful, not arrogant or rude, not insisting on its own way, not irritable or resentful, not rejoicing at the wrong but rejoicing at the right. "It bears all things, believes all things, hopes all things, endures all things" (1 Cor. 13:4-7). Enduring love is the hallmark of the life of beatitude.

---

7. Luther, *LW*, 31:344.
8. Barth, *CD*, 4/2:777.

TALENTS, GIFTS, AND FRUITS OF THE SPIRIT

The work of the Holy Spirit is the work of God personally in each one of our lives through the theological virtues of faith, hope, and love. It is a positive and a creative work that seeks to enlist us to work synergistically and co-creatively in the divine mission on earth. For this the Spirit equips us with talents, gifts, and fruits. These three, of course, are the biblical categories. Later the patristics and medievals drew up a list of seven "gifts," also called "virtues," which included wisdom, understanding, counsel, fortitude, knowledge, piety, and fear of God. This list is an expansion that is based upon the looser and less systematic New Testament categories of talents, gifts, and fruits, which I will look at briefly here.

Talents are our native resources, those potentialities with which we are, so to speak, naturally endowed. They are the givens with which we start out. There are talents that we share with most all members of our race such as intelligence, physical strength, a life cycle that permits learning, an inherited culture, and so forth. In addition we have our own particular talents such as our particular degree of intelligence or strength, wit, beauty, economic circumstance, and so forth. All these belong to the divine economy and whether obvious or not have their place in the divine providence. We also have a responsibility to develop and employ our talents, shepherding them as good stewards, and investing them in the work of the kingdom (Matt. 25:14-30).

In addition to talents the Holy Spirit bestows *gifts*. We are accustomed to looking to 1 Corinthians 12 to see what is meant by "spiritual gifts." Saint Paul gives us a list: the word of wisdom, the word of knowledge, faith, healing, the working of miracles, prophecy, the ability to distinguish between the spirits, tongues, and the interpretation of tongues. Whether the apostle in writing this list had meant to be systematic and exhaustive or whether he was just penning examples of various expressions of the Spirit's grace is not clear from the text. It is my own opinion that the latter is the case. Regardless of Paul's original intention, however, Christians through the ages have from time to time tried to delineate with precision the shape and significance of each gift.

In such delineations the words of knowledge and wisdom are usually designated the "nonremarkable gifts." Perhaps this is because they do not provoke the excited atmosphere of the more remarkable or ecstatic manifestations of the Spirit. We might ask: did Paul have in mind here some sort of supranatural revelation to produce this knowledge and wisdom? Or was he simply offering a thank you to that small group of mature individuals—the knowledgeable and wise elders among us—to whom we should go on occasion for counsel, trusting their ability to deliberate fairly and to render sound judgments? If it is the latter, then perhaps we have an overlap here between talents and gifts. Such people of knowledge and wisdom are found in every society, small in number perhaps, but evidently placed there by God for all to benefit if they only will listen. No doubt the Holy Spirit has given the church some of these people as well, and we should be good stewards of their knowledge and wisdom, because they are God's gifts for the upbuilding of the community.

From here we pass on to the "remarkable gifts." The list begins with healing, and then subsequent to that it mentions miracles. Did Paul intend to contrast these two or to complement them? Would nonmiraculous healing—the kind pursued by scientifically trained physicians and nurses in hospitals—count as a gift of the Spirit? This distinction was probably not important to Paul, but it seems important to some people today to be able to contrast the work of the doctor with the miraculous work of God. For the most part, however, we are usually thankful for whatever healing we get, miraculous or otherwise. This is as it should be. Paul here reminds us that the power to heal originates in God, and that both healers who have this power as well as those healed should be reminded that healing is a gift. It is a special blessing that should not be taken for granted.

The gift of prophecy is described in more detail than the others, and, given the experience of contemporary charismatic prayer groups, it is perhaps better understood. Prophecy as the Spirit's gift does not consist in making sound judgments based upon conventional wisdom. Nor does it consist in making loud criticism of unjust social policies. It is rather a special word from God—usually a word of comfort, although it can contain judgment and admonition as well—delivered verbally through the mouth of one participant during worship. The one speaking has no prepared manuscript and has not thought out in advance what will be said. The message simply runs its course on its own power, the Spirit's power.

The ability to distinguish between spirits also constitutes a gift. Historical criticism can reconstruct what Paul, living amid an ancient and prescientific worldview, probably meant here—namely, some people have the ability to discern the work of the true God from the apparent influences of the various elemental spirits and gods of polytheistic pantheons. This presupposes that it is no easy thing to know for certain whether or not it is the true God who is speaking to us. Other voices sound authentic. Therefore, we need discernment.

Because modernized theologians are intellectually divorced from worldviews that are at home with a panoply of gods and spiritual beings, they are tempted to excise the apparently mythical element to such teaching in order to produce some quite mundane advice. Our temptation is to belittle the idea that the world is full of spiritual realities out of which we need to discern God's Holy Spirit. We moderns tend to think naturalistically and materialistically. We like to employ hermeneutical double-talk so that "discerning the spirits" comes to mean analyzing political options or debating ethical issues. In other words, distinguishing the spirits comes out looking like the word of wisdom or knowledge. This sounds reasonable. Nevertheless, I suggest caution here. As our modern consciousness breaks down and people run off wildly to meditation centers, channelers, reincarnation therapists, psychic healers, exorcists, mediums, and witches, perhaps we will again need someone with the gift of discerning the spirits just as it is described in the Bible. The ability to distinguish the presence of the Holy Spirit amid competing spirits in just the form Paul originally meant it might be what we need most.

Also appearing on Paul's list are speaking in tongues (glossolalia) and the interpretation of tongues. When people speak in tongues, the Holy Spirit prays through them in such a manner as to bypass intellectual limitations and restrictions. They become channels of divinely authored prayer, praise, and thanksgiving.

Contemporary charismatics quote with approval the apostle Paul's remark, "For those who speak in a tongue do not speak to other people but to God; for nobody understands them, since they are speaking mysteries in the Spirit" (1 Cor. 14:2).[9] But a little more reading in the context from which this text is drawn shows that, although Paul certainly approves of glossolalia and actually engages in it himself, he believes that understandable communication is to be preferred. He ranks prophecy higher than speaking in a tongue for the sole reason that it can be understood. He suggests that if Christians insist on speaking in tongues, then the least they could do is provide an interpreter so that other people present could understand what is going on. "I would rather speak five words with my mind in order to instruct others also," he writes with obvious vehemence, "than ten thousand words in a tongue" (1 Cor. 14:19). In short, Paul seeks no compromise in his commitment to understandable communication of the gospel.

In addition to talents and gifts, there are *fruits* of the Spirit. Good fruit comes from a good tree. The tree in this case is a person who through the Spirit has been given faith and hope and who is living the life of love. What bursts forth from its branches are love, joy, peace, patience, kindness, goodness, faithfulness, gentleness, and self-control (Gal. 5:22-23). I doubt if Paul intended that we try to sort out the fine distinctions between these virtues. The very thought of such a thing would return us to the legalistic mindset from which the gospel has liberated us. Instead what we have here is a general character sketch, a spray of color that does not yet have a specific form. It is up to us to draw the picture in detail, creatively and freely, being led and directed by love.

---

9. Kevin Ranaghan and Dorothy Ranaghan, *Catholic Pentecostals* (New York: Paulist, 1969), 199.

SANCTIFICATION

Sanctification, deriving from the Latin *sanctus* and the Greek ἅγιος, meaning "holy," refers to the process by which new life is imparted to Christian believers by the Holy Spirit, a process by which they are increasingly released from the compulsive power of sin and guilt and enabled to love more fully and to love their neighbors selflessly. Although the New Testament nowhere spells out a carefully delineated process of spiritual growth comparable to Gautama's eightfold path, a select group of terms has grown up in the tradition to identify various phases of the Spirit's work of transformation.

The Dynamics of Transformation

I suggest that *sanctification* be the inclusive term for the following elements, which usually fall in this sequence: illumination, regeneration and conversion, obedience and good works, and perfection.

Illumination. The Spirit symbolized by the fire of revelation and the lamp of wisdom begins the transforming work by illuminating the human mind with the knowledge of salvation. This may require external or objective knowledge such as hearing the history of Jesus reported. This is depicted in the book of Acts when Peter and Paul recite the events of Jesus' death and resurrection. But the facts are not enough. Illumination adds to external knowledge an internal knowledge, a conviction of the heart, a realization that this is a truth for me. The Holy Spirit works to open the eyes of the mind so that we can turn from the darkness toward the light (Acts 26:18).

Regeneration and conversion. Illumination along with regeneration make such turning toward the light possible. Regeneration, which literally means "rebirth," is the act of grace by which the Holy Spirit makes the living Christ present to the sinner in faith. It is the act whereby the universal saving event of Christ takes effect in a particular person's life, one's particular sins are forgiven, and the power of the new creation is appropriated. In this way the Holy Spirit gives us the power to turn, to convert. Conversion begins with contrition, a heartfelt sense of sorrow for one's sins, and is followed immediately with repentance, a turning away from one's sin and toward a commitment to living justly. Conversion is the first act of faith, a faith made possible by the Spirit's work of illumination and regeneration.

Obedience and good works. Faith and the power of regeneration continue to act in our lives. They make themselves known internally through obedience to God's will and externally through works of love, both forms of self-giving. A good tree will bear good fruit, so a regenerate faith leads us to appropriate joyfully God's law and to express God's love in the surrounding world. The Spirit of unity that establishes communion within the godhead and that shares communion with us through the divine economy evokes in us a sense of unity with all of God's creation. We realize that there is a bond of love that unites all things, and so we begin to feel sympathetically the pain of others and seek means for healing brokenness and realizing wholeness in every department of life.[10]

Perfection. Sometimes called "entire sanctification" or "holiness," Christian perfection is the presence in the believer of pure love in its fullness. Pure love expels sin and governs the heart and mind totally. The power of pure love comes from the indwelling of the Holy Spirit, which makes it possible to do things not given to ordinary human ability.

The idea of Christian perfection is the answer some denominational traditions have given to certain questions that press for answers. To where does the life of obedience and love lead? Does it consist simply in a number of random intuitions about God's will and a disintegrated series of loving acts? Or do all these things belong to a specific pattern of development that has the aim of perfecting the life of the sinner? Does an act of obedience or a work of love result in an increase in the quantity of holiness in one's soul? Is there here a problem of theological logic: if the life of faith consists essentially in going out of oneself, how can its purpose be to establish itself as holy? Is it the aim of the sanctification process to make a saint at the end, or is one's saintliness simply a byproduct of loving?

John Wesley, with the help of his brother Charles and the rise of Methodism, etched the doctrine of sanctification in many minds and implanted the desire to attain "Christian perfection" in many consciences. Wesley was critical of those who pander what he called "solifidaism," who holler "Believe! Believe!" as if faith alone without pursuing further spiritual growth would be enough. Like the Reformers before him, Wesley believed justification to be wholly distinct from sanctification and necessarily antecedent to it. But the Christian life does not stop with the rebirth belonging to one's state of justification. Faith moves on from infancy toward maturity. He foresaw a spiritual pilgrimage that carries one into a deeper and clearer conviction of inbred sin than is required for justifying faith, and this pilgrimage leads eventually to a decisive experience, namely, the experience of a total death to sin and an entire renewal of life. This renewal consists in a purging of sin, a restoration of the image of God, and a life spontaneously and completely directed by divine love. This is the message of the Wesley hymnbook published in 1742:

---

10. For an expanded depiction of the dynamics of transformation in the context of new age spirituality, see Ted Peters, *The Cosmic Self* (San Francisco: Harper Collins, 1991), 180–88.

> Purge me from every sinful blot;
>   My idols all be cast aside:
> Cleanse me from every evil thought,
>   From all the filth of pride.
> The hatred of the carnal mind
>   Out of my flesh at once remove:
> Give me a tender heart, resigned,
>   And pure, and full of faith and love.

Thus, faith in things unseen is not enough for Christian living, according to Wesley. There must be a concrete experience of the working of the Holy Spirit in one's life. This is what the doctrine of sanctification and Wesley's concept of perfection are about. If it is Jesus who says "Be perfect, therefore, as your heavenly Father is perfect" (Matt. 5:48), then we cannot leave these words lay idle. Despite all our gratitude for God's saving grace, we cannot allow ourselves to be seduced by antinomianism. Jesus has made it clear that the fulfillment of the law is not the annulment of the law. The commandment to love remains, and Jesus does not make it easy. He says we should love God with all our heart, mind, soul, and strength and our neighbor as ourselves. Wesley affirms that even if this sounds difficult, it is possible because the Holy Spirit enables us to do it. Thus, living a life of love is both law and gospel. It is law because God commands it. It is gospel because the power to love is granted to us by God's grace.

Perfection, then, is not just an ideal, according to Wesley. It is not just a forensic imputation, as if the word *righteous* were painted over someone who is in reality guilty. Because God is a God of truth, God will not allow justification to mean declaring as just someone who is in reality not just. The person must become just, must go through an actual transformation.

Wesley describes perfection as "pure love reigning alone" that expels sin and governs the heart and mind of the person of faith. Wesley's critics quibble, of course, that it is impossible for us to expel all of our sin. Critics can invoke John Calvin, according to whom there remains in each regenerate person a fountain of evil, continually producing irregular desires, and a warfare against the Spirit that will terminate only in death. Critics can as well invoke Luther's *simul justus et peccator* as evidence that some vestige of sin will remain in the life of the believer until death accomplishes the final cleansing. But this does not dissuade Wesley. "What, then, does their arguing prove who object against perfection?" he asks. "Absolute and infallible perfection? I never contended for it. Sinless perfection? Neither do I contend for this, seeing that the term is not scriptural." He recognizes that in their mortal lives even perfected Christians will confront temptation, that they are limited by their lack of perfect knowledge, and that they can be subject to mistakes in judgment. They may slip up from time to time. All that Wesley is asking for is that our disposition be perfected, that we "feel nothing but love."[11] This must be possible within our lifespan, he argues, or else scripture would not have enjoined us to "have the mind of Christ" or to "walk in the light as he is in the light."

Wesley's critics have contended that perfection in this life is too much to ask for. Even if the critics are right, however, this should not part our eyes from his central vision: the Christian life can and should actually be lived in love due to the presence of the Holy Spirit.

(1) There is such a thing as perfection; for it is again and again mentioned in scripture. (2) It is not so early as justification; for justified persons are to "go on unto perfection" (Heb. 6:1). (3) It is not so late as death; for Saint Paul speaks of living men that were perfect (Phil. 3:15). (4) It is not absolute. Absolute perfection belongs not to man . . . but to God alone. (5) It does not make a man infallible; none is infallible while he remains in the body. (6) Is it sinless? It is not worth while to contend for a term. It is "salvation from sin." (7) It is "perfect love" (I John 4:18). This is the essence of it. . . . (8) It is improvable. . . . (9) It is amissible, capable of being lost. . . . (10) It is constantly both preceded and followed by a gradual work.[12]

There is no loss of the priority of God's grace here. This is by no means a return to semi-Pelagianism. That John Wesley affirmed the doctrine of Christian perfection but not at the cost of surrendering unmerited grace is seen in his small emendations of his brother Charles's hymns. Most of Charles's staggering output of 6,500 hymns found their way into collections edited by John. One of those hymns, "Love Divine," is routinely found in the "Christian Perfection" section of Methodist hymnals and is known to many:

> Finish then, Thy new creation;
> Pure and spotless let us be;
> Let us see Thy great salvation
> Perfectly restored in Thee:
> Changed from glory into glory,
> 'Till in heaven we take our place,
> 'Till we cast our crowns before Thee,
> Lost in wonder, love, and praise.

When Charles originally wrote the second line above it read "pure and sinless be." John changed *sinless* to *spotless*. Perhaps it was asking too much to think of our existence now, even Christian existence, as "sinless." In the same vein we might note that the phrase "changed from glory into

---

11. See John Telford, ed., *The Letters of John Wesley*, 8 vols. (London: Epworth, 1931), 4:213. See Wesley's sermons "Christian Perfection" (in *WW*, 6:1–19) and "On Perfection" (in *WW*, 6:411–24). See also Wilber T. Dayton, "Entire Sanctification," in Charles W. Carter, ed., *A Contemporary Wesleyan Theology*, 2 vols. (Grand Rapids, Mich.: Zondervan, 1983), 1:528–39.

12. Wesley, *A Plain Account of Christian Perfection* (1767; reprint, London: Epworth, 1952), 106.

glory" for Charles was not a reference to eschatological transformation after death but to sanctification in this life. That Charles was referring to increasing holiness in this life is indicated by the word *'till*, which places the process of glorification prior to one's entrance into heaven. Evidently this aspect of Christian perfection passed John's theological censoring.

Grace and Sanctification

Although critics may be dissatisfied with the apparent Methodist ambiguity on the relationship between free grace and the dynamic of sanctification, the Wesleys sought conscientiously to maintain the priority of a Christ-centered and saving grace in justification to be followed by the purifying work of the Holy Spirit. In later times, however, those proffering the sanctified life seemed to tire from maintaining the careful distinction between the two, and the Reformation emphasis on salvation via unmerited grace slowly dissolved into a new legalism. Despite the fact that "amazing grace" is so zealously shouted in the American revivalist tradition, it is grace itself that seems to get lost among the list of things we have to do to gain personal holiness. Charles Finney, for example, agrees that we are justified by faith. But then he proceeds to redefine faith so that it no longer belongs to sinful persons. It no longer means forgiveness. "Present evangelical faith implies a state of present sinlessness," he writes; "observe, faith is the yielding and committal of the whole will, and of the whole being to Christ. This, and nothing short of this, is evangelical faith.... This is the reason why faith is spoken of as the condition... of salvation."[13] The only reason scripture speaks of faith as the sole condition for justification, Finney thinks, is that included in faith are such things as repentance, obedience, good works, and perseverance. In short, we have come full circle to the medieval position where once again justification and sanctification mean the same thing, and salvation is given not to sinners but to those who are already holy.

I believe the Reformers have bequeathed us a treasure that we ought not let get buried again. The grace of God working through Jesus Christ is total, complete, and sufficient to accomplish our salvation. By becoming Emmanuel, God with us, our gracious God offered justification "while we still were sinners" (Rom. 5:8). By taking our sins onto himself, Christ frees us from all moral impediments to full fellowship with God. In short, faith and God's justness belong to sinners—not to righteous people—as a gift. This is the work of the second person of the Trinity, and it is enough for salvation.

---

13. Charles G. Finney, *Lectures on Systematic Theology*, ed. J. H. Fairchild (1878; reprint, South Gate, Calif.: Colporter Kemp, 1944), 377. The Reformation insight that justification is for the ungodly and is the source of faith seems to have gotten lost in American Protestantism. It has led to a new Pelagianism and to sharp criticisms by the likes of Carl Braaten, *Justification: The Article by Which the Church Stands or Falls* (Minneapolis: Fortress, 1990).

In addition, however, we must celebrate the way in which the work of the Holy Spirit adds grace upon grace. By making Christ present to us through faith, the Spirit fills our heart with hope and love and empowers our lives for effective living. But because love is the greatest of the works of the Spirit within us, and because love as agape is by definition aimed at the betterment of the beloved, the life of love does not have as its end personal holiness. We do not seek to live lovingly in order to prove ourselves obedient and therefore holy and therefore just and therefore deserving of salvation. In the Reformation tradition we must affirm the sanctifying work of the Holy Spirit, to be sure; but we must affirm with equal vigor that this sanctifying work is aimed at making this a better world and not aimed at achieving the salvation of the believer.

This is where holism becomes relevant to current Christian thinking. God's salvation is aimed ultimately at the whole of creation, not just at individual parts of it. We are parts. Our individual blessing is contingent upon God's blessing the whole. It is this sense of belonging to something greater than ourselves that the Holy Spirit communicates to us in the event of illumination, and our conversion consists primarily in a degree of self-denial—of denying our selfness apart from all other things—combined with an affirmation that we belong to someone else. Obedience consists in yielding to God's will, a will that aims to place our own destiny at harmony with everyone else's destiny. Love is stimulated by the whelming sense of belonging to the other, to the one who is the object of our loving work. Hence, the regenerate life cannot have as its end the attainment of ever more holiness for the individual and the achievement of a perfection in isolation from the grand design for salvation that encompasses the cosmos.

THE SPIRIT AND THE TRINITY

As we saw earlier, the church emerged from the Council at Nicea in 325 with a simple assertion, "We believe in the Holy Spirit." But by the time the meeting at Constantinople in 381 was over, this had been expanded to read: "...the Holy Spirit, the Lord and Giver of life, who proceeds from the Father, who together with the Father and the Son is adored and glorified, who spoke through the prophets." What accounts for the change? The controversies during the half century between the councils provoked thinking about pneumatology and elicited more precise formulations of Christian belief. The main challenge came from the Arians, who considered the Holy Spirit more as a creature of God than as the creator God. Against the Arians, Athanasius said that the Spirit belongs to the indivisible Trinity on scriptural grounds; and that because the work of sanctification is a divine and not a creaturely work, the Spirit cannot be thought of as a creature. Basil of Caesarea published the first treatise devoted to pneumatology in 375, *On the Holy Spirit*, in which he contended that "the Holy Spirit is to be ranked with the Father."[14] Gregory of Nazianzus, who followed with his *Fifth Theological Oration*, which deals with this topic, identified a historical progression in the awareness of God. The Old Testament offers an open presentation of God the first person of the Trinity. This is accompanied by oblique references to the Son. In the New Testament the Son is proclaimed, and the deity of the Spirit is suggested. Now in the life of the church the Spirit dwells within Christian communion, and there is an opportunity to make a clearer designation.[15]

Ambrose of Milan offered a more developed pneumatology in his work published at the time of the council in 381, citing scripture to show how the Holy Spirit quickens life, regenerates, sanctifies, and inspires prophets with wisdom. He argued that the Holy Spirit along with the Father and the Son is the "true in the true, God in God, Light in Light, . . . of one nature and one knowledge, . . . [and sharing in] unity of power." Hence, the Spirit is worthy of worship just as the godhead is worthy of worship.[16]

From Nicea to Barth much of the justification for declaring the full divinity of the Holy Spirit has depended upon a spurious argument regarding the term *procession* (ἐκπόρευσις, *processio*). The term comes from the creedal affirmation that the Spirit "proceeds from the Father." Like the term *generation* used to describe the relation between Father and Son, the term *procession* connotes a continuity of essence. This contrasts with the world, which God "creates" or "makes." The creation is not an extension of the creator's essence. But the Spirit is. "What proceeds from God can," says Barth, "only be God."[17] The problem with this apparently exegetical argument is that what it exegetes is not scripture but rather the creed. The Niceno-Constantinopolitan use of *procession* is already an explication of scripture. Hence, what often appears as an argument for the divinity of the Spirit is in fact an illustration of the divinity.

A systematic argument lies behind this apparently exegetical argument. Systematically speaking, we need a term such as *proceed* in order to distinguish the inner life of the godhead from the world which is created or made. We also need a word such as *proceed* in order to distinguish the Spirit from the Son who is "generated." Otherwise, as Augustine fears, the Spirit would turn out to be the Son's brother.[18] What the Spirit and the Son share in common is that they are not created but rather inherent to the divine life proper.

In current theology, with its tendency toward identifying more closely the immanent Trinity with the economic Trinity, the Holy Spirit is be-

---

14. Basil *On the Holy Spirit* 10.25.
15. Gregory of Nazianzus *Orations* 5.26.
16. Ambrose *Of the Holy Spirit* 3.82; 2.125.
17. Barth, *CD*, 1/1:542.
18. Augustine *On the Trinity* 15.27.50.

coming understood as the life-giving force of futurity and relationship for God as well as for the creation. The Spirit of God provides the *telos* for the divine life just as it does for ours. It is not just the case that God is our future. There is a future for Godself. God as the creator Spirit (*spiritus creator*) calls forth what is not yet, drawing something out of nothing, and transforming what is into something else. As the power of the future, the third person of the Trinity is that force that breaks open the present, releases it from the grip of the past, and draws it toward the fulfillment of the past's noble promises. God has a projected goal, an intention that awaits fulfillment, and the attainment or fulfillment of this goal will coincide with our consummate salvation and that of all creation. Here I am offering an understanding of the Spirit as the power of the future. That understanding is not formulated just the way it was by Gregory of Nazianzus or by the Niceno-Constantinopolitan Creed, but it seems to me to be faithful to the scriptural symbols as well as an appropriate form of evangelical explication for our time.

I just made a quick jump from the fourth to the twentieth century as regards the understanding of the role of the Holy Spirit in the Trinity. But in the centuries that immediately followed Constantinople another question arose to which there was more than one answer, and the Western Latin churches have been fighting with the Eastern Orthodox churches ever since. We are still feeling the pain from the wounds inflicted on the body of Christ by this fight. The question is: what is the mode of the Spirit's origin? Does it proceed from both the Father and the Son (*ex Patre Filioque*) or from the Father alone? The statement at Constantinople says simply that the "Spirit proceeds from the Father," but, following up on a remark by Hilary of Poitiers, Augustine began to speculate regarding a double procession. Augustine said that the procession of the Spirit from both is taught in scripture because it speaks of the Spirit of the Son and also the Spirit of the Father. The Father and the Son must then be a single principle in relation to the Holy Spirit. Why should we not then affirm that the Holy Spirit proceeds from the Son as well as the Father?[19] The doctrine of the *filioque* is the result of such interpretive speculation.

By no means was the *filioque* originally intended to be a polemical attack against the Eastern church. Its aim was evangelical explication, the attempt to explain the trinitarian symbols more clearly. But unfortunately, evangelical explication became intertwined with ecclesiastical politics and was employed as a weapon in the Latin fight for papal dominance over the church. The notion of the Spirit's double procession surfaced at the Synods of Toledo in 447 and 589 and was later promoted for popular usage by Charlemagne among the Franks. The Latins and the Greeks were

---

19. Augustine *On the Trinity* 6.10.11; 5.14.15; 15.26.45–48; see Hilary of Poitiers *On the Trinity* 2.29.

competing for influence in newly Christianized areas of Europe such as Bulgaria, so Charlemagne in 809 asked Pope Leo III to rewrite the Nicene Creed with the *filioque* added. Leo III had sufficient integrity to reject this request, citing as grounds that such a unilateral move on his part would violate the authority of the ecumenical Council of Constantinople. The bishops of Rome following Leo III saw things differently, however, and the *filioque* was permitted to slip into Western creedal usage, finding papal approval for use during the mass by 1014. The practice grew and came to a church-dividing climax in 1054 when Pope Leo IX excommunicated the patriarch of Constantinople, Cerularius, on the grounds that the Greeks were omitting the *filioque* from the Nicene Creed.

Photius, a ninth-century patriarch of Constantinople who became a pawn in the game of power between East and West, lashed out at these Latin "blasphemies." Photius raised three arguments against the addition of *filioque*, one ecclesiastical and two theological. The ecclesiastical argument is succinct and clear: when an ecumenical council representing the whole Christian church establishes a statement of faith as was done at Constantinople in 381, then only a similar council has the right to amend or alter it. The unilateral action taken by the bishops at Rome must be considered arbitrary if not scandalous.

Photius's theological arguments have exegetical and systematic components. Exegetically he underscores what Jesus says in John 15:26, namely, that the Spirit comes "from the Father." Photius asks rhetorically: if the Spirit comes from both the Father and the Son, then why did Jesus not add "... and from me"? If "from the Father" was good enough for Jesus, then it ought to be good enough for the church.[20]

His systematic argument focuses on the destruction of the concept of the Trinity that he believes is entailed in the concept of *filioque*. *Filioque* implies that the Spirit is inferior to the first two persons of the Trinity, because the Spirit is produced by them but they are not similarly produced by the Spirit. This means there is no Trinity of three equal persons. It leaves a binity made up of Father and Son. Even worse, if we think of the Son as generated from the Father prior to the Spirit proceeding from the two of them, we may end up with a Father monarch and a Son prince as a mere intermediary. Photius accuses the West of flirting with Sabellianism because *filioque* points to a series of successions leading from the Father to the Son and then, lastly, to the Spirit. He complains that if Christ is the

---

20. Photius, *On the Mystagogy of the Holy Spirit* (Astoria, N.Y.: Studien Publications, 1983), 71–72; 51–52. When Augustine comes to John 15:26, he pauses; but then he goes on to John 20:23, "He [Jesus] breathed on them and said, 'Receive the Holy Spirit' " Augustine remarks that this was done "so as to show that he [the Spirit] proceeded also from himself" (*On the Trinity* 15.26.45). Barth attacks the Eastern exegesis because it isolates John 15:26 from the wider context of texts (*CD*, 1/1:549).

Father's Son, then the Spirit must be his "grandson." *Filioque*, it seems to Photius, cannot help but shortchange the Spirit's divinity.

It seems to me that we must simply grant to Photius the validity of the ecclesiastical argument.[21] The insertion of *filioque* in the West was arbitrary, unfair, and certainly not done in the interest of church unity. The value of an ecumenical council is found in its attempt to decide matters as a whole, to give evangelical explication to the commitments of the entire body of Christ. For Western Christians to ignore such a conciliar decision and to operate as if the East and its concerns did not exist reveal at minimum a lack of integrity and at maximum a divisive spirit. If in the future the Holy Spirit should lead us farther toward a new (or renewed) stage of ecumenical unity, I would hope that Christians in the West would apologize on behalf of their ancestors and seek forgiveness from their Eastern sisters and brothers. It is necessary to invoke the ecumenical principle here and return (at least initially) to the creedal text of 381 as the point of agreement. Once this is affirmed, then the discussion can be advanced.

With regard to the theological import of *filioque*, though, I must say there is much to commend the Western position. If we think of theology as an ongoing process of evangelical explication, then we need not assume that what was somewhat hastily decided at Constantinople in 381 should remain fixed as the last word regarding the Holy Spirit. Continued exploration into the matter and drawing out further the implications of the basic Christian symbols could in principle lead to new insights. *Filioque* is one such insight.

To think of the spirit as proceeding from the Son as well as the Father makes sense on a couple of counts, both having to do with relationality and communality. First, with regard to the life of faith, it ties the Spirit closely to the resurrected Christ. It is the Easter Christ who is present to us in faith, and it is the Spirit that is responsible for this presence. *It is* this presence. When considering this work of transcending and applying the historical event of Jesus Christ to our personal lives, we must think of the Spirit as proceeding from Jesus Christ.

Second, within the divine life proper, whether conceived as the immanent or economic Trinity, the Spirit is the principle of relationship and unity. The separation if not alienation that takes place between Father

---

21. Nineteenth-century Latin defenses of *filioque* almost concede this point. Using historical-critical tools, theologians reviewed the seven universally acknowledged ecumenical councils and determined that none could be cited in support of *filioque*. So we find theologians acknowledging that *filioque* was not "Catholic dogma in the first ages" but "the theologian . . . must contend that the church has always held the doctrine" (Pelikan, *CT*, 5:258). The Faith and Order Commission of the World Council of Churches recommended in 1979 that all recognize the "original form" of the Niceno-Constantinopolitan Creed. Yves Congar favors suppression of *filioque* on the condition that Christian people on both sides prepare for the event by creating an atmosphere of love and that the East stipulate the nonheretical theological content of the Western understanding (*I Believe in the Holy Spirit*, 3 vols. [London and New York: Chapman and Seabury, 1983], 3:206).

and Son and that defines the Father as Father and the Son as Son is healed by the Spirit. The Spirit maintains unity in difference. There is a sort of constitutional dependency of the Spirit upon the twoness or doubleness within the divine life. This is not to posit a temporal priority, as in a modalistic program of three successive stages of divine development. The dependency is rather a logical one. The principle of relationship depends upon having two persons to relate.

This by no means implies that the Spirit of God did not exist in Old Testament times or was absent during the career of the pre-Easter Jesus. The Spirit was not manufactured at the moment of resurrection or ascension. The Spirit is everlasting or eternal in the same sense that the triune godhead is. The Spirit is the principle of relationship within the immanent Trinity, and it is always due to the work of the Spirit that the Father is the Father in relation to the Son and, conversely, the Son is who he is due to a corresponding relationship. The Western picture is not the way Photius so humorously describes it, where God the Father generates the Son and then subsequently produces a grandchild Spirit. The Spirit is the condition whereby the generation of the Son is made possible, yet without the Son to whom the Father relates there would be no divine Spirit.

The position I am advocating here is not one of subordinating the Spirit to the Son. As I will suggest below in my discussion of wisdom (σοφία) and word (λόγος), there is considerable exegetical overlapping between the second and third persons of the Trinity. The creator Spirit is almost interchangeable with the word by which God speaks and things happen. Such observations lend credence to the Orthodox doctrine of procession from the Father alone in a fashion parallel to that of the Son. This indicates that the Bible is not a systematic theology; what doctrinal theologians do is attempt to draw out and develop concepts of God that cohere with one another systematically. An exact understanding of pneumatology is not given in scripture. Gregory of Nazianzus is correct in his historical judgment that our understanding of the Spirit has not been uniform all along. It is something we are working out.

THE COSMIC SPIRIT

In its reaction against the materialism and fragmentary thinking of the modern period, postmodern thinking is much more inclined to apprehend a spiritual and unifying force at work in the natural processes. New age advocates in particular believe that the whole cosmos is being driven forward by creative energies that are leading us toward new levels of individual consciousness and new and more complex forms of interrelationship. This is said to be the work of a cosmic spirit.

Creator Spirit

Such thinking is by no means foreign to Christian theology, which has long held that it is a mistake to dump the responsibility of creation in the lap of the Father alone. Not only is the Son, the Logos, the principle of order in the creation, but the Spirit is the life-giving power of original as well as continuing creation. Ambrose in the fourth century insisted that the Holy Spirit creates just as the Father creates.[22] In the great "Redemption of Man" series of ten giant tapestries produced in Brussels about 1510, a series that now hangs in the DeYoung Museum in San Francisco, the Flemish artists depict the Trinity—Spirit included—as three artisans engaged in the creation of the world. The three are always found together, whether separating the waters and firmaments, placing the sun in the sky, or invoking life through Adam and Eve. There is every reason to think the presence and work of the Spirit are as wide as nature itself.

In Old Testament times it was customary to depict the creative and providential work of God in terms of wisdom. At times wisdom became almost hypostatized as well as feminized, looking quite like a personified agent of God (Prov. 3:19; Jer. 10:12; Matt. 11:19). C. F. D. Moule develops the thesis that an interesting transition in vocabulary takes place in New Testament times. He says that the concept of wisdom breaks down into two concepts: the Logos and the Spirit.[23] Like wisdom the Logos organizes the creation, and like wisdom the Spirit is its life-giving power. Both are the work of the one godhead. Both are universal in scope. The proto-trinitarian thought of Theophilus of Antioch and Irenaeus in the second century may represent a growth still close to these roots when they describe the Trinity as God, word, and wisdom.[24]

This theme is developed in our own time by Jürgen Moltmann. His doctrine of creation is a doctrine of the Holy Spirit. The Spirit who proceeds from the Father and shines forth in the Son is the very spirit of the universe, its cohesive structure, its source of energy. The Spirit is the principle of creativity operating at all levels of matter and life. It is continually opening up possibilities for new realities. It is also a holistic principle. In addition to being the principle of individuation, the Spirit creates interactions and draws things toward cooperation, community, and harmony. The Spirit that gave life in the first place is now engaged in the task of transforming life, in the task of bringing forth the new creation.[25] The Spirit of God did not just create life at the beginning but continues to inspire and evoke wisdom within the cosmos as it makes its way through history toward its appointed destiny.

---

22. Ambrose *Of the Holy Spirit* 2.6.
23. C. F. D. Moule, *The Holy Spirit* (Grand Rapids, Mich.: Eerdmans, 1978), 20.
24. Theophilus *Autolycus* 2.15; see Irenaeus *Against Heresies* 4.7.4.
25. Jürgen Moltmann, *God in Creation* (San Francisco: Harper & Row, 1985), 100.

Christian theology needs to affirm with spokespersons of other religions and of postmodern religiosity that the Spirit of God is present throughout the cosmic process. The divine Spirit is not the private possession of the historic Christian churches. But in saying that, I must affirm as well that this cosmic presence does not take the form of an immanent or impersonal force. There is no such thing as a spiritual nature that exists parallel to physical nature. Rather, the Spirit operates throughout the processes of creation as God's providential activity. As such it is present though hidden in all times and places; yet it is free to surface and enter human experience as a discrete power or identity. Because we understand the work of the Spirit to anticipate proleptically the consummate future by drawing us into the processes of integration and unification in the present, we must recognize and affirm the presence of the Spirit wherever the fruits of the future kingdom are discerned—peace, justice, reconciliation, healing, integrity—both inside and outside the church.

Mystical Oneness and Proleptic Unity

The new age romanticism that characterizes much of emerging postmodern thought implicitly or explicitly assumes something like a doctrine of universal spirit. It relies upon ecstatic experiences in which one's individual consciousness seems caught up into a whelming reality in which one feels a sense of unity with all that is. In times past these were called "oceanic" or "religious" experiences, but these days they are often reported without such labels. Following closely on the heels of the experience itself comes a doctrine of enlightenment, an interpretation of the experience in terms of awakening from sleep or expanding one's consciousness. The result is a conversion or transformation that allegedly leads to a new and more profound understanding of reality and the outright doctrine that all things are in fact really only one thing.

So we need to ask: what, if any, is the connection between the Christian concept of the Holy Spirit and the experiences of those people who are beginning to think with a postmodern or neoreligious mind? We will find that to the extent that postmodernity becomes religious it tends toward mystical monism, a position long advocated by the religious traditions emerging from ancient India. Although Christian symbols lead in a direction of theological explication quite different from those followed by mystical gurus from the East, we need to accept as a given the basic experience upon which Asian thought is based. It seems to me that we cannot deny that individuals from time to time have transcendental experiences. It will be my suggestion here that we should attempt to apply a method of discerning the spirits and, further, that if we do so it will appear that the genuine Spirit of unity and truth has acted to give certain individuals a foretaste of the consummate unity of all things that God is planning for the creation.

Exactly which course we should take in this matter of discerning the spirits is not unambiguously clear. Nevertheless, we can identify some landmarks that if observed might help eventually to point the way. First, the cosmos at present is not an actual unity, either physically or morally. As we saw in the chapter on creation, the cosmos is not a unity physically due to its monodirectional expansion away from a center and due to distances so great that there can be no communication between various parts of it even if such communication were to travel at the speed of light. We know it is not a unity morally because life on earth is rampant with the forces of alienation, destruction, brokenness, and death. Although philosophers spin out idealist conceptions of the universe as a single comprehensive system within which all parts are related to one another according to the doctrine of internal relations, the actual world in which we live is otherwise. The philosophers give us an imaginary picture; our ordinary daily experience and our cosmological theory encompass fragmentation, frustration, and dead ends.

It is therefore important to notice that these oceanic experiences are extraordinary experiences. Those who have them report a temporary departure from ordinary, mundane consciousness. They go on a "trip." We must conclude that what they experience is not the ordinary reality that currently exists. To this they would heartily agree, yet they would add that the ecstatic unity they have experienced is more real than the ordinary one. What can this mean? Is it just more intense, and therefore it seems more real? Or is there a credible metaphysical or ontological assertion being advanced here?

Let us grant that what is going on here is more than a mere hallucination and that something ontological is meant by asserting a deep unity to all things. What then? This leads to my second landmark: the proposition that the unity that is experienced is a proleptic unity. The Spirit of God is the spirit of unity and truth because it is the work of God to bring the creation to a consummate unity in the eschatological kingdom. This is the truth. Perhaps we could understand those extraordinary experiences of unity in the present as blessings, as God-given prophecies or visions of what is to come. The actual ecstatic experience is transitory. Countless meditative techniques and pious slogans have been propounded by gurus in the fruitless attempt to hang on to the experience, to proffer a continuing state of enlightenment that never goes away. But it must go away because the present reality is that we are still on the way to the as yet to be completed work of God with creation, and only upon completion will we be able to experience the unity that does not go away. In our mundane lives we experience fragmentation and separateness. This is the actual state of current affairs. If we are granted one fleeting moment in which we feel the unity of the cosmos, let us consider it a blessing, a Spirit-given advance on a reality that is yet to be.

9

THE CHURCH

Elect from every nation, yet one o'er all the earth
Her charter of salvation: one Lord, one faith, one birth;
One holy name she blesses, partakes one holy food
And to one hope she presses, with every grace endued.
                                                    —Samuel J. Stone (1839–1900)

The church is the historical arc between two terminals, Easter and the consummation. The church has been given the charge of bringing light to the world in this period while we await the full shining glory of God when even the sun will be surpassed in radiance. In the partial darkness of the present aeon, however, we must push on, following the path that the lamp of God's word illumines, a word made audible in the church's preaching, made visible in the celebration of the sacraments, and made tangible in the ministry of reconciling love.

Ecclesiology is the doctrine of the church. Christians believe the church has been called into existence by the Holy Spirit to bear the presence of the risen Christ of Easter until the second coming in glory. The church is many faceted, and each of the facets seems itself to emit a variety of perspectives from which to view it. Because of this, there are more theological disagreements over the doctrine of the church than any other locus.

THE CHURCH DEFINED

We can identify the presence of the church when and where the story of Jesus is being told with its significance, that is, where the word of God is being proclaimed. To elucidate this definition I turn first to an examination of the biblical symbols of the church that still live and thrive in contemporary ecclesiology.

Symbols of the Church

One biblical metaphor for the church is the flock belonging to the good shepherd. The kindly shepherd, God, leads and feeds the sheep and also searches out the lost ones to bring them home; those in the church represent the ones God has already found and placed in the fold (Isa. 40:11; Ezek. 34:11-12; Luke 15:3-7). The church's devoted shepherd is even known to have given up his life for his sheep (John 10:11-15). The New Testament exhorts the elders—who, like the shepherd's dogs, help to keep the flock intact—to be ever mindful of the sufferings of the good shepherd and not be domineering in their charge (1 Pet. 5:1-5).

A second similar metaphor is that of the bride. Christ loves the church so much that "he gave himself up for her," cleanses her and sanctifies her, and "nourishes and tenderly cares for" her (Eph. 5:25-29; see 2 Cor. 11:2). In the apocalyptic visions of John the church is depicted as the bride of the lamb (Rev. 19:7; 21:9; 22:17). Wife of Christ imagery has differentiated a bit so that through the years the church has garnered increased feminine connotations and has come to be known as Mother Church, the source of Christians' life and continued spiritual nourishment. John Calvin expands the metaphor eloquently when writing that "there is no other way to enter into life unless this mother conceive us in her womb, give us birth, nourish us at her breast, and lastly, unless she keep us under her care and guidance until, putting off mortal flesh, we become like the angels (Matt. 22:30)."[1]

A third image is that of branches belonging to the vine that gives them life. The Father is the vinedresser. Christ is the vine. The faithful are the branches who, if they abide in Christ, will "bear more fruit" (John 15:1-11). The vine first gave nourishment to Israel, but some of the branches have broken off. This gives room for the Gentiles to be grafted on (Rom. 11:13-26).

A fourth and similar image is that of the building, the temple of the Holy Spirit. Jesus likened himself to a cornerstone upon which something might be constructed, and—although Jesus seems to have been referring to the kingdom of God—the church has frequently interpreted this to refer to itself (Matt. 21:42; Acts 4:11; 1 Pet. 2:7; Ps. 118:22). This seems to be buttressed by a slightly different use of the metaphor by Paul, who says he himself "laid a foundation" (1 Cor. 3:10) or that the foundation was laid by "apostles and prophets" with "Christ Jesus himself as the cornerstone" (Eph. 2:20). The church thus becomes a "holy temple, . . . a dwelling place for God" (Eph. 2:22).

A fifth metaphor is "the body of Christ." The image of the body is perhaps the most forceful because it has been developed analogically in at least two complementary directions: Christ relates to the church as a head

---

1. Calvin, *Inst.*, 4.1.4.

to its body, while Christians relate to one another as limbs that cooperate. Because he is "the first-born of all creation" and "all things hold together" in him, "he is the head of the body, the church" (Col. 1:15-18). From this head the body is "nourished and knit together through its joints and ligaments," so that it "grows with a growth that is from God" (Col. 2:19). The sacraments indicate this corporal unity. "In the one Spirit we were all baptized into one body" (1 Cor. 12:13), united with Christ in his death and now raised to live the resurrected life (Rom. 6:4-5). Of the eucharist Saint Paul writes, "Because there is one bread, we who are many are one body, for we all partake of the one bread" (1 Cor. 10:17). The unity we share with the head constitutes the unity we share with one another. All the bodily members need one another to sustain a single life. The eye needs the hand and vice versa; therefore, we should cooperate and eliminate discord. If one member suffers, the rest feel the pain too. If a member is honored, all share in the honor (1 Cor. 12:12-26).

One of the problems Christians face today is that these metaphors and symbols are widely thought to be incongruous with the actual church that exists on the plane of world history. The propensity of church leaders to be domineering and unable to recognize their own limits, something feared by 1 Peter 5:3, has plagued the church throughout its history. Potential believers in Christ have found it difficult to accept that submission to God's will requires equal submission to ordained fools and ecclesiastical despots. The general human inclination to be fearful of large authoritarian and apparently impersonal organizations has led to endless suspicions that the institutional church is more interested in preserving its own existence and extending its own influence than in caring for the humble and the downtrodden. The executive efficiency with which ecclesiastical business is conducted gives the impression that spiritual depth and personal warmth have been forsaken in behalf of more worldly forms of institutional success. Roman Catholic ecclesiologist Avery Dulles believes this is the biggest challenge confronting the church in our time. Such fears are discouraging people in the present generation from believing that the church is attuned to their needs. "It seems almost impossible to look upon a huge bureaucracy as a loving mother, yet this, it seems, is precisely what the Church is asking them to do," he writes. "All the biblical imagery about the Church as Bride, as Mother, as Vine, and as little flock appears almost incongruous when applied to the vast clerical bureaucracy.... To large numbers of young people, and to others not so young, the laws and dogmas of the Church seem designed to control and crush rather than to nourish."[2]

---

2. Avery Dulles, "Imaging the Church for the 1980s," *Thought* 56, no. 221 (June 1981): 124.

The Church's Unity

"Word and sacrament constitute the Church," writes Karl Rahner.[3] The Protestant Reformers would agree with Rahner. One of the simplest and most refreshing definitions of the church is found in Article Seven of the Augsburg Confession, a definition endorsed and repeated in Calvin's *Institutes:* "The church is the assembly of saints in which the gospel is taught purely and the sacraments are administered rightly." When it came to the question of the unity of the church—which was the big question during the Reformation—the Reformers said then what should be said again today: for the true unity of the church it is enough to agree concerning the teaching of the gospel and the administration of the sacraments. It is not necessary that human traditions or rites and ceremonies, which have been created at various times and places, should be alike everywhere.[4] The principle of contextualization encourages a pluralism of traditions and practices while affirming with Saint Paul that Christians are still one; they are still one because there is but "one faith, one baptism, one God and Father of all" (Eph. 4:5-6).

This is a simple definition because it designates only one criterion for locating the true church, namely, the gospel, which comes to us in the modes of word and sacrament. Where believers in Christ are assembled and the gospel is present, there is the church of Jesus Christ. Not included in this definition are descriptions of church buildings, the authority of the clergy, ecclesiastical hierarchies, choir anthem schedules, budget directives, committee structures, eligibility for the church softball team, or recipes for Sunday evening potluck dinners. Only the gospel stands as the measure. Roman Catholic Hans Küng speaks out almost like a Reformer when he writes that "ecclesiology can never simply take the status quo of the church as its yardstick, still less seek to justify it. On the contrary, taking once again the original message, the gospel, as its starting-point, it will do all it can to make critical evaluations, as a foundation for the reforms and renewal which the church will always need."[5]

To speak of the church as the "assembly" of believers connotes a more or less eventlike character. This thinking of the church in terms of an event is hinted at in the Dogmatic Constitution on the Church (*Lumen gentium*) of the Second Vatican Council, where the sacramental event is the model. To think of the church as an event, however, seems to undermine the idea of the church as the building within which events take place. It also seems to undermine the thought of the church as a grand and powerful institution, which might be fixed in its ways and enforcing allegedly eternal rules and regulations. Rather, I am suggesting the

---

3. Rahner, *TI*, 4:254.
4. Augsburg Confession, Art. 7; Calvin, *Inst.*, 4.1.9; 4.10.30.
5. Hans Küng, *The Church* (New York: Sheed & Ward, 1967), 28.

church as event is more like a happening, an occasion. The church is a historical phenomenon.

The eventlike character of the church is reflected in the etymology of the word *church*, which is a translation of the Greek ἐκκλησία, from the root "to be called." The church consists of those people who are called by God for something. English terms such as *ecclesiastical* are derived from the Greek, as are the Latin *ecclesia*, French *église*, Spanish *iglesia*, and Italian *chiesa*. In Greece prior to New Testament times the term referred to citizens who were called out of their homes to come to a town meeting—that is, to an assembly or convention. This word is similarly used to describe the crowd on the verge of riot gathered in the theater at Ephesus to defend the union of idol-makers against the criticisms of Paul (Acts 19:32, 41). In the Septuagint ἐκκλησία is used to translate the Hebrew קָהָל (*kahal*), referring to a meeting of people. Paul uses the term to designate particular assemblies or communities of believers, usually located in one or another city. Thinking of all Christians everywhere united in a single ἐκκλησία was a later development. That development is likely to have followed this pattern: first, the believers assembled and became a community in Jerusalem; second, they spread out to other cities, resulting in a diversity of assembling groups—that is, many churches; and third, they realized their extrageographical unity in the Holy Spirit so that a single universal communion of saints could be thought of. To distinguish this universal communion in Christ from secular assemblies, the phrase ἡ ἐκκλησία τοῦ Θεοῦ (church of God) emerged. It would seem that with this scriptural background, then, we should think of the church first of all as an event—that is, an assembly at a given time and place to which Christians are called to experience the gospel through word and sacrament; and, second, as that communion Christians share with one another due to the presence of Christ in word and sacrament.

Although we use the English word *church* to translate ἐκκλησία, its own etymology derives from the Germanic tradition. Its counterparts are *Kirche* in German, *Kyrke* in Swedish, and *carkov* among the Slavs. Luther, writing in the Large Catechism, objects to the use of this term because too many people identify the church with the church building. He argues that the term *Kirche* should refer to the people and not to the building. Then he says the German *Kirche* comes from the same root as the Latin *curia*. He was mistaken about that. *Kirche* actually comes from the Celtic word *kyrk*, meaning what is circumscribed, not from the Latin *curia*. The etymology of *Kirche* goes back to the Greek terms κύριος and οἰκία, which produce the word κυριακόν, meaning "belonging to the house of the Lord." So perhaps the popular identification of *Kirche* with building is not so wide of the mark after all.

Theologically speaking, we need to distinguish the event of the church, which consists of the believers assembling, from the building or institution in which the event happens. The English word *church*, just as the German *Kirche*, is conveniently ambiguous. It can mean both things. The word *congregation*, referring to those who congregate or gather together, reflects more directly the New Testament notion of ἐκκλησία. The heart and center of ecclesial life is the event of worship in the congregation, and it is this that pumps the lifeblood of faith and work throughout all the derivative limbs of the body of Christ on earth. The principal organ or nerve center is not the institution of the clergy, the annual convention, the denominational headquarters, the Vatican, or even some theological ideal of what the church should be. It is rather the concrete event in which the assembled believers in Christ actually hear the gospel and share in the sacramental presence of the living Christ.

The important point here actually has less to do with the difference between assembly and building or institution than it does with the church's mission. That mission consists in one thing: to present the gospel of reconciliation. Whether that is done inside or outside a building is beside the point. Proclaiming God's word and celebrating Christ among us through the sacraments are the events that constitute the church each time they take place. How we go about our mission will differ according to the culture, sophistication, and preferences of the people involved. Not everyone everywhere will do things the same way. Nor should they. The gospel mission can be carried out in a wide variety of forms and still the event of the church will take place in history.

The Church Anticipates the World's Future

To think of the church as a particular historical community with diverse forms still presupposes that there are other communities. The church incorporates part of the human presence in the world, not all of it. This is important to note because Jesus' message regarding the kingdom of God and his salvific work apply to the whole of the world, not just the church. The church is called by God to witness to this wider reality, to witness with high expectation and hope to what the Easter resurrection of Jesus promises for the future of creation. This leads Pannenberg and Braaten to refer to the church as an "eschatological community,"[6] and Letty Russell to dub it an "enclave of the future."[7] Hans Küng sees the church as "an anticipatory sign of the definitive reign of God."[8] Avery Dulles interprets *ecclesia* to refer to "an assembly or convocation and more specifically the convocation of the saints that will be realized to the full at the eschaton."[9]

---

6. Wolfhart Pannenberg, *Theology and the Kingdom of God* (Philadelphia: Westminster, 1969), 74; Carl Braaten, *The Future of God: The Revolutionary Dynamics of Hope* (New York: Harper & Row, 1969), 109.
7. Letty Russell, *The Future of Partnership* (Philadelphia: Westminster, 1979), 105.
8. Küng, *The Church*, 96.
9. Avery Dulles, *Models of the Church* (New York: Doubleday, 1978), 109.

"Christianity does not exist for its own sake," writes Jürgen Moltmann, "it exists for the sake of the coming kingdom."[10] In short, the church is not simply a group of individuals who gather together because of a common faith. Rather, it constitutes a proleptic and ecumenical community that anticipates the fuller reality of God's eschatological and ecumenic consummation.

The church points toward the kingdom that is beyond the church both in scope and time. The church will not last forever. It is a temporal and temporary phenomenon, the work of the Holy Spirit between the first and second comings of Christ. It will eventually be replaced, though not forgotten. The vision of Jeremiah 31:31-34, where the law will be written in our hearts so that all teachers of the law will be out of a job, along with a similar vision in Revelation 21:22, according to which in the new Jerusalem there will be no temple because everyone worships in the full presence of God, indicate the surpassability of the *ecclesia*. The church today is a "called out" group, which is given the task of witnessing in behalf of the gospel to a wider community. In the kingdom of God there will be no need to call out a group for the special task of witness, because full knowledge of God will be as wide as the creation itself. Witness will be a thing of the past.[11]

In distinguishing the church and the kingdom I do not intend to pit them over against one another, as if they were competitors. The former witnesses to, and is fulfilled by, the latter. But this leads to a caution: we must avoid the temptation to equate the church with the kingdom. While amid the fury of finite history we dare not prematurely claim for the church the majesty and authority that belong solely to God and God's reign. As the rule of Christ prepares the way for the rule of the Father (1 Cor. 15:28), so also does the church prepare the way for the kingdom.

The church does its preparatory work as a community called out from the rest of humankind in two ways: as positive proclamation and as negative criticism. Its positive proclamation is its witness to the gospel, the telling and retelling and telling again of the story of Jesus with its significance. In the celebration of the sacraments we similarly "proclaim the Lord's death until he comes." The gospel witness is not simply a look backward toward Jesus. It also looks forward and shares visions of what is to come, visions of the kingdom of justice and love by which the creation will be transformed and fulfilled. This should result in, among other things, works of love in our society that seek to express proleptically the anticipated kingdom of love to be brought by God.

---

10. Jürgen Moltmann, *The Church in the Power of the Spirit* (San Francisco: Harper & Row, 1977), 164.

11. This position is shared by Pannenberg, *Theology and the Kingdom of God*, 76–77, and Küng, *The Church*, 92–93. Dulles disagrees, however, saying that the church will not end at the advent of the eschaton but will live on everlastingly (*Models of the Church*, 109–10).

The negative work of the church has to do with its critical analysis of political institutions. It is the task of the church constantly to remind all consolidated powers on earth that they are strictly penultimate and provisional, that their rule is not absolute but subject to a greater and ultimate rule of God that is yet to come. We need critical vigilance because this truth is easily forgotten, especially by those people who from time to time gain power and then desire to hold it permanently and exercise it ruthlessly. We need to uncover and make visible the limitations and provisionality of all structures of social cohesion and political organization and of the authority assumed by various individuals.

The Visible and Invisible Church

It is necessary to make an observation here regarding how theologians typically discuss the church. Ecclesiological talk is riddled with a variety of pious sounding dualisms such as the wider and narrower definitions of the church, the visible versus the invisible church, the true versus the empirical church, and so forth. But these dualisms are all based on a single widespread mistake, namely, the failure to distinguish properly between the church and the kingdom of God. By tacitly identifying the church with the kingdom and then confronting the contradictions that abound in historical life, misguided theologians have invented concepts such as the invisible church as a repository for fabricated realities that correspond only to their wishes and dreams. The mistake can be corrected and we can return to realistic thinking if we recognize that the tension we perceive in the church's existence is eschatological. The tension is caused by the future kingdom of God challenging the present state of affairs as judge and as lure.

The distinction between the invisible church and the visible church begins quite innocently. It begins with the inability to recognize in our concrete institutional life the marks of the church identified by the creeds. The Niceno-Constantinopolitan Creed identifies four marks: "one, holy, catholic, and apostolic church." Martin Bucer and John Calvin began their dualist thinking by noting how a term such as *catholic* applies to the whole multitude of people spread all over the earth. Because we are finite beings we simply cannot see all of them at one time. The church's catholicity includes saints who have long died as well as descendants who will live after us. We cannot see them now; nor can we even know all their names. But there is a sense in which we share a oneness with them, is there not? Therefore, because the church is inclusive of all these people, and because we cannot actually see them, it follows that the church in its full catholicity must be invisible. It is in this sense that Kallistos Ware can speak for Eastern Orthodoxy and say both that the church "is visible, for it is composed of concrete congregations, worshipping here on earth," and "it is invisible, for it also includes the saints and the angels."[12]

So far, so good. This is a judgment based upon our finitude, upon our inability to perceive the unity of the church over great distances and beyond the barriers of time and death. But this judgment of finitude slips easily and unnoticeably into another kind of judgment, a moral judgment regarding hypocrites. It is here that our theological problem begins. "In this church are mingled many hypocrites who have nothing of Christ but the name and outward appearance," writes Calvin; "there are very many ambitious, greedy, envious persons, evil speakers, and some of quite unclean life. Such are tolerated for a time.... We must believe, therefore, that the former church, invisible to us, is visible to the eyes of God alone, so we are commanded to revere and keep communion with the latter, which is called 'church' in respect to men."[13] Calvin believes that the invisible church coincides exactly with the elect, and only God knows who the elect are. What we perceive in this life, however, is an organization that is a mixture of elect and nonelect, and to this mixed organization we can give the name "church" but only grudgingly "in respect to men." For the theological tradition that followed Calvin, this has meant that the true church has become identified with the invisible church, and the invisible church is the one to which the marks—oneness, holiness, catholicity, and apostolicity—may be applied. It follows that the institutional church experienced in daily life is less than the true church.

What starts out as a theological mistake may lead to social tragedy. Occasionally some leaders arise who are unsatisfied with the split, so they try to purify the visible church to the end of making it coincide completely with the invisible church. The method of purification is called "discipline." One of the chief means for exacting such discipline and purifying the visible church has been to deny access to the Lord's Supper to those judged to be hypocrites. The worst form of hypocrite identified by the Reformation has been the evil-speaker, especially when that evil-speaker is accused of teaching false doctrine. Should two groups of Christians seek purification in behalf of the invisible church simultaneously, and should each think the other group is guilty of evil-speaking and hence subject to discipline, then the result is mutual denial of invitations to share the holy meal. Separate altars for separate heretics! The ironic tragedy is that the sacrament of the altar becomes the symbol of the oneness and catholicity of the true or invisible church at the same time that it fractures and breaks the oneness and catholicity of the visible church.

---

12. Timothy Ware, *The Orthodox Church* (New York: Penguin, 1963), 247.
13. Calvin, *Inst.*, 4.1.7. Augustine, living in the Constantinian epoch where citizenship and church membership could easily coincide, thought the *ecclesia invisibilis* amounted to about 5 percent of the *ecclesia visibilis*.

Is there any scriptural warrant for such thinking and acting? No, I believe there is none. What has happened is that biblical symbols that originally applied to the kingdom have been subtly co-opted by church policy makers. To be sure, Jesus compares the "kingdom of heaven" with a field growing both wheat and weeds: from day to day it is difficult to discriminate between them, but when the harvest comes the weeds will be bundled and burned while the wheat will be gathered into the heavenly barn (Matt. 13:24-30). To be sure, Jesus warns of false Christs who will arise in our midst and tempt even the elect to abandon the kingdom (Mark 13:22; Matt. 24:5, 24). To be sure, Jesus warns us that when the time of fulfillment arrives the sword of judgment will discriminate what we could not clearly distinguish earlier. Is Jesus referring to the church or the kingdom?

I believe Jesus is not referring to the church. He is speaking rather to the relationship between the kingdom of God and the world. The kingdom comes to the whole world (Luke 21:35), not just to the *ecclesia* within the world. Now let me be clear on one point: I am not denying that the principle of discrimination applies to the church. Judgment day will bring a separating of wheat and weeds within the people of God just as it will in the wider arena of God's domain. Yet I am asserting here that there is no warrant for holding that the true church consists only of the wheat while the weeds are grudgingly said to belong to the untrue or empirical church. The realistic position I advocate, in contrast, is that there is one church, the visible church, and that church includes both wheat *and* weeds.

The visible church consists of those who are called to be witnesses to the gospel, and those who are called constitute a mixed group. It is possible that we could apply the notion of *simul justus et peccator* to the people of God as a people as well as to those individuals who have faith. The church is simultaneously graced and sinful, weeds included. We need to accept the fact that the church is a historical reality that stands both in continuity with, as well as in contrast to, the eschatological kingdom of God.[14] It is life in the kingdom that constitutes salvation, not life in an imaginary invisible church.

Jesus as Founder of the Church

Did Jesus found the church? The answer is clearly no if by this we mean that the pre-Easter Jesus established the institution of which modern Christians are now members. Jesus lived as a Jew and died as a Jew. He

---

14. Geoffrey Wainwright's fine work in ecclesiology shows that he is aware of the source of the tension, but he too quickly falls into the traditional trap of contrasting the present state of affairs not with the kingdom but with the "ideal or eschatological church, ... the church as it is meant to be" (*Doxology* [New York: Oxford University Press, 1980], 118). See Küng, *The Church*, 327n.

was never a Christian. What he did was announce the arrival of the imminent kingdom of God and proleptically embody that kingdom in his own person. In an indirect way, however, we might be able to answer yes to the above question if we recall that during Jesus' lifetime disciples gathered around him, and that this group provided a continuity of community through the resurrection and Pentecost down to the present day. But in asking about the foundation of the church, this is less important than has traditionally been thought. What is important is the continuity of symbol, the presence of Christ in the gospel that is publicly proclaimed and sacramentally celebrated in the life of the church. The foundation of the church is the same as the foundation of Jesus' ministry—that is, it is the kingdom of God.[15] The kingdom in the life of the church is remembered as incarnate in Christ and is proleptically anticipated through word and sacrament.

Regardless of whatever else can be said, however, we must admit at minimum that there gathered around Jesus a group of disciples who eventually provided the continuity between the historical Jesus and the subsequent age of the church. Furthermore, within the group of disciples, Jesus appointed a college of twelve and commissioned them with specific responsibilities. They were to remain with him, to preach, and to cast out demons (Mark 3:13-19). Following Easter, Jesus met in Galilee with the eleven disciples who remained after Judas's exit and commissioned them with the all-important charge: "Go therefore and make disciples of all nations, baptizing them in the name of the Father and of the Son and of the Holy Spirit, and teaching them to obey everything that I have commanded you. And remember, I am with you always, to the end of the age" (Matt. 28:19-20). Due to Jesus' sending them out into the wider world, it has become customary to relabel Jesus' followers. Instead of calling them "disciples," which means students, they are now called "apostles," which means those who are sent.

There were hundreds of apostles, many of whom had not previously been disciples. Some ecclesiological interpretations emphasize a priority of authority given to the inner circle of twelve, and then within this group ascribe a still higher priority to just one of the apostles, Peter. The passage in question goes like this: "And I tell you, you are Peter [Πέτρος], and on this rock [πέτρα] I will build my church [ἐκκλησία], and the gates of Hades will not prevail against it. I will give you the keys of the kingdom of heaven, and whatever you bind on earth will be bound in heaven, and whatever you loose on earth will be loosed in heaven" (Matt. 16:18-19). Some scholars dismiss this text as inauthentic, as an obvious redaction in which later ecclesiastical officials found it to their advantage to put

---

15. Hans Schwarz likes to emphasize that, regardless of whether Jesus founded the church, he is its foundation (*The Christian Church* [Minneapolis: Augsburg, 1982], 27–29).

words into the mouth of Jesus that would give divine justification to a later achieved status quo. We cannot determine for certain whether this historical-critical demure is correct.[16] But we can for a moment look at the text as it stands.

The first thing to note is the wordplay regarding rocks. The name Peter in Greek (Πέτρος) means "rock" (πέτρα), which we know in English from such terms as *petrified*. Jesus did not speak Greek, of course. Is this just a pun created by the author of the Gospel of Matthew? Not necessarily. The same pun can be made in Aramaic where the name Peter (Κῆφας) comes from the same root as "rock" (κῆφα). Because the Aramaic name Cephas appears elsewhere in the New Testament (1 Cor. 15:5; Gal. 2:9), the likelihood that Matthew is accurately rendering what Jesus actually said in Aramaic seems quite high.

A building or edifice will stand firm if it is built on a solid foundation such as rock. Is Peter alone the foundation? No. Elsewhere in the New Testament this rocklike or foundational quality is attributed to all of the twelve apostles (Eph. 2:20; Rev. 21:14).

The symbol of the keys is key here. The keys represent permission to enter, in this case to enter the kingdom of heaven. The keys in combination with the concepts of binding and loosing, which in rabbinic tradition refer to forbidding and permitting, would indicate that Peter stands in a position of authority. Christian art as well as jokes through the centuries have identified Peter as the guardian of heaven; and he is frequently pictured as standing before the gates of pearl with keys in hand.

This would tend to make a reader want to ascribe honor and accolades to this very special apostle, Peter. But a brief look at the context will dispel such an impulse. The narrative unit of which this passage is a part is the famous conversation at Caesarea Philippi, which is introduced by Jesus asking his disciples who they think the carpenter from Nazareth really is. After a few flattering but wrong guesses, Peter comes up with the right answer: Jesus is "the Christ, the Son of the living God." Jesus congratulates the son of Jona because of his divinely bestowed insight, an insight akin to an oracle that in other contexts might lead one to think of Peter as a prophet. But that Peter is not yet a prophet is made clear by the mistake he then makes. He is intolerant of the true prophet, Jesus, who predicts his own imminent suffering and death. Peter, hoping for a political messiah to throw off the oppression of the Romans, would be upset if his hero were to meet his demise before the revolution could be accomplished. Peter does not associate the messiah with the suffering servant. So he scolds Jesus. Jesus then

---

16. Oscar Cullmann, New Testament exegete and avid ecumenist, believes that Matt. 16:18-19 reports the actual words of Jesus. Yet, in contrast to what Roman Catholics traditionally say, Cullmann holds they apply to Peter only, not to his successors in Rome (*Unity through Diversity* [Philadelphia: Fortress, 1988], 55).

scolds Peter in return, saying, "Get behind me, Satan! You are a stumbling block to me; for you are setting your mind not on divine things but on human things" (Matt. 16:23). It would be a curious thing indeed to think of giving the keys to the kingdom of heaven to Satan, or to establish the church of Jesus Christ on the leadership of one who is not on the side of God. In retrospect, one might be able to offer various theological reinterpretations of this passage in light of Jesus' resurrection and the concept of justification of sinners that would qualify Peter's rebellious spirit. But it seems quite obvious that even if the Matthean text could be judged historically accurate, one thing is certain: Jesus did not leave Caesarea Philippi with the church constituted and established.

There are a variety of interpretations for the enigmatic statement of Jesus, "On this rock I will build my church." The Second Vatican Council reiterates the traditional Roman Catholic interpretation that Peter is "alone the rock and keybearer of the church" and that the Roman pontiff is "the successor of Peter" (*Lumen gentium* 22). Cyprian and the Anglicans traditionally apply this text to church leadership in general, to the bench of bishops. They do not focus it on the Roman bishop alone. During the controversies emerging from the Reformation period, Protestant interpreters of this passage did two things. First, they assumed that the church in fact was founded at Caesarea Philippi. Second, they asserted that it was founded on the faith of Peter, not on his person or office. What stands out to Protestant eyes is the boldness and correctness of Peter's confession that Jesus is the Christ. This confession of faith is identified as the rock, as the solid foundation upon which the church is built. Whenever and wherever such a confession is made, there is the church. Every member of the priesthood of believers can have faith like a rock, and the church is built upon the faith of the faithful. This implies, among other things, that Peter has no special status superior to others. Any of the disciples who makes such a confession has the keys to the kingdom. This interpretation reinforces the Protestant emphasis on faith (*sola fide*) while undermining the Roman Catholic claim to juridical authority based on claims to have inherited Peter's hegemony over the church. There is a weakness in the Protestant interpretation, however, in that despite Peter's prophetic confession his faith proves to be more like gravel than a rock. No sooner has he uttered his profound statement than he misinterprets it and falls into unfaith.

It is better, in my judgment, to see the Caesarea Philippi incident as a foreshadowing of the church that was to come—a church fraught with the paradoxes of faith. On the one hand, the church boldly confesses the lordship of Jesus Christ. On the other hand, it frequently crumbles under pressure and yields to misunderstanding and spineless self-serving. Peter unknowingly becomes a pattern that the rest of us singly and as a group will follow, namely, *simul justus et peccator*. By no means do we have here the beginning of a formidable ecclesiastical institution.

The church that begins in New Testament times is an event in which the faithful assemble, and in which the word of God is spoken, heard, and responded to. The faithful respond through living worship and loving witness.

WORSHIP AND THE WORD

I now move from the New Testament foundations of the church to its contemporary life. Having defined the church as an assembly, I must be a bit more specific regarding what Christians do when they assemble. Christians ordinarily call what they do "worship." The worship of God is by no means unique to Christians. People of other religions perform parallel rituals that may include singing, chanting, praying, and ambulatory gesturing. The defining characteristics of Christian worship are: the proclamation of the word of God and the celebration of the sacraments of baptism and eucharist.

Worship and Praise

The term *worship* derives from the Saxon *weorthscipe* or *worthship*, which imply homage, that is, an attitude that recognizes the intrinsic value or worth of the person or thing to which homage is directed. When we worship God we begin by assuming that God is worth it, that God is of intrinsic and infinite value, and that as such God is the ultimate target of our praise, thanksgiving, and prayer. God has dignity in that God is the end toward which our homage is directed; God is not simply the means to something else of greater value or importance. The heart and essence of Hebrew and Christian worship are sheer praise for God's majesty supplemented by thanksgiving because God has deigned to dwell with the people whom God has graced. The way God has come to dwell with us is through saving acts in history—especially the Exodus and the incarnation—which we remember and retell amid praise and thanksgiving. Such a sense of divine *worthship* is celebrated in the ancient Psalms that have continued to play a central role in Christian worship down to the present day. "Praise the Lord, for the Lord is good, sing to his name, for he is gracious" (Ps. 135:3). The same exuberance for praise and thanksgiving takes trinitarian form in the Gloria Patri.

> Glory be to the Father, and to the Son,
>   and to the Holy Spirit:
> as it was in the beginning, is now, and ever shall be,
>   world without end. Amen.

Other explosions of liturgical laud such as the Gloria in Excelsis ("Glory be to God on high!") and the Te Deum Laudamus ("We praise thee, O God . . . ") combine praise, recital of the story of Jesus with its significance, and a prayer that petitions God to give us the mercy and grace God has already offered.

The symbolic power of worship is that time and space become collapsed. Past and future become present. Heaven comes down to earth while the shouts of praise bear earth up to heaven. Worshipers recall the mighty deeds of God in the past while delighting in the foretaste of the salvation that is to come. Worshipers recognize the presence of the divine Spirit in the sacraments, song, and celebration of the moment just as it was present in Jesus and just as it will pervade all of creation at the consummation.

Worship and Preaching

Along with praising God and celebrating the sacraments, the worship ministry of the church of Jesus Christ includes teaching and especially preaching the word of God. Preaching includes God's law as well as the gospel. The central task of the church's ministry of the word is to proclaim the story of Jesus with its significance, but one indispensable tool for drawing out its significance is an explication and appropriation of the divine law. The gospel stands in the foreground, to be sure, but the law of God provides the background that helps put the gospel into focus. In what follows I shall first examine the preaching ministry of the church in terms of the political and theological uses of the divine law, and then I shall treat the gospel in terms of the ongoing appropriation of Christ's saving work to the life of faith. I will then need to examine the dialectical relationship between law and gospel within the one word of God.

Phrases such as "the law of God" or "God's commandments" are a bit out of fashion in the vocabularies of modern people. They sound too authoritarian. From the point of view of the modern mind, the biblical call to obey God's will risks self-alienation, risks denying one's true self in order to become dependent upon God for one's self-worth. But we might note two things here. First, the modern assumption that law in general or God's law in particular is alien to true selfhood is itself false. The Christian claim is that it is only through harmony with the divine will that true selfhood can be achieved. Second, we might borrow an element from emerging postmodern consciousness that could help make the concept of law meaningful again. That element is the desire to escape the ghetto of autonomy, to realize what is a deeper truth, namely, that the self belongs intrinsically to other people through love and even to the cosmos through a unity of being. It includes the realization that no person is an island. To be a part of the community means life; to be apart from the community means death. There is no shrinking from the modern commitment to freedom, of course; but there is an acknowledgment that the life of autonomy is a bit lonely. Postmodernity seeks ontological community again. It is at this juncture that we might be able to make an ancient point—namely, the law of God is the vehicle for one's truest and deepest self-expression while it unites the self with the ground of cosmic unity.

The first use of the law. The Bible in general seems to assume that there is a universal awareness of God's will, what some theologians have traditionally dubbed "natural law." It may appear as a vague sense that there is a right way to do things or it may be formulated in the most noble terms of the command to love God and neighbor. The golden rule is not only a teaching of Jesus (Matt. 7:12; Luke 6:31); it also appears frequently in the wisdom literature of ancient China, India, and elsewhere. So, in the opening words of his homily to some non-Jews at Caesarea, Peter can compliment the uncircumcised by saying, "I truly understand that God shows no partiality, but in every nation anyone who fears him and does what is right is acceptable to him" (Acts 10:34). If it is possible to fear God and do what is right regardless of nation, then it must be assumed that the divine law is universally available. Paul similarly observes that Gentiles have consciences, which indicates that "what the law requires is written on their hearts" (Rom. 2:15).[17]

Christian preaching draws upon this natural law, but it is based on positive law. The Torah or Ten Commandments delivered to God's chosen people through revelation constitute the positive law that reiterates with Yahweh's authority what was already more generally known. With the exception of the command to absolute loyalty toward the God of Israel, the rest of the commandments articulate values that in one form or another can be found revered by other peoples, such as respect for one's family and the prohibitions against lying, coveting, fornicating, stealing, and killing. Such laws comprise the simple minimum of mores necessary to establish and maintain community. Without social conventions that protect one from aggressive acts such as theft and murder it would be impossible to maintain order. The result would be chaos and anarchy. Thus, conformity to the law is not intended to diminish the autonomy of the self but to give the individual the opportunity to live with others in a state of peace and cooperation. When the law of God is understood in light of this purpose (the purpose of establishing community—that is,

---

17. We need to be alerted to the multiple use of the phrase "written on their hearts," however, because sometimes it refers to natural law and other times it refers to eschatological salvation (Jer. 31:31-34). This is a most interesting ambiguity. Perhaps it means that inscribed on the heart of every person is a divinely written letter that we like a postal carrier will deliver to the eschaton. The task of the preacher is to encourage us to peek inside and read the mail ahead of time.

272 • THE LIFE OF THE NEW CREATION

the *polis* or *civitas*), it is called the "political use" (*usus politicus*) or "civil use" (*usus civilis*) of the law.

The political use of the law plays an important role in Christian preaching. Preachers begin by summing up the law as Jesus did—that is, they proclaim that we should love God and love one another. There are very few people who would overtly disagree with this. A Hindu could affirm this law just as well as a Christian. Obviously some people take it much more personally and more seriously than others, but even to those who ignore it from day to day it has a ring of truth when they hear it. Something within the human soul wants to say, "That's right!" Consequently, when preachers command their people to love God and love each other they are bringing to public voice something that lies within our preunderstanding about the rightness or fitness of things. In proclaiming the law of God, then, preachers are not delivering news, not telling their listeners about an event. The purpose of preaching law is rather to create or sustain human community.

The second use of law and proclamation of the gospel. I have been describing here the first or political use (*usus politicus* or *civilis*) of God's law. No matter how difficult it might seem from time to time for the preacher to continue trying to encourage human love and community, what comes next is even more difficult. The second use of the law meets with outright resistance. The second or theological use (*usus theologicus*), sometimes called the spiritual or pedagogical use (*usus spiritualis, usus paedogogicus*), functions to accuse, judge, and condemn. It reveals our sin; and because through preaching it comes in the form of existential appropriation, the law seeks us out in our place of hiding, pulls back the camouflage, and exposes us to the full light of God's justice. Like Adam and Eve covering themselves with fig leaves, no one likes such exposure. So we try to prevent the truth from becoming known.

Why the resistance? It is due to the subtle way in which sin in the form of self-justification works. As Prometheus stole fire from the sun so that humans could have it, so also do we seek to steal God's justice and try to possess it for ourselves. Instead of thinking of the law as "thy will," we like to think that it is something we have legislated and executed "within our hearts." It is the move out of community with God and the attempt to establish ourselves as autonomous, as a law unto ourselves. What is good about this is that divine justice has an appeal to us. It is a "delight to the eyes," so we wish to imbibe. But the problem is that we do not want to share the delight. We prefer to possess it. Like stealing an apple off our neighbor's tree, we wish to take what is divine, digest it, and make it constitutive of our own being. This can never be successful, of course, because God cannot finally be robbed. If we are to enjoy true justice and true righteousness, we can do so only in community with

God. We cannot do it on our own. Yet we live with the delusion that we have digested and now embody the righteousness that belongs solely to God. The church preaches the law in its second use in order to unmask this delusion.

It is sometimes said that the function of the law is to reveal our sin and open us up for the grace of the gospel. This is true, but it is true in a certain way. It does not reveal just any old sin. It exposes our fundamental unwillingness to be dependent upon God. It exposes our reluctance to glorify God and to give God thanks. We all know how on some occasions it may be difficult to admit that we are wrong. But cracking the delusion is even more difficult. In fact, it is possible to be confronted with incontrovertible evidence of our guilt that leads us to confession and contrition, yet we may still live on in the delusion that we ourselves are righteous. This is because hypocritical righteousness is a state of mind, not mere action. It is the assumption that because I know what justice and righteousness are, it follows that I am just and righteous. Even in the case where I confess a particular sin and seek absolution, I may approach the matter with the haughty pride that I know confession and absolution are themselves the paths to righteousness. In this case the result is the curious paradox that when I am in the midst of admitting my sin I am actually affirming my righteousness. The more I dwell on my guilt the better the person I am.

Consequently, the second use of the law cannot be identified simply with bringing someone's fault to his or her attention; nor can it be equated with social criticism. Such fault-finding is a necessary activity, to be sure; but in itself it is not a sufficient condition for the second use of the law to be effective. What else is needed? A dialectical relationship with the gospel is required. The gospel means forgiveness. It affirms that our true justness comes from God through the event of Jesus Christ. It is not the product of what we have done. The justness of the innocent Christ—the righteousness of God—is given independently of what we have done. That which we wish to possess, justness, becomes present not as our achievement but as a gift. In faith the kingdom of heaven with its fulfillment of justice is present to us. We do not possess it. We cannot take credit for it. But it is present. This is the good news.

This important dynamic comes to expression liturgically in the sacrament of penance and the ritual of confession and absolution. The ritual's goal is contrition on the part of the worshiper. Contrition consists in the acknowledgment of concrete transgressions against God's commandments. But there is a limit to how many transgressions one can actually list, not just because one has forgotten some but because one may not even be aware of some at the time. This leads to a general sorrowfulness of heart, an awareness of estrangement from God, and a disposition of openness for God's gracious forgiveness. The United Methodist Hymnal of 1989 (entry no. 891), following the Anglican Book of Common Prayer, leads the congregation in traditional language to confess together:

Almighty and most merciful God: We have erred and strayed from Thy ways like lost sheep. We have followed too much the devices and desires of our own hearts. We have offended against Thy holy laws. We have left undone those things which we ought to have done, and we have done those things which we ought not to have done. But Thou, O Lord, have mercy upon us. Spare Thou those, O God, who confess their faults. Restore Thou those who are penitent; according to Thy promises declared in Jesus our Lord.

Confession here consists in admitting violation of God's "holy laws," but not in any simplistic sense, as if one could draw up and compare two lists, one of laws and the other of violations. In addition to seeking forgiveness for "those things which we ought not to have done," the penitent congregation admits sorrow for having "left undone those things which we ought to have done." This list could be infinite. These statements mean that the penitent's basic disposition or state of mind has been out of sync with God's loving disposition. In the Lutheran "Brief Order for Confession and Forgiveness" the parallel reads: "We have sinned against you in thought, word, and deed, by what we have done and by what we have left undone." The attempt here is to exhaust the breadth and depth of our state of estrangement from God due to our sinfulness. It constitutes a thorough spring cleaning for our soul.

Such exposure of our sinfulness in confession is made possible by confidence in the gospel. The Methodist confession opens by describing the Father as "merciful" and ourselves as "lost sheep," exploiting the symbolic imagery of the good shepherd who seeks out his lost sheep. It concludes by asking God to keep the divine promise of restoration, a promise delivered through Christ Jesus. The Methodist minister then follows the general confession with a brief prayer asking God for absolution: "O Lord, we beseech Thee, absolve Thy people from their offenses." The Lutheran pastor is a bit more brash. Instead of beseeching God he or she says to the congregation, "I therefore declare to you the entire forgiveness of all your sins." The difference between beseeching and declaring is not so important. What is of vital importance to both Methodist and Lutheran examples, however, is that in worship the law and gospel—which together constitute the word of God—provide the framework for prayer, praise, and thanksgiving. Only in this way can the gospel be present in its purity—that is, as the good news that it is.

The good news of the gospel is comforting news because it says that even though we deny God, God by grace refuses to deny us. We are liberated from the temptation to ascribe justness and righteousness to ourselves. By understanding what God has done in Christ, we can permit exposure of our darkest secret, our refusal to admit our dependence upon

God. Secure in God's grace, we can allow the second use of the law to take its most critical and accusatory effect. There is no need to hide behind fig leaves or walls of excuses when we know that God loves and accepts us just the way we are.

In sum, we should present the law in its first use so as to inspire cooperation in building community. We should present the law in its second use to render judgment, even if it provokes guilt feelings. Dealing with guilt is necessary in our personal lives. Finally, we should present the gospel so that the truth of God can be heard in light of the truth about ourselves.

The gospel, as we saw earlier, creates the freedom to love. It leads to a creative fulfilling of God's law.[18] This free and creative life lived in accordance with God's law, resulting from the liberation granted us through faith in Christ, was long ago described well by Augustine. "Freedom of choice is necessary to the fulfillment of the law. But by the law comes the knowledge of sin; by faith comes the obtaining of grace against sin; by grace comes the healing of the soul from sin's sickness; by the healing of the soul comes freedom of choice; by freedom of choice comes the love of righteousness; by the love of righteousness comes the working of the law."[19]

WORSHIP AND SACRAMENT

Theologians through the centuries have offered numerous definitions for the word *sacrament*. The Orthodox do not use the term at all, preferring the more ancient Greek μυστήριον—translated "mystery"—with its New Testament roots. In the Latin West, Augustine defined a sacrament as a "visible form of invisible grace" or as "a sign of a sacred thing," and he could apply these definitions to such things as baptism, eucharist, creeds, and the Lord's Prayer. John Calvin thought of a sacrament in terms of an outward sign of an invisible grace that is dependent upon the believer's faith to be effective. The Thirteenth Article of the Augsburg Confession, in contrast to Calvin, says that sacraments are intended to "awaken and confirm faith," which makes them effective regardless of whether one brings faith to the sacrament. Commenting on this article in his "Apology of the Augsburg Confession," Philip Melanchthon defines

---

18. How should this creative response be guided? John Calvin and others have recommended a third use of the law. Once freed from the first two uses, Calvin argued, the Christian should spontaneously and lovingly seek to follow God's law as a guide to moral living (*Inst.*, 2.7.12). It is not clear whether Luther employed a third use or not. Some contemporary Lutherans such as Gerhard Forde, however, repudiate a third use on the grounds that the first use is all Christians need to guide them ("The Christian Life," in *Chr.D.*, 2:449).

19. Augustine "The Spirit and the Letter," 30:52, in *Augustine: Later Works*, The Library of Christian Classics, 26 vols. (Philadelphia: Westminster, 1965), 8:236.

sacraments as "rites which have the command of God and to which the promise of grace has been added."

By the twelfth century some thirty or so sacraments made it onto a list compiled by Hugh of Saint Victor, a list that was trimmed back to seven by Peter Lombard. The list of seven has held constant for Roman Catholics ever since, and parallels the seven mysteries listed by today's Orthodox: baptism, confirmation (chrismation in the East), eucharist, penance, extreme unction, holy orders, and matrimony. The Lutherans began their protest by affirming three: baptism, eucharist, and penance. But they eventually cut that back to two (baptism and eucharist), which most Protestants today hail as the only two sacraments and which the Orthodox along with Roman and Anglo Catholics agree are the primary sacraments because they were ordained by Jesus in the Gospels. The Quakers and the Salvation Army get along with no sacraments. Zwingli and Schleiermacher thought the whole idea of a sacrament had been a plague on the Western churches, and if they had had the choice they would have eliminated the word entirely from theological vocabulary. It is my position that evangelical explication does not require that we proceed by first trying to dream up a definition of sacrament and then attempt to discern what within Christian practice falls under this category. For resources we have the New Testament symbols and the history of explication in church practice. The tacit agreement that extends throughout most of Christendom is that there is something special and even essential about baptism and eucharist, and there is no doubt that these two "mysteries" are quite tightly tied to the wider complex of symbols having to do with the gospel and its place in the *ecclesia*. With his notion of an invisible grace Augustine was trying to get at the work of the Holy Spirit, a special work associated with baptism and eucharist by which the Jesus of yesterday and the kingdom of tomorrow become present to the believer.

This is theologically significant in three ways. First, an important christological truth is at stake here, namely, that God can become Emmanuel. In these two mysteries a physical embodiment of a so-called spiritual reality takes place. Heaven and earth come together in the water, the bread, and the wine just as they did in the Christ of two natures. Second, the physical and ritual character of the mysteries expresses the objective character of God's action in history and in the life of faith. Communion with the divine is not sought by turning inward to subjective contemplation, to the realm of the soul independent of the mundane world. Third, when we think of baptism in terms of initiation and the Lord's Supper in terms of festival, and when we think of both as practices of the church enduring through centuries, they help underscore and establish the existence of Christian communion. They tie us to the transpersonal unity we share with one another because we are members of a single body, the body of Christ. They function socially if not ontologically to identify us as Christian.

Baptism

We baptize because Jesus told us to (Matt. 28:18-20). Even if Jesus had not given the command, we might do it anyway. We might want to copy Jesus, who himself was baptized by John. But there is still a better reason. It has to do with the work of salvation. Through the combination of the word proclaimed and the administration of water, the baptismal action witnesses to the work of the Holy Spirit in personally appropriating to the individual believer the universal saving work of Jesus Christ. This event of appropriation is symbolized by a web of interrelated and overlapping images and concepts.

First and foremost, in baptism we become participants in the death and resurrection of Jesus so that, in an all-important sense, we die to our estrangement from God and rise to everlasting fellowship. "Therefore, we have been buried with him by baptism into death," writes Paul, "so that just as Christ was raised from the dead by the Father, we too might walk in newness of life" (Rom. 6:4; see Col. 2:12). Although the image is one of drowning rather than crucifixion—only baptism by immersion catches the full symbolic significance here—we actually go down into death with Christ and actually come up with him into the resurrected reality. The words of Paul are not just figurative language. Nor is the baptismal rite just a mimesis, just a charade. Luther says, "This should not be understood only allegorically as the death of sin and the life of grace, as many understand it, but as actual death and resurrection."[20] Baptism marks a point of transformation in one's life that is more significant than either birth or death. It is personal Easter. It is the beginning of everlasting life.

The parallel between Jesus' death and resurrection and our drowning and rescue is developed further in the New Testament, and the language gets a bit more figurative. In the water rite we recapitulate Noah's escape from the flood (1 Pet. 3:20-21). Baptism is like emerging from the Red Sea during the Exodus (1 Cor. 10:1-2), like being led by God to the salvation God has prepared.

This brings us to the second cluster of symbols surrounding baptism, the eschatological power of new life. The resurrected life of the eschatological kingdom of God comes back into time, bringing some of the joy and vitality that accompany it. It impacts us proleptically. We experience this as regeneration and renewal. In baptism we are born again (John 3:5). We are renewed by the Spirit (Titus 3:5).

This merges with the third theme of baptism, the gift of the Spirit's presence. The same Holy Spirit who revealed Jesus to be God's Son at his

20. Martin Luther, "The Babylonian Captivity of the Church," in *Three Treatises* (Philadelphia: Fortress, 1960), 190–91.

baptism (Mark 1:10-11) and who empowered the apostles at Pentecost (Acts 2) enters and empowers us as well. We are "sealed" by the Spirit (2 Cor. 1:21-22; Eph. 1:13-14), who gives us confidence and courage within. The Holy Spirit implants, cultivates, and nurtures our faith until the final harvest.

A fourth cluster of baptismal imagery, which is closely allied to the theme of renewal, is that of cleansing. Sins are washed away (Acts 22:16; 1 Cor. 6:11). Water is a natural symbol for purification, and its qualities are exploited to make this vivid. Tertullian waxes eloquent on the virtues of water, mentioning how it was present at the foundation of the world and how out of it came life and all that exists. Water quenches thirst and cleans what is dirty. Because of its abundance and indispensable role in sustaining terrestrial life, it becomes a fit vehicle for God to use in bestowing celestial life.[21] Baptism always requires repentance on our part, and the ablution by water signifies forgiveness, the act whereby the work of Christ for our justification becomes applied to us through faith (Heb. 10:22). Those baptized are pardoned, cleansed, and sanctified by Christ.

This array of allusions to water floods the celebrant's prayer at the font during the baptismal rite of the Book of Common Prayer:

We thank you, Almighty God, for the gift of water. Over it the Holy Spirit moved in the beginning of creation. Through it you led the children of Israel out of their bondage in Egypt into the land of promise. In it your Son Jesus received the baptism of John and was anointed by the Holy Spirit as the messiah, the Christ, to lead us, through his death and resurrection, from the bondage to sin into everlasting life.

The celebrant then prays that the water be sanctified by the Holy Spirit so that it can perform its work of cleansing us from sin.

The fifth element in the baptismal complex is the event of initiation into the Christian church, the grafting of a new branch onto the vine which is Christ, or the surgical addition of a new member to the body of Christ (1 Cor. 12:13). Baptism establishes the communion of saints. We enter a new state of oneness. "There is one body and one Spirit, just as you were called to the one hope of your calling, one Lord, one faith, one baptism, one God and Father of us all" (Eph. 4:4-6). This oneness yields equality within the church, so that "there is no longer Jew or Greek, there is no longer slave or free, there is no longer male or female; for you are all one in Christ Jesus" (Gal. 3:28).

Belief and baptism. Every baptism is a believer's baptism. Repentance, faith, and baptism all belong together. The dominant pattern attested to in the New Testament consists in hearing the proclamation of the gospel, responding with a profession of faith, and then receiving the water rite

---

21. Tertullian *On Baptism* 3.9.

(Acts 8:12-13). One who comes to faith in Jesus Christ normally asks for baptism, just as the Ethiopian eunuch asked Philip to baptize him once he had come to a full understanding of scriptural prophecy (Acts 8:36).

But a number of issues have arisen regarding the precise relationship between faith and the rite. One such issue is this: given that every baptism is a believer's baptism, who is it that has to do the believing? The one being baptized? This is clearly the assumption and the assertion of the Baptist denomination and related groups for whom a public profession of faith on the part of the one being baptized is requisite for receiving the rite. To make such a public profession requires a certain amount of maturity and responsibility, often described as having achieved the "age of accountability." Because infants are not accountable, they must await their trip to the baptistery until they are old enough to take responsibility for it.

But this position is the minority position within Christendom today. In most denominations infants are regularly baptized. It is still believers' baptism, to be sure, but it is the belief of the parents or sponsors that produces the confession of faith in the stead of the child. As the child grows and matures, the time comes when he or she must become accountable for the faith and make public confession. At this point he or she confirms the confession made in his or her stead many years earlier. This public confirmation has over the years become a rite in itself, even given the status of a separate sacrament among Roman Catholics. In origin baptism and confirmation were not separate; nor are they separate today for adult converts to Christianity. Only in the case of baptized infants are they separated, and this for purely practical reasons. Those Christian communions that practice infant baptism seek personal commitment and accountability just as much as the Baptists.

Does the Bible support this practice? A scrupulous reading of the New Testament does not turn up any accounts of babies being baptized. One does find that the profession of faith by one person often accounts for the faith of a whole household. For example, the jailer in Philippi who responded in faith to the words of Paul and Silas was baptized, and along with him so was his whole family (Acts 16:32-33). Now the text does not give the age of his children; nor does it say whether or not the jailer's wife agreed to go along with the idea. The impression is certainly given, however, that his belief sufficed for the entire household. This impression is reinforced by Paul, who contends that an unbelieving husband or wife can be consecrated through his or her spouse and that the children can be regarded as holy (1 Cor. 7:14). With this in mind, it would seem that the confessed faith of parents could include the proto-faith of the children.

Salvation and the nonbaptized. One passage that has stirred concern over the centuries is the remark attributed to Jesus, "Very truly, I tell you, no one can enter the kingdom of God without being born of water and the Spirit" (John 3:5). What does this mean? Does it mean that anyone not having received the rite of the font is doomed to everlasting perdition? Is Jesus here giving justification for the doctrine of *extra ecclesiam nulla salus*, no salvation outside the church (which baptizes)? This is how it has been frequently interpreted. I will look at the larger question of partial versus universal salvation in a later chapter, but for the moment I will explore how the content of the passage impinges on our understanding of baptism.

New Testament scholar Raymond Brown points out that the statement in John 3:5 is a negative universal. It is not a positive statement that says directly that everyone must be baptized. So we must ask: what is being negated here? Brown sees no evidence that the Gospel of John was concerned here with denying the kingdom of God to those who through no fault of their own are unbaptized. Jesus' apparent concern in this text was to contrast flesh with spirit, and to insist that life from above is not the same as ordinary life and cannot be received without the work of the Spirit. The "unless" refers to the general incapacity of the purely natural to achieve fullness. Therefore, neither this text in particular nor the New Testament in general speculates on the fate of the unbaptized.[22]

The issue involves in part the question: does salvation depend upon the performance of a particular rite that has been labeled baptism? Normally such things as repentance, faith, the indwelling of the Holy Spirit, and baptism belong together. With this in mind, we might note a possibly relevant and curious fact about the New Testament—namely, nowhere is it recorded that the twelve apostles were baptized in the name of the Lord Jesus.

Tertullian wrestled with this problem because he was concerned for the apostles' salvation. He notes that some of the Twelve had been followers of John and were likely baptized into repentance. Would this be good enough? No. This is not the same thing as the Christian rite, as indicated by Acts 19 where Paul has to rebaptize those having undergone the water rite under John. Tertullian's solution to the problem is that the Twelve were probably saved by their faith. He cites those miracles in the Synoptic Gospels where Jesus says, "Your faith has made you well" (Luke 18:42; Mark 10:52).[23] That faith might be the key has been the instrument by which most subsequent theologians have sought to solve the problem of the relationship between baptism and life in the kingdom.

Luther tackles a passage that may be even more difficult than John 3:5, namely, Mark 16:16, "The one who believes and is baptized will be saved; but the one who does not believe will be condemned." Modern

---

22. Raymond Brown, "One Baptism for the Remission of Sins—New Testament Roots," in Paul C. Empie and T. Austin Murphy, eds., *Lutherans and Catholics in Dialogue* (Minneapolis: Augsburg, 1965), 2:15–16.
23. Tertullian *On Baptism* 12.

exegetes of critical persuasion can handle this text easily by relegating it to inauthenticity—that is, it is widely accepted that Mark 16:9-20 is a second-century addition to the original text, and many exegetes believe it better to leave the passage out of the Bible. Luther, however, was precritical, so he treated it as if it were canon. Luther argued that Mark 16:16 shows that it is faith that is necessary for salvation and that it can save even without the sacrament of baptism. It is for this reason that the author of Mark did not add "and is not baptized" to the second clause of Mark 16:16.[24]

Tertullian and Luther leave us with a slight wedge driven between faith and baptism that gives us a bit of room in which to maneuver theologically. It is by grace through faith that we are saved, and baptism represents a confirmation of our saving faith. Exactly what direction we should go from here is not spelled out by these thinkers. But what is said just could be relevant to the next problem I wish to examine, namely, the issue of the nonbaptized believers in Christ.

Nonbaptized believers in Christ.   A curious question that goes unasked in Europe and the Americas is whether or not the nonbaptized believers in Christ should be considered Christian. In Asia this question arises with acute force. It arises in Japan because of organizations such as Mukyokaiha, founded by Kanzo Uchimara, a nonchurch Christian sect that does not baptize. Here I would like to note how important issues arise with reference to two other large groups of nonbaptized believers in Christ in Asia.

The first group is those Hindus for whom Jesus Christ has become significant either as an avatar of the god Vishnu or as a teacher of the way to enlightenment. For example, one contemporary Indian philosopher, Guru Nitya Chaitanya Yati, believes that the ground of all reality is the cosmic light, and that each human ego lives in the shadows while striving to transcend the darkness to enter the realm of pure light. Sin consists in narrowness of vision, in being satisfied with living in darkness. The road to salvation begins by recognizing that the divine light is reflected within the shadows—that is, within the human self. As with Boethius, Swami Chaitanya believes each person in this world mirrors the divine light, but the human mirrors reflect this divinity toward one another rather than back toward heaven. An avatar such as Rama or Jesus represents what God would do if God were a human and had to reflect light within the mundane realm of shadows and darkness. By retracing the source of light reflected in the life and teachings of Jesus in the four Gospels (the writings of Saint Paul are of little or no interest to Hindus), one can eventually find the source of light within oneself and then attain liberation from

---

24. Luther, "Babylonian Captivity," 190; see Large Catechism, *BC*, 440.

darkness—that is, *Mukti*. In short, Jesus becomes a vehicle for revealing the truth of one's own inner being, a truth already understood by the Upanishadic philosophers eight centuries before the first Christmas. The upshot of this is that Jesus is taken quite seriously, but because he is understood strictly within the perimeter of Hindu philosophy and religiosity there is no motive to become baptized or to join the Christian church.

Another group for whom the name "nonbaptized believers in Christ" is even more appropriate is also found in Asia both in India and among the Chinese. In the city of Madras in southern India, for example, approximately 10 percent of the population would recognize themselves in this category. These people have some knowledge of Christian teachings, are likely to own a Bible and use it for daily devotions, pray in the name of Jesus Christ, and listen frequently to radio broadcasts of Christian stations or programs. But they will not submit to the rite of baptism or become official members of a Christian church. Why?

To risk a slight oversimplification, they do not approach such matters with quite the individualism characteristic of the modernized West. In India the family dominates. What happens in the immediate and consanguine family is of towering importance to people in India. If a whole family does not convert to Christianity from either Hinduism or Islam, it is extremely difficult for an individual to do so. Should an individual make the jump and join a Christian congregation, it creates confusion and even hostility. It is not unusual for the individual Christian to be excluded from family gatherings and sometimes even disowned in matters of inheritance. In the case of a woman believer in Christ with a Muslim husband, of which there are many cases in Madras, outright conversion to Christianity would mean expulsion from the household. In the heavily patriarchal society of southern India it would be exceptionally difficult for such a woman to become independent, to find satisfactory employment, and to support herself on her own. Hence, the price to be paid for baptism is very high.

Similar situations arise in Chinese society throughout Southeast Asia. Individuals who bolt from the combination Confucianist-Taoist-Buddhist traditions and join a Christian congregation create a tremendous strain on family relations. Typical family festivals such as weddings and funerals and other holidays always include offerings to the ancestors and oblations to the Taoist idols that decorate the house. Even if the family tolerates the individual who has been baptized, it is difficult for the Christian individual to participate actively and with a clear conscience in family rituals. This tends to discourage baptism. Individual believers in Christ are inclined to wait for the whole family to convert before requesting the rite of the font. But often the wait is neverending.

An interesting compromise has become the custom in Hong Kong, where large numbers of teenagers convert to Christian ways of thinking during their high school years. Many are willing to make a verbal commitment but defer baptism until their midtwenties. Having been taught to respect their parents and elders, they feel that while living at home with mother and father they cannot afford the disturbance that would be caused by baptism. So parents and children customarily agree that once the young person has finished schooling and is ready for employment, then baptism and church membership can peaceably take place.

Now to our question: should these nonbaptized believers in Christ be considered Christian? I believe with considerable pain and regret that the answer should be no, they are not Christian. The chief reason for this answer is that we should respect the integrity with which they have made this decision. They are well aware that the badge that identifies a Christian is baptism, and they have consciously and deliberately chosen not to wear this badge. Should we through theological gerrymandering devise such terms as "anonymous Christianity" or something similar so that we can sweep such people into the fold by definition, we would really be doing them a disservice. One of the positive dimensions of the Western doctrine of individual autonomy is that it affords resources for respecting the decisions of others when they do not conform with ours. I believe we must respect the nonbaptized believers in Christ in this regard.

The related issue with which I began this discussion could be reformulated this way: given the maneuvering room between faith and baptism mentioned above, could we think of the nonbaptized believers in Christ as belonging to God's kingdom even though they do not belong to the Christian church? This is a difficult question.

In thinking about it we might recall Raymond Brown's observation that the New Testament does not speculate on the fate of the unbaptized or, more precisely, of "those who through no fault of their own are unbaptized." On this basis could non-Christians be divided into two camps, those who through no fault of their own are unbaptized and those who deliberately reject baptism? Such a division has been offered before and used to condemn those in the second category and provide loopholes for those in the first. Those who deliberately reject baptism are assumed to be those who reject Jesus' lordship in favor of another religion, atheism, or even evil. Hence their condemnation. But the nonbaptized believers in Christ discussed above do not quite fit this picture. They embrace Jesus Christ; they do not reject him. Does this warrant the church taking a condemnatory attitude toward them? I do not see the warrant for this. Rather we in the church need to be grateful that they have heard the gospel and have responded. Perhaps much remains to be considered on their part, but I believe we should thank the Lord for small favors, for small graces. In addition, there just may be some special role these people are destined to play in God's overall writing of this chapter of human history. It just may be that a new truth is emerging here, a truth that is difficult for us to grasp because of our limited vision that has been skewed by our past habits of exclusivism and by our modern individualism. I will take up this issue again in part when discussing the challenge of pluralism, but in the meantime my only advice is that we be cautious about jumping to theological conclusions in this matter.

Eucharist

We eat the bread and drink the wine during the eucharist because Jesus told us to (Matt. 26:26-29; 1 Cor. 11:24). But even if Jesus had not left us with this command, we just might do it anyway. Sharing in the Lord's Supper is like accepting an invitation to a banquet. What is served to the diners is a gift provided by a host who had to make some sacrifice in order to be hospitable. The host is present, of course, just as one would expect at any other banquet. But in this case the host does not dine with us. He is the food itself.

What I am describing here is known as the sacrament of the altar, which goes by many names: the Lord's Supper, the eucharist, the great thanksgiving, the breaking of bread, the holy communion, the mass, or the divine liturgy. By whatever name, the action that takes place during this rite is the central action of the Christian church. It is important because it is the physical communication of the gospel. When we eat the bread and drink the wine, Jesus Christ grants us communion with himself, enlivening the body of Christ and renewing each member. Through the eucharist the Holy Spirit makes the resurrected Christ present and appropriates to us his work of forgiveness of sins (Matt. 26:28) and the promise of everlasting life (John 6:51-58). The significance of the Lord's Supper can best be understood according to the model of the Trinity that is reflected in the eucharistic prayer: namely, (1) it is a gift from the Father for which we render thanks; (2) it is a remembrance of the passion of Jesus and an anticipation of renewed fellowship in the eschatological kingdom; and (3) it is an event of divine presence and fellowship due to the work of the Holy Spirit.

Remembering and anticipating. In the eucharist we remember and anticipate Jesus Christ. According to Paul, Jesus told us what to do: "The Lord Jesus on the night when he was betrayed took a loaf of bread, and when he had given thanks, he broke it, and said, 'This is my body that is for you. Do this in remembrance [ἀνάμνησις] of me.'" In the same way he took the cup also, after supper, saying, "This cup is the new covenant in my blood. Do this, as often as you drink it, in remembrance [ἀνάμνησις] of me. For as often as you eat this bread and drink the cup, you proclaim the Lord's death until he comes" (1 Cor. 11:23b-26). In this key passage that has become the "words of institution" in the eucharistic rite, the central theme is the dialectic between memorial and anticipation. We remember the night on which Jesus was betrayed. We also look forward to a time in the future when with the disciples reassembled we along with Jesus will "again drink of this fruit of the vine" in the "Father's kingdom" (Matt. 26:29).

We remember by imitation, by dramatic re-presentation. We remember the night on which he was betrayed, and we remember the day he was crucified. Yet we also look forward. The convoluted bread of life passages in John 6 develop the anticipated eschatological dimension. Jesus, talking about the bread just consumed at the miracle of feeding the five thousand, contrasts ordinary bread with another kind, the bread of eternal life. "Do not work for the food which perishes," says Jesus, "but for the food which endures to eternal life, which the Son of Man will give you" (John 6:27). This is reminiscent of the assertion that "one does not live by bread alone" (Deut. 8:3), which is quoted by Jesus during his temptation dialogue with Satan (Luke 4:4). In addition to bread, we need to live by the word of God. It is this word of God that the Gospel of John identifies with the person of Jesus through the image of living bread. Jesus says, "I am the bread of life; whoever comes to me will never be hungry, and whoever believes in me will never be thirsty" (John 6:35). He adds, "Your ancestors ate the manna in the wilderness, and they died. This is the bread that comes down from heaven, so that people may eat of it and not die. I am the living bread" (John 6:49-51a). The manna spoke of here refers to Exodus 16, where God fed the people with manna from heaven. In later literature the idea of manna informed the eschatological vision, so that 2 Baruch 29:8 reads, "The treasury of manna will again descend from on high." The Midrash Mekhilta comments on Exodus 16:25: "You will not find it [manna] in this age, but you shall find it in the age that is coming." The message of the Gospel of John is this: Jesus is that future manna made present. To eat his flesh and drink his blood in the eucharist is to participate proleptically in the future consummation of all God's purposes.

This proleptic understanding of the eucharist is tied in an interesting way with the Lord's Prayer as we find it in Matthew 6:9-13 and Luke 11:2-4. The prayer asks for God's kingdom to come. Following this— directly in the Lukan version but with "your will be done" interpolated in Matthew—it reads: "Give us each day our daily bread." But Joachim Jeremias suggests that the more accurate rendering should be, "Our bread for tomorrow give us today."[25] His argument is that the Greek phrase for "daily bread" is an incorrect translation of the words Jesus most likely

---

25. Joachim Jeremias, *The Lord's Prayer* (Philadelphia: Fortress, 1964), 23–25. Arland Hultgren defends the traditional "daily bread" rendering, although he concedes that the Greek phrase τὸν ἐπιούσιον ἄρτον is a puzzle. It most likely means "the coming bread," meaning that it is coming from God ("The Bread Petition of the Lord's Prayer," *Anglican Theological Review*, supplementary series, no. 11 [March 1990]: 41–54).

used in his native Aramaic. In the fourth century Jerome quoted the now lost Aramaic Gospel of the Nazarenes that used the term *mahar* here, meaning "tomorrow." If this Aramaic rendering is closer to the original—assuming that the prayer was memorized and repeated intact—then Jesus originally said, "Our bread for tomorrow give us today." This would fit very well with the petition that precedes it, "Your kingdom come," especially with the Matthean added emphasis of making the reality of heaven in the future impinge upon earth now. In terms of the eucharist, this means that when we eat the bread of life we anticipate the reality that lies ahead of us. Or, as is sung in the Lutheran offertory, "Give us a foretaste of the feast to come."

The question of sacrifice. Some traditions describe the worshipers' relationship to the Father during the sacrament as a "sacrifice." The World Council of Churches study commission that produced the Lima Liturgy believes that "the bread and the wine, fruits of the earth and of human labor, are presented to the Father in faith and thanksgiving."[26] This recalls the medieval Roman Catholic mass, which maintained a mood of sacrifice through the ritual prayer in which the priest would ask God to find the offerings "acceptable." What offerings? The offerings to be judged acceptable are the communion elements: the bread and wine that the Council of Trent describes as "truly propitiatory. . . . For, appeased by this sacrifice, the Lord grants the grace and gift of penitence, and pardons even the gravest of sins."

The Protestant Reformers objected violently to the use of this concept and language of sacrifice because they connote the idea of propitiating God during the worship service. They objected because there is nothing humans can do to propitiate an already gracious and giving Father. To think of propitiating God is blasphemous, say the Protestants, because it seeks to pay for something that sinners have already been given for free. What really happens in the holy communion is that the benefits of Christ, the one and true sacrifice, are offered to the worshipers through the bread and wine. Turning the mass into a human *sacrificium* instead of a divine *beneficium* denies the very qualities of God revealed in Jesus Christ. That the Council of Trent rejected the Protestant protest was made clear: "If anyone shall say that in the Mass a true and real sacrifice is not offered to God, or that what is offered is nothing but that Christ is given us to eat, *anathema sit*."

Many people desperately want the Reformation to be over. They want to put the strife between Christian brothers and sisters behind. Ecumenical conversations have opened up new understandings, not least of which

---

26. *Baptism, Eucharist, and Ministry*, Faith and Order Paper No. 111 (Geneva: World Council of Churches, 1982), 10.

is a greater appreciation on the part of Protestants for the Catholic position on sacrifice. The subtlety of the Roman Catholic mass has always meant that it is Christ who is being offered and that what the priest does in the rite participates ontologically in what Christ has done already on Calvary. The bread and wine the priest offers are in effect the body and blood that Christ has already offered. The celebrant re-presents the sacrifice of Calvary by way of sacramental sign. In *Lumen gentium* 28 Vatican II says that priests "re-present and apply in the Sacrifice of the Mass the one sacrifice of the New Testament."

In recent ecumenical dialogues surprising agreement has been reached on this issue. To the satisfaction of many Protestants, for example, Catholic theologians have stressed that the mass adds nothing by way of propitiation that was not already present in the sacrifice of Christ. The mass does not imply that Christ's work was somehow defective or that we, by rendering acceptable offerings, can somehow earn forgiveness. By using the term *re-presentation*, not in the sense of doing again, but in the sense of "presenting again," Roman Catholics have made it easier for many Protestants to agree wholeheartedly with them.

Yet, the question remains: if the sacrifice of the mass today is a re-presentation of what happened on Good Friday, then is it logically necessary to speak of the mass as itself a sacrifice? The reason Roman Catholics want to keep the language of sacrifice is to emphasize that what happens on the altar is more than a mere memorial, more than keeping a past event in mind. Christ is present, and his saving work is efficacious. The Roman Catholics are right on this. But, I ask, do we need to call the great thanksgiving itself a sacrifice? Would it not be better to think of it as a re-presentation—a making present through the work of the Holy Spirit—of the one final sacrifice of Christ, after which there can be no more sacrifices (Heb. 7:23-28)? What we do during the sacrament of the altar, then, is commune with Christ, receive his benefits (forgiveness and eternal life), and express our gratitude through prayers of thanksgiving.

Christ's presence. Presence is the work of the Holy Spirit. The Greek tradition of the eucharistic prayer includes the epiclesis, the invoking of the Holy Spirit to enter "these gifts here offered." The prayer includes petitions regarding the elements: "Make this bread the precious body of Christ" and "that which is in this cup, the precious blood of Thy Christ." The Lima Liturgy follows the Greek lead. This indicates, among other things, that the Spirit is invoked not to enter the hearts or souls of the worshipers directly, but rather to enter and transform the elements of bread and wine. The Spirit's action makes the body and blood of Christ present to us during the sacrament.

Almost all Christians agree that Jesus Christ is present to us in the sacrament and that it is the work of the Holy Spirit that accomplishes the resulting communion. But there is disagreement regarding just how Christ is present. As we have seen, the Greek liturgy identifies that presence with the bread and wine per se. So does the Latin doctrine of transubstantiation, which spells out in metaphysical detail just how Christ is present. His body and blood are present because they replace the bread and wine. Beginning with Alexander of Hales and running through the scholastic period in Latin theology, Roman Catholics have thought that when the presiding priest says the words of institution a change takes place in the elements. Using Aristotelian categories, Roman Catholics believe that the substance of the bread and wine is replaced with the substance of the body and blood, even though the accidents remain the same. A miracle takes place on the altar. Catholics have taken literally Jesus' words, "This is my body" (Matt. 26:26; 1 Cor. 11:24). Even though the communicants taste bread and wine, they are actually eating the body and blood of Jesus.

This was grossly repulsive to Ulrich Zwingli, who saw the doctrine of transubstantiation as promoting the ignorance and superstition plaguing the medieval church. He found it repugnant to think that in the communion he would tear apart the body of his Lord with his teeth and then masticate before swallowing it. The resurrected and ascended Christ is a spiritual reality, he thought, not subject to physical crudities. The root cause of the medieval error as he saw it was the literal identification of the corporal presence of Christ with the physical elements. Zwingli affirmed that Christ is present in the sacrament, but he argued that Christ is present spiritually and not physically. In "On the Lord's Supper," an essay written in 1526, Zwingli argues that transubstantiation is an erroneous doctrine because there is no scriptural warrant for it. Neither Jesus nor the apostles ever taught that in the mass the bread becomes the body and the wine the blood of Christ. The very important passage, "This is my body" (Matt. 26:26; 1 Cor. 11:24), is obviously a trope and, hence, should be understood metaphorically and not literally. The bread and wine are said to be signs that represent and point to something they themselves are not, namely, the body and the blood. Zwingli does not want us to confuse the sign with what is signified. The result of all this is that although Christ is present in the sacrament, it is a spiritual presence independent of the physical elements.

The Lutheran position represents a much more conservative deviation from the Roman position than that taken by Zwingli. Luther's objection to transubstantiation was not its identification of Christ's presence with the physical elements. He agreed with the tradition on this. He objected rather to the implicit canonizing of Aristotelian philosophy as the means for explaining what Jesus' words ("This is my body") mean. To say that the substance of the bread and wine is transmuted into the substance of body and blood is to say too much. There is no warrant for this in scripture. It is an unnecessary philosophical additive. In a fashion more akin to the Orthodox, Luther believed we should simply assert that Christ is present in the elements but leave the answer to the question of how he is present to mystery. In his Small Catechism he simply says that the body and blood of Christ are "under the bread and wine." This innocuous phrase affirms presence but avoids metaphysical complications. In the Smalcald Articles Luther repudiates transubstantiation as "subtle sophistry" when it teaches that the elements lose their natural substance, because in his view they remain bread and wine while bearing the body and blood. Followers of Luther began to speak of "consubstantiation," another innocuous term, metaphysically speaking, which had the force of affirming both sides of the equation—that is, the bread and wine are fully present and so also are the body and blood fully present.

Some recent ecumenists have sought to reinterpret the sixteenth-century disputes in such a way as to minimize the differences. Edward Schillebeeckx, for example, likes to think that the Council of Trent really wished to affirm nothing more than the real presence of Christ in the mass and that its statement defending transubstantiation was really aimed not at Luther but at Zwinglian spirituality that threatened to disengage the symbolic power of the bread and wine. It seems, however, that the theologians at Trent did in fact have the more conservative Lutheran position in mind, and the canon of 1551 on transubstantiation with its emphasis on the "whole substance" (*tota substantia*) is worded specifically to refute the idea of consubstantiation: "By the consecration of the bread and wine a change is brought about of the whole substance of the bread into the substance of the body of Christ our Lord, and of the whole substance of the wine into the substance of his blood." If the whole substance of the bread and wine is transformed, then there is no longer any bread and wine with which the body and blood can be co-present—that is, no possible consubstantiality.

Over against Zwingli, Luther held that Christ was present in, with, and under the bread and wine. Zwingli thought the Lutheran position was illogical and self-contradictory, based on a primitive literalism that could not apprehend the metaphorical or figurative character of Jesus' words, "This is my body." It is true that Luther did argue on the basis of a literal rendering of this important text. But the issue was metaphysical and christological as well as hermeneutical. At the Marburg Colloquy of 1529 Zwingli argued that spirit and flesh are incompatible. Therefore the presence of Christ can only be spiritual. Luther replied that flesh and spirit can be conjoined, as they were in the incarnate Jesus. Furthermore, they must be conjoined if the work of salvation is to be efficacious. This led to the curious doctrine of the ubiquity of Christ's body, a view scorned by the Reformed, according to which the concept of the *communicatio idiomatum* was expanded to mean that the human nature of Christ now enjoys the omnipresence once reserved for only divine being. Just as God was incarnate in Jesus Christ, so also is Jesus Christ incarnate in the bread and wine of the sacrament. On any given Sunday, the one and the same body of the savior can appear on countless different altars at the same time. This means metaphysically that the Lutherans no longer revered the categorical dualism between matter and spirit that had gone unquestioned for so long in Western tradition. From the Lutheran point of view, the Zwinglian position risked a return to docetism.

The question that pointed in the direction taken first by Zwingli and later followed by John Calvin was this: if Jesus Christ has risen and ascended to the right hand of the Father, then how can his body be found on the many altars of Christendom on earth? These two Reformed theologians made the assumption that because Christ's body is localized in heaven, therefore, it cannot be spread out in various locations on earth. It follows, then, that the presence of Christ in the sacrament must be of a spiritual rather than physical character. Calvin began to depart from Zwingli when Calvin tied this spiritual presence more to the symbols of bread and wine than did Zwingli. In fact, Calvin saw himself in distinctive opposition to Zwingli as well as Luther and Rome, and for some time he pursued his own course with the irenic hope that he could mediate the differences.

Along with the Lutherans, Calvin believed that in the Lord's Supper the body of Christ is really given us to be a food healthful to our souls. Our souls are fed by the substance of his body in order that we may in truth be made one with him. But in saying this, Calvin by no means wished to locate the body of Christ in the physical elements consecrated on the altar. The body of Christ that nourishes us presently sits at the right hand of God in heaven. Christ is not materially present on the altar. How then does he become food for us? By the work of the Holy Spirit who, because of our faith, renders Christ present in the symbolic act of eating and drinking the consecrated elements.

Calvin's dualist presuppositions are important here. Like Zwingli he assumes that matter and spirit are two realities so separated that they cannot be conjoined. Because we humans are stuck in this material and fleshly existence, our spiritual sensibilities are dulled so that we cannot ascertain supraphysical truths directly. But God in divine grace has condescended to employ earthly symbols as a mirror that reflects heavenly blessings.

As our faith is slight and feeble unless it be propped on all sides and sustained by every means, it trembles, wavers, totters, and at last gives way. Here our merciful Lord, according to his infinite kindness, so tempers himself to our capacity that, since we are creatures who always creep on the ground, cleave to flesh, and, do not think about or even conceive of anything spiritual, he condescends to lead us to himself by these earthly elements, and to set before us in the flesh a mirror of spiritual blessings. For if we were incorporeal (as Chrysostom says), he would give us these very things naked and incorporeal.[27]

It appears that to Calvin the sacrament is a grudging concession on the part of God. If it were not for human feebleness, God would not use mundane physical elements for the purpose of communicating with us.

Hence, Calvin assumes that real truth is spiritual, and by this he means incorporeal. A genuine enfleshment in the physical realm would apparently compromise the spiritual reality; therefore, what is physical can at best "mirror" the other reality. It cannot embody it. Thus, for Calvin the bread and wine are symbols that represent but do not embody the body and blood. They point to this heavenly reality but they themselves are physical and thereby cannot actually participate in what is spiritual.

How then is Christ present in the sacrament? After all, there is an infinite distance between Christ who is in heaven and us who are on earth. The distance is overcome by the Holy Spirit, who makes Christ present through the faith of the believer in the act of communing. Therefore, we can say that whereas for the Lutherans there is an objective co-presence of body and blood with the bread and the wine, for Calvin the body and blood of Christ are present in the faith-act whereby the believer consumes the elements. We might describe the Lutheran position as incarnationalist, because Christ is present to the physical elements themselves. We might describe the Calvinist position as parallelist, because the earthly elements and the heavenly Christ are consumed simultaneously but separately in the action of the believer. The weakness in the Lutheran point of view is that there is no openness to considering the obviously metaphorical or figurative structure of Jesus' words, "This is my body." This combined with their rejection of scholastic metaphysics leaves the Lutherans with no tools for explaining what they mean by the objective presence of Christ in the elements. The weakness in the Calvinist view is a lack of consistency. Given the dualist assumption and the position that the work of the Holy Spirit comes through the communicant's faith and not through the physical elements, it is difficult to see why Calvin insisted on any connection at all between the bread and wine and the body and blood of Christ. Despite these strengths, weaknesses, and differences, Lutheran and Presbyterian theologians meeting at Princeton during the 1960s found that both Reformation positions agreed that Christ and his saving work are present in the sacrament and that fellowship could and should exist across these denominational lines.[28] I could not agree more.

---

27. Calvin, *Inst.*, 4.14.3.

28. Paul C. Empie and James I. McCord, *Marburg Revisited* (Minneapolis: Augsburg, 1966), 103–4. The same mood of reconciliation appears in the Leuenberg Agreement of 1973. Yet, writes George Lindbeck humorously, "The struggle continues. There is a saying in Bavaria that lay people are Zwinglians, the pastors Calvinists, and only the theologians *echt* ('kosher') *Lutheraner* in their understanding of the real presence. In areas less traditionally

In recent times the Roman Catholic concept of transubstantiation with its change in *tota substantia* has come to be deemed anachronistic, out of accord with modern understandings of physics and the natural world. Aristotelian cosmology is now outdated. Some Catholic thinkers are tempted to reconsider a more open approach that affirms the real presence of Christ in the sacramental elements but without giving any specific philosophical or scientific formula for explaining the actual process. Karl Rahner, for example, distinguishes between logical explanations, which try to make things precise strictly on the basis of what is given, and ontic explanations, which seek to make things intelligible by asserting something else, usually of a metaphysical nature. Rahner then argues that transubstantiation is really a logical explanation of Jesus words, "This is my body." It is a way of affirming Christ's presence in the sacrament. Thus, transubstantiation need not be understood ontically—that is, it need not be tied to Aristotle's metaphysics. Where does this lead? It leads to a real ecumenical breakthrough. Rahner reexamines the Council of Trent and then says: "It seems to me that with regard to the real presence in the sacrament itself... there is no essential difference between the Catholic and the Lutheran faith."[29]

What all of these different and bitterly contested views have in common is confidence in the work of the Holy Spirit to unite us with the salvific accomplishments of Jesus Christ. What is present in the sacrament is not only the present. The past is there. We do not just remember the last supper or Calvary. We share in its reality. Similarly, the future is there. We do not just await God's kingdom. In the sacrament it comes ahead of time, partially but proleptically. It comes as the power of new life that invigorates and revitalizes the body of Christ. This is the life-giving work of the Holy Spirit.

THE MARKS OF THE CHURCH

The concept of the marks of the church derives from the parallel statements of the Apostles' Creed, which recognizes "one holy catholic church," and the Niceno-Constantinopolitan Creed, which tells of "one, holy, catholic, and apostolic church." It is customary to choose the longer list, giving us four marks.

It has never been clear just what theological role the marks are to play. Are they criteria that distinguish a true from a false church? According to what I have presented here, they do not constitute criteria, because

---

orthodox than Bavaria not even the theologians can be counted on" ("The Reformation Heritage and Christian Unity," *Lutheran Quarterly* 2, no. 4 [Winter 1988]: 493).

29. Rahner, *TI*, 4:294, and see 302; see also "The Eucharist: A Lutheran–Roman Catholic Statement," in *Lutherans and Catholics in Dialogue* (Minneapolis: Augsburg, 1967), 3:187–98.

that is the role assigned to proclamation of the word and celebration of the sacraments. Are they then signs or characteristics that let us know when the church is present? Not likely. Not only are some marks—such as oneness—never empirically present, but this creedal list is not even remotely exhaustive. Luther offered a modest list of seven characteristics that overlap with the criteria. They include preaching the word of God, administering baptism, celebrating the Lord's Supper, the power of the keys, the clergy, prayer and hymn singing, suffering and persecution. Perhaps still more signs could be listed. Are these four then ideals after which we should strive? Yes, to be sure. But I think it even a bit more accurate to say: the marks of the church are dispositions of moral resolve that should characterize the various members of the body of Christ.

The One Church

The church is one. It may have been easier to think of just one Christian church during the era when the creeds were being formulated than it is today. Like the builders of the Tower of Babel before the Lord confused their language, the first three centuries of church life experienced rapid geographical spread but considerable unity of language, culture, politics, and communication. It was still possible to hold a truly ecumenical council—that is, a meeting in which virtually the whole church was represented. The battles that irretrievably broke the church into the Latin West, the Greek East, the monophysites, the Nestorians, the Coptics, and such, came later. The twin forces of the Protestant Reformation and the modern mind smashed any remaining sense of institutional unity because they so elevated the individual conscience that it seemed to give theological justification for a neverending process of splintering and fragmenting. Through the centuries we have been witnessing not the unity of the church but the surgical dismembering of the body of Christ into smaller and smaller segments. It is a curiosity of history that after the creeds saddled Christians with the commitment to unity each group ran off in a separate direction confessing the oneness of the church. In sum, the writers of the Niceno-Constantinopolitan Creed could afford to be a bit naive regarding the oneness of the church because they could see it. We today can only dream about it.

But dream we must. Because all Christians are baptized into one name, the name of Jesus Christ, Paul says they should think of themselves as belonging to the one catholic church and not to one or another sect or party centered around a favorite leader or teacher (1 Cor. 1:13). It is the separatist mentality, which Paul calls "party spirit," that is so destructive to church unity. Paul lists the qualities of character that are worthy of our "calling"—lowliness, meekness, patience, forbearing one another in love—and he includes something indispensable to the unity of the church, namely, eagerness "to maintain the unity of the Spirit in the bond of peace" (Eph. 4:3). On the one hand, our unity derives from the fact that one and only one savior, Jesus Christ, has bestowed grace upon all of us. This is symbolized by the one baptism in which all Christians have participated. On the other hand, Paul calls us to walk wet, to live out the oneness into which we have been called. Walking wet with the water of our baptism includes, among other things, eagerness to maintain the unity of the Spirit in the bond of peace.

In our own era, the mark of oneness stimulates ecumenical resolve. Pope John Paul II believes "Christ is guiding us to the unity of that flock of which He alone is the one and sure shepherd." Karl Rahner and Heinrich Fries stress that "unity is a matter of life or death for Christendom" now as faith in God is being attacked by militant atheism and relativistic skepticism.[30] So intense is ecumenical resolve in some quarters that structural unity is being advocated while at the same time permitting considerable diversity in theological or confessional stances.[31] This thrust is healthy. Granting that theological diversity is inevitable, we must honor the mark of oneness by permitting disagreement without dividing the church.

Ecumenical oneness also has implications for ecumenic oneness. It is true that the *ecclesia* has been called out from the rest of society and is distinguishable from it. But this distinction is a means to a further end, namely, the establishment of God's kingdom. God's kingdom is inclusive of the whole *ecumené*. The unity of the church represents the unity of the world. The 1968 Uppsala assembly of the World Council of Churches dubbed the church the "sign of the future unity of mankind."[32]

The Holy Church

Christians confess that the church is holy. Despite what is said when reciting the creeds, however, the New Testament does not generally speak of a "holy church." Baptism and the Lord's Supper are not referred to as "holy." There are no holy objects to be venerated or holy places to which pilgrimages should be made. Hence, the holiness of the church does not seem to be rooted in the symbol at its compact level. It is rather a theological construction, and as such we must understand it as a track taken by evangelical explication. There are three reasons that it is appropriate to follow this track and use the adjective *holy* when speaking about the church.

The church can be thought of as holy, first of all, because as the ἐκκλησία it is a people called out by God for a particular purpose. This

---

30. Fries and Rahner, *Unity of the Churches* (Philadelphia: Fortress, 1985), 1.

31. This is Cullmann's position in *Unity through Diversity*.

32. The correlation of the unity of the church with the unity of the world is a major theme in the ecumenical theology of Wolfhart Pannenberg, *The Church* (Philadelphia: Westminster, 1983), 151–52.

reflects the basic understanding of what holiness is. Whether the Old Testament קָדוֹשׁ (*qadosh*) or the New Testament ἅγιος, the term means being separated out or consecrated for God. The idea of a holy people called from among the nations (Exod. 19:6; 1 Pet. 2:9-10) persists into the New Testament. Thus, the people of God are holy because God has consecrated them for specific purposes in history. The church, which currently makes up part of this holy people, has been set apart for the specific mission of spreading the gospel of Jesus Christ.

Second, we can think of the church as holy in the same way that we can think of an individual Christian believer as holy, namely, as a forgiven sinner.[33] Ephesians 5:25b-27 contains a combination of images (Jesus' sacrifice, the happy exchange, washing by baptism, and readying the bride of Christ), all converging on an understanding of the church: "Christ loved the church and gave himself up for her, in order to make her holy [ἁγιάσῃ]...and without blemish." To be holy is to be cleansed from sin, to be forgiven. This is what Christ has done on Calvary and what is appropriated through baptism.

Third, the church strives for holiness in the same sense that an individual believer strives for sanctification. The tension created by *simul justus et peccator* can be restated eschatologically: holiness in the sense of the new creation is a gift of God already given in baptism, yet its realization has yet to be striven for. What emerges is for all practical purposes an ethical imperative for Christians to be holy: "As he who called you is holy, be holy yourselves in all your conduct" (1 Pet. 1:15). The writer of Ephesians says we should be "imitators of God" and offers a long list of dos and don'ts. Among the don'ts are hardness of heart, deceitful lusts, covetousness, clandestine "works of darkness," bitterness, stealing, evil talk, and filthy talk. The dos include putting on the new nature of the likeness of God, speaking the truth, not letting the "sun go down" on one's anger, giving no opportunity to the devil, tenderheartedness, forgiving one another, addressing one another in psalms, hymns, and spiritual songs, and all this while "making melody to the Lord in your hearts" (Eph. 4:17—5:20). These are the qualities befitting a saintly life. They are also the qualities Christians strive to embody in the life of the church, the communion of saints.

The Catholic Church

Augustine enjoyed painting heretics into a corner by forcing them to make verbal obeisance to the one catholic church. He wrote: "Whether they will or no, heretics and schismatics use no other name for it than the name of

---

33. Hans Küng and Jürgen Moltmann describe the church as a *communio peccatorum* (community of sinners) as well as a *communio sanctorum* (community of saints) (Küng, *The Church*, 327; Moltmann, *Church in the Power of the Spirit*, 353; see also Wainwright, *Doxology*, 132).

Catholic, when they speak of it not among themselves but with outsiders. They cannot make themselves understood unless they designate it by this name which is in universal use."[34] Evidently there is no getting around the use of the term *catholic* to describe the church. This has caused considerable consternation on the part of some Protestant groups who wish to delete the term from the creeds and substitute "Christian" or "universal" in its place. Their motive is to establish the confessional legitimacy of their own denomination and declare their independence from the church centered in Rome. This tactic fails, however, because then in other contexts when such Protestants use the term *catholic* it cannot but help refer to the church of Rome. So, finding themselves painted into Augustine's corner, they end up granting verbal legitimacy to the Roman church as the one referred to by the original creeds.

What does this enigmatic term mean? How should we use it in our time? If we start with the Bible, we will note that the New Testament never describes the church as catholic. The term is only used once (Acts 4:19), and in this instance it takes the form of an adverb usually translated "at all." The adjectival form, καθολικός, composed etymologically of κατά and ὅλον, means "according to the whole." It was used in classical Greek to distinguish general or universal statements from those applying to particular individuals. It is rendered *catholicus* or *universalis* in Latin, and has come to denote the general, the whole, the entirety, or what is complete or total. The phrase "the whole catholic church throughout the world" appears in an early document, The Martyrdom of Polycarp (8:1), and it seems clear that here it is referring to the composite or inclusive church rather than to local congregations.

Thus, the most useful understanding of "catholic" is its reference to the Christian church as a whole, to the church understood as inclusive of all persons of faith and all local assemblies over all periods of time. Catholicism, in short, is a wholeness principle. But in saying this, I do not wish to imply that the primary reality is this inclusive whole so that individual persons assembled for word and sacrament are considered mere expressions or vehicles by which this greater reality makes itself known. Rather, I take the position that the local congregation is the church in the fullest sense. The presence of Christ in the word and in the sacrament and in the faith of those gathered together as the local congregation defines the church. Without the local parts there would be no universal whole. Curiously enough, one of the earliest uses of the term *catholic* in reference to the church ties it to the local assembly. In his "Epistle to the Smyrneans," Ignatius of Antioch writes that "wherever Jesus Christ is, there is the Catholic Church."[35] Thus, it seems that the word *catholic* applies both to the

---

34. Augustine *Of True Religion* 7.12.
35. Ignatius of Antioch "Epistle to the Smyrneans" 7.2.

church as a composite whole and to the local part. How, then, can we understand the relationship between these two dimensions of catholicity?

Let me suggest a postmodern model of wholeness for explicating the whole-part relationship of catholicity, namely, the printed hologram. A printed hologram differs from ordinary types of pictures. If you have a photograph of a dog, for example, and cut off one corner, what appears on that corner is just part of the dog, such as a foot or a leg. If you show someone the removed corner, the viewer cannot tell from the picture what the whole dog looks like. The part is just a part apart. But a hologram is different. If you cut away just a part and blow that part back up to original size, you will see the whole dog. Each individual part of the picture contains the whole in condensed form. The same is true for catholicity. There is one catholic church that is inclusive of all local congregations, but in each time and place where the believers congregate and Christ is present, so also is the whole catholic church present in its fullness.

Inclusivity is one of the most potent ways in which the moral resolve of catholicity can express itself in our day. The concept of inclusivity is a tool for grappling with the issue of pluralism in the emerging postmodern world. Having taken the concept of dignity from the modern period and combining it with the global consciousness of postmodern holism, we now seek comprehensive unity while becoming acutely aware of the integrity and value of particularity indicative of each of the various racial groups and ethnic traditions that constitute the human race. Or to put it more bluntly, we use catholicity as an antidote for the poisons of prejudice and discrimination. There is good biblical support for this. The struggle between Peter and Paul in Acts 15 and Galatians had to do with the inclusivity of the church. The victor in this struggle was the Gentile who could then be included in the church along with the Jew. There could be no clearer affirmation of inclusivity and prohibition against prejudice than Paul's words, "There is no longer Jew or Greek, there is no longer slave or free, there is no longer male or female; for you are all one in Christ Jesus" (Gal. 4:28). The principle of inclusivity is clearly present in Paul's philosophy of mission, according to which the church can be different things to different people (1 Cor. 9:19-23). In our time this means that congregations should strive for racial integration, foster social unity between labor and management, create fellowship between rich and poor, and encourage mutual respect between male and female. *Lumen gentium* 28 enjoins us to "wipe out every kind of division, so that the whole human race may be brought into the unity of the family of God."

The Apostolic Church

The church is apostolic. The word *apostolic* has come to mean that the church has a direct link with the apostles, and the apostles in turn have a direct link with Christ. In New Testament times the Greek term ἀπόστολος referred to someone sent as a representative, such as an ambassador. This was applied to those ambassadors for Christ who experienced the resurrected Jesus and who were given the commission to witness to the gospel to the four corners of the world. The church is the successor to the apostles. It continues shouldering the task of presenting the gospel to the world, of witnessing to the significance of the resurrected Christ. The church does not receive this gospel message or the commission through direct inspiration, however. Rather, it receives them indirectly through the witness of the first apostles. Apostolic succession in the life of the church consists fundamentally, then, in attending to the indispensable testimony of the scriptures in which the original apostolic message is found.[36]

Apostolicity usually involves two things: loyalty to the scriptural testimony plus the institutionalized clergy, whose task it is to foster this loyalty. Carl Braaten dubs these "canon" and "ministry." He says that "the maintenance of the canon as the norm of apostolicity is essential for the church, and so is the office of the ministry that continues the primacy of the apostolic service of the Word to the whole community of Jesus Christ."[37] Service here means specifically service to the apostolic message.

Hans Küng adds to this a healthy antiauthoritarian note. The continuing apostolic ministry not only submits itself to the original testimony of the apostles found in scripture; it also submits itself to service in the broad sense. Ministry means service. It means serving the truth of the gospel, and it means serving people in all walks of life with the love befitting the message ministers bear. As a call to service, the call to apostleship ought not to be construed as a call to power and authority over others. It is wrong to use such things as the episcopal succession of bishops, for example, as an excuse for bishops to gain power over people's minds or lives. "Apostolicity can never mean power through which the Church might rule," writes Küng; "it is not a question of others submitting to the Church; the Church must itself submit by accepting the authority of the apostles and of the Church's and the apostles' Lord."[38] "What, then, are the priests and bishops?" asks Luther in his 1523 treatise entitled *Temporal Authority*. "Answer: their government is not a matter of authority or

---

36. Marjorie Hewitt Suchocki temporalizes the church's marks in an interesting fashion. "Apostolicity is the sense in which the church is continuously affected by and responsible to its past, beginning with the testimony of the apostles to the life, death, and resurrection of Jesus. Unity comes to the church from its future, because of the dynamics of identity in Christ. Holiness is the present result as the church exists in faithfulness to both its past and future" (*God, Christ, Church: A Practical Guide to Process Theology* [New York: Crossroad, 1982], 134).

37. Carl Braaten, *The Apostolic Imperative* (Minneapolis: Augsburg, 1985), 129.

38. Küng, *The Church*, 358. Although Braaten thinks of ordination as sacramental and associates apostolicity with the ordained clergy, he too is wary of authoritarianism. "There is a need for an equilibrium of authority and power at every level in the church" (*Apostolic Imperative*, 135).

power, but a service and an office; for they are neither higher nor better than other Christians."[39]

In short, true apostolicity is found in the church's ministry of witness and service. As such the term *apostolic* applies to the whole church, not just a few individuals within the church charged with oversight. The Nicene Creed speaks of an "apostolic church," not an "apostolic clergy" or "apostolic episcopacy" or "apostolic hierarchy" or whatever. In our own time with the relentless advance of modern ideals such as equality, dignity, inclusivity, delegated authority, and a rising sense of entitlement, nothing could make the church appear more anachronistic than to try to use the concept of apostolicity to justify an intraecclesial aristocracy.

MINISTRY IN A POSTMODERN WORLD

The problem is not that a hierarchy within church structures might exist. The problem is that the people in it are tempted to take it too seriously, are tempted to think that it has some eternal or everlasting validity, which it does not. The apostolic ministry is strictly a temporal and ephemeral affair. It is serious, but it is not eternally serious. People in the church may need a hierarchy from time to time, not because God has ordained it, but because they need a form of order for organizing efforts to carry the gospel to the world. In the modern era hierarchical authority has largely been transformed into delegated authority—that is, the tendency is that those who govern do so only with the consent of the governed. As we move into the postmodern era, even delegated authority may be gradually replaced with networking. The institutionalized ministry as we have known it exists due to practical exigencies, because it facilitates Christian practice. Any effective ordering of the ministry is permissible because it is the gospel—not the forms of ministry of the gospel—that is essential and foundational. Or, to put it another way, each generation should organize the ministry in such a fashion as to be a good steward of the gifts God bestows to carry out the apostolic ministry in its time and place.[40]

This is where stewardship of gifts or charisms (χαρίσματα) becomes important. Each member of the church—all lay people included—has been given something by the Holy Spirit that has value for the life of the whole body. To bury one's talent (Matt. 25:14-30) by leaving a gift undeveloped and unexploited is to sin against the Holy Spirit and to maim the body of Christ. In our time we by no means need a repressive

---

39. Luther, *LW*, 45:117.

40. The authors of *Baptism, Eucharist, and Ministry* pine: "A common answer needs to be found to the following question: How, according to the will of God and under the guidance of the Holy Spirit, is the life of the church to be understood and ordered, so that the Gospel may be spread and the community built up in love?" (20–21). I caution against the assumed need to find a single, common answer to the question of church order that would prohibit flexibility and variety in structuring ministry.

hierarchy but rather a ministry of humble leadership that will help unwrap these divine gifts wherever they are found and spend their wealth in the service of the church's overall mission.

Five Forms of Ministry

There is no need here to recite the long and sometimes bloody history of competition between Christians to establish their respective doctrines of the ministry. We now need an openness of spirit and a creativity to assess the needs of the current and the future generation and to plan a form of ministerial preparation and organization that is appropriate. In what follows I will sketch five general forms in which we can plan and execute the apostolic ministry to which the church as a whole has been commissioned.

Secular vocation. The ministry of secular vocation applies primarily to lay people, but even ordained clergy have some dimensions to their lives in which secular responsibilities are to be exercised. This is ministry outside the province of the institutional church but well within the province of the universal kingdom of God. It is exercised in the professional, political, and familial realms of life. When our profession emerges from our confession, we refer to it as our vocation.

The word *vocation*, which means literally "the calling," has two theological meanings. It can refer to the call of the gospel to repentance and faith. Or it can refer to God's call to the faithful to live out their faith in the world, especially as it has to do with routine, daily work. It is the second theological meaning that applies here. Through our professional work we can fulfill the commandment to love our neighbor. Constructive work contributes to the betterment of life on earth as a whole, and being a good steward of our native talents consists in training, self-discipline, development of skills, and the exercise of our skills to the best of our ability. Doing high-quality work is a mandate from God even if the boss does not require it.

Personal evangelism. *Evangelism* basically means sharing the evangel, sharing the gospel. It consists in something very simple yet very profound, namely, giving to one's family and friends a frank witness by word and deed to God's loving action in Jesus Christ. It consists in introducing one's comrades to the life of a healthy Christian congregation. It need not be complicated or detailed or exploitive, only forthright.

Surprisingly enough, personal evangelism is the single most significant factor influencing the growth of congregations. Its importance cannot be overestimated. This truth unmasks a popular misconception regarding evangelism. The image many people have is that of a professional clergyperson such as a priest, missionary, or evangelist who stands up before a crowd of people and delivers a persuasive speech, following which convicted individuals come forward and ask for church membership. Something like this seems to have happened at Pentecost in Acts 2, and something like this appears to be happening when watching an evangelism crusade on television. But this is not the way most people come to a knowledge or appreciation of the gospel today. It is almost always through a friend or family member. Whether it be due to the influence of modernity or whatever, evangelism occurs almost solely on a one-to-one basis.

Congregational stewardship. It is here that the careful unwrapping and sharing of God's gifts to each individual need to take place for the upbuilding of the community as a whole. Good readers should be asked to be lectors. Good teachers should be asked to teach. Singers should sing and cooks should cook. Sensitive and patient people should visit the sick, and those good with figures should count the money and keep the books. Those who have been blessed in their secular employment with large incomes should with the cheerfulness of which Paul speaks provide as much financial support as is possible (2 Cor. 9:7; Rom. 12:8). Experience teaches that a congregation is much healthier when everyone, no matter how poor, contributes something to the common fund and general welfare. Even so, large contributions enable the congregation to engage in still more creative forms of ministry and social service.

Diaconal service. A deacon is a servant. According to Vatican II a deacon is one who obtains authorization from the priest to administer the sacraments and assist or officiate at marriages and funerals. According to John Calvin the deacon is entrusted with the ministry to the poor. Either definition is technically satisfactory because *diakonia* (διακονία) in Acts 6 simply means service—originally service at table—and the church applies *diakonia* to the service of the word as well as service to those in need. Here I have in mind Calvin's understanding of deacon. I will leave the service of the word to the next category of ministry.

The dire situation today cries for help for the poor of the world. The twin problems of uncontrolled population growth and the steady loss of natural resources exacerbated by economic exploitation and oppressive political systems are leaving in their wake unparalleled human carnage and devastation. Malnourishment and starvation are now the fate of millions of the poor in drought-ridden regions of Africa. Refugees from central and southeastern Asia are condemned to live for unknown periods of time in crammed and undersupplied camps. Landlessness and joblessness in the increasingly overcrowded cities of Latin America are creating unimaginable squalor. Unemployment and unpayable medical bills in the United States are sucking people out of the middle class and dropping

them into the ranks of the homeless. Poverty on a global scale is staggering in proportion, and just because so much in our world is interrelated
we are compelled to think of poverty on this global scale if we are to be
realistic. We need to find a way to break the back of the system that is
currently breaking the human race.

One way to do this might be to form a worldwide network of deacons. Under the banner of "deacon" we could gather from churches and
church organizations those devoted souls who have enough moral resolve
and creative energy to make good deacons.[41] Then we would bring them
together and underwrite them as they make plans and execute programs
of service and aid. We would also encourage them to engage in revolutionary thinking, to come up with theories and leads in the practice that will
liberate the peoples of the globe from the highly productive but largely oppressive world economic system that dominates our lives. We need a new
world economic order founded on the principles of justice and dedicated
to the elimination of poverty and the promotion of a higher quality of life
for every sentient being on the planet. I believe it is part of the church's
ministry in our time to give top priority to this form of diaconal service.

Word and sacrament.   Whether they are called bishops, presbyters, pastors, or ministers, Calvin says they have two particular functions: "to
proclaim the gospel and to administer the sacraments."[42] Article Five of
the Augsburg Confession says that the office of the ministry has been instituted by God for these two purposes. A great deal about these two
purposes has already been said in this chapter. In contrast to the personal evangelism just mentioned, the ministry of the word takes the form
of public evangelism. It is public both within and without the church,
whether it consists in pastoral preaching from the pulpit or in presenting
the gospel on the air waves to unknown audiences. The church cannot be
the church without the public telling of the story of Jesus with its significance or the memorial and prolepsis embodied in the celebration of the
sacraments. For this the church needs leadership.

To provide this leadership the church needs an ordained clergy. Ordination signifies here that the minister of word and sacrament performs his
or her duties with the full support and blessing of the wider constituency
that makes up the body of Christ. Self-appointed prophets and preachers do not necessarily speak for the church. Yet we need ministers who

---

41. Braaten suggests the revival of the order of deacons, but his purpose is to provide
a meaningful office for those people who would like to be ordained pastors but who lack
the talents of leadership (*Apostolic Imperative*, 158). This would, in effect, make the office
of deacon a consolation prize for those who view ordination as a status symbol. It would
use the word *deacon* to describe the retinue of helpers who hang around churches. What I
am suggesting here, in contrast, is to pursue talented people in order to establish a group
of professionals who are competent to deal with the problems of poverty.

42. Calvin, *Inst.*, 4.3.6.

do. Therefore, a process of careful selection of candidates on the basis of their devotion and gifts, combined with rigorous theological education and personal self-discipline, is necessary to make ready the voice we want to hear from our pulpits. The rite of ordination is a sign that the people of God are entrusting the ordinand with representative responsibility as well as an opportunity to serve in congregational leadership.

It should be noted, however, that this setting apart of the ordained from the lay creates a bit of tension in our modern and emerging postmodern culture due to deeply held egalitarian and antiauthoritarian values. Some advocates of a postmodern society stress the need for networking to replace hierarchies. Despite this challenge, it seems to me that the practical need for responsible leadership will require the church to sponsor an ordained clergy or its equivalent for the indefinite future. Ministers of word and sacrament will have the delicate task of exercising responsibly their particular authority yet doing so in a genuine mood of communal cooperation with their lay partners in ministry.

Three patterns of setting apart by ordination rite are familiar. First, the onefold or unitary ministry distinguishes between lay people and a single category of ordained pastors whose function is to preside over word and sacrament. Second, the twofold ministry separates out both deacons and pastors (sometimes called presbyters) by special rite. In the event that the polity of either the onefold or twofold pattern includes the office of bishop, the bishop is usually considered one ordained pastor among others. The bishop, like other pastors, is ordained to the ministry of word and sacrament, and then later is singled out for the particular service in the office of bishop. Third, in the threefold ministry pattern, the bishops are added as a distinctive class. The three ministries are divided into three functions: *diaconal* ministry to the world; *presbyteral* ministry of preaching, teaching, and pastoral care in the local congregation; and *episcopal* ministry of oversight, continuity, and unity in the church to be carried out by the bishops. The threefold ministry pattern may include the belief that the church's apostolicity is guaranteed through the laying on of hands—not at presbyters' ordinations, but at bishops' installations—from one generation of bishops to the next. Certain pastors graduate, so to speak, to the rank of bishop and gain the task of episcopacy or oversight. When debates arise regarding authority in the church, they usually indicate a struggle on the part of bishops to gain authority over pastors, deacons, and the laity.

In my judgment, the threefold pattern has more problems than the onefold or twofold. First, as indicated, the scheme of three offices usually includes the doctrine of the historic episcopate that restricts apostolic succession to bishops, rendering them a distinct class set apart from other ordained clergy. There seems to be little or no scriptural warrant for this, noting that *bishop* and *presbyter* are interchangeable terms in the catholic epistles. More importantly, the association of apostolic succession with the bishop's office sets up an institutional rival to the teaching of the gospel as the norm for Christian thought and practice. It is my judgment that bishops should be considered a subclass within the more inclusive category of ordained pastors. What distinguishes a bishop is the particular function he or she performs, not the task of shouldering apostolic succession for the rest of the church. Second, the traditional threefold pattern has underemployed deacons so that their effectiveness in the wider world has been minimized. The hierarchical structure of the ordained has made deacons servile to the whims of the higher-ranked clergy and has directed the diaconal ministry toward secondary roles in the sphere of worship. My proposal, in contrast, is to encourage deacons to specialize in ministry to the world at large with a focus on the problems of poverty and injustice. Therefore, I support either the onefold ministry that includes nonordained deacons or, preferably, the twofold ministry of pastors (including bishops) and deacons.

When it comes to the selection of candidates for ordination to word and sacrament, the churches have the right and the responsibility to search out the most appropriate gifts to enhance the ministry. Potential pastors ought not to be disqualified because of economic, racial, ethnic, or gender discrimination. Where the wounds of division and schism exist in society, those in the church should try to heal such wounds rather than exacerbate them. The right choice of clergy just may help in the healing process. In the Church of South India many of today's pastors were previously the poverty-entrapped outcastes—also known as untouchables—of the Hindu caste system. Caste should be no barrier to recognizing a gift of leadership.

In the modern and emerging postmodern context, this applies as well to the issue of women in ministry. Although most ecclesial traditions have for centuries limited the ranks of the ordained clergy to men, in our time we are witnessing a widespread change. Women are studying at theological institutions in record numbers, and many are assuming full responsibilities as congregational pastors. One could attribute this change to the impact on the church by the general rise in the sense of entitlement that pervades the modern world. No doubt this has been a sociological factor. But the chief reason—a theological reason—for asking women to come into the pulpits is stewardship. The pool of gifts, skills, sophistication, and dedication doubles in size as soon as women are included. The Holy Spirit has bestowed valuable talents upon women, and the church would risk burying many talents if on the basis of gender discrimination it excluded them from engaging in the ministry of word and sacrament.

Given all I have said about eschatology and the open future, it is logical for me to stress that as regards women and ordained ministry there is room to be creative and to make changes even where traditions have been long ensconced. Creative change often produces some resistance, and this certainly has been the case with regard to women in the ordained ministry. Yet women's ordination seems right for our time and for a healthy understanding of stewardship. So the church should push on with confidence, seeking to persuade the resistance within the church to see the light, while trying to avoid the darkness of fracture and schism. This takes a combination of courage and humility in the face of God's apostolic commission.

KINGDOM AND RECONCILIATION

The central concern of the church is the kingdom of God, and the way to show this concern is through carrying out its apostolic ministry of reconciliation. This is done through presenting the gospel in word and sacrament. Like an electric arc between two terminals, the church is called to bear the light between Easter and the consummation.

The church is provisional, not eternal, except in the proleptic sense of finding its place as a part in the more inclusive whole that is the kingdom. As the Easter Christ is the future made present, so also our communion with that Christ makes his future present in the life of the community called to be the church. That communion takes place in the preaching of the word, whereby God's grace exerts upon us the power of transformation, the power of the new creation that moves us here and now from citizenship in the old aeon to citizenship in the future city of God. That communion also takes place in baptism and eucharist, where through the physical elements of water and bread and wine the Spirit makes Christ incarnately present in our presence.

10

ESCHATOLOGY

We must desire that the kingdom of God should not be only "over" all (for it is that already), but also "in" all, that God should be "all in all" and that "all should be one in him."

—Vladimir Sergeevic Soloviev

Salvation is already present to us in faith. It is present in faith but not in experience, at least not in uninterrupted, continual, plenary, uncontradictable experience. Faith is under continual attack by temptation from within and suffering from without due to the warfare between the two aeons, due to the conflict between the present and the future. Beatitudinal living is living between the times: we both have and await the blessings that Christ has wrought. We live out of the power of salvation that dwells within our hearts while yet awaiting salvation to come in its fullness. We express the vitality and power of new life while yet awaiting that new life to transform our existence. Faith has this proleptic structure that permits us to live now with confidence and hope while expecting still greater things to appear in the future.

This brings us to the locus on eschatology. Eschatology is that region of Christian contemplation in which we ponder the last things, τὰ ἔσχατα. Usually included here are topics such as the everlasting kingdom of God, the second advent of Christ, resurrection of the dead, the final judgment, heaven, hell, purgatory, and related concerns. Such things are considered "last" only from the point of view of the present aeon. They mark the end of our aeon. But with respect to the new creation, they mark a beginning.

Eschatology begins at Easter. At Easter the end appeared ahead of time. It appeared proleptically. Thus, the resurrection of Jesus Christ is the foundation upon which we must build our constructive thoughts regarding the future. It also provides a sort of limit. Beyond what we know about the resurrection of Jesus we have little or no knowledge that penetrates the shroud of mystery protecting the divine secrets of what is to come. We ought not pretend we know more than we do.

Before I proceed with my discussion of eschatology, perhaps I should add a word about theological method with regard to the subject. Rudolf Bultmann saw eschatology as so fraught with myth that he believed it, more than any other doctrine, had to be demythologized in order for the gospel to have an existential impact for modern people.[1] Although when he used the term *demythologizing* he did not intend to "eliminate" but rather to "interpret" the mythical worldview of the Bible, Bultmann for all practical purposes imposed an existentialist hermeneutic that has restricted eschatological assertions to the sphere of personal faith and has eliminated any reference to cosmic history. This is not the method followed here.

Based on the earlier discussion on the significance of Jesus' resurrection, it would seem clear that Easter cannot be understood rightly except as prolepsis, except as an anticipation in Jesus' person of what God will do to transform and renew the whole of creation. Eschatology is not restricted to the personal sphere of life, and cannot be limited to present experience. Karl Rahner is right when he insists that the Christian understanding of the faith

must contain an eschatology which really bears on the *future*, that which is still to come, in a very ordinary, empirical sense of the word time. An interpretation of the eschatological assertions of Scripture, which in the course of simply demythizing would de-eschatologize it in such a way that all eschatological sayings of Scripture, explicit or implicit, only meant something that takes place here and now in the existence of the individual and in the decision he takes here and now, is theologically unacceptable.[2]

To treat eschatology proleptically, we must treat time and the future cosmically as well as individually.

TIME AND THE FUTURE

In my attempt to determine the heart of the gospel at the beginning of this study, I argued that the originary symbolization of the Christian message was so intimately tied to the context of Hebrew prophecy and Jewish apocalyptic thinking that some commitments regarding the future of the cosmos are unavoidably implicit. I argued we must part company with any theological method that proposes that it can so totally demythologize the gospel as to extricate it completely from all cosmological commitments.

---

1. Rudolf Bultmann, *Jesus Christ and Mythology* (New York: Scribners, 1958), chap. 2.
2. Rahner, *TI*, 4:326; Rahner's italics.

Although the gospel does not create its own Weltanschauung independent of other linguistic and cultural factors, evangelical explication cannot
avoid taking certain stands regarding the nature of the wider reality of
which human consciousness is a part. In particular, the gospel understood
as the proleptic anticipation of the future kingdom of God in the person
of Jesus Christ must determine to some extent our understanding of time
and the future. The most distinguishing characteristic of time, when explicated in terms of the gospel, is that it leads in one direction—toward
a single divine future for the whole of creation.

In examining the various doctrinal areas of Christian theology, I have
explained how this works out. In each locus analyzed thus far in this book,
the concept of time that leads toward a final cosmic future has been vital
to my explication. Revelation from God that is mediated to us through
symbols and concepts is open to the future in a double sense: first, the
symbols provide an intellectual home for interpreting new experiences
and making sense out of them; and, second, we await divine confirmation of the validity of our beliefs that can only come with the advent of
the consummate kingdom of God. With regard to human understanding
of God and creation, I have argued that we cannot think of the cosmos
as having been created just once and then left to run on its own forever;
rather, it is necessary to think of continuing creation (*creatio continua*) on
the part of a God who is free to alter the course of natural and historical
events and to create new things in the future. In discussing Christology
I proposed that it is best to understand the divine incarnation in Jesus
as the future made present, as the universal reign of God in our midst
in this person, bringing the power and reality of the new creation to
bear upon our lives amid the old creation. For anthropology this means
that we cannot define what a human being is on the basis of present
factors alone; we must anticipate the future and acknowledge that true
humanity is defined by its relation to the new Adam, to the eschatological Christ. The Holy Spirit makes the reality of the new creation and
of our true nature available ahead of time by making the risen Christ
present to us through faith, through the proclamation of the word of
God, and through God's real presence in the sacraments celebrated by
the church. In each and every doctrinal region of theological thinking
we find we cannot explicate the gospel without thinking eschatologically,
without pondering the link between the present state of affairs and the
ultimate future.

The link is the prolepsis that ties together two otherwise disjunctive
understandings of the future, *futurum* and *adventus*. Our modern view
presupposes *futurum*, the assumption that the future will be the result of
causative forces coming from the past. The future actualizes a potential
that is already present, just as a cherry tree actualizes the potential already
in the stone or seed we plant in the ground. With the term *adventus*, in

contrast, we think of the appearance of something absolutely new. It is not merely the effect of past causes or the actualization of existing potential. The kingdom of God that cleanses our world of its original sin, for example, cannot be simply the product of present causes, because all such present causes are corrupted and unable to shed their corruption. The kingdom of God must then come as an advent, as an act of divine grace whereby the creation undergoes genuine renewal. The future renewal of all things that the advent of the divine kingdom will bring has already appeared ahead of time in the person of Jesus from Nazareth, the proleptic advent of the ultimate rule of God.

A third Latin term for the future, *venturum*, is helpful here. We find it paired with *futurum* in Romance languages—*il futuro* and *l'avenire* in Italian, *futur* and *l'avenir* in French, and *futuro* and *porvenir* in Spanish. We know it from the Latin phrase *vitam venturi saeculi* (life in the world to come). It is the coming that I emphasize here. In its coming this future has an impact on us before its full advent. *Venturum* gives us the sense of prolepsis, the invasion of the present by the power of what is yet to come.[3]

Thus, time itself becomes christologized and eschatologized. This interweaving of future and present in the Christ-event cannot be explicated fully within the strictures of the Western notion of linear time with its three successive stages of past, present, and future and the assumption that the future is the product of the past. To try to do so would consign the Christ-event to just one point on a time line and would limit it to being strictly a past for us today. The Easter resurrection did occur at one point on the line, to be sure, but it also transcended the circumscription of its own historical period. Somehow the everlasting future was collapsed and compressed and appeared in seed form within the soil of that temporal moment. Therefore, celebrating Easter is not simply a matter of remembering and recapitulating it in Sunday worship services or at special festivals as other historical watersheds might be recalled. It is rather a matter of participating in an as yet outstanding universal reality that has taken on the limits of finitude, in the eternal and everlasting kingdom that has taken on the limits of temporality and ephemerality. Just as in Christ himself, so also in the eucharist, the future arrives ahead of time but is not exhausted upon its arrival. It is the proleptic presence under humble conditions of the yet to be consummated fulfillment of all things in their ultimate glory.

---

3. I distinguished *futurum* and *adventus* in an earlier book, *Futures—Human and Divine* (Atlanta: John Knox, 1978), 20–22. The use of *venturum* to connote prolepsis is the helpful suggestion of José Lana, "Eschatology and Utopia" (Th.D. diss., The Graduate Theological Union, 1988).

DEATH AND THE SPIRITUAL BODY

To speak of the new in terms of *adventus* inevitably implies that what is old will have to die. The future holds an element of death as well as the promise of new life. Death, however, is not a subject that frightens Christians who have faith. They can afford to be realistic about the subject. It belongs indelibly to the heart of Christian originary symbolism—that is, a person of faith identifies with the one who died on the cross. Death to the old aeon is necessary if the new creation is going to have the quality of newness required to make it a fulfillment.

To understand the tie between death and the old aeon we will need to visit once again the Garden of Eden.

The Destruction of Evil in Eden

There were two trees of special importance in the Garden of Eden, the tree of the knowledge of good and evil and also the tree of life. The violation of God's command to avoid the knowledge of good and evil precipitated the fall into sin. In response to this disobedience God threw Adam and Eve out of the garden and placed the cherubim at the gate with a flaming sword. This kept them from getting back in. Why did God do such a thing? Was this a case of a divine short temper, a celestial temper tantrum whereby the insult to the throne of grace was met with vengeful wrath? Did God decide to rid paradise of this first human prototype because of hurt pride, because of divine reluctance to love a race that did not respond in kind? Not quite. That God did not cease to love the woman and man is made clear by Genesis 3:21, an easily overlooked passage where the Lord replaces the rapidly wilting fig leaves with divinely tailored leather clothes. God still cares for these sinners.

Why then did the creator of paradise cast them out? The answer has to do with that other tree. Although Adam and Eve had eaten the fruit from the tree of the knowledge of good and evil, they had not yet gotten around to the tree of life. This is fortuitous, because had they eaten that fruit they would "live forever" (Gen. 3:22). Having fallen into sin and brought upon themselves the enmity between humans and wild beasts, the sweat of the brow by which a living must be arrested from nature, pain in childbirth, and all manner of suffering, the last thing one would want to add to this list is that it all go on forever. It is out of love, then, that God separates Adam and Eve from the tree of life. Death is a gift of divine grace because it marks the point at which the consequences for sin come to an end. There is no suffering in the grave. Death is the door that God slams shut on evil and suffering within creation.

When Paul says that "the wages of sin is death" (Rom. 6:23), we may interpret this negatively to mean that death is the appropriate penalty for disobedience. We may think that just as high treason is a capital crime punishable by the electric chair or firing squad, so eating forbidden fruit is similarly punishable. Death signals the deserved loss of divine grace. But it may not be quite so simple. There may be a long-range, positive interpretation as well. In light of Genesis 3 and in light of Easter, it seems that death plays an important role in the divine plan of salvation. It is even conceivable that we like Paul might desire death in order to realize that salvation sooner (Phil. 1:23). Death can be evaluated according to either the law or the gospel. According to the law it is our just deserts for acting sinfully. According to the gospel, it is a gift that opens the door to an everlasting life free of the sufferings we undergo in this life.

In saying this I do not want to diminish in any sense the reality or totality of death; nor do I want to disregard the fear if not outright terror with which many of us face our own demise. The Bible clearly states that we humans are mortal. We really do die and cease to exist. We will not be saved by a heroic soulechtomy, that is, by extracting an immaterial soul from our material body. Sin is a cancer that eats away at the totality of human existence, leaving no organ, whether physical or spiritual, uninfected. The resulting death means true extinction.

The Destruction of Evil in Gethsemane

This applies to Jesus as well. He was born a mortal and died a mortal, and he knew it. The death of Socrates and the death of Jesus have much in common. Yet there are some notable differences that are relevant to the present discussion. Jesus did not face death with the comfort Socrates had. Socrates accepted death peacefully believing in his own imminent soulechtomy, looking forward to the future as an immortal psyche in the bliss of philosophical speculation. The death of Socrates, as described by Plato, was a beautiful death. It was free of anxiety and terror. Like shedding one's coat Socrates rid himself of his body and slipped quietly off into a better existence.

Not so with Jesus. Death for him was the end. In Gethsemane he was "distressed and agitated," saying to his disciples, "I am deeply grieved, even to death" (Mark 14:33-34). Praying in agony "with loud cries and tears" (Heb. 5:7), "his sweat became like great drops of blood falling down on the ground" (Luke 22:44). Whereas Socrates took the cup of hemlock calmly and voluntarily, Jesus petitioned God: "Remove this cup from me" (Mark 14:36). "Jesus is afraid," writes Oscar Cullmann. "He is afraid in the face of death itself. Death for him is not something divine; it is something dreadful.... Here is nothing of the composure of Socrates, who met death peacefully as a friend."[4] Whereas Socrates went out drinking the hemlock in sublime calm, Jesus cried from the cross, "My God,

4. Oscar Cullmann, "Immortality of the Soul or Resurrection of the Dead?" in Krister Stendahl, ed., *Immortality and Resurrection* (New York: Macmillan, 1965), 14–15.

my God, why have you forsaken me?" (Mark 15:34). This is not a death of liberation but death in all its frightful horror. It is genuinely the "last enemy" of God (1 Cor. 15:26).

I do not wish here to picture Jesus as a coward. His bravery is stalwart. Despite his petition in the Gethsemane prayer that he not have to drink the cup of death, he still concludes his prayer to God: "Yet not what I want, but what you want" (Mark 14:36). This signals courage, and despite his agonizing sense of abandonment on the cross, he still utters: "Father, into your hands I commend my spirit" (Luke 23:46). Death is terrible, but Jesus' faith is strong.

God confirmed Jesus' faith by raising him from the dead on Easter. Jesus died a mortal, but God the creator acted with the power of new creation. God bestowed new life, and this new life is different from the old life that Jesus gave up. The new life is no longer subject to sin, suffering, or death. It is this that makes Jesus' resurrection salvific. In this regard what happened to Jesus differs from other reported resurrections such as the widow's son at Nain (Luke 7:11-17), Jairus's daughter (Mark 5:21-43), and Lazarus (John 11:38-44). These three were not raised to immortality. They were simply returned to normal life. They would all have to face death again just like the rest of us. But Jesus was not restored to ordinary life. His resurrected existence is eschatological. He will not have to die again. When those who enjoyed fellowship with the risen Jesus reported what they saw, they did not say, "The Nazarene is back." Rather, they reported that they had seen "the Lord" (Luke 24:34; John 20:18). Jesus died the death that slammed the door on sin and suffering, and God's raising him from the dead opened another door, the door to new life.

Resurrection and the Spiritual Body

When reciting the Nicene Creed we say we believe in the "resurrection of the dead"; and when we recite the Apostles' Creed we say the "resurrection of the body and the life everlasting." What does this mean? It does not mean resuscitation of a corpse in the sense that one recuperates from surgery and goes back to the daily routine of life. Nor is this referring to a soulechtomy. We note that the Greeks in Athens thought Paul's discussion of resurrection at the Areopagus to be so preposterous that they mocked him (Acts 17:32). This rejection might indicate that whatever Paul said, it did not sound to the Greeks like a description of immortality of the soul. If the Athenians present that day were disciples of Socrates, they may have had a low opinion of the physical body. If so, when Paul spoke of a raised body they would naturally have objected.

If resurrection is neither a resuscitation of a corpse nor a soulechtomy, could that which is resurrected look like a ka depicted on frescoes in Egyptian pyramids? Or might it resemble the occult understanding of the astral (star) body? Both the ka and the astral body, according to ancient Egyptian and contemporary occult belief, duplicate the shape of the physical body but have no material substance. In introducing his great discussion of resurrection, Paul speaks of heavenly bodies (σώματα ἐπουράνια) with their glory or luster (δόξα) and identifies them with the resurrection of the dead (1 Cor. 15:40-42), which might indicate that he has an astral body in mind. But we cannot press this too far, because there is a problem here. Occult thinking presupposes a cleavage between the physical body and the supraphysical locus of selfhood in the astral body so that when one dies one does not really die. The self simply sheds its physical body and goes on, maintaining continuity between this world and the next on the basis of some built-in principle. There is no genuine death or destruction in alleged astral existence. An element of the person abides. But for Paul there is no element that perdures through death. If there is resurrection, it is new creation. Therefore, the resurrected body of the New Testament must be something different from the astral body as ordinarily understood.

When Paul attempts to describe resurrection, he employs the image of the seed sown in the ground. That which rises above the ground looks quite different from what had been planted. But in order to guard against any possible misinterpretation in terms of soulechtomy, Paul exploits the deadlike appearance of the typical seed to say, "What you sow does not come to life unless it dies" (1 Cor. 15:36). Hence, there is a delicacy to this analogy. Paul wishes to affirm continuity and discontinuity between the present and future realities. What happens is not creation out of nothing, but creation of something out of something else. A dead seed is sown, but new life is harvested. Then he describes the eschatological harvest in terms of four complementary contrasts. "So it is with the resurrection of the dead. What is sown is perishable [corrupt, φθορᾷ], what is raised is imperishable [incorrupt, ἀφθαρσία]. It is sown in dishonor [ἀτιμία], it is raised in glory [δόξῃ]. It is sown in weakness [ἀσθενία], it is raised in power [δυνάμει]. It is sown a physical body [σῶμα ψυχικόν], it is raised a spiritual body [σῶμα πνευματικόν]" (1 Cor. 15:42-44). To be raised "imperishable" is to be raised to everlasting life. It is not to have one's body resuscitated so as to return to one's daily toil. Δόξα, which in reference to the heavenly bodies usually means luster, here means honor—that is, we will be raised to honor. The power into which we will be raised, δυνάμι, is the same power by which miracles of healing are wrought (1 Cor. 12:28).

Most interesting is the last of these four antitheses in Paul's list, namely, the contrast between the earthly and the spiritual bodies. Paul does not describe the earthly body as one of flesh (σῶμα σαρκικόν), as one would have expected, but rather as σῶμα ψυχικόν. Literally this is the ensouled body that would usually be identified with the Greek philosophical tradition. This is what is sown but not raised. Hence, the soul dies. As if to rub it in, Paul says it is not the ψύχη that we find in the resurrection; it is the σῶμα.

What is raised is a "spiritual body." We can tell from other writings of Paul that he assumes there is a war going on between the flesh (σάρξ) and the spirit (Gal. 5:13-26). Flesh is the power of sin that leads to death. The spirit is its great antagonist; it is the power of creation and new creation. Both powers attempt to invade and control us. It is important to discern here that when Paul uses these terms he does not intend to make metaphysical statements regarding human nature—that is, he does not hold that flesh and spirit are distinct ontological components of each human being. This is not another version of the Greek body-soul dualism. Rather, flesh and spirit are proclivities or forces that contend for domination of the whole person, body and soul included.

One way to get at Paul's underlying conceptuality here is to think of the σῶμα as the form that can exist with one or another substance, either flesh (σάρξ) or spirit (πνεῦμα). Hans Conzelmann advocates this form-substance theory and contends that there is no such thing as a σῶμα all by itself. Σῶμα always exists in a specific mode of being, either as σάρξ or as δόξα. The form is always related to its concrete mode of being. It is always either heavenly or earthly. It does not constitute the individual human being as such. Σῶμα exists on its own only as an abstract concept.[5] This theory is of some help, but Conzelmann is not careful to show just how his idea takes account of the fact that Paul's contrast is actually between a psychic body and a spiritual body, not between a fleshly and a glorified body.

Therefore, more needs to be said. The spirit is not simply one substance interchangeable with others. It is the power of God whereby reality itself is determined. The σῶμα πνευμάτικον is the resurrected body that is determined by the Holy Spirit. It is the reality that we will be because God will have created us—that is, re-created us—in this form. Because it is an eschatological reality that belongs to the new creation, and because we still live amid the old creation, we cannot expect to apprehend clearly just what this means. Now we can only look through a mirror darkly; and Christ is that mirror reflecting the light of future glory amid our present darkness. What one can say with confidence is that there will be a resurrection of the human self. What one cannot say at this point is precisely what that resurrected mode of existence will look like.

It is also worth observing that Paul is apparently thinking this out for the first time in his dialogue with the Corinthians. He is by no means simply reiterating an already existing set of ideas that previously belonged to the Jews, the Gnostics, the Corinthians, or any other group we know of. His is not one theory of immortality among others; this is a case of evangelical explication at work. Paul has already confronted the gospel and is now trying to re-present it to an audience that probably believes

---

5. Hans Conzelmann, *I Corinthians* (Philadelphia: Fortress, 1978), 282.

the material body is inimical to the spirit. The Christians in Corinth, probably heavily influenced by the Greek intellectual tradition, have misunderstood the significance of the gospel for human mortality and eternal life. We today do not know exactly how Paul thought of the gospel before explicating it to the Corinthians, so for us this epistle serves as a primary symbol bearing the gospel and, hence, is subject to further explication, both critical and evangelical.

The Great Transformation

We cannot separate human destiny from cosmic destiny. Religious traditions that advocate some sort of soulechtomy deal with the question of human destiny in partial isolation from that of cosmic destiny. For Plato, for example, it seems that one's own soul may exercise its philosophical wings and fly to heaven and there enjoy the beatific vision. Or for Hinduism, through strenuous meditative effort one might attain enlightenment and realize oneness with Brahman. In such cases the affairs of this mundane world will simply go on as a matter of course without these now-departed human souls. Not so with the Christian vision. What happens to persons depends on what happens to the cosmos. The resurrection to a spiritual body can occur only at the advent of the eschaton. If there is no cosmic transformation, then there is no resurrection; and if there is no resurrection, then Christian faith is in vain and of all people believers are most to be pitied (1 Cor. 15:14, 19).

The eschatological parousia—the second coming of Christ—is the context of Christian thinking about the issue of life beyond death. Paul speaks of an order to things. First comes Christ, the first fruits (1 Cor. 15:23). This probably refers to Easter. Then at his coming "the dead in Christ will rise first. Then we who are alive" (1 Thess. 4:16-17). The Lord Jesus Christ "will transform the body of our humiliation, that it may be conformed to the body of his glory" (Phil. 3:21; see Rom. 8:29). "Then comes the end, when he hands over the kingdom to God the Father, after destroying every ruler and every authority and power.... The last enemy to be destroyed is death" (1 Cor. 15:24, 26).

In the closing book of his *City of God*, Augustine speculates on all the questions we would like to ask regarding just what this transformation means. Will everybody be raised? Yes. What about abortions? Yes, they will be raised. Will we get our own bodies back or will we be issued new ones? Augustine answers that the actual physical elements that composed the first body will be retrieved for the new one. What condition will our physical bodies be in? All blemishes and infirmities will be removed. How old will we be, the age at which we die? No. We will be at our healthiest mature age, which Augustine guesses is about thirty. Will some of us be bigger than others? Yes, as in this life, but we will have the same youthful vigor regardless of age at death. Will there be two sexes in heaven? Yes, but lust will be gone. Will we remember our past tragedies and sufferings? Yes, we will remember them intellectually but we will no longer feel the pain.

How does Augustine know all of this? He does not really. He is speculating. But, then, that is what theologians are supposed to do. On the basis of the witness of scripture to the gospel, systematic theologians try to construct reasonable answers to questions that may not have been directly posed and answered within the pages of the Bible. Augustine offers a carefully thought out explication of the New Testament. His thoughts regarding the great transformation have been quite widely accepted over the last millennium and a half. But this is a mysterious area, and some questions almost defy a coherent answer.

Although one cannot make univocal assertions in answer to questions regarding what happens beyond death, there is a fund of symbols tied to the New Testament upon which to base reflections. Of special importance are the last judgment, heaven, and hell. To these I now turn.

OUR FINAL DESTINIES

In the history of religions it is not unusual to find doctrines of an afterlife spent in heaven as a reward for a life well lived on earth. Nor is it difficult to find hell understood either as punishment or as a place where the effects of one's sins are purged through torture. Such images live in the Christian tradition as well. How they are to be understood, however, depends upon the destiny of Christ.

The Judgment

The concept of a final judgment is one of the apocalyptic elements in the New Testament worldview, and it functions significantly in the teaching of John the Baptist, Jesus, Paul, and the book of Revelation. According to the vision of Daniel, the new aeon will be brought in by Saint Michael—whom the book of Revelation identifies with Jesus Christ—at which point the resurrection will take place. "Many of those who sleep in the dust of the earth shall awake, some to everlasting life, and some to shame and everlasting contempt" (Dan. 12:2). In the New Testament, the final judgment is located at the point where this parting of the destinies occurs, and this is followed by everlasting life in heaven or unending perdition in hell.

Based on all I have said above about the gospel, it would seem at first that a final judgment would be unnecessary. The cosmic court has already heard humankind's case. We have been found guilty. The punishment in the form of a sentence to death has already been meted out, although it was inflicted on Christ, not us. The trial and execution are over. Because of Christ our sins have been forgiven. Before God we stand justified. There is no double jeopardy. "Very truly, I tell you," are the words we hear from Jesus, "anyone who hears my word and believes him who sent me has eternal life, and does not come under judgment, but has passed from death to life" (John 5:24).

It would seem, especially from the point of view of the Gospel of John, that the final judgment is a thing of the past, having occurred already on Calvary (John 12:31). But it is likely that the same author wrote 1 John 4:17, where we find the sense of the still-outstanding future: "We may have boldness on the day of judgment, because as he is so are we in this world." The day of judgment is yet to come as well. Might this be another case of prolepsis? The freedom from the law that one experiences in the present state of justification is a freedom that anticipates the declaration of justness at the advent of the eschaton. If so, I suggest that we try to think of the final judgment as a single act of God that begins on Calvary and concludes on the last day. Our entire existence is found amid this one inclusive act of God.

Earlier in the present work I employed a temporalized version of the microcosm-macrocosm correlation to suggest that what happened in the person of Christ will happen to the whole of creation and that these two are of a single piece. If this is applied now to the concept of the judgment, then one would expect the eschaton to have a structure that corresponds to that of justification—that is, one would experience the condemnation for sin at the same time that one receives the pronouncement of grace. The psychological or spiritual significance of this at the present time is that one can look forward to the day of judgment with joy, confident that in Christ the believer has already passed through the judgment and been declared just. The Westminster Shorter Catechism gives the following answer to Question 38: "At the resurrection, believers being raised up in glory, shall be openly acknowledged and acquitted in the day of judgment, and made perfectly blessed in the full enjoying of God to all eternity."

To press the question farther as to just why there must be a judgment in the future, it should be noted that it is not for the purpose of determining each person's destiny. That will have already been determined prior to physical death. The purpose is rather to reveal the justice and sovereignty of God. Up until this time the truth of God's justice will have been hidden under the ambiguities of history. The wheat and the tares have been growing together, and within history one can catch only occasional glimpses of the difference between them. The final sifting needs to take place so that one can see clearly what has been the case all along. In short, the final judgment is an act of revelation more than an act of salvation.

This explanation of judgment does not completely tie up all the loose ends in the New Testament symbolism, however. One item that remains is the question of the relationship between faith and works. If one asks about the criterion for judgment, faith in Jesus Christ is repeatedly offered. For those who reject the Son of God it will be worse than it was for Sodom

(Matt. 11:20-24; Luke 10:10-16), but "everyone who believes in him may not perish but may have eternal life" (John 3:16; see 3:36; 12:48; 1 John 2:23). Another New Testament answer is that judgment will be according to works: "For the Son of Man is to come with his angels in the glory of his Father, and then he will repay everyone for what has been done" (Matt. 16:27). Paul tells the Romans they are storing up wrath for the day of judgment when God will render to everyone according to his or her works (Rom. 2:6; see Rev. 20:12; 22:12). The texts are unmistakably clear: what we do counts.

Now which is it: faith that justifies apart from works or the works themselves? The best way to handle this dilemma is to examine the close relationship between faith and works. Faith must give rise to works of love (Gal. 5:6) because love is its natural form of expression. Works, in turn, are evidence of true faith. Faith without works is dead (James 2:26). Jesus, ever ready to expose a hypocrite, takes his stand: "Not everyone who says to me, 'Lord, Lord,' will enter the kingdom of heaven, but only the one who does the will of my Father in heaven" (Matt. 7:21). The judgment on the basis of works, it might be said, is really a judgment about faith because works are the evidence of genuine faith in God. Anthony Hoekema follows John Calvin in putting it this way: "It is faith alone which justifies, and yet the faith which justifies is not alone."[6]

Heaven

Heaven seems a very pleasant place to go. To get there it appears that we need to go up. The general assumption made in biblical times was that heaven (שׁמים [shemayim], οὐρανός) is located up in the sky where the clouds are. That is where God and the angels dwell (Gen. 28:12; Ps. 11:4; Matt. 6:9), although the "heaven and the highest heaven cannot contain" God (1 Kings 8:27), who is omnipresent (Ps. 139:8-10). Similar to occult spiritualism today, many in the ancient world assumed there was a hierarchy of heavens (2 Cor. 12:2-3), some planes of which were ruled by demonic powers (Eph. 6:12), and beyond which Christ was raised when he "ascended far above all the heavens" (Eph. 4:10). The Soviet cosmonaut who mocked the religious people of the world by saying he had gone to heaven but could not find God was making the false assumption that the religious mind takes such things literally. Some people do, of course. But even in ancient and medieval times it was the symbolic—not the literal—power of the heavens that communicated things divine. In the rabbinic tradition contemporary with the New Testament, heaven was thought of as the dimension of God from which salvation emerges, as the source of blessing. Luther could think of heaven as coextensive with

6. Anthony A. Hoekema, *The Bible and the Future* (Grand Rapids, Mich.: Eerdmans, 1979), 261.

God's omnipresence and, hence, as a dimension of the present life. Jürgen Moltmann thinks of heaven as the openness of God to grant potentiality for the earth to transform itself; that is, heaven is the earth's future.[7] What all this means, in short, is that heaven is not simply a place to which we go.

The symbol of heaven represents the transformed reality promised by the resurrection of Jesus Christ. It does not refer to a geographically remote region to which disembodied souls fly when released from their anchor on earth. It is present here and now amid bodily life in a proleptic way. It will be present here fully when the ultimate future—the kingdom of God—is finally established.

The Christian tradition has communicated the meaning of heaven through four dominant images or symbols: the ecstasy of worship, the vision of God, the garden of paradise, and the new Jerusalem. As to the ecstasy of worship: there is no need to have a temple in heaven because the worship of the almighty God explodes spontaneously from every quarter of creation (Rev. 21:22). Living creatures never cease to sing, "Holy! Holy! Holy!" The twenty-four elders cast their crowns before the throne of grace intoning, "You are worthy, our Lord and God" (Rev. 4). That songs of praise will fill our heavenly home is anticipated in Johann Meyfart's seventeenth-century hymn "O Jerusalem, du hochgebaute Stadt":

> Saints robed in white before the shining throne
>> Their joyful anthems raise,
> Till heaven's arches echo with the tone
>> Of that great hymn of praise,
>
> And all its host rejoices,
>> And all its blessed throng,
> Unite their myriad voices,
>> In one eternal song.

The desire to experience ecstasy has led to the second significant image of heaven, the beatific vision of the godhead known as the *visio Dei*. The New Testament is not without its references to seeing God. One of Jesus' beatitudes says that the pure in heart will "see God" (Matt. 5:8), and Paul contrasts present and future by saying, "Now we see in a mirror dimly, but then we will see face to face" (1 Cor. 13:12). The prospect of apprehending the full truth of God is an exciting one, but by no means is this a dominant motif in the New Testament.

The *visio Dei* comes into Christian tradition primarily from Plato. In the *Phaedrus* Plato says that the disembodied soul of the philosopher between incarnations is able to follow "in the train of Zeus" and behold the "beatific vision ... shining in pure light." When "enshrined in that

---

7. Moltmann, *God in Creation* (San Francisco: Harper & Row, 1985), 165.

living tomb [the body] which we carry about," however, the philosopher can only see "through a glass dimly." Plato wants to know the truth as God knows it, and to know it he must escape the finite limits of his bodily existence.[8]

Plato's concept of the beatific vision eventually became Christianized. Irenaeus identifies seeing God with the cause of immortality. Augustine thinks of it as a reward for faith, but he is not sure whether it will be an objective seeing or not. Thomas Aquinas develops the notion in Aristotelian terms so that the *visio Dei* consists in the intellectual knowledge of the divine substance. This is not an objective seeing, of course, but rather a suprasensible or ecstatic knowing in which we see all things not in succession but simultaneously. The beatific vision is a seeing from the point of view of eternity. It is a participatory knowledge because in heaven God will not remain outside us but will dwell within the depths of our souls. Will this way of looking bore us? No, argues Thomas. Nothing viewed with wonder is tiresome, and the wonder of the vision will never cease.

The essential problem with the *visio Dei* doctrine is not that it comes from Plato rather than the Bible. Many good things come from Plato. The problem has to do with its basic gnostic and world-denying structure. It presupposes that the problem causing our alienation from God is ignorance due to finitude and not due to sin. It assumes the limitations to finite knowing are what prevent us from having fellowship with God. What would then heal the rift is infinite knowing, or what amounts to a merging of the human and the divine into a single union of intellect. As we saw earlier, the human problem is not finitude, but sin. There is nothing wrong with finite or mediated knowledge of God.

The problem of the human condition is not essentially one of ignorance. Ignorance is only a symptom. The real problem is sin. Sin expands the ego of the individual to the point of harming other individuals, and this in turn destroys harmonious community within God's created order. The problem is a lack of love; for without love the various parts of the creation collide with one another and destroy the harmony of the whole. Yes, there will be truth in heaven. Yes, there will be the pure light of knowledge. But this does not necessarily mean the elimination of finitude or, what comes with it, the community of finite beings. The fulfillment of this community is at the heart of salvation. Knowing the full truth of God will be an immense delight for us, no doubt. But this does not constitute the heart of heaven. New community does. Let us turn then to two other images of heaven that depict it as the healed community. One image is rural, the other urban.

The rural image is that of paradise, usually depicted as a great garden in which all the animals and plants and spiritual realities exist together

---

8. Plato *Phaedrus* S.250.

in natural harmony. The New Testament word παράδεισος comes from an old Persian term meaning "park" or "garden." Its use to designate heaven (Luke 23:43; 2 Cor. 12:3; Rev. 2:7) usually connotes a return to the Garden of Eden prior to the fall, to a state of pristine innocence. It may as well connote Plato's isle of the blessed, because the name of that island, μακάριος, is the same word used by Matthew's Jesus in the Beatitudes to describe the blessings of God's kingdom. Human alienation from nature resulting from primitive farming or modern technologized agriculture will be healed in heaven. In the words of the sixteenth-century hymn "Jerusalem, My Happy Home," we sing,

> Thy gardens and thy gallant walks continually are green;
> There grow such sweet and pleasant flowers as nowhere else are seen.
>
> There trees for evermore bear fruit, and evermore do spring;
> There evermore the angels sit, and evermore do sing.

The implicit love of nature and its inherent beauty makes this a theme shared by Christian and secular artists alike. Renaissance art experienced a flowering of depictions of the Garden of Eden with Adam and Eve, nude but unembarrassed, enjoying its nonhostile environment of blooming bushes and tamed animals and even the abiding presence of God. Adam and Eve represent our future in God's grace as well as our past. Sometimes it is not Adam and Eve but rather a joyous orgy amid lush greenery that is depicted. Titian's *Bacchanal* and Watteau's *L'Embarquement pour Cythere* are attempts to go back behind the Christianized paradise to the classical myths in order to emphasize the joys of erotic love, which the artists believed represented the harmony between humanity and nature as a whole. The symbol of paradise—a a garden of harmony, fecundity, and beauty—seems to be rooted deeply in the human psyche and that makes it an apt medium for communicating the nature of heaven.

The fourth image of heaven is urban: heaven is viewed as the new Jerusalem, which is a variant on the kingdom of God theme. In Matthew the phrases "kingdom of heaven" and "kingdom of God" are used interchangeably, so there is every reason to think that all these images belong together in a single symbol complex. I call it the "heavenly polis" because it derives from a vision of God's intention to establish an eschatological body politic. It is the capital city of God's new creation whose descent is described amid the magnificent conclusion to the whole of what is Christian scripture:

Then I saw a new heaven and a new earth; for the first heaven and the first earth had passed away, and the sea was no more. And I saw the holy city [τὴν πόλιν τὴν ἁγίαν], the new Jerusalem, coming down out of heaven from God, prepared as a bride adorned for her husband. And I heard a loud voice from the throne saying, "See, the home of God is among mortals. He will dwell with them as their God;

they will be his peoples, and God himself will be with them; he will wipe every tear from their eyes. Death will be no more; mourning and crying and pain will be no more, for the first things have passed away." (Rev. 21:1-4)

Certain features of the new Jerusalem are worth pointing out. It does not stay up in heaven. At the point of destruction and renewal it takes up its abode where we are. We do not go to it. It comes to us; and when it comes it means salvation, the healing of sorrow, the drying of tears, the forgetting of suffering, and dwelling in safety with God forever. This leads Augustine to extol a vision of the polis of God that includes worshipful praise, the *visio Dei*, and the holistic community:

> How great shall be that felicity, which shall be tainted with no evil, which shall lack no good, and which shall afford leisure for the praises of God, who shall be all in all!...All the members and organs of the incorruptible body, which now we see to be suited to various necessary uses, shall contribute to the praises of God....Into that state nothing which is unseemly shall be admitted....True honor shall be there....True peace shall be there....[God] shall be the end of our desires who shall be seen without end, loved without cloy, praised without weariness.[9]

Political symbols such as the new Jerusalem and the kingdom of God imply a community of interacting individuals, not simply a sublime knowledge present to the individual soul. Rather than a mystical union we have a political communion. It is made up of transformed men and women who continue their personal identity and mutual recognition into the resurrection; and yet they transcend most of the other categories of this finite and time-bound world. Johann Casper Heterich's turn-of-the-century painting *Himmlisches Wiedersehen* depicts family members from scattered generations recognizing and joyfully greeting one another upon arrival in heaven. Although, as Augustine made clear, God is "the end of our desires," salvation also consists in the redemption of the creation and of the community to be shared by the creatures within it.

Hell

Hell, in contrast to heaven, is not a very pleasant place to go. It is the abode of the damned. There are two overlapping concepts of hell in the New Testament. Hades (ἄδης) is the Septuagint translation of the Hebrew שְׁאוֹל (*sheol*), referring to the shadowy realm of the underworld where it

---

9. Augustine *City of God* 22.30. Carl Jung puts such images of the kingdom of God into the category of archetypes of the golden age, where everything is provided in abundance for everyone. However, he writes, "The sad truth is that man's real life consists of a complex of inexorable opposites—day and night, birth and death, happiness and misery, good and evil. We are not even sure that one will prevail against the other, that good will overcome evil, or joy defeat pain. Life is a battleground" (*Man and His Symbols* [New York: Doubleday, 1964], 85). Jung is certainly correct that the contrast between our daily reality and the envisioned utopia is sharp. The issue is: has God's revelation actually promised us that the envisioned city of God will one day become a reality?

was originally thought that all the dead went, both good and bad (Ps. 89:48; Matt. 11:23). The other concept is Gehenna (γέεννα), where only the bad go. Connoting the image of the fire of judgment burning in the Valley of Hinnom, John the Baptist and Jesus warn of Gehenna as a place where an everlasting and unquenchable fire burns (Matt. 5:22; 13:42), and where there are darkness and gnashing of teeth (Matt. 8:12; 22:13). Paul's language is a bit more abstract. He describes hell in terms of destruction, perishing, and loss of relationship with God (Rom. 9:22; 2 Thess. 1:9; 2:10). Hell is the punishment meted out to the devil and his angels and to those who persist in a reluctance to show love to the needy or who refuse to repent and accept God's offer of newness of life (Matt. 5:29; 25:41). Medieval art is replete with pictures of the mouth of hell—usually depicted as an enormously ugly monster with jaws agape, giant fanglike teeth, and a throat belching the red hot flames of the nether-world—and of relatively tiny sinners overwhelmed with their fate being swallowed up by the monster of everlasting perdition.

What happens once sinners enter the mouth of hell? If hell is sixty times hotter than any earthly fire, as it was described in ancient rabbinic tradition, then will sinners simply be consumed? Will they be utterly destroyed and be done with it? No, contends Augustine, who asks whether or not our eternal bodies can be burned without becoming consumed. In the world to come humans will be clothed in flesh that can suffer pain but cannot die. "The first death drives the soul from the body against her will," he writes, but "the second death holds the soul in the body against her will. The two have this in common, that the soul suffers against her will what her own body inflicts."[10]

Does this mean there really is an everlasting fire, or are we to think of it metaphorically? Thomas Aquinas does not beat around the bush. Hellfire is literally fire. "The fire of hell is not called so metaphorically, nor an imaginary fire, but a real corporeal fire."[11] Karl Rahner disagrees with Thomas, warning us against such literalization. What the Bible says about hell should be interpreted in keeping with "its literary character of 'threat-discourse' and hence [is] not to be read as a preview of something which will exist some day." Rahner prefers the metaphorical over the literal on the grounds that the reference to hell's fire is "something radically not of this world."[12] Whether literal or metaphorical, the function of hellfire in the New Testament is clearly that of a warning and a challenge for us to make a decision in the face of the possibility of being everlastingly separated from God. Hell signifies that our rejection of God can result in everlasting estrangement.

---

10. Augustine *City of God* 21.3.
11. Thomas Aquinas, *Summa Theologica*, III, q. 70, a. 3.
12. Karl Rahner, "Hell," *Encyclopedia of Theology* (New York: Seabury, 1975), 603.

From the time of Jesus down to the opening generations of the modern era the doctrine of hell has been used as threat-discourse in two ways. First, it was used to prod morality. Without morality we would lose social cohesion and our society would dissolve into anarchy. So even rationalist religion in the eighteenth century made good use of the fear of eternal punishment. Second, the threat of hell was used to persuade people to become "born again." This was important to the revivalist tradition that extended the pietist emphasis upon deep personal faith, drawing a sharp contrast between the formal or perfunctory Christians and those who had made a deep commitment that led to becoming "born again." Jonathan Edwards in his famous sermon "Sinners in the Hands of an Angry God" employs threat-discourse for this purpose. Imagine, he says,

that world of misery, that lake of burning brimstone, is extended abroad under you. There is the dreadful pit of the glowing flames of the wrath of God; there is hell's wide gaping mouth open; and you have nothing to stand upon, nor anything to take hold of; there is nothing between you and hell but the air; it is only the power and mere pleasure of God that holds you up.... Thus all of you that never passed under a great change of heart, by the mighty power of the spirit of God upon your souls; all that were never born again, and made new creatures, and raised from being dead in sin, to a state of new, and before altogether unexperienced light and life, are in the hands of an angry God.[13]

What Jonathan Edwards had to say offends our more modern sensibilities. The liberal minds of the last two centuries have been pricked by a moral conscience that finds such threat-discourse undignified and revolting. Those who hold modern and more genteel standards of morality are appalled at the thought that God might punish for eternity someone who committed a temporal sin. We ask: how could the very concept of hell with its everlasting punishment fit coherently with the concept of a loving God? Does it make moral sense to think of the God of love, perhaps together with the saints in heaven, watching for all eternity hopeless, pitiless, cruel, and apparently loveless suffering? Could a God of love be so hardhearted? Even apart from love, could God be so unjust? Is it just to mete out an infinite punishment for a finite sin? Even the crimes of an Adolf Hitler or a Joseph Stalin are not bad enough to warrant all that hell exacts. Thus, in our time hell is more and more thought to be incompatible with the idea of God as infinite love, because it lodges the existence of suffering right into the creation for all eternity. Would not a God of both love and power put an end to suffering?[14]

---

13. Jonathan Edwards, "Sinners in the Hands of an Angry God," in *The Works of Jonathan Edwards*, 2 vols. (London: Ball, Arnold, and Co., 1860), 2:9.

14. See John Hick, *Death and Eternal Life* (San Francisco: Harper & Row, 1976), 201; Hans Küng, *Eternal Life?* (New York: Doubleday, 1984), 136; and John S. Mbiti, *New Testament Eschatology in an African Background* (Oxford: Oxford University Press, 1971), 70.

Such thoughts have led many in our time to an outright rejection of the doctrine of hell in favor of universal salvation. But a Christian doctrine should not be rejected simply because it rubs against the grain of modern sensibilities. An argument that appeals to modern sensibilities can be raised in defense of the doctrine of hell: it affirms an important modern value, namely, freedom. "Since we have free will," argues Kallistos Ware, "it is possible for us to reject God. Since free will exists, Hell exists; for Hell is nothing else than the rejection of God."[15] In short, the affirmation of human freedom seems to require the affirmation of a possible realm that eternally rejects the love and grace of God.

Whether or not an everlasting hell exists is a difficult matter to settle. Nevertheless, we cannot just drop this concern, because how we develop the idea of hell has to do with the evangelical explication of such concepts as divine love and divine justice. I will take up this issue directly in the next chapter when considering the implications of the concept of universal salvation. In the meantime we cannot overlook the fact that the threat of hell belongs indelibly to the New Testament symbol system and that its purpose, like that of the judgment, is to reaffirm the justice of God in a world of sin.

DESTINATION AND PREDESTINATION

When are the tickets to heaven and hell passed out? Or better, when is our final destination entered into the computer of the celestial travel agent? Are our seats already reserved so that we just pick up our tickets on judgment day, or do we still have time to decide where we would like to go? In short, is our future open or is it predestined?

This opens the question of predestination, a doctrinal concern that usually does not appear in a chapter on eschatology. I will look at it here, however, because the very notion of destination has futuristic implications and because I believe proleptic eschatology can help us escape from some blind alleys into which the concept of predestination has previously led us.

Interpreted in its most unfavorable light, the doctrine of predestination makes God seem like a tyrant who arbitrarily consigns helpless souls to hell in order to maintain an image of being the almighty one. Of course this is a perversion of the doctrine's intention. Nevertheless, it would seem that there must be something wrong in the formulation of the concept of predestination in the first place if it would lend itself to this perverted interpretation. Yes, there is something wrong. I believe the principal weakness in the concept of predestination is its assumed notion of time and causality, so that the determining power of God comes prior to events rather than subsequent to them. This archonic theory of time makes

---

15. Ware, *The Orthodox Church* (New York: Penguin, 1963), 266.

God look like a despotic monarch who casts unwilling subjects in directions they have not chosen. If we shift temporal causality from the past to the future, however, instead of predestination we get destination.

The Gospel's Universal Scope

The doctrine of predestination consists in an explication of the concept of justifying grace put on a cosmic scale. In order to avoid any hint of works-righteousness by which we might contribute to our salvation, this doctrine holds that all of our eternal destinies were predetermined by God. Therefore, we do not determine them. What happens to us is solely the result of divine grace, or lack thereof. When referred to as "double" predestination, this position is that God has already actively determined who will eventually be granted admittance to heaven and who will be consigned to hell. When referred to with the softer term "single" predestination, the emphasis is on God's active decision to save some of the people; but then the doctrine of single predestination pleads only a passive divine role with regard to the fate of the reprobate. That is, God does not actually send people to hell; rather, God simply does not rescue them from their own proclivity to go there. The concepts of both single and double predestination share the prefix "pre," which means that the decision of grace is made ahead of time.

It is assumed that unless God were to make a decision in behalf of human salvation, then, due to human depravity, hell would be our only and necessary fate. Having made the extremely important and decisive assumption that apart from divine intervention everyone without exception is subject to condemnation, the overriding emphasis becomes the gracious act of God by which some sinners are saved. Without the assumption that eternal perdition is the given, God looks more like a tyrant than a savior. The Reformers were thankful that God is a savior, and the doctrine of predestination is their attempt to explain just how God saves.

Some people have mistakenly thought that the notion of predetermination emerged from the concept of God's omnipotence. It might seem logical that if God is all-powerful, then every event in the causal nexus must be due either to an exercise of God's power or to a refraining from exercising that power. But this by no means is the starting point for thinking about predestination. Rather, for Augustine and Calvin the basic question emerges from the observation that when the gospel is preached only some respond in faith and others reject it. They ask: why? The answer, they submit, is predestination.[16] Now how did they get from this question to that answer?

The intervening premise is that saving faith in Jesus Christ is not a human work but rather a gift of divine grace. Grace is the free gift of

---

16. Augustine *On the Predestination of the Saints* 15.8; Calvin, *Inst.*, 3.21.1.

God. It is not the reward for human merit. If some respond to the gospel in faith but others do not, then it follows that God has bestowed faith in some instances but withheld it in others. It is an act of predestination, a divine act before the foundation of the world by which God out of grace chooses to rescue some individuals from reprobation. "We call predestination God's eternal decree," writes Calvin, "by which he compacted with himself what he willed to become of each man. For all are not created in equal condition; rather, eternal life is foreordained for some, eternal damnation for others."[17] The result of this train of thought is the doctrine of the limited atonement, according to which Christ's saving grace applies to some but not all of the human race. The work of Christ has no effect on those who were not foreordained for faith and rescue.

Now what about those who are not rescued? When we press the question as to why this gift of faith unto eternal life is given to some but not others, theologians typically respond by appealing to the mystery of God pointed to by Paul when exclaiming, "How unsearchable are his judgments, and how inscrutable his ways!" (Rom. 11:33). This means that we ought to be thankful to God for those who by divine grace have been spared from their well-deserved damnation. It also means that we have no right to question God's judgment regarding those who were not given this grace.

One might raise the question as to whether the heavier term *predestination* must be used here. Why could one not simply say that an omniscient God could foresee who would respond to the gospel and who would not? This would allow us to say that Christ died for all and also allow us to hold that every individual is free to either affirm or deny Christ through faith. Foreknowledge would then relieve God of the responsibility of appearing arbitrary, and a person's faith would remain the responsibility of his or her own free decision. But Augustine rejects this option outright. This was the position held by Pelagius, a position that did not fully comprehend the significance of saying that faith, justification, and salvation are gifts from God. Only the concept of predestination connotes a free act of God (from the human point of view free acts of God necessarily appear arbitrary) by which God grants salvation for no reason whatsoever. There is no reason external to the nature of God.[18]

This position regarding predestination has its strong opponents. Jacobus Arminius in the seventeenth century and John Wesley in the eighteenth century each attacked the idea of limited atonement. Christ died for all, they insisted. Wesley attacked Calvinism because it appeared to be a "direct antidote to Methodism." According to the pernicious doc-

17. Calvin, *Inst.*, 3.21.5.
18. Augustine *On the Predestination of the Saints* 38.19.

trine of predestination, Wesley complained, "The absolutely elect must have been saved without him [Christ]; and the non-elect cannot be saved by him."[19]

Karl Barth objects to Calvin's version of predestination because it seems to make Christ's salvific work apply only to some people and not all. Because the decision was made by God that some would be elected and others would not, it follows that Jesus died only for those already elected and not for the unelected sinners.[20] Barth's solution is to conflate the doctrines of creation and redemption almost into one, so that election begins with the Father electing the Son, and through the Son the whole of creation is in turn elected. This includes all people, because Christ is the new Adam by whom true humanity is defined. Furthermore, Barth says that the divine electing means only one possibility is "basically open," namely, the salvation of all. The whole purpose of the gracious act of election is "not to shut but to open, not to exclude but to include, not to say No but Yes to the surrounding world." With this concept of universal election hiding away in his premises, one would think that Barth would then conclude that salvation is universal. But he is reluctant to draw this conclusion, consigning the next step in theological reasoning to the unsearchable mystery of God.[21] Thus, although reluctant to affirm universal salvation, Barth's position is that saving grace applies to everyone. Everyone is elected. At this point it would seem that Barth separates himself from the traditional doctrine of double predestination. When he answers the question regarding those who are not saved, however, Barth falls in with Augustine and Calvin to consign this to the impenetrable divine mystery.

The arguments of Wesley and Barth are salutary, I think, in that they rightly defend the universal scope of Christ's atoning work. We must take account of some important and relevant biblical commitments: Christ's "act of righteousness leads to justification and life for all" (Rom. 5:18), or God is "merciful to all" (Rom. 11:32), or God our savior "desires everyone to be saved" (1 Tim. 2:4). The gospel that should be preached is the gospel of God's unlimited love and grace. Some people will like what they hear. Others might not. But in anticipation of those who are likely to reject it, I see no good reason for going back and changing the scope of the gospel. In effect, this is what Calvin's doctrine of predestination does— and this is just why we should criticize Calvin at this point—insofar as it leads to the conclusion that Christ's salvific work is directed at only part but not all of the human community.

---

19. Wesley, *WW*, 8:336.
20. Barth, *CD*, 1/2:111.
21. Barth, *CD*, 2/2:416–19.

Predestination and Spiritual Comfort

The clear intent of the doctrine of predestination is to explicate the gospel and to do so in such a way as to provide comfort and assurance to the person of faith. The logic goes like this: if we recognize that our salvation is based not just upon the amorphous good will of God but rather upon a specific decision of God to save us, then we can be confident that once elected to salvation we will not later be denied it. God's decision will not be revoked. To John Calvin[22] and other Reformers such as John Knox this brought comfort borne out of the assurance of salvation.

But in many instances the doctrine backfires. Rather than assurance, it brings anxiety. Rather than comfort, it produces confusion. The anxiety and confusion result from the existential question: am I one of the elect? Once the premise is laid down that God has already made up God's mind and cannot change it, all we need to do is to open the door to doubt just a crack and in rushes the overwhelming terror of a possible lost eternity.

The difficulties this wreaks upon spiritual care are vividly illustrated by the attempts made by John Knox to bring comfort to the tortured soul of Elizabeth Bowes. While on the continent in 1559 Knox had published a 170,000-word treatise that repeated and extended the basic position being then taken by John Calvin on predestination. Later, back in his native Scotland, Knox wrote numerous letters to Mrs. Bowes, counseling her on deep introspective concerns. She lacked assurance that she had been placed among the elect. She doubted. Her faith was weak. Mrs. Bowes was in great spiritual agony.

The pastoral approach taken by Knox was to try to demonstrate that she in fact belonged to the congregation of the elect. Through a series of clever reversals of logic, Knox sought to turn negatives into positives. Instead of berating Mrs. Bowes for her lack of assurance, he told her that her doubts served as evidence of her election. Although she thought her faith was weak, the very fact that she was turning to a minister of the church for help was a sign of God's grace at work in her. The reprobate, after all, despised ministers. Even assaults from the devil should not frighten Mrs. Bowes, Knox explained. The devil would not bother the reprobate. The devil seeks to tempt only the faithful. The very fact that she was turning to Christ amid her crisis was a sign of her elected status. Knox was certain Mrs. Bowes was safe.

But Mrs. Bowes was not convinced. She continued to worry. Some have described her as "weariful and much-afraid," with a character akin to that of John Bunyan's Mr. Fearing. Others have perhaps unkindly dubbed

---

22. William Bouwsma makes the observation that Calvin "was a singularly anxious man and, as a reformer, fearful and troubled" (*John Calvin* [Oxford: Oxford University Press, 1988], chap. 2). For Calvin personally, then, the doctrine of predestination was a message of comfort, "our only ground for firmness and confidence." The doctrine functioned to liberate one into life, but only, of course, if one avoided speculating about it.

her "the inveterate spiritual hypochondriac."[23] Near the end of his life Knox himself admitted that she had been something of a burden to him, spiritually as well as physically.

We cannot with fairness after four centuries second guess Knox's practice of pastoral care. But one point within the horizon of this concern needs to be focused upon: once we place the decision of God into an atemporal eternity or into a prelapsarian point of origin and make it invincible, we are going to run into the spiritual problem of how to relate to a nonrelational God, to a God Beyond but not Intimate. It is one thing to say that God's will is eternal; yet we still need the comfort of knowing that divine decisions vis-à-vis our world take the course of our individual lives into account. Once God's decision of how to relate to each of us seems locked up into a past event, then our future is over and done with. God is prevented from responding to how we feel or what we think or which actions we take.

The Problem of the Archonic Beyond

This problem with the doctrine of predestination is caused by its inherently archonic structure—that is, it assumes that God determined the nature of reality at the beginning, back at the *arché*, and that nothing subsequent can change things significantly. Thus, my concern with the traditional doctrine of predestination is that it inadvertently teaches that God is temporally removed from the course of human history and, even worse, that God is not a living Lord but rather a prisoner to a mechanistic working out of God's own will. The problem is that this mechanistic working out of a pretemporal decision by God seems to disregard any form of personal relationship between God and the course of events. It is an appeal strictly to the God Beyond with the total elimination of Emmanuel.

But in fact the life of God is not separated from the world in process. Eternity is not pretemporal, as if it were finished and no longer effectual at the point when time began. As we saw during the earlier discussion of continuing creation, the world is in the process of coming to be. It is not done yet. Nor will it be done until the eschaton, until the consummate end. We are living amid the creative and re-creative work of God right now. This means that divine decrees can be made in response to the actual course of events, that God's relationship to the world is an ongoing drama in which the various acts make a genuine contribution to what will become the climax.

In this drama, the living God remains free. The divine does not give up freedom to make new decisions in response to temporal movement.

23. Richard L. Greaves, *Theology and Revolution in the Scottish Reformation: Studies in the Thought of John Knox* (Grand Rapids, Mich.: Eerdmans, 1980), 22, 68.

God acts and reacts. What we humans experience as continuity in nature or history is the product of divine faithfulness.

What about the term *predestination* then? Can we still use it? Yes, I believe we can, but we need to alter its meaning by changing the concept of time that it presupposes. In doing so we must keep in mind that the term was always intended to communicate the gospel, the good news. The problem has been that by being identified with a fixed pretemporal decree, it has become bad news because it eviscerates the notion of human freedom while making God look like a tyrant for condemning otherwise innocent people to eternal damnation.

I believe we need to start with destiny. What is our destiny? It is ultimately to live with God in the new creation. The meaning of all events and the definition of all actualities will be determined by the context of the whole of history, a whole that will be established only at the advent of God's kingdom. That destiny will determine who we will be. Retroactively, it determines who we are today. We are now on the way, becoming who we will be. Hence we know who we are proleptically—that is, in anticipation of our final reality yet to be established by God.

Let me distinguish between *that* and *what*. That our identity is yet to be determined by our relationship to the whole of God's creation through our relationship to Christ is the destiny into which the gracious God is drawing us. Just what that identity is will be forged by us through the course of our actual life stories as they converge into the one cosmic story. What we do, think, feel, hope for, weep over, and love are in the process of constituting our part that will be integrated into the divine whole. We actually contribute to the material makeup of that whole. This is not works-righteousness. This is divine grace understood as fulfillment rather than annihilation, as *adventum* fulfilling *futurum* through *venturum*.

This understanding of our destiny opens up a new understanding of our predestiny. Jesus Christ is the predestiny of all humankind. He is the new Adam. He is who we too shall be in relation to God. To live in Christ through faith is to share his proleptic reality, to know our destiny in advance. This means that to feel predestined is to feel the joy and confidence of knowing who we are on the basis of who we will be.

This proleptic interpretation by no means simply replaces a pretemporal determinism with a posttemporal determinism. The point is that God is a living God, and our destiny will be the result of the intertwining of the divine life with the creative world process. What gives us confidence regarding the final outcome in the future is not the existence of a pretemporal decree engraved in unerodable concrete. It is rather the personality of God. It is the faithfulness of a God who makes promises and keeps them. It is the divine word that has announced in advance that our salvation draws nigh. Our guarantee is not the execution of a mechanical process. It is rather the living God.

PART FIVE

PROLEPTIC
CO-CREATION

INTRODUCTION

Theology is an ongoing task with which Christians are never finished because something new is always placed on its agenda. Although it is the thinking discipline whereby faith seeks to understand itself, it is also a part of the church's ministry. Its peculiar ministry is to provide intellectual leadership. The present work in systematic theology has sought to explicate the significance of the gospel so that what Christians say is intelligible within the context of emerging postmodern consciousness. Thus, a methodological foundation was laid and the doctrinal content clarified. In turning to ecumenics and ethics now, much more can yet be done.

In a world that feels fragmentation and brokenness so acutely, Christians can offer a bold vision of union and communion. In a world that stands on the brink of gradual disintegration through the ruin of the ecosphere, and even at times on the brink of imminent immolation through nuclear geocide, a vision of global unity and peace is worth projecting. On the basis of such visions the ends and goals toward which the human race should be dedicated can be brought to inspiring effect. In short, theology can enhance the quality of social life in the world at large by offering a vision of ecumenic wholeness and a proleptic ethic.

11

ECUMENIC PLURALISM

Christ transcends all cultures.
—S. J. Samartha

The holism so precious to the postmodern mind is by no means intended to eliminate particularity and individuality. Postmodernity seeks a dynamic whole, a cooperative whole, a synthetic whole. The dynamism of the whole contributes to the vitality of the parts just as the parts constitute the substance of the whole. Instead of union we think of communion. I have argued that the universality and comprehensiveness of the kingdom of God lend some theological support for employing such holistic and communal categories.

I believe it is within this framework that the issue of pluralism should be placed on the theological agenda for the medium-range future. The term *pluralism* has many meanings and connotations, but theological usage seeks to avoid sheer plurality or anarchy, on the one hand, and unity beyond discrimination, on the other hand. Particularity needs affirmation but not at the expense of community. In the present chapter, I will argue that an anarchic force is at work in current theology. I label it "radical pluralism." Radical pluralism is an ideological stance that tends to lose sight of the whole while advocating an inviolate plurality of parts. I will recommend that the better vision is that of "ecumenic pluralism," which affirms the unity of the human race as an article of faith even though empirical differences and divisions seem so strong.

ECUMENIC VERSUS RADICAL PLURALISM

The contemporary situation, whether one views it as modern or postmodern, is dominated by the reality of pluralism. Speaking descriptively, the spectrum of plurality ranges from simple differences of opinion at one end to mutually exclusive definitions of reality and allegiances to differing value systems or lifestyles on the other end. When we deal with commitments to symbols of ultimacy, we are dealing with a plurality of rival religions.

The plurality of religious traditions constitutes one of the most potent challenges to Christian faith in our time. The challenge is more acute now than before. In times past religion was so closely identified with culture that the other religions of the world just seemed to belong to other lands and other cultures that lay beyond the border of our immediate concerns. We thought they belonged to a different history from ours. But things are changing rapidly in this regard. The religious atlases of the world are becoming obsolete. No longer can we label North America "Christian" or India "Hindu" or Indonesia "Islamic." More and more Americans and Europeans are investigating Asian philosophies and adopting the mystical disciplines of the East. Third World Christian churches have come into their own and, in the case of the Church of South India, are showing exceptional leadership in ecumenical affairs. In any given geographical location, increasing numbers of alternative commitments to ultimate reality can be found. We now have pluralism right in our hometown.

Not only are these alternatives all around us. They exist within us as well. We have begun to internalize pluralism, so that the confrontation between the various reality-defining agencies takes place within us as we wrestle with truth questions. This is possible because there speaks within our soul the still small voice of the *ecumené*, the sense that we belong to a single universal humanity sustained by a mysterious but single divine reality. Even if we are not fully clear regarding the proper relationship between Christianity and the other religions, we still work with the assumption that all human beings share a common status before God and in relation to one another.

I call this ecumenic pluralism because it makes the assumption that there is only one human race to which people in diverse times and cultures belong. Whether it is immediately visible or not, we believe all people have something in common. It is this transcultural and even transreligious unity that makes pluralism possible, that provides the warrant for respecting and appreciating people who differ from ourselves. This is sometimes difficult to see when differences in language and culture seem to run so deep and when violent conflict between peoples seems unavoidable. Nevertheless, I believe we need to affirm through faith that the eschatological kingdom of God will reveal a oneness to the human race, a oneness that may be invisible to us at present.

Ecumenic pluralism tackles a somewhat different problem from that which we know under the term *ecumenical movement*. Coming from the Greek root οἶκος, meaning "one house," the term *ecumenical movement* refers to the attempt by the various Christian churches to understand all Christians as belonging to the single household of faith. This is a perfectly legitimate use of the term, but what I have in mind here is a bit broader. I suggest that we think of the whole creation as God's house and that all of us are guests of equal stature in the divine living room. Corresponding to God's oneness is a oneness of humanity.

The concept of ecumenic unity goes back to the epics of Homer. There *oikoumené* (οἰκουμένη) referred to the inhabited world, consisting of islands and continents. Surrounding the *oikoumené* on all sides is the *okeanos* (ὠκεανός), the ever-running river that returns to itself. The *oikoumené* is our cosmic habitat. Looking out over the *okeanos* we see the horizon, the boundary that distinguishes our world from the mysteries that lie beyond our cosmic order. Turning around, we see that there is but one world this side of the far horizon.[1]

Since Galileo and the rise of the modern mind, we have come to think of our *oikoumené* in terms of a single sphere and the *okeanos* in terms of the infinity of outer space. Looking outward toward the unfathomable horizon of intergalactic mysteries, we are awed by our relative minuteness and insignificance. Yet turning with camera in hand and looking back from the moon toward earth again, we get the picture that the shiny blue sphere that is our world is but one world. The satellites cannot see the lines between nations that we draw on our maps; nor can they report the parochialism of the human mind that imagines the *okeanos* to flow around the borders of one's own country, one's own race, one's own culture, or one's own religion.

Ecumenic pluralism is a perspective that sees all the differences that divide the human race as but outlines of the parts that constitute the whole. It is the recognition that this side of the horizon there is but one inhabited world and that it is a shared world. It is the condition that makes pluralistic thinking possible. Without the assumption of an ecumenic unity, we have no pluralism. We have only anarchy.

The reason pluralism and the human *ecumené* should appear on the theological agenda today is that they are currently being undermined by the ideological stance I have identified as radical pluralism—that is, a pluralism that fails to shoulder responsibility for its corresponding unity. Although the problem is by no means unique to theology, we have our version of it in current North American liberation rhetoric. Religious literature during the 1970s and 1980s told readers that white people simply cannot understand black people, that the rich cannot understand the poor,

---

1. See Eric C. Voegelin, *The Ecumenic Age*, vol. 4 of *Order and History* (Baton Rouge: Louisiana State University Press, 1956–1987), 201–7. Postmodern theorist Jean Gebser develops the notion of "oceanic thinking" based upon *okeanos*, in which the "not-only-but-also" sense of inclusivity is emphasized. This contrasts with the alleged "either-or" attitude of the modern mind (*The Ever-present Origin* [Athens: Ohio University Press, 1985], 253).

and that men cannot understand women. A hands-off policy has emerged. To some extent this is justified. Past wrongs need to be righted. Nevertheless, if left to persist in its own logic, such thinking will lead to baptizing a radical pluralism that will justify a return to tribal parochialism and the loss of a sense of responsibility to the shared *ecumené*.

Radical pluralism espouses the belief that plurality, variety, and diversity are in themselves a positive good. In its extreme form, radical pluralism defends what is different just because it is different; so it opposes the combining of various traditions. It judges the integrity of any existing approach to life inviolate; so any attempt to change it in behalf of transcultural or transethnic unity is considered culturally immoral. Radical pluralism is antiholistic.

When the logic of making an "ism" out of cultural integrity is pressed to the extreme, the principle of supracultural human unity evaporates. Anthropologist Clifford Geertz gives us a hint regarding which way things might go. He suggests that "the basic unity of mankind" might become an empty phrase. To view the diversity of custom across time and over space not merely as a matter of garb or appearance but rather as an affirmation that humanity itself is various in its essences and expressions, he contends, "is to cast off the moorings of philosophical humanism, thus leading to an uneasy drifting into perilous waters."[2] In other words, if we are so intent on emphasizing the diversity or plurality, we will lose the sense of unity. We will sacrifice the very idea that there is one house for humanity. Geertz as an anthropologist is speaking as a social scientist. He is speaking descriptively. Pluralistic ideologists turn radical pluralism into a prescription, and this cannot but help somewhere down the line to fuel the flames of competition, division, and disunity.

What we need to affirm, I believe, is ecumenic pluralism. Ecumenic pluralism is based upon a vision of the whole. While from day to day on the surface of our earth we encounter the dividing walls of culture and the barriers of prejudice, we can still imagine the one world seen by the astronauts looking back from the horizon. Therefore, ecumenic pluralism affirms descriptively the side by side existence of various and contradictory perspectives, worldviews, or approaches to human understanding and living. In conjunction it affirms prescriptively that we should act as if all this plurality belongs to a greater whole. Such acting would be founded not upon what can be observed from our day to day perspective, nor upon the judgments of academic anthropologists, but rather upon our faith in God's unifying and fulfilling plan. The vision of one world is an anticipation of things to come.

---

2. Clifford Geertz, *The Interpretation of Cultures* (New York: Basic Books, Harper Colophon edition, 1973), 36–37.

All this comes down to this: the concept of a universal humanity must become an article of faith. We cannot prove this universality empirically on the basis of present terrestrial experience, yet it is something we both assume and strive after. Like other proleptic realities, the envisioned fullness of human unity will be realized only in the consummate kingdom of God. Now, amid the old aeon with its cultural conflicts, hierarchies, racism, and discrimination, it is not easily demonstrable that all people are equally and fully human. But we must assume it on the basis of a holistic vision, on the basis of a trust that God will eventually reveal that it has always been so.

This vision of a single universal humanity has already served as a driving force in the modern era. This belief in the unity of humanity ignited the fires of religious liberty, energized revolutions against monarchical tyrannies in the name of democracy, burned in the hearts of abolitionists and civil rights martyrs, still stokes the fires of opposition to apartheid and the caste system, and keeps ablaze the desire for equality between the sexes and the generations. This vision of human unity, whether an implicit or explicit article of faith, burns with the explosive power for transforming society.

This power may become defused, however, if the principle of radical pluralism like a Trojan horse makes its home within the citadel of theology, let alone within our culture. In the face of challenges in the past, the Christian faith has responded with confessional statements. Perhaps the time is coming when we will need to confess our faith in the existence of a single universal humanity, a faith not based upon empirical proof but upon trust in God's will for the consummate unity of the creation.

INTERRELIGIOUS DIALOGUE AND THE UNIVERSALITY OF CHRIST

Now we need to ask: just what might be the implications of ecumenic pluralism for interreligious dialogue? One of the general themes indicative of the postmodern consciousness is the reemergence of an appreciation for things religious. Modern scientism, secularism, and materialism are now losing currency. A new respect for ancient traditions, a curiosity about esoteric symbolism, and a desire to learn mystical techniques are gaining in currency. Interreligious dialogue is just one of the many exciting opportunities spawned by this new atmosphere.

Confessional Universalism

Given what I have said about ecumenic pluralism, it seems to follow that Christians should have nothing to fear from engaging in interreligious dialogue. In fact, the opportunity to converse with people of other religious traditions about the things of greatest importance to our respective faiths should be greeted with enthusiasm. I suggest that one approach this matter with what I call a confessional universalist position, one that does not shrink from stating the authentic claims of the Christian faith while at the same time open-mindedly listening to and learning from the insights of others. It is confessional because it takes a stand regarding the gospel that has been borne through history by only one religious tradition, namely, Christianity. It is universal because its claims are ultimate—that is, they are thought to be valid for all people of all times and all places. In short, Christians have something to say. But in dialogue, they also listen.

This suggests certain conditions necessary to make interreligious dialogue fruitful. In addition to a cheerful and courteous demeanor that helps to make any conversation pleasant, there are four theoretical conditions necessary for genuine dialogue to take place. First, each party to the dialogue must have a position to put forth. This is the pluralist assumption. If everyone were to agree with each other, or if the parties were to so waffle on their commitments that the issues became either blurred or lost, a pleasant discussion and a friendly visit might result. But unless there are two or more distinct positions represented there can be no real dialogue.

The second condition is a genuine disposition toward openness combined with the willingness to listen sympathetically to the position being advanced by representatives of the other tradition. It requires in principle the openness to consider seriously the possibility that there is validity to the claims being made by our partners in dialogue. It requires a readiness to be persuaded that reality is not the way we have assumed it to be, that there is some truth for us yet to learn, and that this dialogue just may provide the time and place where our understanding will be expanded and enriched. This is a situation in which the self-critical principle of systematic theology is appropriately invoked.

Attitude is important. Interreligious dialogue is not based on the model of a labor-management negotiation that, although it has two parties in conversation, is strictly an adversarial debate. Labor-management negotiations are approached for the sole purpose of seeking the best interests of the side one is representing. They assume there is a finite pie of wealth and that each side wants the biggest slice it can get. There is no gain in losing. Dialogue, in contrast, is not adversarial. Here, ironically enough, losing could be winning. The spiritual pie is infinite in the wealth it offers the human soul. To lose—which consists in giving up some aspect of one's position because a new and better insight has come to replace it—results in a net gain of knowledge and understanding and perhaps even a strengthening of faith.

Third, genuine dialogue requires the disposition of love. Openness to new possibilities requires imputing integrity at the outset to one's partner in the discussion. It also elicits a desire to make the entire conversation serve to enrich all parties involved. This issues from love. By love here I mean a genuine enjoyment of the sharing that is taking place, the hope for affirming some degree of unity, and the desire to see the other partners in the discussion edified.

The fourth condition is sufficient time and stamina to discuss matters in depth and with thoroughness. Superficial banter about forms and practices in which each side feigns interest in the trivia that plague all ethnic and religious traditions is something less that genuine dialogue. Time and energy must be given for claim and counterclaim regarding the cardinal foundations and pillars of each position to be explicated, analyzed, criticized, defended, and discussed again. Depth and thoroughness are the tools with which we mine the dialogue for its precious jewels of enrichment.

I offer an etymology of the word *dialogue* to make my point. *Logos* (λόγος) is commonly known to be the Greek word for "word" or "conversation." The prefix *di* (δί) attached to words such as *dipolar* means "two," so it might seem obvious that a dialogue is a conversation between two parties. But a closer look will show that the prefix is *dia*, not *di*. Δία is the Greek preposition meaning through or throughout. Could we think of a dialogue as a conversation in which we talk a subject through, in which we exhaust its details and nuances and implications and draw out its full significance?

Confessional Exclusivism

There are a number of alternatives to the proposal I am offering here. One we might call the confessional exclusivist position. This is the view that once I have affirmed my faith in the centrality of Jesus Christ and the absoluteness of the revelation that he is "the way, and the truth, and the life" (John 14:6), then it would follow that interreligious dialogue is unnecessary if not outright apostasy. The assumption here is that the revelation that the Christian church possesses is complete and sufficient; hence, interreligious dialogue cannot add anything new or essential. In fact, it may even lead to some compromise and deterioration of the faith. The net result is that someone holding the confessional exclusivist position is not likely to show up for a dialogue with Buddhists or Hindus.

Confessional exclusivists seem to fear that in dialogue they will learn of new truths that will change their minds about things. Yes, it must be admitted: it is quite likely that dialogue will lead its participants to change their minds. But there is absolutely nothing to fear on this score. If the God in which Christians believe is in fact the creator of the cosmos and the gracious reconciler of all that is disparate, then there is no truth—if it be genuine truth and not partisan propaganda—that one could ever learn that could possibly lead away from God. "I am the way, and the truth, and the life," said Jesus (John 14:6). This faith is in the truth. Dialogue and the honest listening for truth cannot knock one faithful to Christ off the track. To have the "Spirit of truth" (1 John 5:7) is to have truth's testimony within one's soul. A person of faith can live and converse with confidence—not arrogance—in this.

For the confessional universalist this means that the presentation of the claim to truth in Jesus Christ can be open, aboveboard, without tricks or gimmicks, and nondefensive. If one is genuinely concerned with the truth, and if the Spirit is in fact the truth, then one can speak with a certain attitude of letting go, of letting the truth do its own work. This is in part what Paul means when he says that "we refuse to practice cunning or to falsify God's word; but by the open statement of the truth we commend ourselves to the conscience of everyone in the sight of God" (2 Cor. 4:2). The temptation to employ techniques of persuasion such as belittling, brow-beating, cajoling, flattering, or verbal bribing should be resisted because they tend to deny the integrity of the dialogue partner and even give evidence of one's lack of confidence in the truth. In the long run, truth for both ourselves and for our friends in other religious traditions must be a matter of the heart, and a conviction of the heart cannot be won by force or trickery (Ps. 51:6; 1 Pet. 1:22).

What happens if amid dialogue the partner refuses to accept the gospel or perhaps makes a flat and categorical denial of the lordship of Jesus Christ and the gracious promises that accompany this lordship? What happens if our partner says that what we say is untrue? Such a repudiation should come as no surprise, of course. This opposition to the gospel is generally implied by the very presence of non-Christians in interreligious dialogue, and it occasionally surfaces and becomes the issue under discussion. If at this point one has already become fully committed to the dialogue process, the temptation will be great to modify and weaken the Christian position, to reduce or eliminate its demands so as to avoid offending the others. This is a genuine and heartfelt temptation because the Christian does not want to appear to be uncompromising or inhospitable. Such a temptation is actually a healthy sign because it signals that love and a sense of ecumenic unity are present. Nevertheless, it is in fact a temptation and as such deserves caution. Giving in to this temptation would sever the tie with the very reason one entered into dialogue in the first place. Therefore, I suggest that the temptation to surrender one's commitment to Jesus Christ for the sake of a contrived unity of belief should be resisted. Regarding this commitment, the confessional exclusivists and confessional universalists have something important in common.

Yet at this point in the dialogue—the point of position and counterposition—the Christian conversant ought to probe further and ask for the fullest possible exposition of the alternative position. Through listening carefully he or she should employ the tools of critical consciousness to apprehend how the world looks apart from the gospel of Jesus Christ. Rather than looking for those features of religion that Christianity and the other religious tradition hold in common so as to make agreement appear easy, one should ask for a critical appraisal of the very heart of the Christian faith's foundations, the gospel itself. This means listening with such a degree of openness that the question is honestly asked: is the Christian claim regarding the universality of Christ wrong? There is room for this question because on this side of the eschaton we still live by faith. We await God's confirmation. It is logically possible that Christians are wrong in what they believe, and should the temporal process roll on and on with no parousia it would in principle disconfirm the Christian faith. One cannot cover up this realm of doubt with a phony claim to certainty. At its very heart the Christian belief system has made itself subject to a still outstanding truth, and the believer must not waver in trusting in the truth when confronted with the most direct challenges. This openness to divine confirmation or disconfirmation has a byproduct—that is, it permits and even encourages honesty in assessing the claims of non-Christians.

This is by no means a license to be gullible or a call to surrender faith's most cherished beliefs in advance. It is a simple plea to remove the dogmatic wax from Christian ears long enough to hear what is being said and to reassess honestly one's own confessional commitment. The process of making this reassessment should be carried on out loud and in light of the perspective and logic of the counterposition in the existing dialogue. There is nothing to hide. No violent defense is called for. What is called for is a careful and thoughtful rethinking amid the context of the open dialogue that critically and evangelically reassesses the symbols of Christian faith. The process itself, whether one restates the original Christian claim or not, will carry its own integrity and power.

Supraconfessional Universalism

Not all who advocate interreligious dialogue agree with the confessional universalist position I offer here. Confessional exclusivists do not. Neither do theologians in the camp of John Hick, Paul Knitter, Wilfred Cantwell Smith, or Hans Küng, who represent a school of thought that would prematurely abdicate Christian universalism. This group is critical of the emphasis on the centrality and universality of Jesus Christ in the confessional faith of historic Christianity. Hick in particular argues that the Chalcedonian two-natures Christology represents an unwarranted deification of an otherwise human Jesus, and this he believes has led to the unconscionable Christian attitudes of exclusivity and triumphalism. To have genuine interreligious dialogue, Hick contends, Christians must overcome this tendency toward exclusivity at the outset, and that can be done by removing Jesus Christ from his position at the center of God's revelation and from his position in the divine Trinity.

In this position there is a shift away from a christocentric religion toward a theocentric model of a universe of faiths. Rather than advocate one or another existing religious perspective, this supraconfessional theology would see the existing world religions as different human responses to the one divine reality. Like Ramakrishna in the last century, who saw all the religions of the world as different roads up the same mountain, today's supraconfessional universalists see the various religions as different roads to the same center. What is at the center? The godhead. There is one divine noumenon (transcendent religious reality) behind all the religions, they say, that provides for the cognitive or informational input for each tradition. This divine input is interpreted by the minds of each tradition in terms of its own categorical system of thought, so that the one numinous reality becomes expressed in different modes of historically conditioned interpretation. The Christian religion allegedly consists in one of the many such historical modes of expression for this one divine reality. Thus, the claims of confessional Christianity can be said to be true for Christians in Western society, but what Hindus and Buddhists believe in the East is equally true for them.

Hick writes again and again that we need to get beyond what he calls the "older view"—which I take to be the confessional exclusivist view—where we see the non-Christian religions as "outside the sphere of God's saving activity.... And so the older assumption that all human beings must be converted to Jesus as their only Lord and Saviour, if they are to become acceptable to God, has given place to dialogue with people of other traditions on a basis of full mutual respect." He quotes Bishop John V. Taylor with approval, "We believe now that the Ultimate Reality upon which the faith of all believers is focussed in every religion is the same."[3]

I have been calling this position supraconfessional universalism because it seeks to supersede previous confessional commitments within Christianity in order to embrace what we might call an extrareligious or perhaps philosophical affirmation regarding a universal or comprehensive perspective. Hick's metaphysical thesis, expressed clearly in the title of one of his books, *God Has Many Names*, is that there is only one very transcendent divine reality that is partially revealed in Christianity and is similarly revealed in non-Christian religious traditions as well.[4] According to Hick

---

3. John Hick, "A Response to Hebblethwaite," in Michael Goulder, ed., *Incarnation and Myth* (Grand Rapids, Mich.: Eerdmans, 1979), 193; see John Hick, *God and the Universe of Faiths* (New York: St. Martin's Press, 1973), 131; idem, "Jesus and the World Religions," in *The Myth of God Incarnate* (Philadelphia: Westminster, 1977), 179, and in *God Has Many Names* (New York: Macmillan, 1980), 73–75; see also Paul Knitter, *No Other Name?* (Maryknoll, N.Y.: Orbis, 1985), 147, 208–9. Also in this genre belongs Wilfred Cantwell Smith's *Theology of the World* (Philadelphia: Westminster, 1981) and Hans Küng's *Christianity and the World Religions* (New York: Doubleday, 1986). A critical alternative can be found in Carl E. Braaten, *No Other Gospel! Christianity among the World's Religions* (Minneapolis: Fortress, 1992).

4. On some occasions this transcendent reality is depicted theistically by Hick, especially when he advocates theocentrism in opposition to Christocentrism. Nontheistic religions

there is not only universal revelation—what has traditionally been called natural revelation—but also universal salvation. Every religious tradition is said to be salvific. How does Hick know that every tradition is salvific? It is important to note that this assertion regarding the presence of salvation in all the religions is a philosophical assumption. It is not the result of an empirical investigation of existing religious traditions to see if salvation is actually present. That each religion has salvific efficacy is imputed as a condition for establishing mutual respect in order to pursue dialogue.

Once this position is assumed, then the ground for the centrality and universal normativity of Jesus Christ as well as for the Christian mission of evangelism is undercut. Why would anyone want to give up this confessional commitment to the centrality of Christ? Answer: for the purpose of redefining mission in terms of interreligious dialogue. Paul Knitter makes this explicit when he says that intellectually and psychologically it is not possible to give oneself wholly to Jesus and at the same time recognize the possibility that other saviors have carried out this same function for other people. In order to avoid being hamstrung by the exclusivist mindset that prevents dialogue, we need to consign claims for Jesus' exclusive role in salvation for humanity to a past and now outdated thought-pattern. Knitter invites us to consider a new thought-pattern belonging to a new minority of theologians who consider taking the position that Jesus Christ is no longer normative for Christian faith.[5]

The method seems to be that if we can spread the assumption that all religious retailers are brokers in the commodity of salvation, then the Christian monopoly will be broken. Once the monopoly is broken, then the quality of interreligious dialogue will improve because the Christian conversants will then allegedly be pursuing truth rather than stating their confessional positions. Instead of carrying out their mission to evangelize, they will be going to school.

If we were to use a food analogy to track the scope of salvation envisioned by the ancient Hebrews, by the teachings of Jesus, and by the supraconfessional universalists, I think it would look something like this. According to the mindset of the ancient Hebrews, only the chosen people of God would be invited to eat. According to the teachings of Jesus, God's messengers would go out to the highways and hedges to bring people in so that no one goes hungry. According to the supraconfessional

---

such as Buddhism may find this a dubious concession, however, because they do not affirm the God of Judaism, Christianity, and Islam. So, Hick kicks himself up into a higher level of abstraction and speaks of "reality-centrism" or the "Eternal One" so as to include both theists and nontheists. The effective result is a transcendental agnosticism in which we posit a noumenon without any qualities. Gavin D'Costa criticizes Hick here for cutting his moorings with all of the Semitic religions ("Theology of Religions," in David F. Ford, ed., *The Modern Theologians*, 2 vols. [Oxford and New York: Basil Blackwell, 1989], 2:281).

5. Knitter, *No Other Name?* 146, 230.

universalists, we would simply declare that everyone has already eaten, eliminating the need to offer them any food.

Now, people such as John Hick and Paul Knitter certainly offer a refreshing freedom with which to reassess critically the Christian symbols, and their desire to place dialogue on a foundation of mutual respect is no doubt well intentioned. However, there is also a glaring non sequitur in the argument. The logical inconsistency of the argument can be demonstrated by showing how if pressed very far it first destroys the heart of the Christian commitment and, thereby, second, destroys the ground for interreligious dialogue itself.

First, let us ask if we can have genuine Christian faith if we remove the universal and normative significance of Jesus Christ that is already present within the most compact forms of Christian symbolization. Beginning with Yahweh hardening pharaoh's heart during the Exodus—which means that the God of Israel was also the God of Egypt even if the Egyptians did not know it—and extending through the competition of Elijah with the prophets of Baal on Mount Carmel to the repudiation of idol worship in Isaiah, the Hebrew tradition that the Christians inherited consistently affirmed the universal reach of the God revealed to Moses in the burning bush. The New Testament claim is that this same God has become Emmanuel, has entered the finite confines of human history at a particular time and place, and has acted decisively in Jesus of Nazareth. "No one comes to the Father except through me," says Jesus in the Fourth Gospel (John 14:6). One of Peter's addresses implies an undeniable uniqueness: "There is salvation in no one else, for there is no other name under heaven given among mortals by which we must be saved" (Acts 4:12). That name has been exalted "above every name," writes Paul, so that "at the name of Jesus every knee should bend, in heaven and on earth and under the earth, and every tongue should confess that Jesus Christ is Lord, to the glory of God the Father" (Phil. 2:9-11).

This bold confession, "Jesus Christ is Lord," is itself a phrase that accounted for numerous martyrs amid a climate in which it was thought that only Caesar was lord. Would it have helped in the pursuit of truth for the early church to make it clear that it believed there was a single nameless and transcendent divine reality that was revealed equally through Caesar and Jesus, and that salvation could be found in both? Should Christians have affirmed the saving efficacy of Caesar right along with that of Jesus Christ? The New Testament Christians could not do this because the very truth to which the symbols pointed would not permit such compromise. One needs to ask: would Christianity actually be Christianity without its commitment to the universality of the truth regarding Jesus, a commitment so strong that death is preferable to its denial?

All this adds up to the observation that the universality of Jesus Christ belongs indelibly to the basic symbols of the faith. We have no picture of the historical Jesus apart from his universal significance. Should we remove all claims having to do with his close relationship to God the Father and the creation as a whole, then like sand flowing through our fingers the identifiable Jesus would dissipate. There is no getting around the Christian explication of the evangel that holds that Jesus Christ is not just one son of God among many; he is the only begotten Son of God. He is not a savior but the savior. He is not one lord sharing his lordship with other rulers divine or human or both; he is the Lord. In the words of Carl Braaten, "He is the one and only Christ, or he is not Christ at all. He is the one and only Son of God, or he is not God's Son at all. He is the one and only Savior, or he is no Savior at all."[6]

Consequently, the supraconfessional universalist position in effect asks Christians to deny an essential element in their identity. Christians are being asked to repudiate the significance of Jesus inherent in scripture's most basic symbolic formulations. Christian representatives are being asked to enter into dialogue but not to represent the full tradition of which they are a part. By denying the unique and universal relationship that exists between Jesus and the ground of all being at the outset, people holding the supraconfessional position are hoping—hoping in vain in my view—that the dialogue will yield more truth.

Yet this position overlooks the problem of belief versus unbelief. "Do you not believe," asks Jesus, "that I am in the Father and the Father is in me?" (John 14:10). This passage implies that it is possible—perhaps even likely—that some people might not believe what is said about Jesus or what Jesus says about himself. It must be admitted that the claim is a bit outrageous, so outrageous that some who heard it but did not believe it became angry and "sought all the more to kill him" (John 5:18). From New Testament times on the question has been: do you believe it? There are two possible answers, yes and no. Both have been given with considerable frequency.

The supraconfessional universalist position would alter this to read: I no longer believe it, so I wish to enter dialogue to find a different truth I have already presupposed, namely, that revelation and salvation can be found equally in the various religious traditions. What this does, first, is water down the yes-no conflict within Christendom. Supraconfessional universalists say no to Jesus' uniqueness and universality, but yes to the general presence of revelation and salvation within the Christian religion. Then they do the same for non-Christian religions, denying them the opportunity to say no to Jesus by affirming that they have already said yes to the same revelatory and saving power. It is all quite positive and upbeat. According to the supraconfessional agenda, interreligious relations

---

6. Braaten, "The Person of Jesus Christ," in *Chr.D.*, 2:561.

will have left the yes-no conflict behind and entered a Shangri-la of yes, yes, yes.

This brings us to the second implication of the supraconfessional non sequitur. Without a genuine Christian position taken and represented, a genuine dialogue between Christians and non-Christians cannot take place. Dialogue requires two different perspectives or positions of understanding that face and engage one another. But if we look at the Christian chair and find it empty, it will leave the non-Christian to engage in a monologue. What would make the Christian chair empty is not the absence of a theologian, but the presence of a theologian who has given the position away before the dialogue has begun. For authentic dialogue we need theologians, priests, and laypersons whose lives are guided by their respective religious symbol systems to engage one another, not philosophers or even scholars of the world's religions.[7] The quest for supraconfessional universals belongs to the province of the philosophy of religion and should not be mistaken for interreligious dialogue.

The supraconfessional universalists are actually a tertium quid. They could not represent either of the religious traditions engaged in a given dialogue. Consequently, conversations between supraconfessional universalists are not likely to yield much in the way of new truth regarding basic religious perspectives. Why? Because they believe they have already established an unassailable truth at the level of assumption—that is, they have taken the equivalent of a confessional stance. The cardinal doctrine of this stance is this: there is a mysterious and transcendent reality that has only partially revealed itself in each of the various religious traditions, and the normative claims of each tradition are due to human narrow-mindedness and not to the validity of any of the claims. Therefore, one need not investigate the possibility that normative claims—whether Christian, Muslim, or whatever—are true. This assumption prevents dialogue because it denies in advance the possible validity of any normative claim made by one tradition over against a competing claim made by another tradition. No normative claim by any particular religion can be the result of an actual normative revelation on the part of the divine. In other words, the a priori inclusivist position taken by these philosophers of religion has ruled out in advance the possible validity of any of the exclusivist claims. This is hardly open-mindedness.

I am not trying to discourage dialogue. I am rather trying to encourage it. The issue is whether a Christian needs to give up his or her commitment to the universality and normativeness of Christ before entering into dialogue. I say no. Nor does a Muslim have to give up commitment to the normativeness of the Qur'an. Nor does a dialogue partner from any other

---

7. Fortunately, Knitter agrees that in dialogue theologians (not history of religions scholars) should represent their traditions (*No Other Name?* 203–4). So does John Cobb in *Beyond Dialogue* (Philadelphia: Westminster, 1982), 45.

religion—even if it makes exclusivist claims—have to surrender key commitments before dialogue begins. What is necessary for dialogue is critical consciousness, the willingness to listen carefully to the other party and openly consider what valuable things might be said. This implies willingness to look at one's own religious commitment from the point of view of the other tradition, exploring the broadening of one's own horizon of understanding. We may in the process of conversation discover the presence of revelation or even salvation in another tradition. It is also possible that we may not. But we cannot decide in advance. We need the actual dialogue in order to find these things out.

In sum, interreligious dialogue is eviscerated by the supraconfessional universalist position on two counts. First, there is the loss of two distinctly different perspectives. Second, the dogmatism of the supraconfessionalist position assumes a universalist doctrine that is itself immune from criticism by any particular religious tradition.

Thus, I believe the confessional universalist position I advocate here is more honest regarding the nature of the unity that must be presupposed if dialogue is to take place. The supraconfessional universalists seem to assume they already know what that unity is—that is, it is an eternal transcendent noumenon. The confessional universalist position entertains this as a hypothetical possibility, but it goes on to posit that such a unity does not in fact exist as a historical phenomenon. It has yet to become actualized. Our historical experience is in fact one of plurality. What turns plurality into ecumenic pluralism is our act of faith in the one God who promises to actualize a unity that we now can only anticipate.

The confessional universalist position is also more honest regarding the fundamental claims of the Christian faith; and it is better able on this count to understand sympathetically the normative if not exclusivist claims of other traditions such as Islam. On the one hand, it grants the realistic possibility that dialogue just might end with a standoff, with a set of claims and counterclaims with no resolution, and with no pretense of an invisible higher unity of agreement. On the other hand, this is by no means inevitable. Christians must remember that the basic symbols of their faith are open and protean in character. The explicated doctrines of faith are not engraved in everlasting cement. Growth and change can be expected, even encouraged. Dialogue just may help in this growth. One does not know unless one engages in it. One can enter into the conversation with nothing more than the desire to see what comes of it.

THE QUESTION OF UNIVERSAL SALVATION

We must work our way through the smoke screen to see just what in fact is burning in this issue of supraconfessional universalism. The smoke might make us think at first that the issue is that of universal revelation;

but a bit of fanning the smoke then makes us see it is really the issue of universal salvation that fuels the flame. What is really hidden in the smoke and what is really creating the heat is the underlying intolerance of the supraconfessional universalist position toward certain ideas belonging to one religious tradition, Christianity. John Hick is intolerant of the Christian idea that some people might spend eternity in hell. Let me try to trace the steps through the smoke to the fire.

First, the supraconfessionalist position acknowledges in its own way what scholastic theologians used to call natural revelation—that is, the knowledge of God available to other religious traditions and philosophies apart from revelation in Jesus Christ. Then it proceeds to assert that salvation is universal too.

I have some sympathy here. The mood of the present work in systematic theology, concerned as it is with an ecumenic faith, is somewhat critical of Christian churches for narrow-mindedness when they assert *extra ecclesiam nulla salus* (no salvation outside the church). Such criticism appears pertinent from time to time when Eastern Orthodoxy, Roman Catholicism, or some Protestant denominations claim excessive authority and so closely identify themselves with the church that the slogan comes to read: no salvation outside our denomination. I criticize this position because it is presumptuous, because it puts a human institution in the position of doing Christ's work of saving people.

Curiously enough the supraconfessionalist position seems to be assuming the same authority. Only instead of withholding salvation from those outside the church, it now distributes it willy-nilly. John Hick seems to be passing out salvation to the various religions as indiscriminately as a street preacher passes out tracts to pedestrians. Everybody gets it. But how do we know that everybody gets it? We know it evidently because we assume it, not because we have studied all the religions and drawn this conclusion. It is the assumption of a philosopher of religion, not the product of empirical study.

Yet in pondering this assumption, we cannot help but wonder: if so many billions of people for so many centuries in so many religious traditions all have had salvation, why is our world in the shape it is today? In practically every nation we have domestic quarrels, alcoholism, drug abuse, petty crime, felonious crime, disappointment, want, guilt, anxiety, fear of death, suffering, and strife. In some countries millions if not billions are plagued by hopeless poverty, oppression, famine, and starvation. The whole world trembles in the grip of the technological and political forces that threaten geocide through thermonuclear war. Whether from a nonmaterialist or spiritual point of view, the peoples of our world continue to walk in the darkness of selfish desire and narrow-mindedness without even the zest for seeking enlightenment. With all this salvation everywhere, why are we in such a mess?

Salvation Defined

The question needs to be refined because the term *salvation* or its equivalent does not mean exactly the same thing in every religious tradition. In fact, what constitutes salvation can vary so significantly from tradition to tradition that various traditions seem hardly to be speaking about the same thing. The contrast between materialism and mysticism can serve as an example. According to a materialist ideology such as Marxism, the equivalent of salvation consists in the satisfaction of economic needs and the triumph of the oppressed class over bourgeois exploitation. If that is so, then certainly salvation could not be universal because millions and billions of people have died and are dying amid a state of economic injustice. They will never live to see the success of the revolution. In mystical schools of ancient Asian traditions such as Hinduism or Buddhism, in contrast, the equivalent to salvation consists in some form of egoless enlightenment, in the realization of the oneness of the self with the whole of the cosmos, and with escaping the wheel of rebirth so that the finite material world can be left behind forever. Now these two views of salvation are mutually exclusive. There is no way to reconcile mysticism with materialism because, according to the mystic, the materialist's very preoccupation with economic well-being and temporal justice is exactly what precipitates karma and prevents the soul's release. If the finite material world brings only ephemerality and grief, as Asian mystics think, then the materialist doctrine of economic liberation would point to just the opposite of salvation. What, then, does it mean to say we find salvation everywhere?

The Christian understanding of salvation differs from both of these. Here the concept of salvation emerges from the compact symbol of the gospel itself. In brief, salvation consists in Christ's forgiveness of sins and the gift of a transformed and renewed life in the kingdom of God. "Salvation in the New Testament is what God has done to death in the resurrection of Jesus," writes Carl Braaten. "The gospel is the announcement that in one man's history death is no longer the eschaton, but was only the second-to-last thing.... Our final salvation lies in the eschatological future when our own death will be put behind us."[8]

This Christian doctrine of resurrection appears problematic from the point of view of materialists and mystics. Marxism accuses the Christian emphasis on the resurrected life of being escapist, of fostering belief in the happiness of another world that eliminates motivation for improving this one. As I will argue later in my discussion of proleptic ethics, the Marxist interpretation is simply wrong on this; but the important point here is that materialists believe it. Similarly, from the mystical point of view, the Christian hope in resurrection appears to be an impediment to true salvation because it amounts to the illusory hope for an eschatological

---

8. Braaten, "The Person of Jesus Christ," in *Chr.D.*, 1:566.

return to ego-consciousness. If, as the Hindus or Buddhists think, salvation consists in enlightened knowing beyond ego-ness, then the Christian gratitude for forgiveness would appear irrelevant. In short, the content of salvation differs from tradition to tradition, and salvation in one case rules out salvation in other cases.

Even with these observations, we have not yet taken account of what happens within a given religious tradition. Within each tradition one can sometimes discriminate between those who get salvation and those who do not. What rational sense would it make, then, to say that all religions are salvific? Whose definition of salvation would we use? If we use the definition of only one of the various religions, then we are right back where we started.

Therefore, the problem is not merely one of asserting the existence of salvation everywhere. It is knowing what it is.

It is also knowing what it is not. Salvation is not going to everlasting hell. Here is the fire that has been sending up all that smoke regarding universal revelation and universal salvation. Hick opposes the traditional Christian doctrine of hell, which he says "is as scientifically fantastic as it is morally revolting."[9] He opposes the very concept of a double destiny and the exclusivism and religious discrimination that he believes are produced by it. Hick thinks a universalist position will foster more humane treatment of non-Christians by Christians. This is a noble intent. I can only applaud his desire to foster mutual respect and friendship in social relationships. Yet, this position creates confusion because Hick's own philosophical position actually functions as one position within interreligious dialogue while pretending to serve as the inclusive framework for dialogue itself.

How do we get out of this confusion? We need to clear the smoke and fully accept the reality of pluralism. This means we must recognize Hick's proposal for what it is, namely, one confessional position within the plurality of positions regarding the nature of revelation and salvation. It is not a precondition that all must accept in order for dialogue to take place. We must keep in mind not only that there are different concepts of salvation in the different traditions, but that within a given tradition it is not necessarily the case that everyone is thought to attain salvation. A particular religion might conceive of more than one ultimate destiny, such as heaven and hell, and disagree with the premise that everyone goes to heaven. If there is no doctrine of universal salvation already within a given confessional tradition, to force it upon such a tradition from a supraconfessional point of view violates the integrity of dialogue. The acceptance of pluralism means, among other things, that if a given religious tradition teaches double or multiple ultimate destinies,

---

9. Hick, *Death and Eternal Life* (San Francisco: Harper & Row, 1976), 199.

then it should be permitted to express that position without an attack on its integrity at the outset. This should include all major religions, Christianity included. There is no reason to discriminate against Christianity just because it may teach double destiny. Many other religions do too.

The Universality of Christ's Saving Work

After all this is said, I must thank Hick for the insight and courage to question critically the Christian understanding of salvation and damnation. Let us for a moment continue the questioning along this track.

I raise again the question of double destiny versus universal salvation. For centuries the Christian church has taught that the existence of an everlasting heaven and an everlasting hell is necessary for the execution of divine retributive justice. But in the modern period this has been challenged by nonreligious Marxists who deny the existence of heaven and by religious universalists who deny the existence of hell. This is one of those issues that stretch to the limits the theological method of symbol explication. It is stretched necessarily because of an inconsistency that seems to be built into the compact symbol structure itself. One could easily line up passages in the New Testament that say three different—and perhaps even incompatible—things.

First, the New Testament seems to say that salvation will apply to some people and not others on the grounds that one must have faith in order to be saved and only some people have faith while others obviously do not. Saint Paul says salvation is for "everyone who has faith" (Rom. 1:16), and the oft-quoted John 3:16 says eternal life is given to those who believe in Jesus. Now we just might ask: what happens to those who do not have faith? Do such passages imply that those without faith are condemned to everlasting perdition? If so, then salvation is by no means universal.

Second, a double destiny is clearly articulated by those passages that claim that salvation is dependent upon the virtuous works we perform. The most forceful statement of this position is Jesus' parable of the last judgment in Matthew 25. The sheep are separated from the goats. What is the criterion? Love of neighbor. The saved sheep go to the right hand of the Son of man because they visited the sick and imprisoned and gave food and drink to the hungry and clothes to the destitute. The goats who failed to love their neighbors in this way follow the direction the left hand is pointing. It points to everlasting hell. Faith and belief are not mentioned in this passage. Only good works determine if a person goes to heaven or not.

There is a third category of passages that tend to support the position of universal salvation. These so emphasize that salvation is dependent upon God's grace and not human works that all conditions are precluded. Paul repeatedly emphasizes that we are saved by grace. "It is the gift of God" (Eph. 2:8; Rom. 3:24). God's grace is universal. It knows no bounds. Christ "died for all" (2 Cor. 5:15), "so all will be made alive in Christ" (1 Cor. 15:22). How should we interpret this "all"? Does it refer to everybody? To those without faith as well as the faithful? To non-Christian as well as Christian? It would seem to. "The act of righteousness of one leads to acquittal and life for all" (Rom. 5:18; *ILL*).

It appears that we have three irreconcilable positions within the New Testament: whether we are granted everlasting salvation depends on (1) whether or not we have faith; (2) whether or not we love our neighbor; or (3) neither of the above, because salvation is totally a free gift of God's grace and hence cannot be earned by anything we do. Are these three positions just three different ways of saying the same thing, or is there a real incompatibility here? Unfortunately for the theologian, the differences seem to run deep. Certainly these three approaches as they stand could not be taken up into a theological system without introducing inconsistency and incoherence. What shall we do?

Based on all I have said above, I think most favorably of the third alternative, a universalist interpretation of *sola gratia*. But before I develop this any further I need to be honest and admit that all of the New Testament cannot simply be swept into this basket with nothing left over. Strict exegesis would lead in more than one direction. Therefore, any systematic theology that seeks to harmonize everything so that all the elements cohere with one another must be alert here. It will be difficult if not impossible to do successful systematics without doing injustice to one or another path taken by exegesis.

Nevertheless, let us proceed and ask where evangelical explication might take us. John Hick's sensitive question is worth repeating: is it credible that the loving God and Father of all of us has decreed that only those born within one particular thread of human history shall be saved? It would not seem credible. Why? Because as we try to explicate the meaning inherent in the gospel, we begin to think of God in certain ways. Rather than a ruthless and capricious despot, God is a loving Father, gracious in disposition, just in his judgment, sympathetic in feeling, and caring in action. Furthermore, the very concept of forgiveness of sins so tempers justice with mercy that one wonders if there is room left for exacting as fierce a punishment as the concept of hell seems to imply. To consign persons to hell for not loving their neighbors when they have been forgiven seems to remove the force of forgiveness. To consign some people to everlasting damnation because they do not confess that Jesus is Lord, which may be because they just happen to have been born in an Islamic or Buddhist or Shinto setting, sounds unjust, unfair, unbefitting the God of mercy we have come to know through the saving work of Jesus Christ. These considerations tend to lead toward a doctrine of universal salvation.

Let us for a moment follow where the logic of evangelical explication might lead, even if it prescinds from something less than the whole counsel of New Testament symbols. I suggest that a focus on divine love and grace would lead to offering two complementary hypotheses. First, salvation will be universal—that is, it has been given in Christ and will be applied to all human beings regardless of their sinful behavior on earth. Second, hell, if it does exist now, cannot last forever. Only God's kingdom is everlasting. Why does evangelical explication lead in this direction?

Let us mention the two attributes of God that are called into question by the theodicy issue, namely, God understood as both all-powerful (omnipotent) and all-loving (omnibeneficent). If God is all-powerful, then the forces of evil cannot have ultimate power. If hell or hades represents the domain of the devil, and if this domain is understood as the kingdom of evil standing over against God, then it cannot be as enduring as the kingdom of God. If hell were to remain forever, it would also remain as a constant reminder that God's will is not completely done, that God's power is less than complete. Unless God's kingdom is universal and all-inclusive, God is not all-powerful. Therefore, hell, if it exists, must be temporary, and once it passes out of existence all will be taken into the consummate kingdom of God.

Now, one might counter: what if we think of hell not as the domain of the devil that exists contrary to the will of God, but rather as existing under the domain of divine power itself? What if we think of hell as God's means for executing retributive justice? Then we would have to ask what it means to say that God is all-loving. This divine love is understood by the Christian gospel to apply even to sinful people, even to those who have not loved God in return. "Christ died for the ungodly" (Rom. 5:6). Hence, this love is expressed in terms of mercy, grace, and forgiveness. If God's love is capable of extending grace and forgiveness even to those most detestable to God, then it seems that this love would effect the elimination of hell. Thus, to posit that God uses omnipotent power to establish a place of everlasting torment and suffering as retribution for sin would appear to draw a limit to this gracious loving.

This leads to another much more delicate argument in behalf of the concept of universal salvation in heaven, when heaven is understood as the kingdom of God. It has to do with the nature of love and the New Testament observation that "we love because he first loved us" (1 John 4:19). Love is holomorphic—that is, it is more than simply a quality of an individual's personality. It is a participatory power or energy that unites one individual with another and both to the whole. One of the significant characteristics of holomorphic love is sympathy. Combining *syn* (σύν) with *pathos* (πάθος), the word *sympathy* means feeling someone else's pain with him or her. The precedent begins with God. Yahweh of Israel saw the sufferings of the chosen people in Egypt and "heard their cry" (Exod.

3:7) and responded with the Exodus deliverance. So also Christians believe God has responded to the sufferings of the whole world by sharing in them through Jesus' sufferings, and by using such sufferings as a means of deliverance. To love is to feel the pain of the other. To feel someone else's pain is to be pained in oneself; and we cannot be released from sympathetic pain until healing has occurred. Just as God so loved this world (John 3:16), so also do those who love God groan in travail (Rom. 8:22) in behalf of the healing of all things. This is the interconnectedness and wholeness of things coming to expression through sympathetic love. Love will not rest from sympathetic suffering until all things are made whole.

This implies universal salvation and the end to hell. How? Suppose heaven were populated with persons who genuinely love others just as God first loved us. Further, suppose these loving souls were aware that somewhere beyond the walls of heaven there existed another place, hell, where the souls of the damned were undergoing continuous and everlasting suffering from incessant, hot flames that neither consumed them nor let them lose consciousness. How would those people in heaven feel? If they loved sympathetically, they too would feel the pain of the damned. So anxious would they be to see the sufferings of the damned stopped and their souls released from agony, that they would find heaven a miserable place; and if heaven is miserable, then it is not truly heaven. It is intrinsic to the nature of love that it be complete and whole. Partial fulfillment—fulfillment for oneself while others remain unfulfilled—runs contrary to the very nature of the love that we believe we have been bequeathed by God. In short, heaven could not be heaven if there existed a hell alongside it.

The pair of hypotheses I am suggesting here does not try to answer the question of whether hell exists now or not, although it is obvious that if hell does exist it belongs to an interim period prior to the consummation. Certainly Jesus and the New Testament writers assumed that hell does exist. My point here is that one path evangelical explication can take is toward the position that hell, if it does exist, cannot last forever and that salvation is for the whole of God's creation. The power and love of God would forbid the everlasting existence of hell. For textual evidence, one can cite the dramatic conclusion of the Apocalypse of John where the devil, death, and hades itself are all destroyed when they are thrown into the lake of fire (Rev. 20:14). Perhaps this is a vivid way for the New Testament to make the point that when the kingdom of God arrives in its fullness, there will be no more room left for hell.

Now let me repeat a methodological caution mentioned earlier. The hypothesis regarding universal salvation is just that, a hypothesis. It is not dogma. It is an attempt to explicate evangelically the New Testament symbols. But in pursuing this line of theological reasoning I have never ceased to be aware that some other biblical texts seem to lead in another direction, in the direction of an everlasting double destiny. In fact, through the years the double destiny position has dominated Christian thinking and become the orthodox position in many circles.

To be more precise, the hypothetical position I suggest here is a form of an ancient doctrine that has often been repudiated, namely, apocatastasis (ἀποκατάστασις), which holds that Satan and all sinners will ultimately be restored to God. Even in our own time apocatastasis has been rejected, but when it is rejected, curiously enough, there seems to be considerable pussyfooting around it. Karl Barth argues, on the one hand, for the universal saving work of Jesus Christ for all persons while, on the other hand, he will not permit us to say that God's salvific intention will "finally be coincident with the world."[10] Barth will say yes without equivocation to the universality of God's grace, but the answer to the question of universal salvation he consigns to divine mystery. Karl Rahner waffles in a similar fashion. In his article on hell in *Sacramentum Mundi* he takes a firm stand against apocatastasis. But in his *Foundations*, where the weight shifts a bit toward universalism, he shrinks from positively endorsing double destiny, saying that "the existence of the possibility that freedom will end in eternal loss stands alongside the doctrine that the history of the world as a whole will in fact enter into eternal life with God."[11] Now one could sharply criticize Barth and Rahner on systematic grounds for lack of consistency and coherence, for their inability to bring universal grace and double destiny together. But it is not the fault of the systematicians here. The ambiguity lies in the biblical symbols themselves, and this ambiguity continues to be reflected in the systematic yet faithful explication of those symbols.

---

10. Barth, *CD*, 2/2:417.

11. Karl Rahner, *Foundations of Christian Faith* (New York: Seabury, Crossroad, 1978), 444; see idem, *TI*, 5:121–22.

12

PROLEPTIC ETHICS

Still your children wander homeless; still the hungry cry for bread;
Still the captives long for freedom; still in grief we mourn our dead.
As you, Lord, in deep compassion healed the sick and freed the soul,
By your Spirit send your power to our world to make it whole.
—Albert F. Bayly

The spirituality that accompanies a proleptic understanding of the Christian faith is what I call the life of beatitude. The name comes from the structure of Jesus' Beatitudes in Matthew 5:1-12, where the blessings of the future kingdom of God are mysteriously present now in anticipation. Those who are poor in spirit, or who mourn, or who are meek are blessed in some enigmatic way, says Jesus, because these dispositions somehow anticipate the salvation that God has promised will come. Those who hunger and thirst after justice, show mercy, and make peace already participate even if unknowingly in the wholeness that will imbue the new creation.

The ethical thinking appropriate to the life of beatitude, I think, should lead in the direction of proleptic ethics. In this chapter I will describe the ethics of a Christian life influenced by postmodern ecumenic consciousness as holistic, creative, ecological, and proleptic. It is probably obvious that the proleptic ethic I plan on developing here will be an evangelical ethic—that is, it takes as its point of departure the freedom won for humankind by the gospel, by the evangel. Having been freed from the tyranny of the law and having received the indwelling of the Holy Spirit, Christians can develop an ethic that seeks to give co-creative expression to the power of love.

Co-creative love is crucial for meeting the challenges of the present global crisis, what some futurists call the *world problematique*. World leadership desperately needs middle axioms that bridge the gap between the universal imperative to love and the concrete actions that individuals and groups must decide to take. In the following discussion I will suggest seven such middle axioms. I will call them proleptic principles, and they are intended to provide guidance in the face of international strife, the environmental crisis, and economic injustice. The remaining step is for Christian individuals and groups to make creative application—that is, to engage the world passionately yet with wisdom and sound judgment.

PROLEPTIC PRINCIPLES

As we move from the primary biblical symbols toward a proleptic ethic for our emerging postmodern world, we will follow the trajectory of evangelical ethics. The twin emphases of evangelical ethics are freedom and love. The gospel as justification has liberated us from subservience to things alien to our true self. The evangel has freed us from condemnation by a divine law that demands that we behave contrary to our disposition. The gospel as new creation, as presence of the Holy Spirit within the heart of the believer, yields a life of love that becomes authentic self-expression. Our life of loving service today anticipates ahead of time what will be our reality tomorrow, namely, our eschatological oneness with the new life of Christ, the same Christ who gave himself on the cross. Our love today is homologous with whom we will become in the everlasting tomorrow.

Liberated Love for Created Co-creators

This is the basis for what is normally called an evangelical ethic. Luther formulated the paradox of liberation and servanthood by saying that a Christian is perfectly free, subject to none, yet at the same time a Christian is a perfectly dutiful servant of all, subject to everyone. The point is that because the gospel declares us fully holy on the basis of what Christ has done, the life of love we lead can add nothing to our own status before heaven. We are already of infinite value in the eyes of God, so whatever good deeds we perform cannot increase our value. This sets our love free from any self-serving motives that would diminish its giving or sacrificial quality. Hence, we love as God does. We serve as Jesus did.

An evangelical ethic is not concerned primarily with discerning the proper rules and then fulfilling them. It rather seeks out opportunities for love to become expressed and to do its work in edifying God's creatures and in building community. There are no ledgers to measure the degree of responsibility fulfillment. Nor is there a straight road of moral self-discipline down which we should march, looking to neither the left nor the right.

The dynamic movement of love within this world has a creative character because it seeks constantly to create wholeness where previously there was only brokenness. Hence, an ethic based upon liberated love establishes a new relationship with law. Instead of determining what is right by measuring its degree of conformity or nonconformity to an already established law or moral precept, a proleptic ethic leads us to create new laws for the purpose of fostering new levels of community.

This approach is very practical. We might call this a teleological or even a "holophronetic" approach. It consists in making judgments and taking actions in the present situation that we believe will serve the long-range good of the whole. We confront concrete problems, and the most loving thing we can do in most cases is pursue the solution that works best, that is most effective in light of the long-range view. In the social and political sphere this most often means the creation of positive laws that aim at bringing people together peacefully so that they can best enhance one another's well-being. Love produces positive law for the purpose of "creating new forms of human community and uniting those who have been separated," writes Wolfhart Pannenberg. "The law that is produced by love is not some ideal order with a claim to timeless validity (and thus, in this case, it is not natural law) but the specific, concrete solution of concrete problems until something new arises; that is, until a new situation demands new solutions."[1] Thus, the production of just laws is not the end. It is the means for creating a wholesome community.

Creative love may require radical change, even revolution. The oppression and tyranny of the black underclass in South Africa calls for a radical transformation of apartheid. Wholesome community may be the long-range goal, but the overcoming of injustice and the creation of justice constitute the immediate and unavoidable means. The 1985 *Kairos Document* reveals the boldness and the subtlety of Christian ethics: "The fact that the State is tyrannical and an enemy of God is no excuse for hatred. As Christians we are called upon to love our enemies (Matt. 5:44).... But then we must also remember that the most loving thing we can do for both the oppressed *and* for our enemies who are oppressors is to eliminate the oppression, remove the tyrants from power and establish a just government for the common good of *all the people*."[2]

Given the dramatic changes in Western culture since the Enlightenment, given the avalanche of social transformation the world has undergone in the 1980s and 1990s, and given the philosophical necessity for formulating a dynamic ontology to understand our world, it is difficult now to conceive of an ethic based on some immutable set of precepts or rules. Because of the continuing creation, the rules must change too. This temporal fluidity may leave us with a sense of insecurity, a sense of loss without any safe moorings. We can tolerate this fluidity, however, if we understand that God is present to us amid the fluidity. Our trust is in the

---

1. Wolfhart Pannenberg, *Ethics* (Philadelphia: Westminster, 1981), 54.
2. *The Kairos Document: Challenge to the Church* (Grand Rapids, Mich.: Eerdmans, 1985), 4.3.

God of the future who is present now. We cannot rely on a rule book or set of commandments that we have inherited from the past. Divine love ties us to the ultimate future and gives us the security we need; that love has been liberated within our souls by the power of the gospel to create new life amid the present aeon of death.

Eschatological Justice and Temporal Politics

Amid the present aeon of death human beings can experience a modest degree of God's life-sustaining and life-enhancing power through the orders of justice operative in social institutions and government. Because of that, biblical writers could assume obedience to civil law to be normative for Christian life. "For the Lord's sake accept the authority of every human institution, whether of the emperor as supreme, or of governors, as sent by him to punish those who do wrong and to praise those who do right" (1 Pet. 2:13-14). Or, "Let every person be subject to the governing authorities; for there is no authority except from God, and those authorities that exist have been instituted by God" (Rom. 13:1). These New Testament writers encourage civil responsibility on grounds of divine authority— that is, on the grounds that our governmental leadership is exercising a God-given mandate to establish and protect justice in society. The legal system functions to sustain community and to enable constructive social intercourse because its task is "to punish those who do wrong and to praise those who do right." We use civil authority in anticipation of the final justice of God, according to which the disharmonies of the past will be reharmonized into the synthetic unity of the future kingdom of God.

One could interpret this biblical understanding in a minimalist fashion, asserting that the civil order has an essentially negative function, namely, to curb evil. At least this seemed to be the emphasis of the Protestant Reformers who saw the primary function of government as punishing criminals, encouraging good citizenship, permitting domestic freedom, and providing for public security against the scourges of war. What Luther called the "civil use of the law" had as its aim the bridling of evil forces that otherwise might get out of control and lead to social anarchy. Such a minimalist understanding of human government is essentially conservative. It emphasizes the discontinuity between the kingdom of this world and that of the world to come.

In our emerging postmodern context we have a tendency to look for greater continuity. Hence Pannenberg argues that the Reformers' teaching is too narrow. By limiting the role of secular government to curbing evil we might overlook "the correspondence between the justice of the state and the divine will to do justice." God's will for justice is more than simply a negative reaction against sin. We need to look to the order that God wants to see realized in the communal life of God's creatures. This divine ordering is not something alien to us. It is built right into our nature, so that Pannenberg can appeal obliquely to natural law theory to make his case. "The creator's will to order is imprinted in creation itself," he writes; "not only in the laws of nature but also in the communal life of human beings does order emerge from the concrete life of creatures themselves, and this despite all the antagonism between individuals.... The political order is thus based on human nature insofar as this is intrinsically disposed and oriented to a communal life."[3] What we experience as the general human tendency toward the forming of community and the ordering of community life around principles of fairness and justice is the eschatological call ringing in the ears of everyone in organized society. Life in the temporal body politic can offer us a positive foretaste of what will be our final destiny in the everlasting polis of God.

In terms of ethics this means that as citizens of the eschatological polis we are called to support just political structures in the present and to transform those structures when they fail to embody and enhance justice. The New Testament writers encouraged obedience to governing authorities, but not at all cost. When a government becomes perverted and punishes the righteous while praising wrongdoers, then it is time for a change. Disobedience if not resistance may even be required, as Peter told the high priest that he would have to obey God rather than a human authority (Acts 5:29). Both Luther and Calvin cite Peter's bold defense and confirm that there may be times when our loyalty to God's kingdom cannot be reconciled with the principalities and powers of this world. "A wise prince is a mighty rare bird," writes Luther in his treatise entitled *Temporal Authority*. So he asks: "When a prince is in the wrong, are his people bound to follow him then too? I answer, No, for it is no one's duty to do wrong; we ought to obey God."[4] Calvin too, especially when seeing the persecution of his Reformed brothers and sisters at the hands of French nobles, concludes his *Institutes* by recognizing that there are times when we must choose between obedience to secular rulers and obedience to the "truly supreme power of God."[5]

The proleptic dimension of this is that by choosing the future of God over the present existence of any given body politic we are in fact choosing what is best for that body politic. We are choosing what may appear to be divisive and destructive, but we hope its divisiveness and destructiveness will be relatively short-lived. What we want to endure are social and political institutions that better embody and anticipate the justice of God's eschatological community. Ethical action in light of this eschatological vision may require transformation of the present order of things in behalf of what we see coming in the future.

---

3. Pannenberg, *Anthropology in Theological Perspective* (Philadelphia: Westminster, 1985), 449.

4. Luther, *LW*, 45:113.

5. Calvin, *Inst.*, 4.20.32.

Although, on the one hand, we want to affirm a positive continuity between the future of God's justice and its political embodiment in the present time, on the other hand, we need to keep them sufficiently distinct so as to be able to render critical judgment against failures in the present. "The role of the political order is to point ahead to the kingdom of God as a reality distinct from itself," says Pannenberg rightly.[6] The worst mark of a tyrannical state is that it tries to blur this distinction by seeking religious validation of its present authority. Once it is successful in convincing its subjects of its eternal validity, there is no recourse to transcendence to the system, no vantage point from which to render critical judgment. Then tyranny is almost unstoppable. Consequently, the theology of the future kingdom of God—a kingdom that is sharply distinguishable from both the secular government as well as ecclesiastical organization—is necessary to remind human governments of their limits and responsibilities.

From Ecumenics to Eco-ethics

Included in the responsibilities of governments—and the responsibilities of all other individuals and institutions, including the church—is the welfare of the world, the whole world. Striving to maintain military security for one's own nation is understandable. So also is hungering and thirsting after political enfranchisement or economic justice for a particular underclass. These are important items on parochial political and ethical agendas. But at this moment, they are not enough. More is being called for. The needs of the moment are calling for the appearance of an ecumenic ethic—an ethic dedicated to the welfare of the world as a whole.

The call is coming from a developing crisis that is enveloping the world. The Club of Rome has aptly named the current crisis the world problematique, emphasizing that the whole globe shares in the anxiety created by overpopulation, maldistribution of wealth, dwindling non-renewable natural resources, pollution, massive starvation, international terrorism, and the ominous threat of thermonuclear war. Here we see that some of the most important ethical challenges of our time are virtually universal in scope. We cannot deal with them by simply retreating into the community of Christian truth to listen again to the old stories and reestablish our particular identity. Nor can we cope with them if we limit our ethical agendas to class economics or national politics.

We need an ecumenic scope, and I suggest here that we gain that ecumenic scope by founding ethical thinking on a vision of the eschatological kingdom of God. Beginning with the vision of God's future kingdom as the source and ground of value, I will attempt to discern what we should do by developing principles based upon this vision. Our present world situation reveals how badly we need middle axioms, princi-

---

6. Pannenberg, *Anthropology*, 450.

ples that mediate between our vision of ultimate harmony and the realistic appraisal of what we can actually do. We need some principles for guidance. Based on a proleptic ethic, in what follows I will try to develop a set of provolutionary principles.

PROVOLUTIONARY PRINCIPLES

The proleptic structure with which I am working begins with the promise of the coming kingdom of God and the fulfillment of all creation that it will bring. It begins with the future and works back to the present. It begins with heaven and works back to earth. It begins with eschatology and works back to ethics.

The Question of Escapism

Before proceeding farther, I need to pause and raise an unavoidable critical question. Does this advocacy of a strong eschatology necessarily result in escapism? Is this a version of premillennialist fundamentalism that seems to endorse the bourgeois status quo while awaiting the rapture? Is this a return to the religion rejected by the Marxists as the opiate of the people? No, it is not. The eschatological vision is not a sedative. It is a stimulus to action.

Lenin thought of religion per se as a sedative that prevented the believer from acting creatively. Karl Marx, however, saw the eschatological element within religion as consciousness of the need for change, as the "sigh of the oppressed" and the "protest against real distress."[7] It is my belief that a strong eschatology stimulates a strong ethic.

It is important to note that eschatology is an essential element of Christian liberation theology. African American theologian James Cone contends that it is only when oppressed people take seriously the promise of resurrection that they can see clearly the contradictions of present injustice and "fight against overwhelming odds."[8] Feminist Letty Russell uses the term "advent shock" to refer to the sense of maladjustment in the present when compared to the anticipated future fulfillment. "Because of advent shock we seek to anticipate the future in what we do, opening ourselves to the working of God's Spirit and expecting the impossible."[9] Gustavo Gutiérrez reports that "the attraction of 'what is to come' is the driving force of history. The attraction of Yahweh in history and his action at the end of history are inseparable."[10] South African antiapartheid leader Allan Boesak argues forcefully, "New Testament eschatology is a call to

---

7. Karl Marx, "Contribution to the Critique of Hegel's Philosophy of Right," in Reinhold Niebuhr, ed., *Marx and Engels on Religion* (New York: Schocken, 1964), 42.

8. James Cone, *A Black Theology of Liberation* (New York: Lippincott, 1970), 248.

9. Letty Russell, *The Future of Partnership* (Philadelphia: Westminster, 1979), 102.

10. Gustavo Gutiérrez, *A Theology of Liberation* (Maryknoll, N.Y.: Orbis, 1973), 164.

arms, a summons not to be content with the existing situation of oppression, but to take sides with the oppressed and the poor and subsequently for the new humanity and the new world."[11]

Liberation theologians by no means have a monopoly on eschatologically based ethics. C. S. Lewis, popular in evangelical circles, made the point in 1943 in his widely read book *Mere Christianity*. He argued that looking forward to eternal life is not escapism and that history will show that it has been just those Christians with a vision of the new world who have been most effective in reshaping the present world. "It is since Christians have largely ceased to think of the other world that they have become so ineffective in this. Aim at heaven and you will get earth thrown in; aim at earth and you will get neither."[12] Or, in the words of Wolfhart Pannenberg, "The striving for God as the ultimate good beyond the world is turned into concern for the world."[13] The ethical value of the eschaton is that it locates the *summum bonum*, the highest good, the lure toward which we are being drawn, the ideal of the future we wish to make actual in the present.

Carl Braaten refers to ethics in this context as eschatopraxis—that is, doing the future ahead of time. He writes, "In proleptic ethics it may truly be said that the end justifies the means, because the end is proleptically present and operative beforehand, rehearsing the qualities of the eschatological kingdom—peace, love, joy, freedom, equality, unity—in the course of history's forward movement."[14] I am saying here that not only does eschatology stimulate action; it is the very foundation of ethics. Once we apprehend God's will for the consummate future, we seek to incarnate that future proleptically in present human action.

Middle Axioms for Action

Recognizing our advent shock and the need for eschatopraxis, we need to think in terms of an action program made up of middle axioms that will move us from the comprehensive vision to the challenges we face amid current future consciousness. Jürgen Moltmann says such action planning in church circles is too often oriented toward the past, thinking in the category of *re*—for example, revolution, return, renewal, revival, reformation. He advocates using the future-oriented category of the *pro*, replacing revolution with "provolution." Moltmann maintains that "in *pro*volution,

---

11. Allan Boesak, *Farewell to Innocence* (Maryknoll, N.Y.: Orbis, 1977), 145.

12. C. S. Lewis, *Mere Christianity* (New York: Macmillan, 1943), 118.

13. Wolfhart Pannenberg, *Theology and the Kingdom of God* (Philadelphia: Westminster, 1969), 111.

14. Carl E. Braaten, *Eschatology and Ethics* (Minneapolis: Augsburg, 1974), 121. Although Braaten is less than fully sympathetic to liberation theology, he defines the church's mission in terms of proclaiming "the message of Jesus about the future of God's approaching kingdom," which includes the charge to change the world for the better (Braaten, *The Flaming Center* [Philadelphia: Fortress, 1977], 76–77).

the human dream turned forward is combined with the new possibility of the future and begins consciously to direct the course of human history as well as the evolution of nature."[15] Taking a cue from Moltmann, let me draw out seven further "pro's" for Christian provolutionary strategy.

1. Project a vision of the coming new order. This is the prophetic task of the Christian church. The redemption of the historical and the natural order is coming and someone needs to say so. This first "pro" is perhaps the single most important element in the strategy of proleptic ethics. It reflects faith in the divine promise as well as provides the starting point for significant human action.

According to futurists and other postmodern ethicists, the key to tackling the world problematique is found in our projection of, and adherence to, a vision of new reality. Visions are akin to ideas or ideals, and many practical minds are reluctant to embrace great ideals. The fact is, however, that projecting visions and ideals is the first and necessary step to any significant cooperative action. Dutch sociologist and pioneer futurist Fred L. Polak contends that positive images of the future are the primary causal factor in cultural change.[16] Such positive images pull a civilization together and unite its people in a single task. Nothing is more practical than a good idea, an idea that inspires and directs.

What is our image of what is to come? If we look at the biblical symbols we find it is the vision of Isaiah 58:6-9, where the rich share their bread with the hungry. It is the promise of natural harmony in Isaiah 11:6, where "the wolf shall live with the lamb." It is the vision of Amos 5:24, where justice and righteousness roll down upon us like an ever-flowing stream. It is Micah's vision of no more war, where swords are beaten into plowshares and spears into pruning hooks. It is John's vision in the Apocalypse, where God wipes away every tear from our eyes, and where death and mourning will have passed away (Rev. 21:4). Our hope flows from such visionary symbols and is based not on unfounded wishes for an idealist utopia, but on the promise of God confirmed in the proleptic revelation of the future in Jesus Christ.

Projecting such visions creates advent shock. The contrast between what is promised for tomorrow and the actuality of today creates tension. If in God's future there will be no more war, then why have war now? If in God's future the hungry will be fed and the mourning comforted, then our proleptic task is to minister to the hungry and the mourning today.

---

15. Jürgen Moltmann, *Religion, Revolution, and the Future* (New York: Scribners, 1969), 32. I have begun developing this notion of provolutionary principles in *Futures—Human and Divine* (Atlanta: John Knox, 1978), 170–81, and in "Creation, Consummation, and the Ethical Imagination," in Philip Joranson and Ken Butigan, eds., *Cry of the Environment* (Sante Fe: Bear & Company, 1984), 401–29.

16. Fred L. Polak, *The Image of the Future*, trans. and abr. Elise Boulding (New York: Elsevier, 1973).

If in God's future the lion will lie down with the lamb, then perhaps now we should seek to the degree possible to live in the realization that human harmony depends upon harmony throughout all of nature.

Can we go still farther? On the basis of this promise and on the basis of what we know to be the crying needs of our present world, can we project a tailor-made vision? I believe we can say prophetically that there is a new world coming that will be, among other things:

1. organized as a single, worldwide, planetary society;

2. united in devotion to the will of God;

3. sustainable within the biological carrying capacity of the planet and harmonized with the principles of the ecosphere;

4. organized politically so as to preserve the just rights and voluntary contributions of all individuals;

5. organized economically so as to guarantee the basic survival needs of each person;

6. organized socially so that dignity and freedom are respected and protected in every quarter;

7. dedicated to advancing the quality of life in behalf of future generations.

This is the schematic outline of a constructed vision. It is rational and terse, to be sure. But if it could be amplified and molded with beauty and drama by committed artists into symbols, songs, poems, pictures, and architecture, then its heuristic power would be increased and it could become an inspiration and guide.

With regard to a theological concern that might arise when making such a proposal, I believe there is no irreconcilable conflict here between divine action and human imagination. There is no hidden Pelagian agenda here. The ethical action being proposed is our response to God's promise; it is not itself the fulfillment of that promise. While retaining sublime mystery, God has promised that the kingdom will come. Exactly what that kingdom will look like we humans can only imagine. And imagine we must. Our imaginative projections of the perfect society are influenced by our sensitivity to the needs of our present context, to the crisis posed by future consciousness. Our thoughts are conditioned and finite, to be sure. Nonetheless, we understand God's salvation as fulfillment, as meeting the actual needs of us creatures as experienced historically. This means that the content of God's eschatological kingdom—who and what will be there—will be made up of the very course of historical events in which we are presently engaged. The who of the kingdom is us. The what of the kingdom is what we do. Therefore, the projection of future fulfillment based upon present understandings is as theologically legitimate as it is morally necessary. Our only caution is to avoid the premature absolutizing of our vision—that is, we must retain the proleptic and provisional character of anticipatory visions.

2. Promote a sense of global community. The second proleptic principle is an extension of the first. A significant element in the vision we project is the sense of unity. The type of unity I speak of here is not an amorphous, cosmic oneness but rather "com-unity"—that is, unity-with. It is a unity we share with one another, with the world of nature in which we are enmeshed, and with God.

Aspiring toward this unity requires that we replace "we-they" thinking with "us" thinking. The German term for community, *Gemeinschaft*, connotes intimacy and loyalty within a group of people. It connotes the qualities one would expect to find in a close family unit wherein each member's identity is so tied up with the *Gemeinschaft* that the success and happiness of the group are simultaneously the success and happiness of the individual. Can we think of the whole world this way?

Postmodern futurists are accustomed to thinking holistically, recognizing that the various peoples of the world no matter where they live are becoming increasingly interdependent. International trade is no longer a luxury; it is now the norm. Natural resources and agricultural production are in constant movement, and this movement is necessary for each civilization simply to be itself. In addition, trends such as continued depletion of nonrenewable natural resources and environmental pollution impoverish the whole world. Their effects crisscross borders and ignore the separation of continents. Localism, parochialism, and nationalism are all forms of avoiding this truth. There is only one future for all of us. The promotion of a sense of worldwide community places a high value on the futurist observation that everything is interconnected, that no part is divorced from the whole. Any attempt at aggrandizement of the part—any attempt by a portion of the world to garner more than its share of terrestrial blessings—is disintegrative for the whole and will finally result in self-destruction. The way to express *Gemeinschaft* in our present circumstance is to care; it is to treat peoples previously thought foreign as parts of one's own family. Such caring actually incarnates and represents the good of the ultimate whole. Ecumenic caring today proleptically anticipates the divine unity of tomorrow.

We may call this the "ecu-ethic" because it seeks to include all peoples in a single ecumenic world. Yet this *Gemeinschaft* need not refer solely to interhuman relationships. We humans share community with nature as well. The complement of the ecu-ethic is the very comprehensive eco-ethic. The eco-ethic incorporates into its vision the health of the whole biosphere. It recognizes that there is value in loving nature because humans are an indelible part of nature, and because all that God is in the process of creating is a target of divine love.

Global *Gemeinschaft* means, among other things, a revered sense of the oneness we humans share with nature and of the call to care in behalf of God. The World Council of Churches, which first gave attention to futurology at Geneva in 1966 and later sponsored an international conference on the theme "Faith, Science, and the Future" at MIT in 1979, has astutely characterized the global *Gemeinschaft* as participatory; it is also a "just" and "sustainable" society. Justice points to the necessity of correcting the maldistribution of the products of the earth and of bridging the gap between rich and poor countries. Ecological sustainability points to humanity's dependence on earth. An ecologically sustainable society that is unjust can hardly be worth sustaining socially. A just society that is ecologically unsustainable is self-defeating. A proleptic eco-ethic means that the *imago Dei* within us—that is, the dominion that the human race has been given—be employed to bring justice to the needy and sustainability to the biosphere and thereby anticipate the consummate whole toward which we are being drawn.

3. Provide for posterity. The unity sought in global *Gemeinschaft* implies a community over space, a worldwide community. But what about community through time? What is our relationship to future generations whom we ourselves will not live to see? Given the prognostications of futurists regarding depletion of nonrenewable resources and uncontrolled pollution of the biosphere, I pose the ethical question this way: does the present generation have the right to go on one last gluttonous industrial fling, using up all the earth's fecund ability to support life, and then leave our grandchildren with only a cesspool of pollution for a home? Unless decisions are made to alter current trends, this is just what will happen. Once we are dead, our children will attend the reading of the will only to find out that we have bequeathed them a garbage dump instead of a home.

If we are to provide for our posterity, we must begin by recognizing an important fact: the future of life on earth is in jeopardy. We are confronted by threats on many fronts. One such threat is the heating up of the earth's atmosphere due to the greenhouse effect. Burning fossil fuels and forests releases carbon dioxide and other chemicals. Currently, activities such as generating electricity and driving cars as well as producing steel release five billion tons of carbon and ten million tons of sulfur into the atmosphere each year. The accumulation of carbon and other similar emissions traps solar radiation near the earth's surface, causing global warming. This could mean a planetary temperature increase of three to nine degrees over the next forty-five years, leading to a melting of the polar ice caps. This would eventually cause sea levels to rise, inundating many low-lying river deltas and coastal cities. This is where much of the food is grown in many of the overpopulated Third World countries. In June 1988 James Hansen, an atmospheric scientist who heads NASA's Goddard Institute, told the U.S. Congress that the greenhouse effect has already begun. During the first five months of 1988, he said, the average worldwide temperatures were the highest in the 130 years that records have been kept. He believes this is due primarily to pollution produced by power plants and automobiles.[17]

Another threat is the deterioration of the ozone layer of earth's atmosphere, most likely from gases released during the production of foam and the use of refrigerants and aerosols. A substantial loss of ozone may lead to an increase in skin cancer and negatively effect the health of livestock as well as some life forms at the base of the marine food chain. The 1986 discovery of a hole in the ozone layer above the Antarctic suggests the possibility that ozone deterioration is moving at a faster rate than previously predicted.

A third threat is the combination of acidification, deforestation, and desertification. Acid is being released into the atmosphere from the burning of sulfur fuels. It falls back to earth in the form of acid rain and kills fish in the lakes and plant life on the land. Animals then eat the poisoned plants. Entire species of animals are being lost. Central Europe is currently receiving more than one gram of sulfur for every meter of ground each year. This has begun to lead to the loss of forests; and the loss of forests will eventually leave in its wake disastrous erosion, siltation, floods, and local climate change. It will produce deserts where once there was green. Each year right now six million hectares of land are degraded to desertlike conditions.

A fourth threat is the disposal of toxic wastes, especially radioactive wastes from the nuclear industry. This is worth a paragraph or two here because the ethical issues surrounding the nuclear power industry raise quite acutely the issue of an eco-ethic aimed at bridging the generations. Looking just at high level wastes (HLWs), one asks about what should be done with the nonuseful remainder produced by nuclear power plants in the form of spent fuel rods and liquids of highly intense and penetrating radioactivity. HLWs generate considerable heat and must be handled remotely, without human contact. The relevant technical data include the fact that the potential danger from nuclear waste will endure beyond the life-span of all those making disposal decisions. The time it takes for most fission products to decay to manageable levels of toxicity is about seven hundred to one thousand years. Staggering in its implications, however, is the fact that long-lived actinides such as plutonium 239 will not decay to safe levels for 250,000 years. Some experts even estimate 500,000 years.

---

17. Reported by David Brand, "Is the Earth Warming Up?" *Time* (July 4, 1988): 18. See Lester R. Brown, et al., *State of the World 1989*, chap. 1, and *State of the World 1990*, chap. 2 (New York: W. W. Norton, 1989, 1990).

Permanent disposal would mean isolation from the biosphere for this entire period. No human beings to this point have had sufficient long-term experience with such containment processes to be able to guarantee with integrity that proposed disposal plans will be permanently safe. Hence, we must operate on the presumption that we are risking the health and safety of our descendants for hundreds of millennia to come.

Even if it is possible to achieve safety for an indefinite period, the achievement will not be easy or automatic. Future generations will have to care for today's waste in order to protect themselves. How long will the repositories have to be monitored? Opinions vary. Some believe that if nothing goes wrong within the first ten to thirty years after disposal, then nothing is ever likely to go wrong. Others believe we need institutional arrangements for monitoring for as long as 200,000 years at sites where plutonium is buried. Finally, there is an intermediate position that sees the necessity for monitoring during the first one hundred to seven hundred years. (This is roughly the time it takes for most HLWs to decay to levels of toxicity equivalent to that of natural uranium ore.) After that time information posted at the site could prevent accidental intrusion into the repository. Regardless of which estimate contains the most truth, it appears that vigilance will be required by our descendants for extensive periods of time to protect themselves from dangers we have created. How much vigilance the present generation can rightly require of them is a moral question.

An important middle axiom generated by our wider vision of eschatological holism is the principle of intergenerational community, which might be developed in its minimalist form in terms of the golden rule: do unto others as you would have them do unto you. We need to ask: if the generations were reversed, would we want our foreparents to bequeath us an inheritance of depleted natural resources and a dump of dangerous and expensive-to-manage waste? Do we have the right to take wealth from our children and leave them our waste? Would we consider it just if our predecessors had treated us this way? Population ecologist Lester R. Brown uncovers the tacitly assumed we-they thinking of our generation this way: "We have not inherited the earth from our fathers, we are borrowing it from our children."[18]

I believe we today must make some commitments to future generations. With regard to radioactive waste in particular, we must at minimum commit ourselves to the very best technology and waste management program of which we are capable, even if it is very expensive. We have no right to jeopardize future generations' health and safety because the present generation wishes to cut corners to make a profit. This applies to all forms of pollution that we are bequeathing them. To drive this point

18. Lester R. Brown, *Building a Sustainable Society* (New York: W. W. Norton, 1981).

home, we may even propose that long-term financial institutions be set up to manage an endowment fund. Contributions to this fund would come from present profits, be invested, and the original investment plus interest would be available in the centuries to come to cover the almost inevitable costs of dump maintenance. If this appears to be too expensive to us now, then we must force the ethical issue: can we rightfully exploit today's resources at such a cost to tomorrow's children?

Stretching the global *Gemeinschaft* over time would replace the current we-they thinking with a form of "us thinking" that would foster a sense of unity between the present and future generations. It would enjoin us to try to protect our posterity.

4. Protect human dignity. By *dignity* I mean what Immanuel Kant meant, namely, that we treat each person as an end and not as a means. Dignity in this sense is at present basically an ideal. It does not fully exist. The industrial and emerging postindustrial society in which we live is organized around hierarchical structures and job descriptions, which makes persons interchangeable with one another. Value is derived from a giant economic machine, and persons function as cogs in the wheels that keep this machine rolling. To compound the indignity, whatever cog one becomes is often due in part to discrimination on the basis of one's race, age, or gender, all impersonal factors irrelevant to the integrity or value of the person. Dignity is not a widespread present actuality.

Although this fact has gone unobserved, dignity is in reality future-dependent. In the wake of the Enlightenment we have come to think of dignity as being inherent. But this is not quite true. Our experience tells us that before dignity can be inherent, it must be conferred. Dignity must first be bestowed. Then it becomes owned. Dignity has a grace or gift quality to it. This is because it is a social phenomenon. To experience dignity is to experience self-worth through being respected, honored, loved, or served—that is, to be treated as an end and not as a means. This self-worth is gained through intercourse with a world of meaning that confers this worth. Dignity is dependent upon the web of interconnectedness that will finally unite all things, upon the anticipated whole of redeemed reality wrought by a God whose love for us makes us ends rather than means.

This emphasis on dignity sets the proleptic position I am developing here apart from other eco-ethicists who advocate abandoning so-called anthropocentrism and making nature or some suprahuman category the locus of value. Hence, my proposal differs in part from the ecological ethic proposed by John Cobb in concert with Charles Birch. What my proposal and the Cobb-Birch proposal have in common is a sense of holism, a sense of dependence upon the interconnectedness of the web of life. The difference is that Cobb and Birch place the locus of value in the experience of biological life in general, thereby subordinating human dignity to a further end. "The locus of intrinsic value is not in persons as such," Cobb writes, "but in experience. All experience has intrinsic value."[19] Although he might not wish to label it this way, Cobb's position is in effect an experiential hedonism that holds that value is intrinsic to life because life experiences. This leads to gradations of value due to the relative "richness of experience" within life. The greater the richness the greater the life and, hence, the greater the value. "To have richer experience is to be more alive."[20]

One ominous implication of this position is that it raises again the specter of comparative or relative human worth instead of intrinsic dignity. Belief in human dignity had eliminated this question by positing human equality on the grounds that every person has equal dignity. In Cobb's scheme, however, we may now discriminate between human persons, valuing more highly those with richer experience and valuing more lowly those whose experience is restricted. "There is no substantial reason to believe that all persons have equal intrinsic value," write Cobb and Birch.[21] Although Cobb and Birch are quick to deny it, it seems inevitable that an ethic of triage would follow from these premises. People could devise a scale of richness of experience against which they could measure every person they know. In time of crisis due to limited resources they would have a ready-made calculus for eliminating those people with relatively less richness up to the point of bringing resources and population back into balance. If such a calculus were widely accepted, a ruthless leadership could use it prematurely to increase the power and wealth of a privileged class to the elimination of those they would define as deficient in richness of experience. This is certainly not the intention of Cobb and Birch, who are seeking a holistic ethic that can meet the needs of the ecological concerns that we have. Nevertheless, any position that withdraws support for human dignity risks a dangerous setback.

I believe that whatever ecological holism we aim for must include human dignity, even if it goes beyond it. Dignity is not just an aberration of the Enlightenment. It has a biblical foundation on three counts. First, although God creates the whole cosmos, there is a special "delight" in humanity (Prov. 8:27-31). Second, God delights enough in humanity to sacrifice for it. The incarnation and the atonement amount to a divine conferring of dignity, to a divine act wherein humans are treated as an end and Christ is the means. Third, human beings are created in the image of God. In light of what was said earlier about proleptic eschatology and creation from the future, what I mean by the *imago Dei* is Christ, the second

19. John B. Cobb, Jr., "Process Theology and Environmental Issues," *The Journal of Religion* 60, no. 4 (October 1980): 449.

20. Charles Birch and John B. Cobb, Jr., *The Liberation of Life* (Cambridge: Cambridge University Press, 1981), 146; see 106.

21. Ibid., 164.

Adam. Who we as humans are is dependent upon who we will be, namely, new creatures in Christ. Our dignity is christologically grounded. Even though we may not see or perceive actual dignity in people we presently encounter because they may be poor and deprived of rich experience, we must—if we are to live in the truth—impute Christness to them. Today dignity is conferred. Tomorrow it will be inherent.

Such a proleptic ethic is necessary to ground a movement to liberate the oppressed. The first step in the liberation process is the conferring of dignity where it does not presently exist. Victims of injustice and poverty lack dignity in the sense that they are not ends—and may be simply the exploited means—of the world economic system as a whole. The millions if not billions of poor people in the world can be defined almost by their deprivation of rich experience, or at least their deprivation of experience of richness. They lack actual dignity because, as the forgotten and exploited ones, they are not the ends of the dominant social systems. The dignity of the poor and the oppressed must be conferred upon them—that is, imputed to them—even though it runs contrary to their experience up to now. The basis for conferring such dignity is faith, faith in a future where this dignity will become actual and inherent. The basis of this faith is God's promise. Without such a divine promise, the whole enterprise of striving for liberation would consist of an empty ideal that flies in the face of our current experience of injustice and oppression. As promise, however, the tension between the ideal and the present reality becomes the very inspiration for vigorous provolutionary work.

The dignity I am supporting is not intended to justify an anthropocentrism that in turn justifies the wanton destruction of nature. It does imply, however, that any dignity ascribed to the natural order at large is derived from human dignity. We need to resist current sentimental and romantic appeals to an alleged holism in nature that would flower in purity apart from contamination by human exploitation, an ecologist's version of the ideal of the noble savage. The fact is that violence and destruction occur every moment in the biosphere even apart from human intervention, as life feeds on life and blood is "red in tooth and claw" (Tennyson). Nothing indicates that if there were no humans on earth, then earth would suddenly become the Garden of Eden. The current interdependence of all strands that constitute the single web of life is in fact a competitive and violent interdependence. One living thing is not an end for another living thing; it is treated as a means. It is devoured. That the whole of life in all its complexity can be viewed as beautiful and revered depends upon the perspective of the viewer. The only viewer who can do this as far as we know is the human being, or perhaps God. Amid the constant violence and destruction that characterize natural life we can confer dignity on the biosphere only because of God's promise that someday the lion will lie down with the lamb rather than devour the lamb. We humans live proleptically when we say grace at table, showing thankfulness for the life of the animal or plant sacrificed so that we can eat, a life sacrificed because it still belonged to the old aeon, the aeon of death that will someday pass away (Rev. 21:1).

5. Proffer the distinction between needs and wants. One of the reasons the wealthy First World overconsumes and is slow to share with the Third World is that marketing blurs the distinction between needs and wants. We pretend that everything we desire has the status of a need. I submit that needs should be understood as those things that all people require just to be human: food, shelter, sleep, exercise, protection from danger, and such. These are the survival and security requirements at the bottom of Abraham Maslow's hierarchy of human needs. They are satiable.

Wants, in contrast, have to do with our desire to be unique or superior. They are insatiable. The more we get the more we want. An ancient Upanishadic saying puts it this way: to believe you can cure a person's desire for wealth by giving him or her money is like thinking you can put out a fire by pouring butterfat on it.

Basic needs have a moral priority over wants and desires. Ian Barbour says that "all persons have a right to life and therefore *a right to the basic necessities of life*, including adequate food for survival."[22] Given the maldistribution of wealth in the world, this could mean that the rich will have to live more simply if the poor are simply to live. Unless we can distinguish our wants from our needs—unless we can stop wrongly calling them all "needs"—we will not be able to fulfill our moral responsibility to meet first the needs of all and only then meet the wants of some.

We must apply this kind of ethical thinking to the weapons industry. Wealth wants power, and power wants wealth, and weapons are a key link in this cycle. Each year countries spend a combined $560 billion on nuclear and conventional arms, an average of $1.53 billion per day. Compare that with the lack of resources controlled by poor people. Nearly a billion people on our planet live in abject poverty, with illiteracy undercutting their opportunities and malnutrition rendering them physically handicapped and mentally weakened. If we were to think holistically, and if we were to apply our principle of distinguishing the want for military power over against the need for the basics of life, we could ponder what good work a reallocation of resources would do in our world today. Just one day's weapons' budget could buy food relief for the starving, and a few weeks' budget if carefully spent could help establish the foundation for the economic independence of millions who need it.

---

22. Ian G. Barbour, *Technology, Environment, and Human Value* (New York: Praeger, 1980), 250; Barbour's italics.

6. Propose alliances. Pope John XXIII wrote in *Pacem in terris* that Catholics could cooperate with "all men of good will" in working for world peace. So also, I believe, Christians of every stripe should link arms with all women and men who share a positive vision of the future and who are willing to exert effort toward making it a present actuality. Members of churches should be willing to form alliances with whomever shares a complementary commitment to all or any part of their vision of a planetary *Gemeinschaft* and of living at peace with nature.

Just as God raised up the prophet Amos from the unlikely little village of Tekoa, so also prophetic voices are rising in unexpected quarters of our society to announce the coming of something new and better. If we listen through the church doors to the noises of the outside world we hear passionate talk of world peace, a new economic order, political justice, a sustainable society, ecological balance, a new holism, an Aquarian age. The chimes of the future are being rung by the left hand of God. Those in the churches need to listen and join in the music. When others in the secular realm or others in non-Christian religions seem to be humming in harmony, Christians should not scramble to rewrite the notes so that their own song sounds exclusive or unique. There is no virtue in the solo per se. Rather, people of faith should join the chorus.

In doing so, however, it should be remembered that what we humans sing is not yet identical to what the angels sing. At the same time that we cooperate with other people "of good will," the critical power of the Christian vision of God's ultimate future will remind us that all human approximations to it—although good and meaningful—are still provisional and not absolute. We must always be vigilant so that we do not fall into ideology, so that we avoid embracing an already engineered system of thought that eliminates our critical faculty and leads us to forget the transcendent judgment of the kingdom of God. We must always be on guard against fanaticism, against the unflagging belief in one's own rightness that idolatrously absolutizes one human individual or institution. No present political system or even the church itself should ever be identified isomorphically with the as yet transcendent kingdom of God. To claim prematurely such ultimacy within the confines of human finitude leads to totalitarianism, a demonic unity at the expense of personal dignity. Proleptically speaking, that which we value now as a right or a good is done only in the light of the as yet coming absolute good. The positive trends and plans of the present are provisionally good, that is, dependent for their goodness on the future eschaton.

Because of this, society needs the preaching of the church. Such preaching—especially as law—does two things. First, it reinforces the already healthy visions of a positive future produced by secular visionaries. Second, it reminds secular society that it is secular. The church as a distinct institution is in a position to remind the present political (and natural) order that it is provisional. There is more coming.

7. Profess faith. If we allow futuristic forecasts that extrapolate from present trends regarding the spread of starvation or the growing prospect of ecological disaster to get us down and sap our energies, then we will have surrendered our faith in God. I have defined faith as trust in the God of the future, trust in the God who raised Jesus to new life on Easter and who promises to transform the present world into a new creation.

Even if doomsday should come—as it did for Jesus on Good Friday and for the persecuted first readers of the book of Revelation—the New Testament promise is that God will not fail. God has the power of resurrection. The burden of our errors and evils, although heavy, will not last forever. The good news of the Christian evangel is that sin is met by forgiveness, that hurt is met by healing, that death is met by new creation. The new humanity and new ecology for which we yearn will not ultimately be stillborn. Our visions are not vain illusions. Our praxis is not without meaning. The new world will finally come. It will come with God's power.

Professing this faith may itself help to bring the projected new order into being ahead of schedule proleptically—that is, fragmentarily yet authentically. It is our way of embodying the prayer, "Thy will be done on earth as it is in heaven." Professing proleptic faith could make the faith itself contagious. Others might catch on and join the project of bringing the future reality of God's kingdom to bear on the present crisis.

THE LIFE OF BEATITUDE

Professing one's faith is intrinsic to the life of beatitude, and thinking about one's faith is intrinsic to the nature of theology. In our time theological thinking must be engaging. It must confront the world in and around the church and interpret the fundamental symbols of our faith in light of the contemporary context. This contemporary context is feeling the impact of an emerging postmodern mind accompanied by a global future consciousness—the consciousness of a potential avalanche of disasters about to thunder down upon us. We need a faith that can face the future.

This faith is something Christians can share with the world around, because faith in Jesus Christ is rooted in God's future. It is rooted in the future redemption of the entire creation, the consummate fulfillment of all things, which has appeared ahead of time in the person of Jesus of Nazareth. The destiny of Jesus is a microcosm of what we can expect for ourselves and for the macrocosmic order, namely, passing through destruction to resurrection and new creation. The present aeon is experiencing the brokenness and fragmentation of a fallen world, of a world yearning for a wholeness that it does not yet have. In Jesus Christ, God has given us a promise that the present yearning for wholeness is not in vain. Actually, God has given us more than a mere promise. In the Easter resurrection of Jesus, God has given us a prolepsis of what is to come, a preactualization of the eschatological wholeness that will imbue all things.

Christian faith is an ecumenic faith. It recognizes that redemption is aimed at the whole of the created order of which we are a part. It is not limited to the extraction from the world of individual souls; nor is it limited to the triumph of the Christian church in worldly affairs. Christian faith places trust in the faithfulness of God and in the divine promise that as God raised Jesus from the dead on Easter so also will God bring the whole of creation to its consummate fulfillment in the new creation.

The resulting life of beatitude is a life lived between the times—that is, a life lived now with the future new creation in, with, and under our present faith. It is a life of courage that is able to be realistic about the world problematique and its ominous prospects, yet it is a life of hope in the knowledge of God's appointed destiny. This courage and this hope release into our daily activity the power of creative love, a Spirit-inspired love.

INDEX

Abelard, P., 208–10
advent shock, 363–65
adventus, 308–10, 331
agnosticism, 119
Alexander of Hales, 288
Althaus, P., 57 n.14, 217
Ambrose of Milan, 152 n.13, 231, 248, 253
Amin, Idi, 167 n.32
analogy of being, 90
animal rationale, 146
Anselm of Canterbury, 28, 212–15, 217
anthropocentrism, 371–73
anthropology, doctrine of, 140–70, 308
antinomianism, 244
anxiety, 156–57, 159, 161, 164, 168, 170, 238, 329
apocalyptic vision, 46–47, 74, 183, 188, 316
apocatastasis, 356
apophatic statements, 88–90, 114, 116
Apostles' Creed, 3, 40–41, 45, 62, 69–70, 81, 85, 292, 312
archonic view, 133, 137, 330
Aristotle, 4, 37, 142
Arius of Alexandria, 99–100, 247
Arminius, J., 327
Athanasius, 52, 54, 100–101, 103–4, 106, 146, 151, 247
atheism, viii, 7, 12, 119, 125, 283, 294
atonement, 175, 202–22, 372
Augustine, 6, 90, 102, 106, 129 n.8, 146, 154, 158, 160, 168–70, 176, 248–49, 250 n.20, 264 n.13, 275–76, 295, 315–16, 320, 322–23, 326–28
Aulen, G., 210, 214, 216–17

Babai the Great, 208
Babcock, M. D., 110
baptism, 35, 269, 275–84, 294–95, 305
Barbour, I. G., 134 n.17, 136 n.20, 374
Barr, J., 96 n.9
Barth, K., x, 59, 94 n.8, 105, 106 n.19, 126 n.3, 147, 155 n.19, 194 n.19, 200, 236 n.6, 238, 248, 250 n.20, 328, 356

Basil of Caesarea, 56, 103, 247
Bayly, A. F., 357
beatific vision, 315, 319–20
beatitude, life of, xii–xiii, 19, 77, 230, 234–35, 238, 306, 357, 376–77
Becker, E., 157, 161
Beker, J. C., 58 n.15
Berdyaev, N., 130 n.9
Betz, H. D., 189 n.13
Bible. *See* scripture
big bang theory, 131–32, 134, 135 n.18, 136
Birch, C., 371
bishop, office of, 303–4
blasphemy, 156, 165–68
Boesak, A., 363
Boethius, 90, 104, 142, 281
Boff, L., 212
Bohm, D., 124
Bonhoeffer, D., 5
Bornkamm, G., 188
Bouwsma, W., 329 n.22
Bowes, E., 329
Braaten, C., 58 n.15, 134 n.18, 146, 246 n.13, 261, 298, 302 n.41, 343 n.3, 346, 350, 364
Brand, D., 369 n.17
Brock, R. N., 153 n.15
Brown, L. R., 369 n.17, 370
Brown, R., 280, 283
Bucer, M., 263
Buddhism, 344 n.4, 350–51
Bultmann, R., 5, 188, 192–94, 307
Bundy, T., 167 n.32
Bunyan, J., 329

Calvin, J., 6, 52, 55, 62, 66, 106, 147, 150, 157–58, 176, 176 n.3, 199–200, 215, 216 n.13, 220, 234, 236, 244, 257, 259, 263–64, 275, 275 n.18, 290–91, 318, 324, 326, 328–29, 361
Cameron, C., 122
Campbell, T., 40
canon, 52–54, 56–62

378